zondag maandag dinsdag woensdag donderdag vrijdag zaterdag
7 8 9 10 11 12 13
hemelvaart
MEI

zondag maandag dinsdag woensdag donderdag vrijdag zaterdag
14 15 16 17 18 19 20
MEI

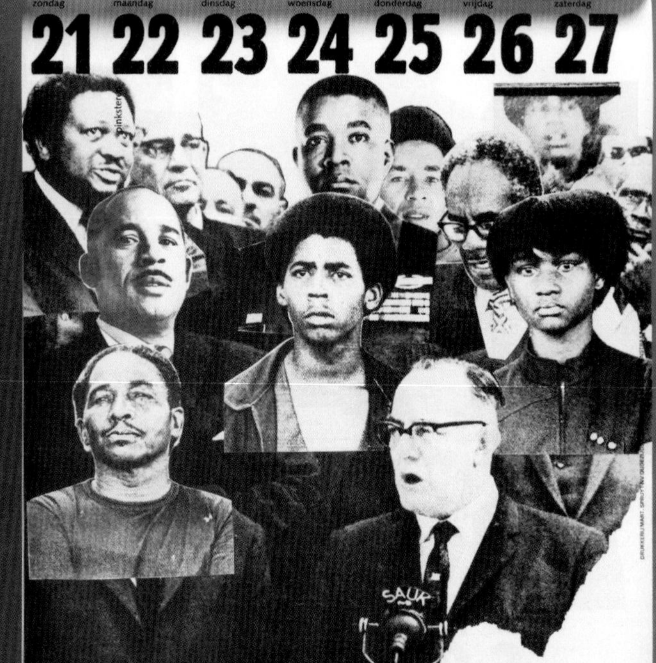
zondag maandag dinsdag woensdag donderdag vrijdag zaterdag
21 22 23 24 25 26 27
pinksteren
MEI

MEI
JUNI
zondag maandag dinsdag woensdag donderdag vrijdag zaterdag
28 29 30 31 1 2 3

JUNI
zondag maandag dinsdag woensdag donderdag vrijdag zaterdag
4 5 6 7 8 9 10

JUNI
zondag maandag dinsdag woensdag donderdag vrijdag zaterdag
11 12 13 14 15 16 17

JUNI
zondag maandag dinsdag woensdag donderdag vrijdag zaterdag
18 19 20 21 22 23 24

JUNI
maandag woensdag donderdag vrijdag zaterdag
25 26 27 28 29 30 1

JULI
zondag maandag dinsdag
2 3 4 5 6 7 8

JULI
zondag
9
maandag
10
dinsdag
11
woensdag
12
donderdag
13
vrijdag
14
zaterdag
15
DRUKKERIJ MART. SPRUYT NV OUDEZIJDS VOORBU
L 82 ELEMENTENSTRAAT 18 AMSTERDAM

JULI
zondag
rdag
vrijdag
zaterdag
16 17 18 19 20 21 22

en
BERNADETTE DEVLIN
zondag
maandag
dinsdag
woensdag
donderdag
vrijdag
zaterdag
23 24 25 26 27 28 29

AUGUSTUS
zondag
maandag
dinsdag
woensdag
donderdag
vrijdag
30 31 1 2 3 4 5

AUGUSTUS
zondag
maandag
dinsdag
woensdag
donderdag
vrijdag
zaterdag
6 7 8 9 10 11 12

AUGUSTUS

DRUKKERIJ MART. SPRUYT NV OUDEZIJDS VOORBURGWAL 82 ELEMENTENSTRAAT 18 AMSTERDAM

zondag maandag

13 14 15 16 17 18 19

AUGUSTUS

DRUKKERIJ MART. SPRUYT NV OUDEZIJDS VOORBURGWAL 82 ELEMENTENSTRAAT 18 AMSTERDAM

zondag	maandag	dinsdag	woensdag	donderdag	vrijdag	zaterdag
20	**21**	**22**	**23**	**24**	**25**	**26**

AUGUSTUS
SEPTEMBER
zondag
maandag
dinsdag
woensdag
donderdag
vrijdag
zaterdag
27 28 29 30 31 1 2

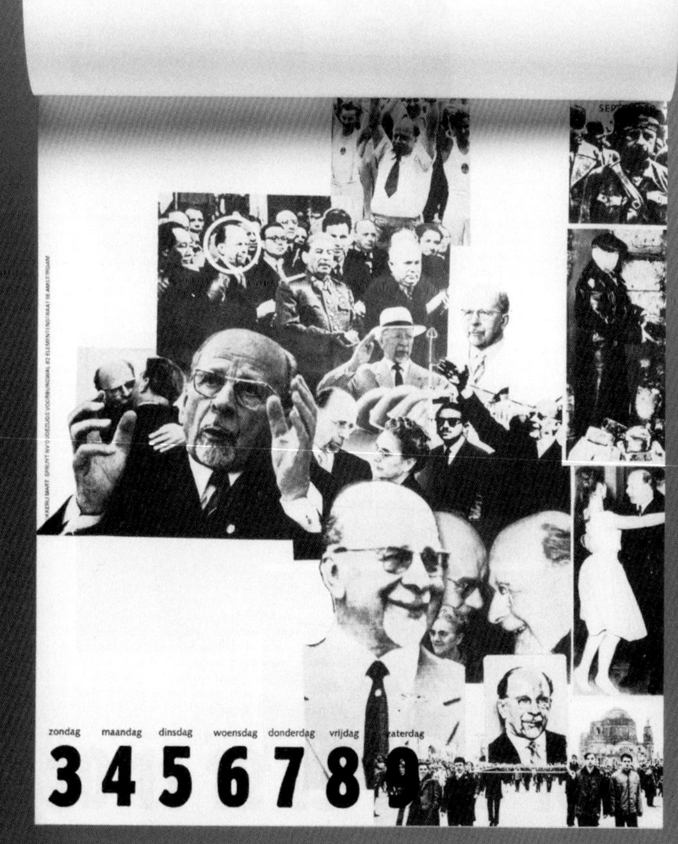
zondag
maandag
dinsdag
woensdag
donderdag
vrijdag
zaterdag
3 4 5 6 7 8 9

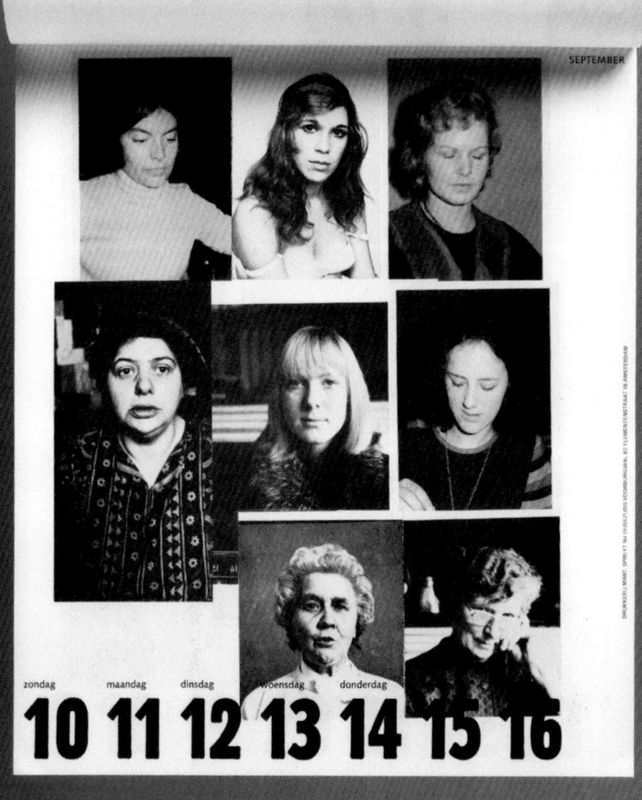
SEPTEMBER
zondag
maandag
dinsdag
woensdag
donderdag
10 11 12 13 14 15 16

SEPTEMBER
zondag
maandag
dinsdag
woensdag
donderdag
vrijdag
zaterdag
17 18 19 20 21 22 23

SEPTEMBER
zondag maandag dinsdag woensdag donderdag vrijdag zaterdag
24 25 26 27 28 29 30

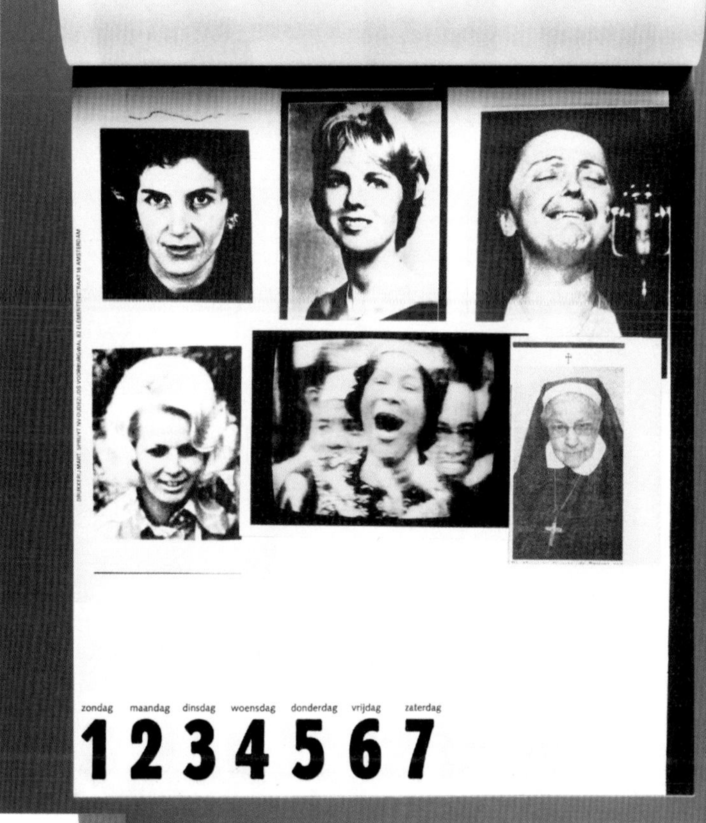
zondag maandag dinsdag woensdag donderdag vrijdag zaterdag
1 2 3 4 5 6 7

WANTED BY THE FBI
INTERSTATE FLIGHT - MURDER, KIDNAPPING
ANGELA YVONNE DAVIS
zondag maandag dinsdag zaterdag
8 9 10 11 12 13 14

OKTOBER
zondag maandag dinsdag woensdag donderdag vrijdag zaterdag
15 16 17 18 19 20 21

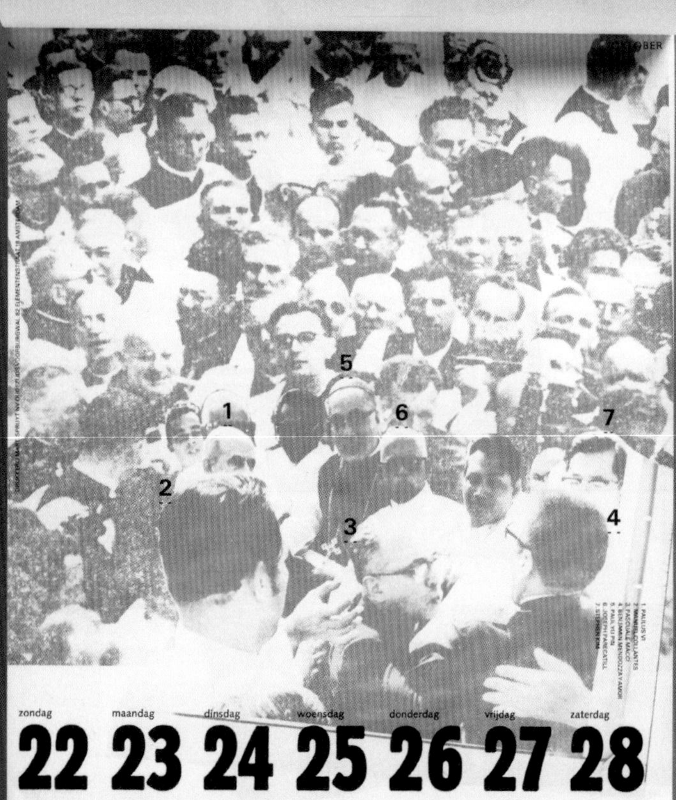
OKTOBER
1
2
3
4
5
6
7
zondag maandag dinsdag woensdag donderdag vrijdag zaterdag
22 23 24 25 26 27 28

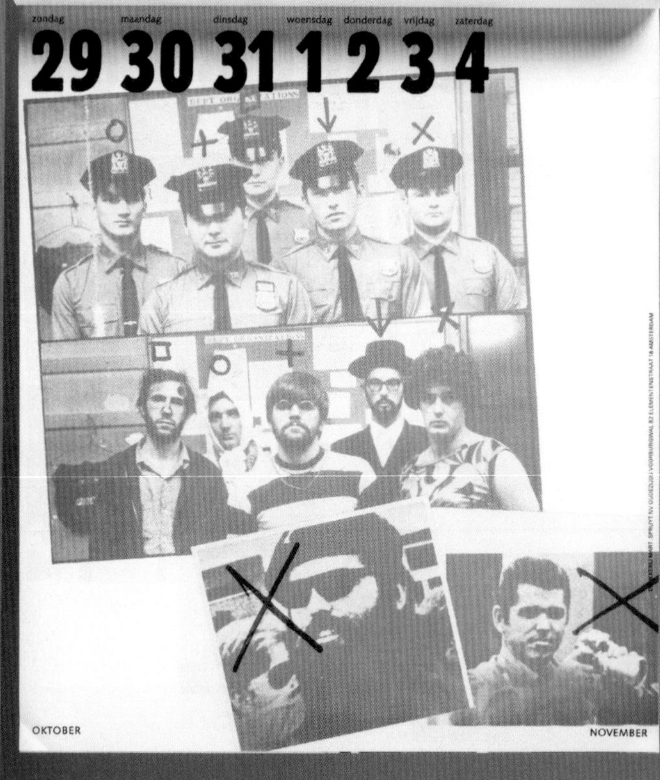
zondag maandag dinsdag woensdag donderdag vrijdag zaterdag
29 30 31 1 2 3 4
OKTOBER
NOVEMBER

zondag maandag dinsdag woensdag donderdag vrijdag zaterdag
5 6 7 8 9 10 11
NOVEMBER

zondag maandag dinsdag woensdag donderdag vrijdag zaterdag
12 13 14 15 16 17 18

zondag maandag dinsdag woensdag donderdag vrijdag zaterdag
19 20 21 22 23 24 25

NOVEMBER
DECEMBER
zondag maandag dinsdag woensdag vrijdag zaterdag
26 27 28 29 30 1 2

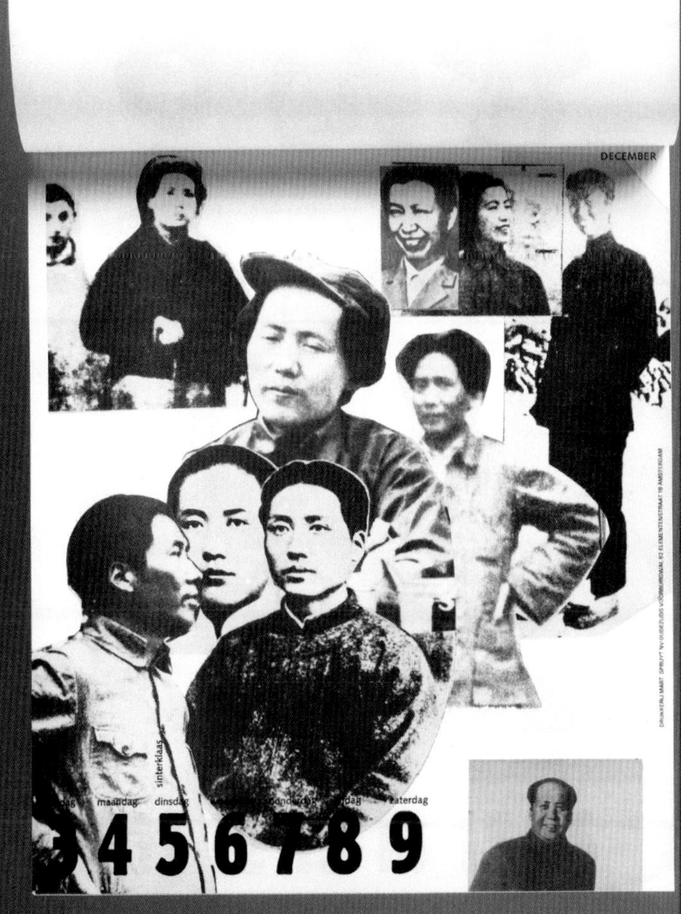
DECEMBER
sinterklaas
maandag dinsdag zaterdag
4 5 6 7 8 9

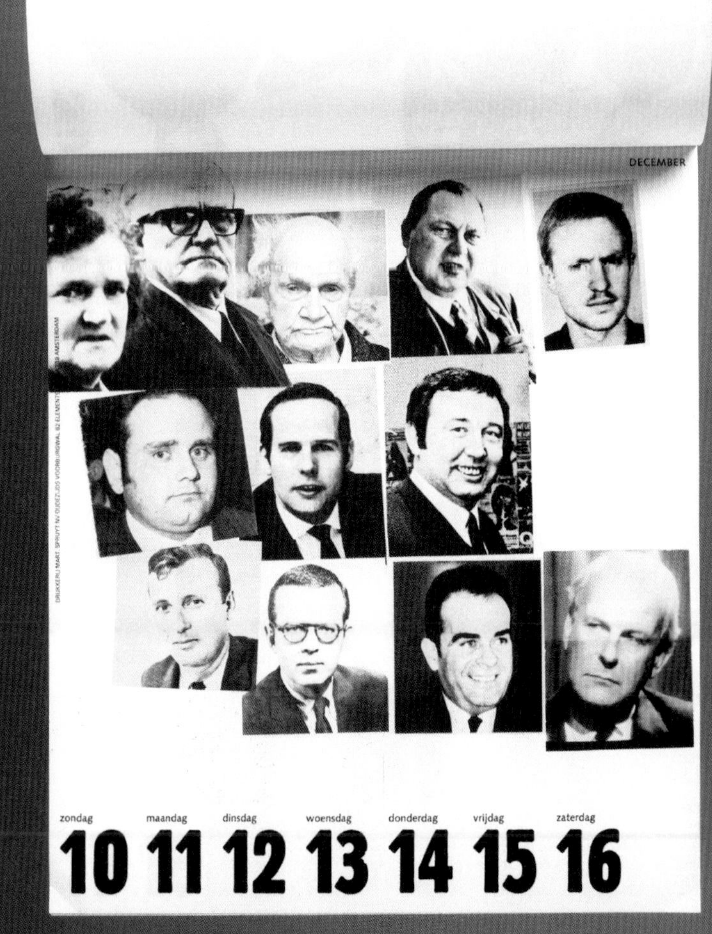
DECEMBER
zondag maandag dinsdag woensdag donderdag vrijdag zaterdag
10 11 12 13 14 15 16

DECEMBER

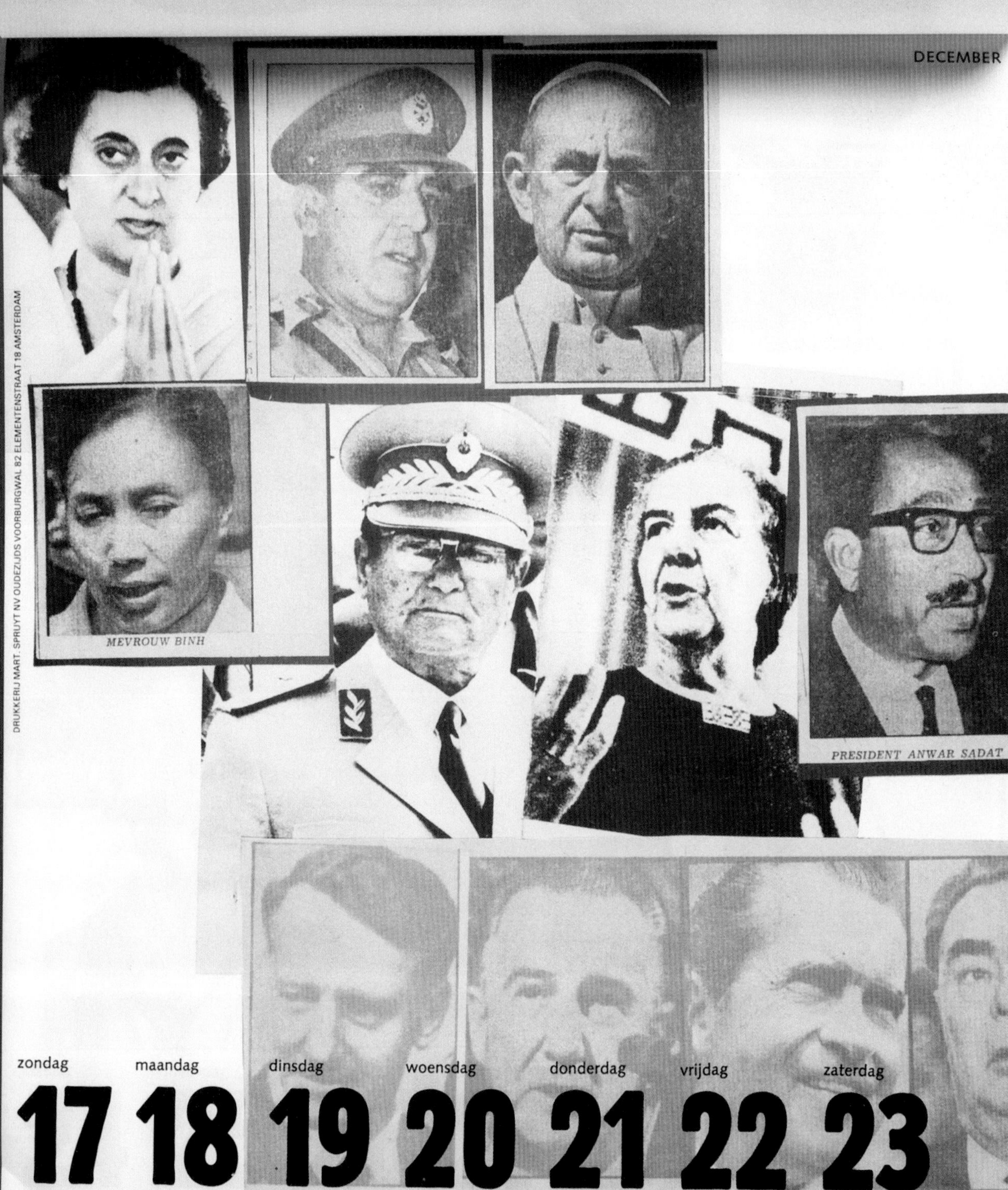

DRUKKERIJ MART. SPRUYT NV OUDEZIJDS VOORBURGWAL 82 ELEMENTENSTRAAT 18 AMSTERDAM

zondag	maandag	dinsdag	woensdag	donderdag	vrijdag	zaterdag
17	**18**	**19**	**20**	**21**	**22**	**23**

DECEMBER
zondag maandag dinsdag woensdag donderdag vrijdag zaterdag
24 25 26 27 28 29 30

JANUARI
zondag
31 1 2 3 4 5 6

JANUARI
zondag maandag dinsdag woensdag
7 8 9 10 11 12 13

JANUARI
zondag maandag dinsdag woensdag vrijdag
14 15 16 17 18 19

zondag maandag dinsdag
21 22 23 24 25 26 27

JANUARI
FEBRUARI
zondag maandag dinsdag woensdag donderdag vrijdag zaterdag
28 29 30 31 1 2 3

FEBRUARI
zondag maandag dinsdag woensdag zaterdag
4 5 6 7 8 9 10

FEBRUARI
zondag maandag dinsdag woensdag
11 12 13 14 15 16 17

zondag	maandag	dinsdag	woensdag	donderdag	vrijdag	zaterdag
18	**19**	**20**	**21**	**22**	**23**	**24**

DRUKKERIJ MART. SPRUYT NV OUDEZIJDS VOORBURGWAL 82 ELEMENTENSTRAAT 18 AMSTERDAM

FEBRUARI

FEBRUARI
MAART
zondag maandag dinsdag woensdag donderdag vrijdag zaterdag
25 26 27 28 1 2 3

MAART
zondag maandag dinsdag woensdag donderdag vrijdag zaterdag
4 5 6 7 8 9 10

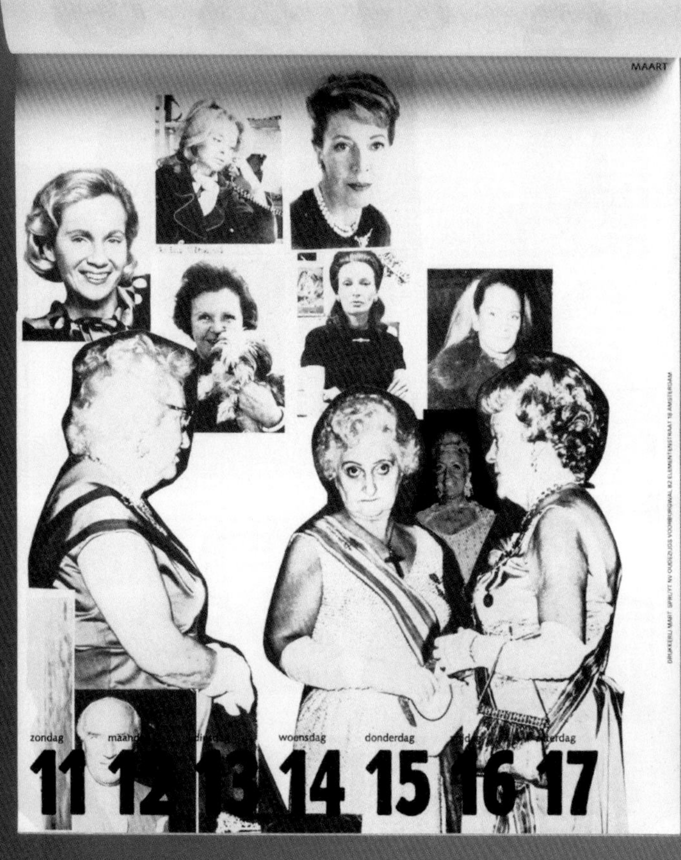
MAART
zondag woensdag donderdag
11 12 13 14 15 16 17

MAART
zondag maandag dinsdag woensdag donderdag vrijdag zaterdag
18 19 20 21 22 23 24

samenstelling en ontwerp Jan van Toorn
foto's Geertjan Dusseljee, Anpfoto en anderen
litho's Biegelaar & Jansen nv, Utrecht

MART. SPRUYT NV AMSTERDAM
oudezijds voorburgwal 82 en elementenstraat 18

APRIL

zondag	maandag	dinsdag	woensdag	donderdag	vrijdag	zaterdag
8	9	10	11	12	13	14

1972/73 calendar. Complete publication shown.
Publisher and printer: Mart.Spruijt. Photographs:
Geertjan Dusseljee, Anpfoto and others

Jan van Toorn: Critical Practice

Rick Poynor

010 Publishers, Rotterdam 2008

Jan van Toorn: Critical Practice is the third volume in the series "Graphic Design in the Netherlands". This series of monographs is an initiative of the Prins Bernhard Cultuurfonds in Amsterdam. Editorial board: Max Bruinsma, Simon den Hartog and Frank Tiesing.

The publisher wishes to thank Jan van Toorn for his generous cooperation. All work shown in this book is by Van Toorn unless otherwise indicated.

The author wishes to thank Els Kuijpers and Professor Dan Fern at the School of Communications, Royal College of Art, London, where a research fellowship made the completion of this book possible.

Text by Rick Poynor
Design by Simon Davies
Image editing by Simon Davies and Rick Poynor
Text editing by Max Bruinsma
Translation Dutch / English by Jan Wijnsen
Photography by Ole Eshuis

All work shown in this book is by Jan van Toorn, except for: p. 18 and 78: Michel Boesveld, portraits of Jan van Toorn; p. 79: Paul Schuitema, poster for Van Berkel; p. 84: David King, design for *The Sunday Times*; p. 100: Wim Crouwel, poster for Stedelijk Museum, Amsterdam; p. 101: Wim Crouwel, cover for *Fodor 8*, 1972; p. 103: Wim Crouwel, calendar for Erven E. van der Geer; p. 103: Exhibition "De Straat", Van Abbemuseum, 1972, photographs by H.J. Schröter and v.d. Bichelaer.

Printed by Die Keure, Bruges

ISBN 978-90-6450-565-2

Also published in this series
Otto Treumann (1999) ISBN 90-6450-311-7 (Dutch edition) / ISBN 90-6450-312-5 (English edition)
Sandberg, Vormgever van het Stedelijk (2004) ISBN 90-6450-463-6
Sandberg, Designer and Director of the Stedelijk (2004) ISBN 90-6450-481-4 (English edition)

"DESIGNERS ARE CONNECTED TO THE EXISTING ORDER. THAT'S THE REALITY AND YOU HAVE TO DEAL WITH IT."

Visual reporting

Jan van Toorn

Range no. 25. Magazine cover, 1964. Publisher: Philips' Telecommunicatie Industrie

Range no. 27. Magazine cover and spreads, 1965.
Publisher: Philips' Telecommunicatie Industrie

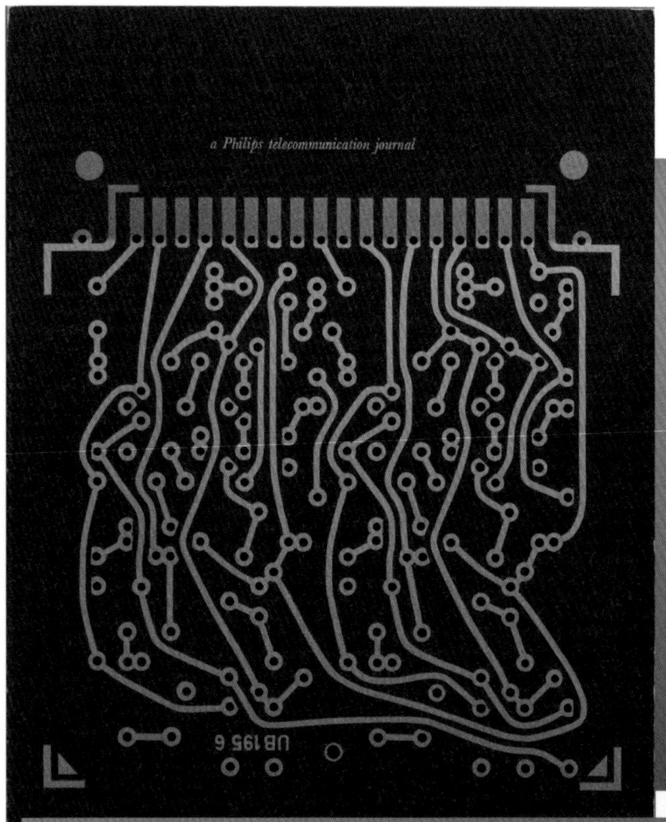

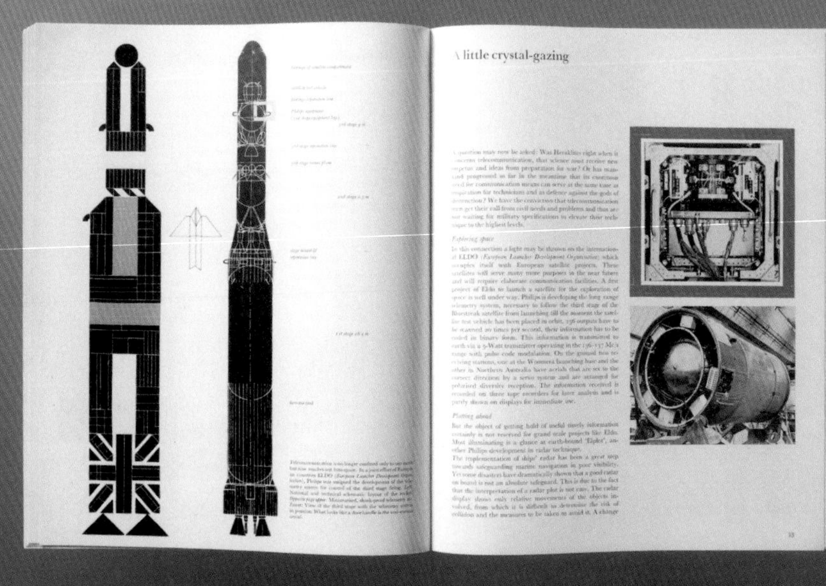

in course and/or speed and the consequences that may eventuate with respect to other moving objects within range, are better estimated from a picture giving absolute speeds and courses. A device which translates the normal radar picture and estimates the courses of all vessels in the area for more than a half-hour ahead, will be a great help in solving this problem. Elplot, in fact, is a simple analogue computer into which data from the radar screen is fed by very simple manipulations and which will show the possible consequences when a certain development of the existing situation occurs. It goes even a step further and can show what form the new display will take when a certain change in course or speed is made and what new consequences would then arise regarding risks of collision with other vessels in the area. A number of changes in course or speed may be tried out on the Elplot so that the best solution can be chosen before giving orders. The procedure takes little time and relieves the operator from all calculations and plotting.

Old services, new methods

More and more old effective services will be affected by new methods that may change operational practices completely. Railways, for instance, are quite aware of the necessity to introduce new means to cope with the increasing problems of today and of tomorrow. They now make use of modern means like television and mobile radio in their marshalling yards. A great problem is the collection of information of the composition of goods trains and the forwarding of it to the marshalling yards before the arrival of the train, in order to prepare a switching plan well ahead. Spoorweg Sein Industrie, associated with Philips' Telecommunicatie Industrie, has developed a system which electrically collects and despatches automatically all the required information when the train leaves the point of departure for the point of destination, while the train is running on the track. Thus the information reaches the next marshalling yard well in time to have a switching plan prepared before the train's arrival, when the points-switching can start without delay.

More data, more traffic

It is one thing to secure data, another thing is to store it, but from an operational point of view success is only achieved if and when the right data is presented to the right man (or machine) at the right time. For that reason it is to be expected that in the near future data traffic will become of more importance, some even expect it will take a dominating position in telecommunications. At first, existing means such as telex will be able to handle the volume of traffic, but the time is not far off when many enterprises will need the service of a

To assist in the interpretation of a radar display, an analogue computer is incorporated in the console of Elplot equipment which adds to the positions of neighbouring vessels the courses these vessels are following, thus indicating what future situations may occur. The navigator gets his information at a glance instead of after the long and tedious calculations which he had to make.
Railways also have their data communication problems. Traffic controller at a marshalling yard wants to know the formation of trains to be expected well ahead of their arrival in order to make a switching plan in time. Data is collected by means of wagon identification apparatus when trains leave departure yard and is transmitted to the destination yard where the cars have to be switched according to type and destination. *Opposite:* Schematic diagram of railway car switching on the basis of wagon identification at the departure station. (Small frames indicate wagon identification equipment placed close to rail tracks.)

34

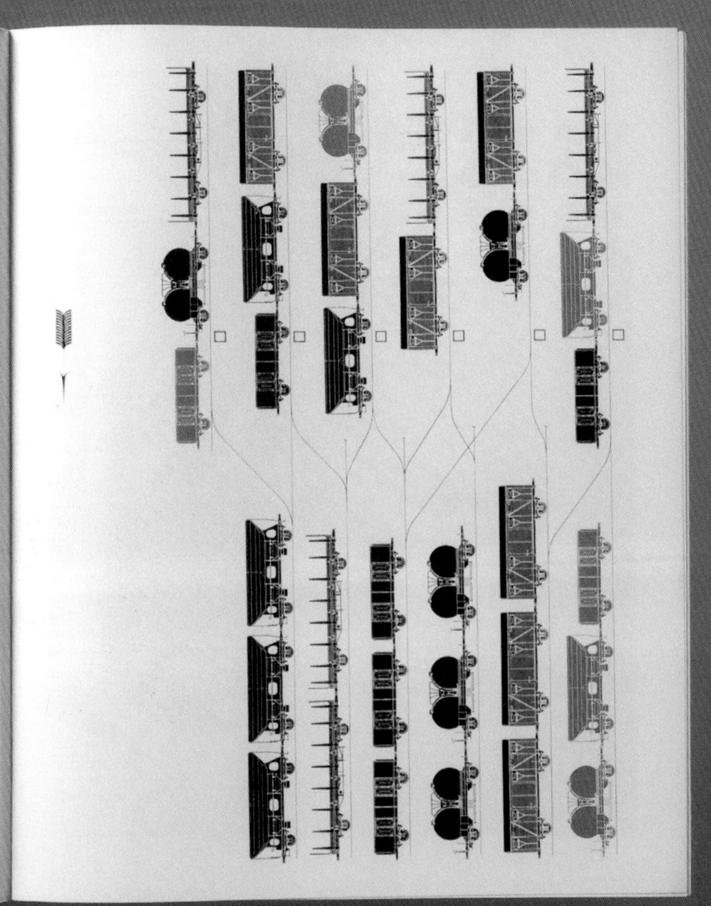

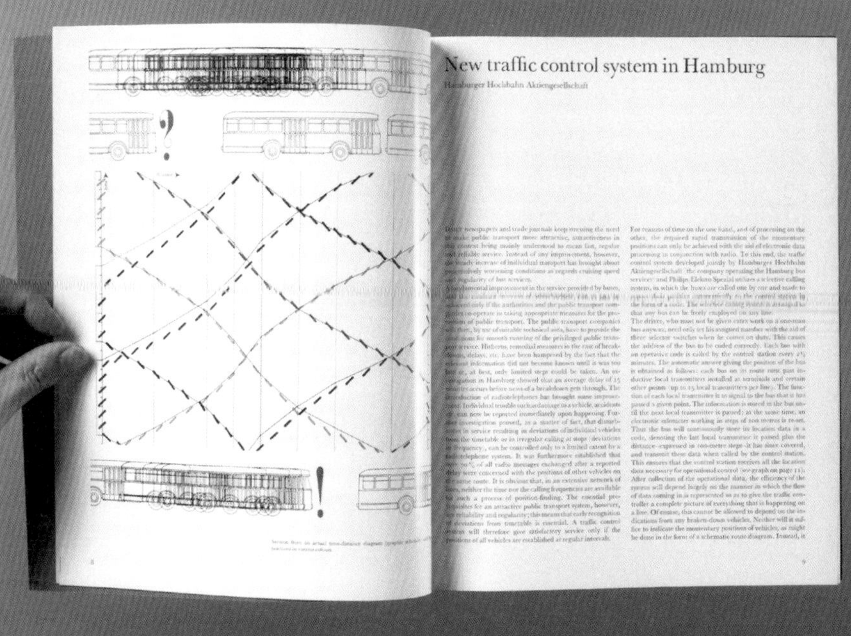

Range no. 28. Magazine cover and spreads, 1965.
Publisher: Philips' Telecommunicatie Industrie

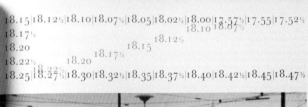

must be possible to compare the position of a faulty vehicle with the position of the preceding bus and that of the subsequent one. The idea of using an electronic computer, which would indicate any deviations by constantly comparing the target timetable and the actual one, was dropped because of the large storage capacity it would require. In addition, the display methods so far mentioned do not meet the requirement that it should be possible to forecast the development of conditions on a line. This requirement in particular seems to be imperative with a view to taking effective action.

A comprehensive display system can be built up if the target schedule can be run off at the right speed by a suitable transport mechanism in the form of a time-distance diagram printed on a paper strip, and if the positional data received from the buses can be automatically printed on this strip at the right time and place.

An operationally useful comparison between target and actual conditions appears to be obtained when the distance covered is counted in 100-metre stages and the position reports are made at 2½-minute intervals. If the display area of the recording apparatus is suitably arranged, the traffic controller on duty will be in a position to survey the recorded operational data up to the instant, and to detect trouble as soon as it starts to develop.

The high resolution of distance in use necessitates a display unit of correspondingly high resolving power. A recorder satisfying these requirements is the Philips 12-channel pen recorder, which is a compensation type of recorder. The digital position data received are translated by a digital-analogue converter into a voltage representing the location of a bus, and the voltage is fed to the recorder. The relatively long adjustment time of the compensation recorder (approx. 3 seconds) was overcome by finding a suitable calling sequence for the selective calling system. To avoid inconvenience to the operator, recording takes place on the underside of transparent paper. A further note of interest is that the buses are represented by eight different colours, so that they can be clearly distinguished. Each bus retains its assigned colour for the duration of its duty. An additional distinction, namely between buses travelling from *a* to *b* and those travelling from *b* to *a*, is made by the positions of the printed lines (*see page 8*).

This visual display of bus positions permits the traffic controller to evaluate the operating conditions and to decide when and how he will take action if anything goes wrong. Any such action, however, will be effective only if it can be taken without delay. Automatic change-over of the vehicle radio sets from data to speech transmission allows of direct communication with any bus driver by means of the selective call normally used for data transmission.

The nature of the corrective measures determines the value of a traffic control system. Graphic representation permits anticipatory action by means of extrapolations (*see illustration with legend alongside*).

A further advantage of this method of representation lies in the fact that the traffic controller can check the effectiveness of any action taken. This means that any incorrect evaluation or later changes in operating conditions may result in a subsequent correction.

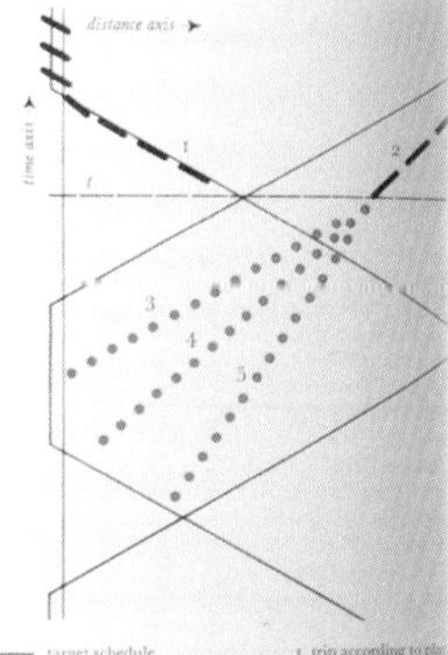

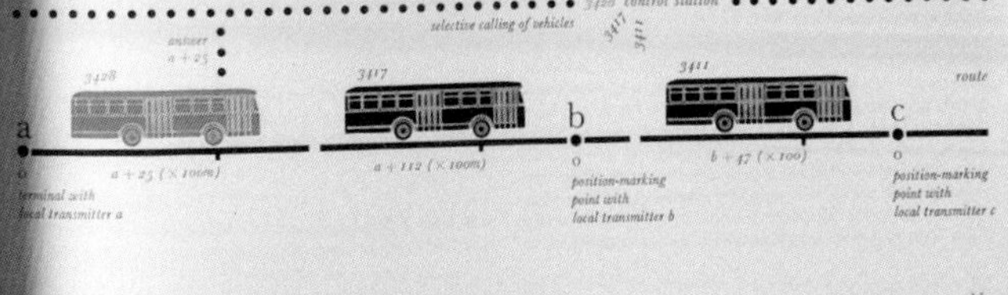

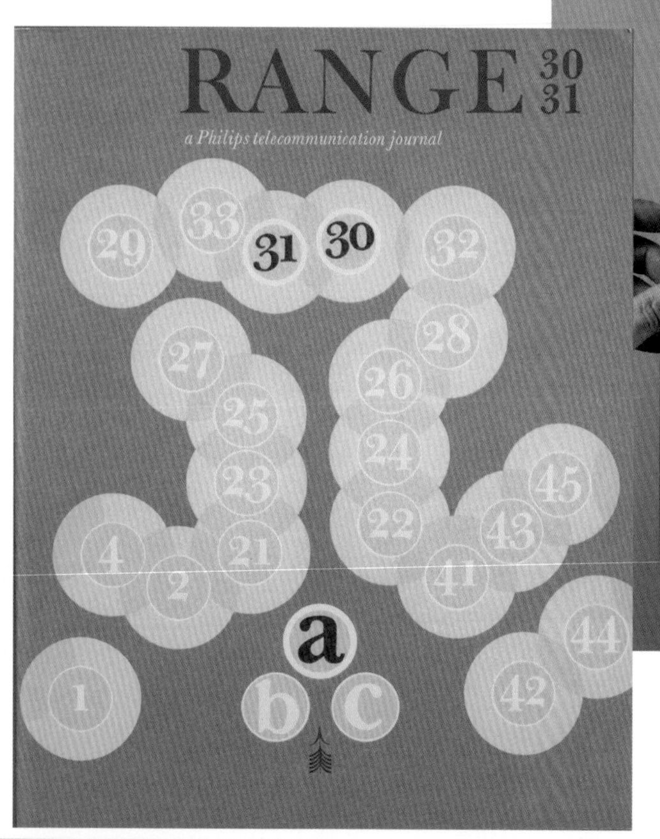

Evolution in the PABX family

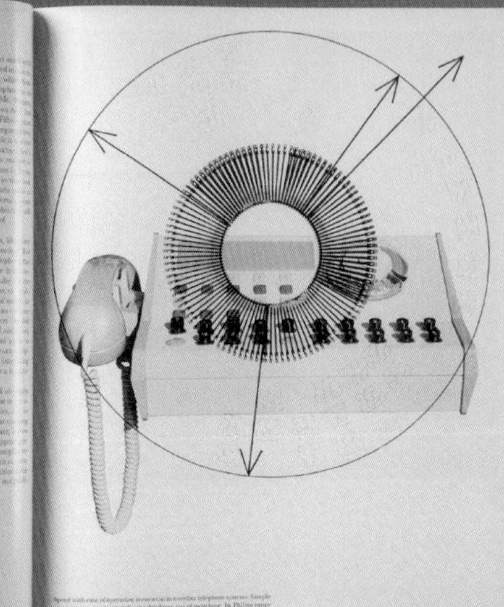

Range no. 30/31. Magazine cover and spread, 1967. Publisher: Philips' Telecommunicatie Industrie

Range no. 32. Magazine spread, 1968. Publisher: Philips' Telecommunicatie Industrie

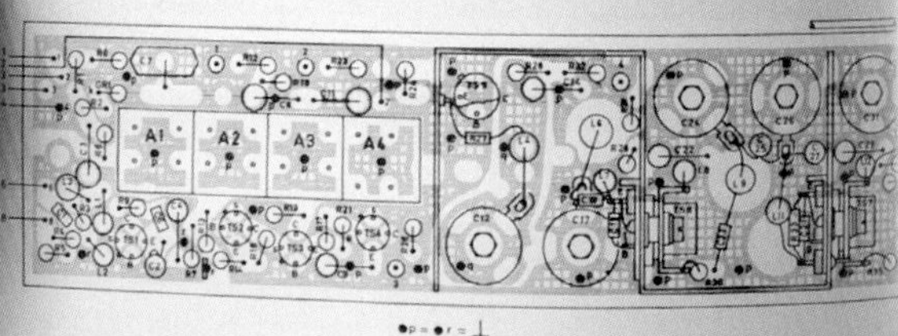

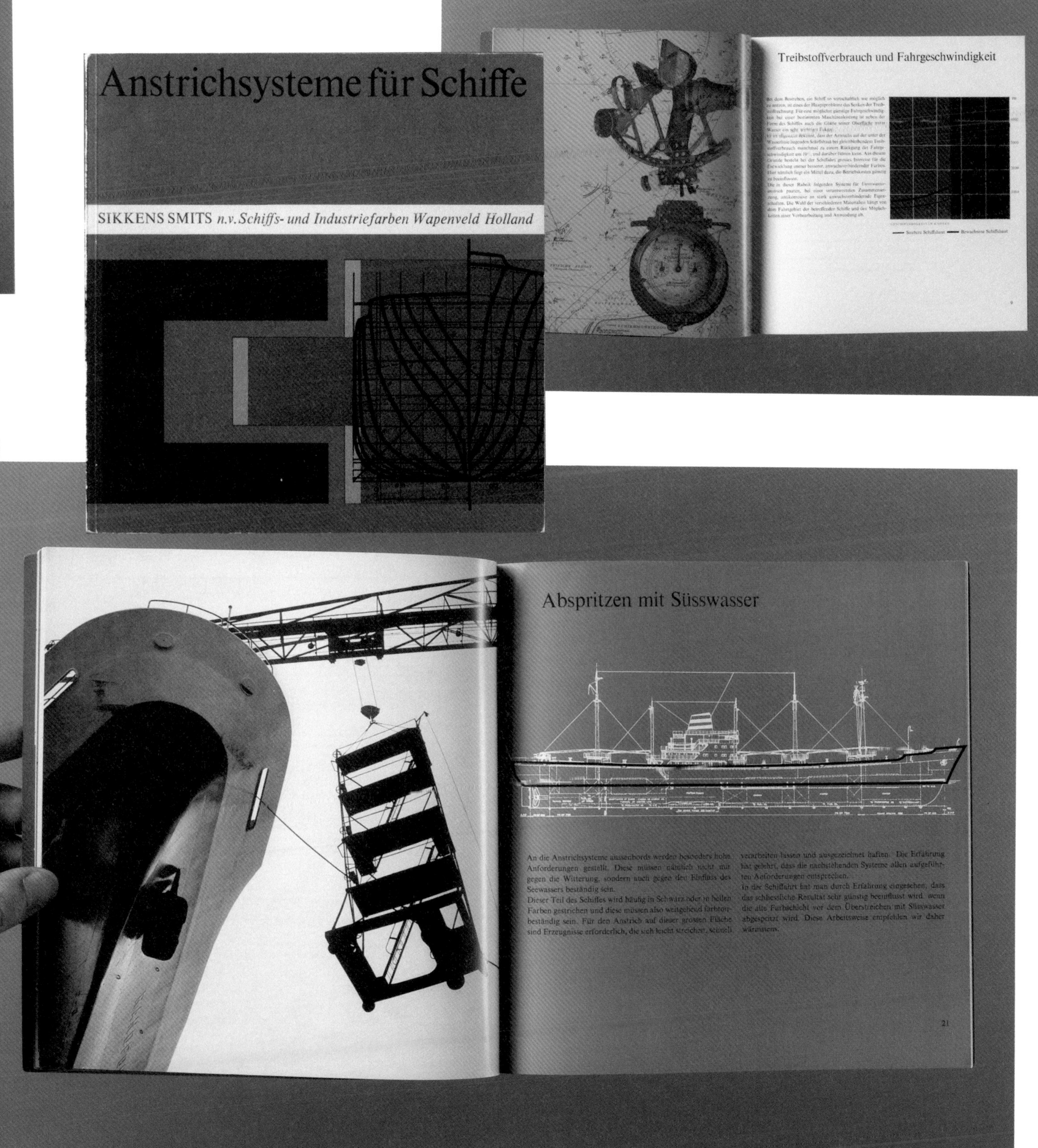

Anstrichsysteme für Schiffe (Painting programme for ships). Brochure cover and spreads, early 1960s. Client: Sikkens Smits. Photographs: Hans de Boer

NAVIGARE NECESSE EST
werd het motto voor onze drukkerij-
kalender 1961, die in druk een beeld
hoopt te geven van noodzakelijk varen

NAVIGARE NECESSE EST
werd het motto voor onze drukkerij-
kalender 1961, die in druk een beeld
hoopt te geven van noodzakelijk varen

Navigare Necesse Est (Navigation is vital). 1961 calendar cover and pages. Publisher and printer: Mart.Spruijt

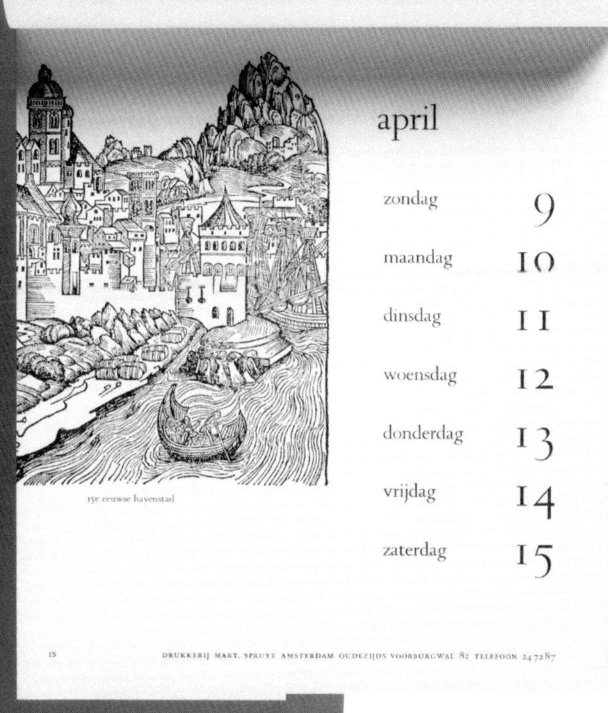

15e eeuwse havenstad

april

zondag	9
maandag	10
dinsdag	11
woensdag	12
donderdag	13
vrijdag	14
zaterdag	15

15 DRUKKERIJ MART. SPRUYT AMSTERDAM OUDEZIJDS VOORBURGWAL 82 TELEFOON 247287

VOORBEELDEN

VAN HET DRUKWERK TEN DIENSTE VAN DE SCHEEPVAART

druk VOOR WAL EN SCHIP

mei

zondag	7	
maandag	8	
dinsdag	9	
woensdag	10	
donderdag	11	HEMELVAART
vrijdag	12	
zaterdag	13	

19 DRUKKERIJ MART. SPRUYT AMSTERDAM OUDEZIJDS VOORBURGWAL 82 TELEFOON 247287

oktober|november

a b

Spaanse kompasrozen van *a* Rodrigo Çamorano (1581) en *b* Ferdinandus Oliverius de Sancta Columba (1550-1560). Uit A. Schück, Der Kompass

zondag	29
maandag	30
dinsdag	31
woensdag	1
donderdag	2
vrijdag	3
zaterdag	4

44 DRUKKERIJ MART. SPRUYT AMSTERDAM OUDEZIJDS VOORBURGWAL 82 TELEFOON 247287

Letter. 1963 calendar cover and pages. Publisher and printer: Mart.Spruijt

1969/70 calendar cover and pages. Publisher and printer: Mart.Spruijt

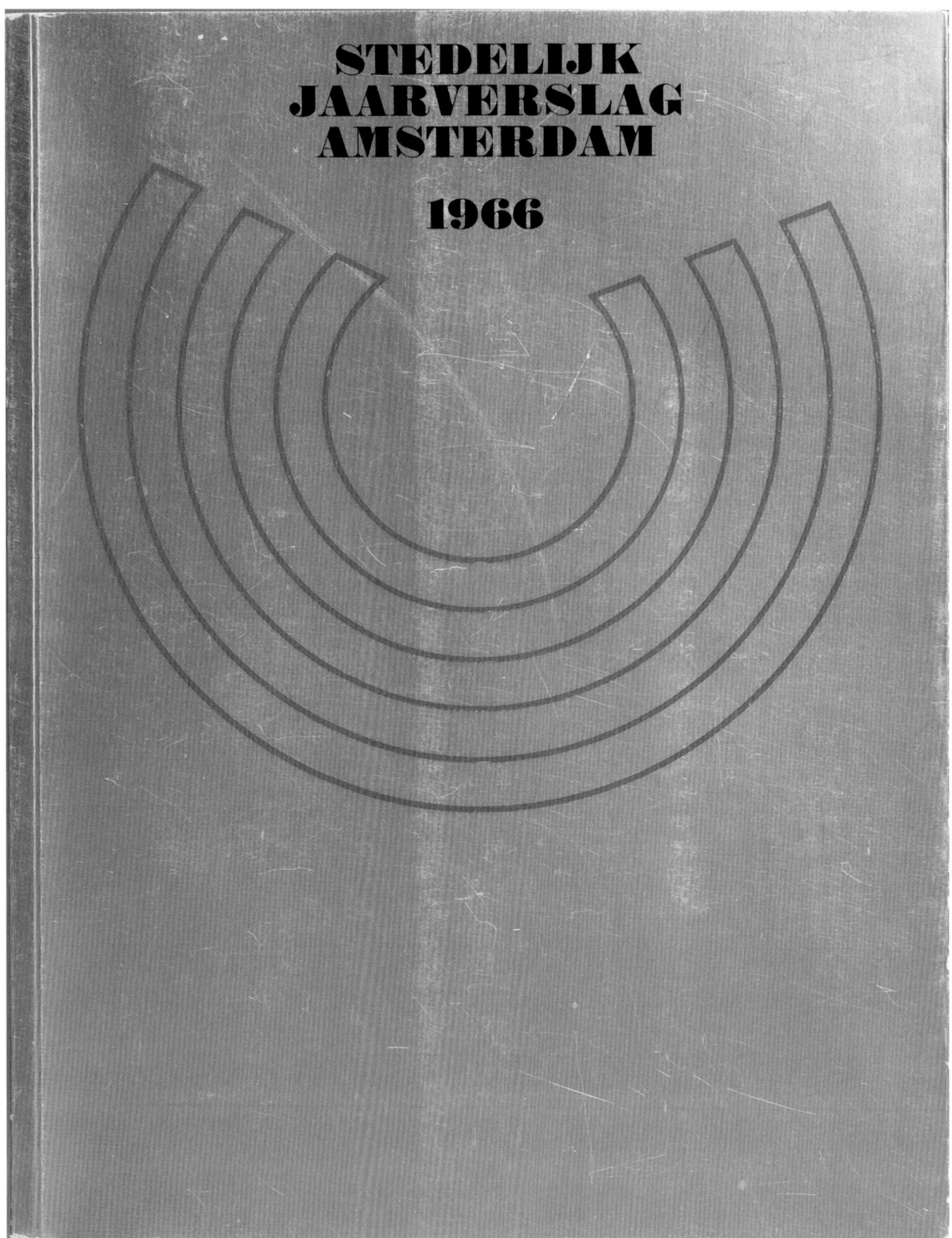

Stedelijk Jaarverslag Amsterdam 1966. Annual report, cover and spreads, 1967. Photographs: Paul van den Bos, Cor Jaring and others

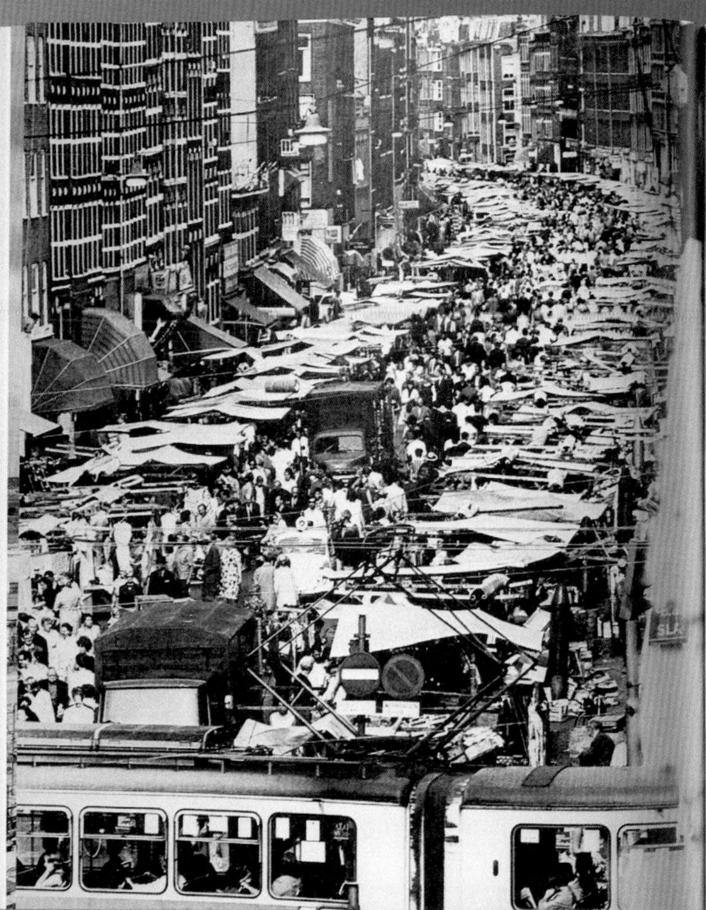

nen, goed wonen, kan men in iedere gemeente van ons land. Maar wonen in Amsterdam is léven in sterdam. Dat door de burgerij vaak chauvinistisch bezongen leefklimaat wordt bepaald door de veel- igheid van de stad, het conglomeraat van uiteenlopende beroepen, de aanwezigheid van talrijke turele en wetenschappelijke centra, de internationale contacten en een aangenaam decor, dat zich strekt van de oude binnenstad tot de meest moderne woonwijken en waarin speelplaatsen en parken, egen en kerken, theaters en clubhuizen mogelijkheden bieden voor creatie en recreatie, bezinning en cussie.

wen aan de toekomst van Amsterdam is meer dan het ontwerpen en doen uitvoeren van bouwplannen. is tevens waken over de cultuurhistorische monumenten en over het behoud van alle facetten, die sterdam tot een leefbare stad maken. Het is ook het opvangen en inpassen van nieuwe stromingen in levenspatroon van de bevolking, hetgeen zich kan uiten in de behoefte aan een winkelcentrum, aan stadsspoorweg of aan een speakers corner.

3

Amsterdam-woonstad

Amsterdam, stad van grachten, bomen, torens, terrasjes; stad van arbeiders, zakenmensen, kunstenaars, studenten; kleurrijke gemeenschap van mensen; leefstad: Woonstad.

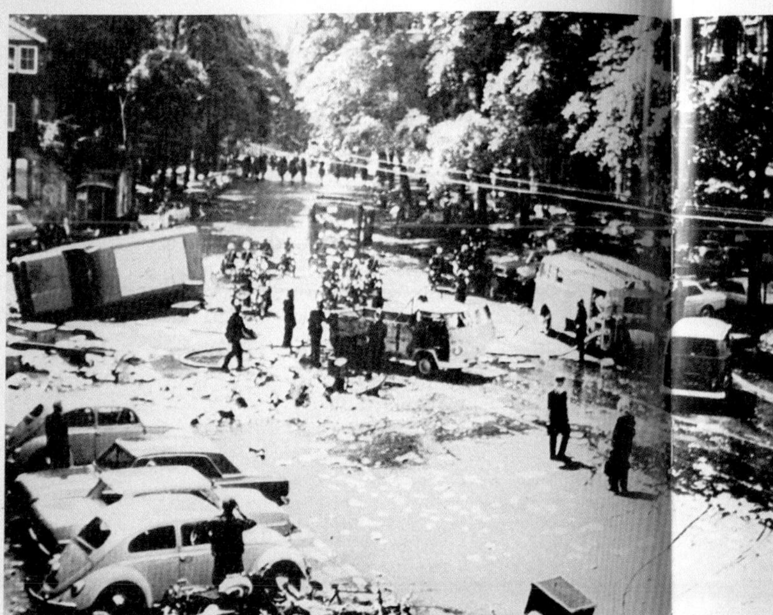

De Nieuwezijds Voorburgwal na de bestorming van het gebouw van dagblad De Telegraaf, de inleiding tot een dag, die aan een revolutie deed denken.

van 90 man rijkspolitie gevraagd; hij kreeg er 30. Op 22 mei bracht hij de aanvrage, in overleg met het ministerie van Binnenlandse zaken, terug tot 60 man, doch vroeg tegelijkertijd per 31 mei tevens bijstand van 100 man koninklijke marechaussee. Dit laatste verzoek werd niet ingewilligd.
Op 14 juni echter, toen de vlam in de pan sloeg, werd de assistentie onmiddellijk tot ruim 1400 man rijkspolitie en koninklijke marechaussee verhoogd.
De eerste onderdelen van de toegezegde versterking arriveerden in de middag van 14 juni in Amsterdam, waar zij onmiddellijk werden ingezet om te zamen met de mobiele eenheid van de hoofdstedelijke politie de onlusten in de binnenstad, die tot in de nacht duurden, te bestrijden. Hierbij werd gebruik gemaakt van traangashandgranaten. De politie werd met stenen bekogeld door groepen jongelui, die uit pure baldadigheid ruiten van warenhuizen en winkels vernielden en verkeersborden en parkeermeters uit de grond rukten. Er deden zich gelukkig geen ernstige ongelukken voor. De 'juni-opstand' leidde tot 63 gewonden onder de burgers en 28 onder de politie. Er werden 43 personen gearresteerd.
Ook op de avond van 15 juni lokken groepen jongeren, onder wie velen, die uit sensatielust van elders naar Amsterdam zijn gekomen, ongeregeldheden uit door het uitdagen van de politie, het gooien van stenen en opwerpen van barricades. Twee personen worden gewond en 19 gearresteerd.

Per advertentie, die overigens door een aantal kranten wordt geweigerd, publiceren dan 850 Nederlanders (hoogleraren, schrijvers, acteurs, journalisten, studenten) een manifest, waarin zij van de regering, kamerleden, burgemeesters en rechters verlangen 'dat al het mogelijke wordt gedaan om rede en billijkheid in onze rechtsbedeling te herstellen. Die rede en billijkheid zijn nu zoek'.

14|6

89

Drukkersweekblad en Autolijn, Christmas issue. Journal cover and spreads, 1968. Publishers: Federation of Master Printers and the Netherlands Photo-Engravers Association. Photographs: Joost Guntenaar, Aart Klein and Hans Samson

61 Fles, Islamitisch, middeleeuwen. 62 Drinkbeker met reticella-werk (kant-glas). Venetië omstreeks 1560. 63 Vleugelglas, façon de Venise. Nederlands of Duits 17e eeuw. 65 Slurfbeker, Frankisch, 6e eeuw. Gemeentemuseum, Den Haag. 64 Guttrolf, façon de Venise, Waarschijnlijk Duits 17e eeuw. 66 Vaas van geëmailleerd glas, Spanje 16e/17e eeuw. 67 Roemertje, versierd in diamantgravure. Getekend 'Anna Roemers, anno 1621'. Nederlands. Rijksmuseum, Amsterdam. 68 Fles met versiering van gekleurde glasdraden. Romeins, Keulen 2e eeuw. 69 Glazen potten. Romeins 1e of 2e eeuw. Rijksmuseum G. M. Kam, Nijmegen. 70 Voorraadfles, 19e eeuw. Door bolling van het glas lijken de eieren groter. 71 Links: Kogelflesjes, Nederland 1906 tot ongeveer 1935. Rechts: Glasplastieken van H. P. Berlage, Leerdam 1926. Stichting nationaal glasmuseum, Leerdam.

61 Bottle, Islamitic, medieval. 62 Goblet in reticella technique. Venice ca. 1560. 63 Wing glass, façon de Venise, probably German 17th cent.
64 Elephant's trunk goblet. Frankish, 6th cent. 65 Guttrolf, façon de Venise, probably German 17th cent.
66 Enamelled glass vase, Spain 16th/17th cent. 67 Small rummer, decorated with diamond engraving. Signed 'Anna Roemers, anno 1621'. Netherlands. 68 Bottle with decoration in the form of coloured glass threads. Roman. Cologne 2nd cent. 69 Glass pots. Roman 1st or 2nd cent. 70 Glass jar, 19th cent. The con vexity of the glass makes the eggs look bigger. 71 Left: Stopper bottles, Netherlands 1906 to ca. 1935. Right: Glass 'sculptures' by H. P. Berlage, Leerdam 1926.

76 Altaarvleugel met voorstellingen uit het leven van Maria. Boven: Verkondiging en visitatie. Beneden: Geboorte en aanbidding der wijzen. Middelrijns meester, omstreeks 1410. Aartsbisschoppelijk museum, Utrecht.
76 Wing of altarpiece displaying scenes from the life of the Virgin Mary. Above: Annunciation and visitation. Below: Birth of Jesus and adoration of the magi. Middle-Rhine master, ca. 1410.

Kunsthistorische museums

Temidden van de 436 officieel erkende museums die ons land kent, bevindt zich een groot aantal, die wij veelal als kunstmuseums betitelen, doch die door velen als 'het museum' in de ware zin des woords worden beschouwd. Ideeën als: 'het lijkt daar wel een museum' en de term 'museumstuk' vinden waarschijnlijk hier in ons spraakgebruik hun oorsprong.
In dit museum-nummer is het haast vanzelfsprekend, dat niet al te diep ingegaan kan worden op de collecties van al deze kunstmusea; evenmin kan incidenteel worden ingegaan op hun ontstaan en verzamelgebied, en een uitgebreide kunsthistorische beschouwing zult u ook moeten ontberen. Hiervoor bestaan uitermate goede handboeken, door de verschillende museums uitgegeven. Al bladerende door dit kaleidoscopisch museumboek zal u de lust bekruipen, of ontvallen!, om meer gedetailleerd ingelicht te worden over een bepaald museum. Toch moeten vooraf enige algemene historische feiten worden vermeld, die de ontwikkelingsgang van de museums gekenmerkt hebben gedurende de laatste 150 jaar.
Het eerste openbare museum dat in Nederland geopend werd, was het Teylers museum in Haarlem, een 'universele collectie' omvattende voorwerpen als wetenschappelijke instrumenten, fossielen, naturaliën e.d. doch men legde zich later toe op het verzamelen van prenten en tekeningen. Het werd in 1798 opengesteld. In 1769 werd in Zeeland en wel te Vlissingen de grondslag gelegd voor een archeologisch en natuurhistorisch museum. Het eerste openbare kunstmuseum 'de Nationale kunst-gallery' in het Huis ten Bosch te Den Haag werd in 1800 opengesteld, daarna in 1805 naar het Buitenhof in Den Haag verplaatst.
In de hierna volgende jaren werd door Lodewijk Napoleon besloten tot oprichting van één of meer museums, hetgeen o.m. resulteerde in de openstelling van het Koninklijk museum te Amsterdam in 1808, waarin, naast de haast volledige collectie van de Nationale gallery uit Den Haag, aankopen van de koning, archeologische voorwerpen en schilderijen uit het bezit van de gemeente Amsterdam waren samengevoegd. Na 1815 vond gelukkig een verdeling plaats van al deze ver uit elkaar lopende zaken en zo ontstonden in 1821 het Mauritshuis te Den Haag, tussen 1820 en 1830 het Rijksmuseum van oudheden in Leiden en in 1837 eveneens in Leiden het Rijks etnografisch museum.
Dat in de loop van deze 100 of 150 jaar de gehele presentatie en soms ook het verzamelgebied veel verandering onderging behoeft geen betoog. Men hoeft slechts afbeeldingen van het museumbezoek anno 1870 en foto's van de hedendaagse openingen te vergelijken om in één oogopslag deze mentaliteitsverandering te onderkennen. Was het museumbezoek vroeger een privilege, weggelegd voor de verfijnde personen, behorende tot een bepaalde, welgestelde klasse, thans blijkt het museum meer en meer te worden een open ontmoetingscentrum waar kunstenaars en publiek elkaar kunnen treffen, soms kunnen botsen. Toch blijkt er nog, met name in de eigentijdse kunst, een grote niet te overbruggen kloof tussen kunstenaar en publiek, het vele goede werk van de educatieve diensten ten spijt. Integratie van beeldende kunst in het onderwijs zou wellicht hierin verandering kunnen brengen.

Temidden van deze kunstmuseums vinden we er, die zich gespecialiseerd hebben op een richting of een tijdsduur in de beeldende kunst, zoals bijvoorbeeld het Frans Halsmuseum te Haarlem en het Rijksmuseum Mesdag te Den Haag en het nieuw te bouwen Van Gogh museum. Opmerkelijk is echter dat het nationale karakter van onze museums, en wel voornamelijk dat van het Rijksmuseum, sterk benadrukt is. Dit in tegenstelling met de ontwikkeling van de grote museums in het buitenland, die hun verzameling specialiseerden op internationale scholen. Dit heeft tot gevolg gehad dat men in het Rijksmuseum een beeld kan krijgen van bijvoorbeeld de Nederlandse schilderkunst van de 15e tot en met het eind van de 19e eeuw. Veel van de hierachter in beeld gebrachte museums zijn ontstaan uit stichtingen, gegroeid uit particuliere verzamelingen of initiatieven. Naderhand werden deze verzamelingen of stichtingen onder provinciaal- of gemeentebestuur gesteld. Het is opmerkelijk dat al vroeg de overheden het belang van een stedelijke of provinciale collectie inzagen. Zo zien wij bijvoorbeeld dat reeds in 1856 het Gemeentemuseum Arnhem, in 1862 het Frans Halsmuseum in Haarlem en bijv. in 1899 het Stedelijk museum van Schiedam gesticht werden.
In het begin van dit artikel stelde ik al, dat het ondoenlijk is om in zo'n kort bestek aan te geven, wat de hoogtepunten in collecties van de Nederlandse kunstmuseums zijn. Bovendien zijn er vaak speciale voorkeuren voor niet het bekende of beroemde werk, maar juist bewondering voor het onverwachte, het vertederende of fantastische van wie door het publiek 'kleine meesters' worden genoemd. Daarom zou ik eenvoudig willen zeggen, dat in de Nederlandse kunstmuseums van vroeg middeleeuwse sculpturen tot mobiles en van primitieven tot minimal-art te genieten valt, met tussen deze uiterste polen in één grote staalkaart van stijlen en opvattingen, zó rijk geschakeerd, dat wij terecht internationaal gezien een bijzonder boeiend museumland zijn. Het is verheugend te constateren, dat wij zowel op het gebied van de oude kunst als op het gebied van de eigentijdse kunst enige museums bezitten met een wereldberoemde vermaardheid om hun collecties, doch de laatste tientallen jaren ook om hun exposities. Exposities, die vooral in de

Museums of art

Among the 436 officially recognized museums in this country, are a large number often referred to as 'art galleries', but regarded by many as 'museums' in the true sense of the word. Phrases such as 'the place is like a museum' and the term a 'museum piece' probably originate in our speech usage on this point. Obviously in this museum number no very detailed discussion of the collections in all these museums can be entered on. Nor can the reader expect a circumstantial account of their origins and what they specialize in, nor an extensive treatment of them in terms of art-history. Such aspects are to be found in the excellent handbooks published by the various museums themselves. As the reader leafs through this kaleidoscopic museum book the urge will no doubt come over him (or leave him!) to learn more about a particular museum.
Among the museums of visual art we find some that have specialized in one school or period, like the Frans Hals museum at Haarlem, or the National museum Mesdag at The Hague, or the planned Van Gogh museum. One striking fact, however, is that the national character of our museums, and in particular that of the Rijksmuseum, is strongly emphasized. This contrasts with the way most of the big foreign museums have developed, with their collections specializing in international schools. What it means is that in the Rijksmuseum one can find a survey of Dutch painting, for example, from the 15th century to the end of the 19th. Many of the museums illustrated in the pages that follow were started by foundations developed from private collections or private initiatives. At some later date these collections or foundations were placed under the management of town or provincial councils. It is remarkable how early the authorities became aware of the importance of having municipal or provincial collections. For example the Municipal museum at Arnhem was founded as early as 1856, the Frans Hals museum at Haarlem in 1862, and the Municipal museum at Schiedam in 1899.
At the beginning of this article I stated that it was out of the question in the limited space available to list the highlights of the collections in the Dutch museums. Moreover what people want to see is often not the works that are well-known or famous, but the unexpected, the charming or fantastic works by the artists whom the public calls 'minor masters'. I would therefore simply like to say that whether it is early-medieval sculpture or mobiles, primitives or minimal-art the visitor is looking for, he will find it in the galleries of the Netherlands, and, in between, a great range of styles and schools, so richly varied that this country is rightly regarded from an international standpoint as an exceptionally exciting field for the museum-goer. It is encouraging to note that we possess museums of both older and contemporary art that have become world-famous not only for their collections, but also in the last few decades for their exhibitions. These exhibitions, especially those put on by the museums of contemporary art, have been particularly interesting as regards their style of presentation, a completely new aspect of museum management. Photographs of older exhibition lay-outs in this number provoke in us a sympathetic smile, and prompt us to ask whether in such labyrinths anyone could really have enjoyed the exhibits.
Comparision with other countries shows that where the presentation of objects in museums is concerned, the Netherlands stands in the front rank. Unfortunately the same cannot be said for our acquisition of important objects. In this respect other countries are often far in advance of us.
If we go on to take museum-goers themselves, over the last 150 years shall we say, one of the things that strikes us immediately is how the dignified visitors striding into the museum in the painting by A. van Allebé, have made way for more ordinary people who drop in to the museum 'en passant' as it were.

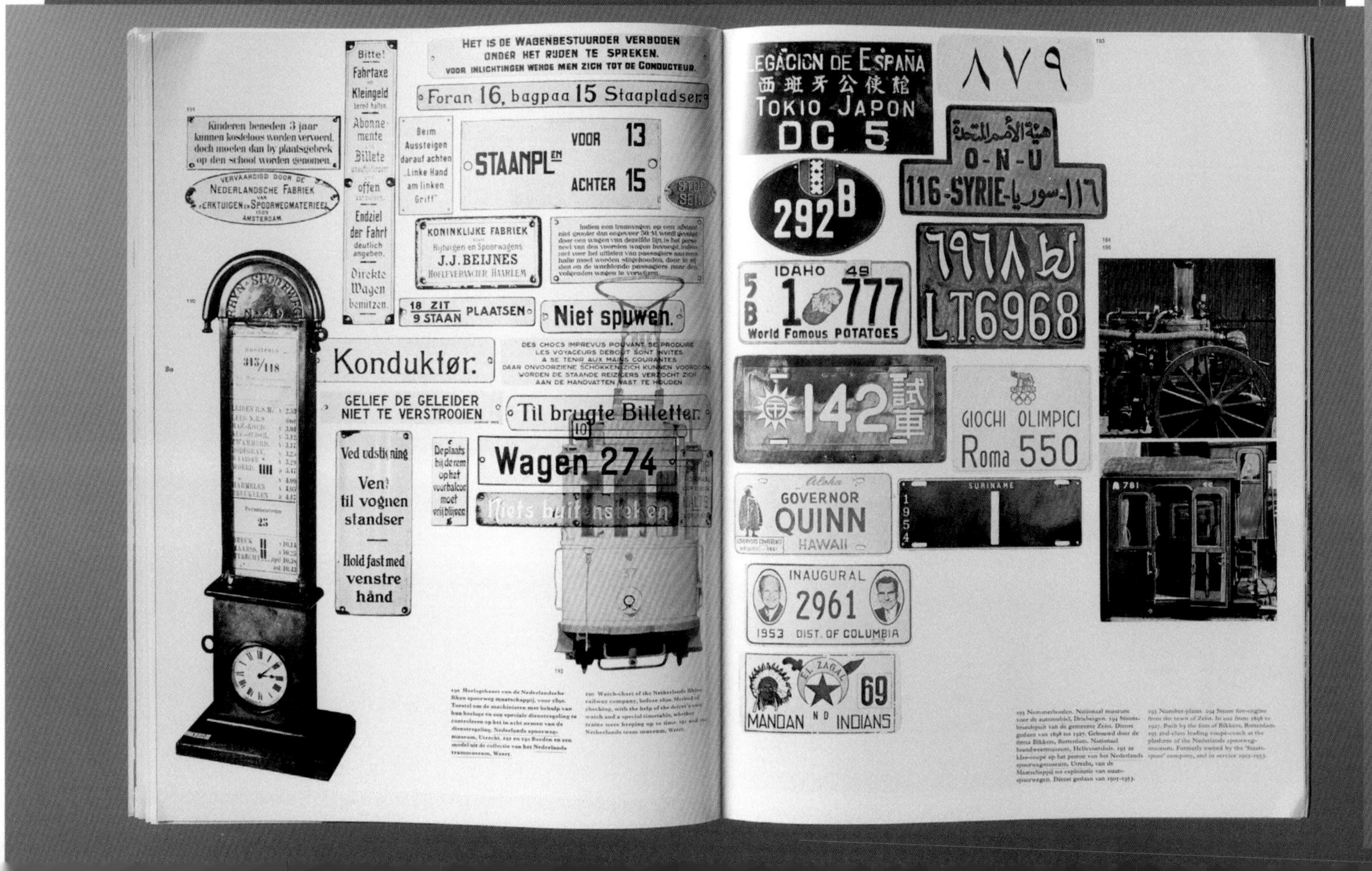

Drukkersweekblad en Autolijn, Christmas issue. Journal spreads, 1968. Publishers: Federation of Master Printers and the Netherlands Photo-Engravers Association. Photographs: Joost Guntenaar, Aart Klein and Hans Samson

Chronique Sikkens Varia no. 56. Journal cover and spreads, 1968. Publisher: Sikkens Groep

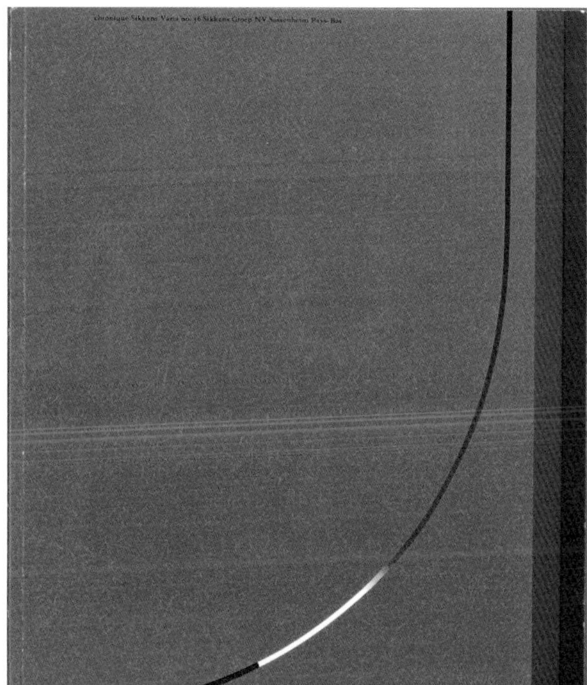

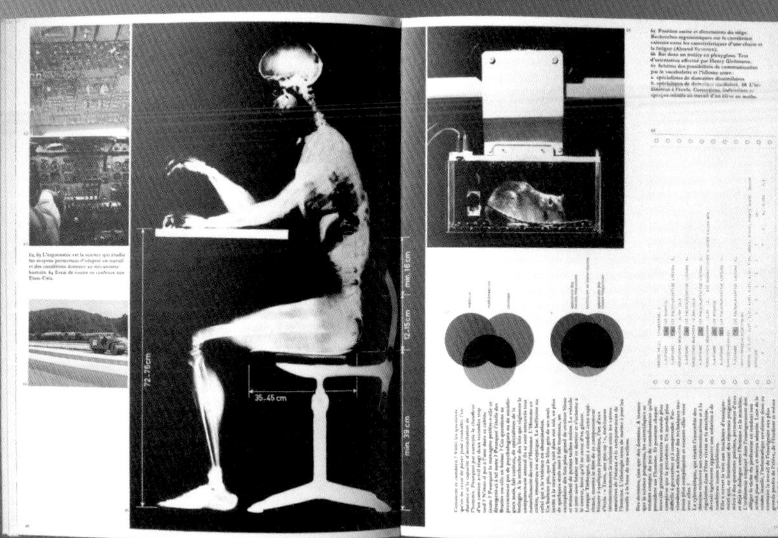

36 Beat of Blood, le battement du sang, est une enluminure symbolisant les dieux hindous. C'est une « ambiance » d'USCO, New York. USCO est une expérience de coexistence sans dogmatisme, se recommandant de l'amour universel et utilisant toutes les techniques : peinture, sculpture, photographie, acoustique, radio, cinéma, télévision.
Ses adeptes, dont une douzaine habitent dans une église désaffectée de New York, maîtrisent tous l'une de ces techniques. USCO nous concerne tous, au même titre que les douze habitants de l'ancienne église new-yorkaise.
37 Nébuleuse photographiée avec le télescope à miroir 5,08 m du Mont-Palomar.
38 L'astronaute Allen Shephard.

Que découvriront les futurs astronautes en pénétrant toujours plus loin dans les blancs du cosmos ? La vie ? L'absence de vie ?

Que la vie existe à l'état extra-terrestre est un fait confirmé par les experts présents au Congrès de la Biologie tenue en 1967 à Londres.

Des chercheurs de la NASA ont déclaré que des sondes lancées à 15 000 mètres avaient permis de déceler 70 à 100 micro-organismes dans 1 000 m³ d'air. À 45 000 mètres ces sondes avaient encore découvert des sporules de moisissures.

Plus modeste que le cosmonaute affirmant qu'il n'avait pas vu Dieu, le professeur Freudenthal de la Faculté d'Utrecht a mis au point un langage cosmique qui nous permettrait de communiquer avec des êtres intelligents sur d'autres planètes. Cette langue est basée sur des formules mathématiques représentées par des signaux de plus ou moins forte amplitude.

Le projet Apollo, démarré il y a quelques années, visé à envoyer trois Américains sur la Lune. Le vaisseau et ses trois hommes d'équipage représentent un poids total de 40 tonnes, c'est-à-dire presque autant que la Nina, la plus petite des caravelles de Christophe Colomb.[1]

1 Der Spiegel, 1966-67

"THE MUSEUM SHOULD RELATE TO THE PUBLİC AS A PARTNER İN DİALOGUE, NOT AS A TEACHER." Jan van Toorn

vijf jonge grafici Dick Cassée Ko Oosterkerk Rob Otte Zoltin Peeter Marte Röling vijf jonge grafici Dick Cassée Ko Oosterkerk Rob Otte Zoltin Peeter Marte Röling vijf jonge grafici D ick Cassée Ko Oosterkerk

Stedelijk van Abbemuseum Eindhoven

8 januari tot en met 13 februari 1966

vijf jonge grafici Dick Cassée Ko Oosterkerk Rob Otte Zoltin Peeter Marte Röling vijf jonge grafici Dick Cassée Ko Oosterkerk Rob Otte Zoltin Peeter Marte Röling vijf jonge grafici D

dagelijks geopend van 10-17 uur
zondag van 14-18 uur
dinsdag- en donderdagavond van 20-22 uur

Posters for Van Abbemuseum, pp. 39–68

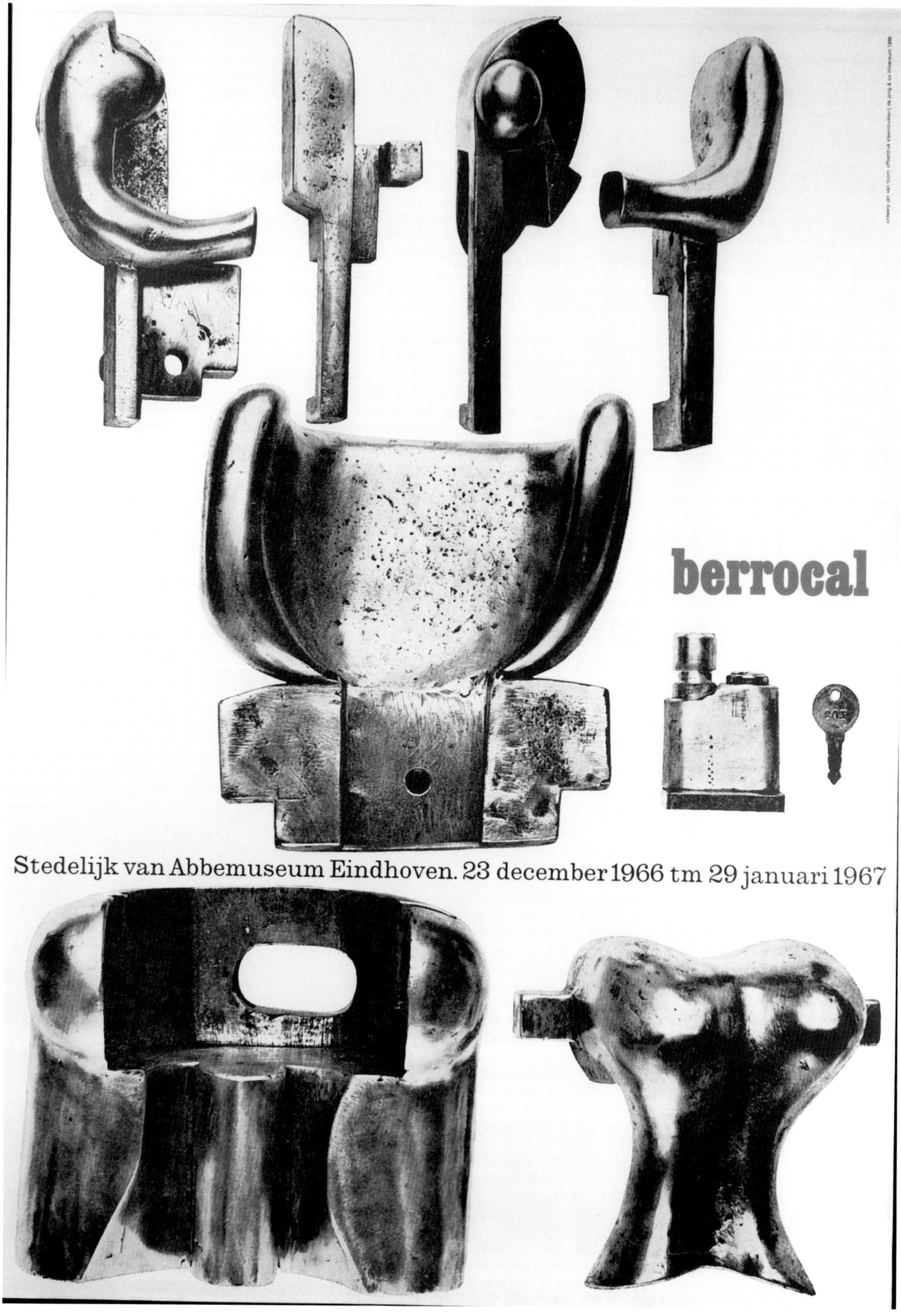

berrocal

Stedelijk van Abbemuseum Eindhoven. 23 december 1966 tm 29 januari 1967

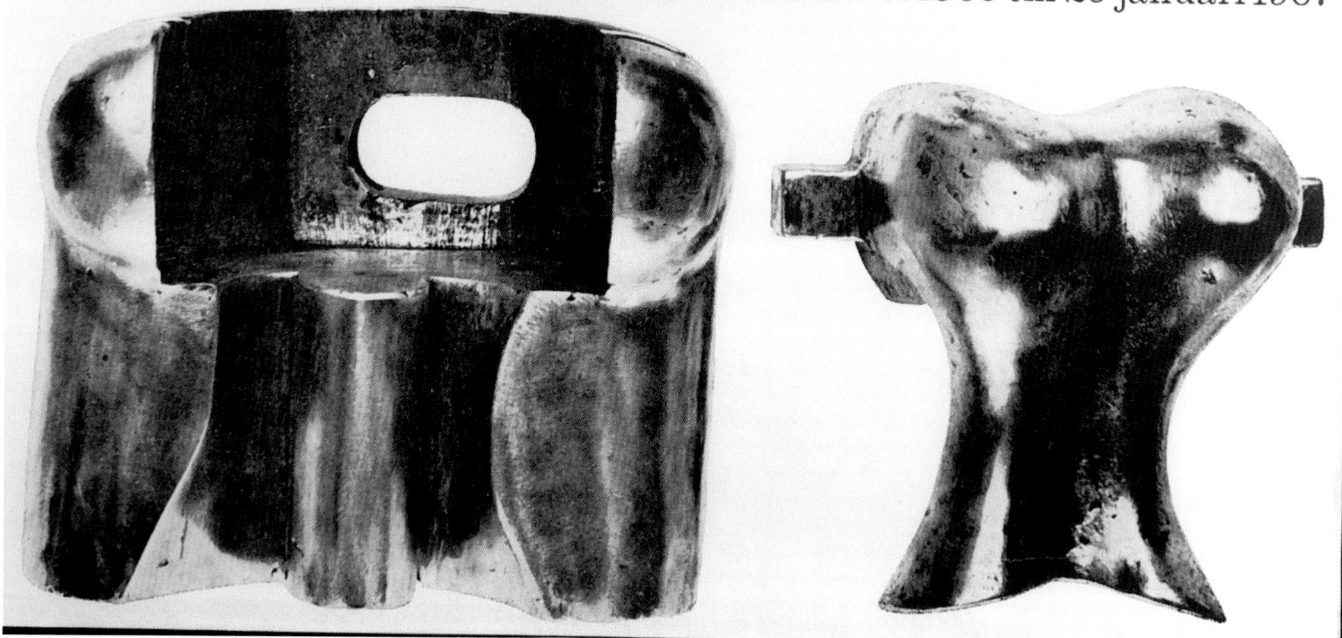

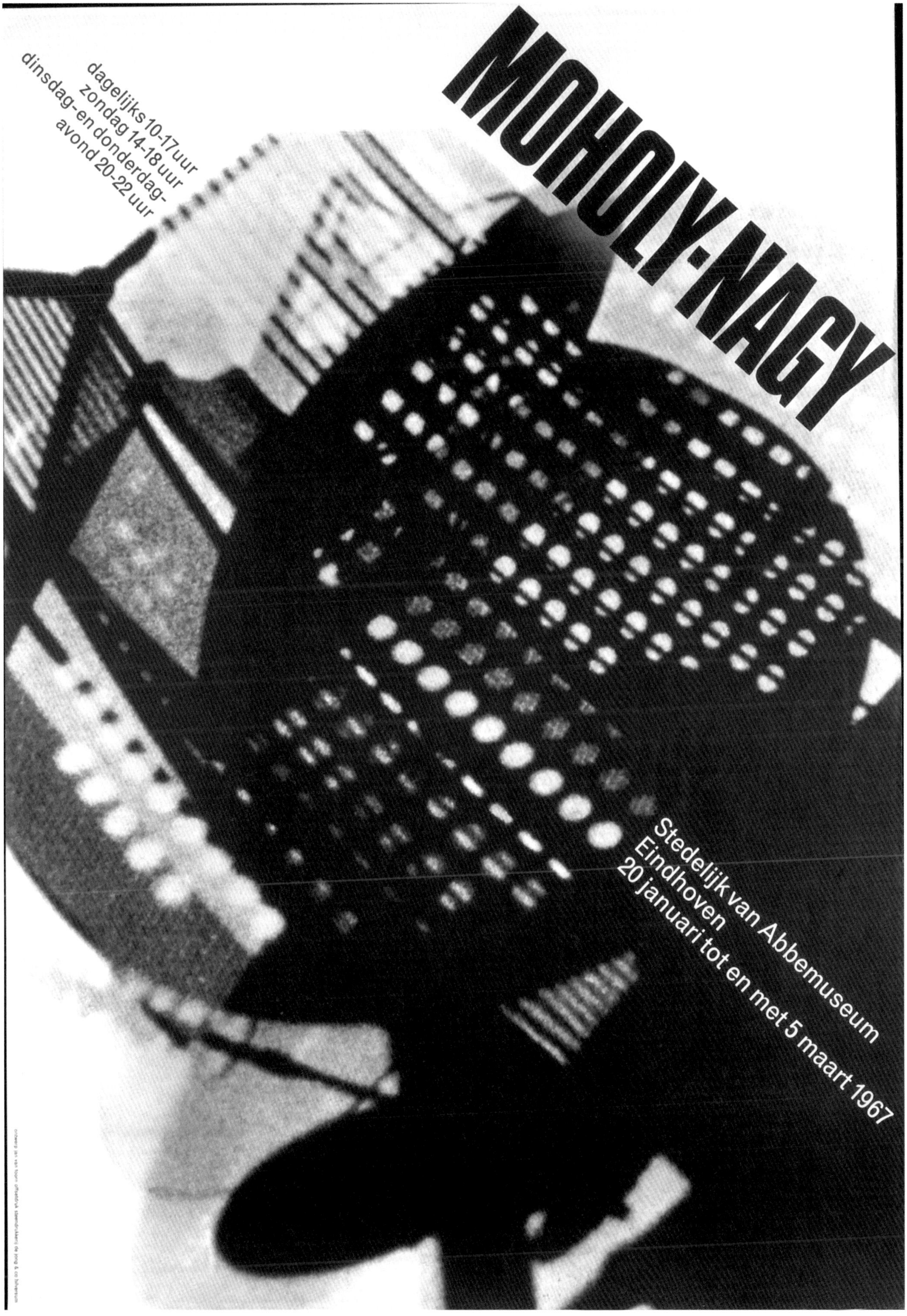
MOHOLY-NAGY
dagelijks 10-17 uur
zondag 14-18 uur
dinsdag- en donderdag-
avond 20-22 uur
Stedelijk van Abbemuseum
Eindhoven
20 januari tot en met 5 maart 1967
ontwerp jan van toorn offsetdruk steendrukkerij de jong & co hilversum

Stedelijk van Abbemuseum Eindhoven 17 maart tot en met 23 april 1967
Groninger Museum voor stad en lande 28 april tot en met 28 mei 1967

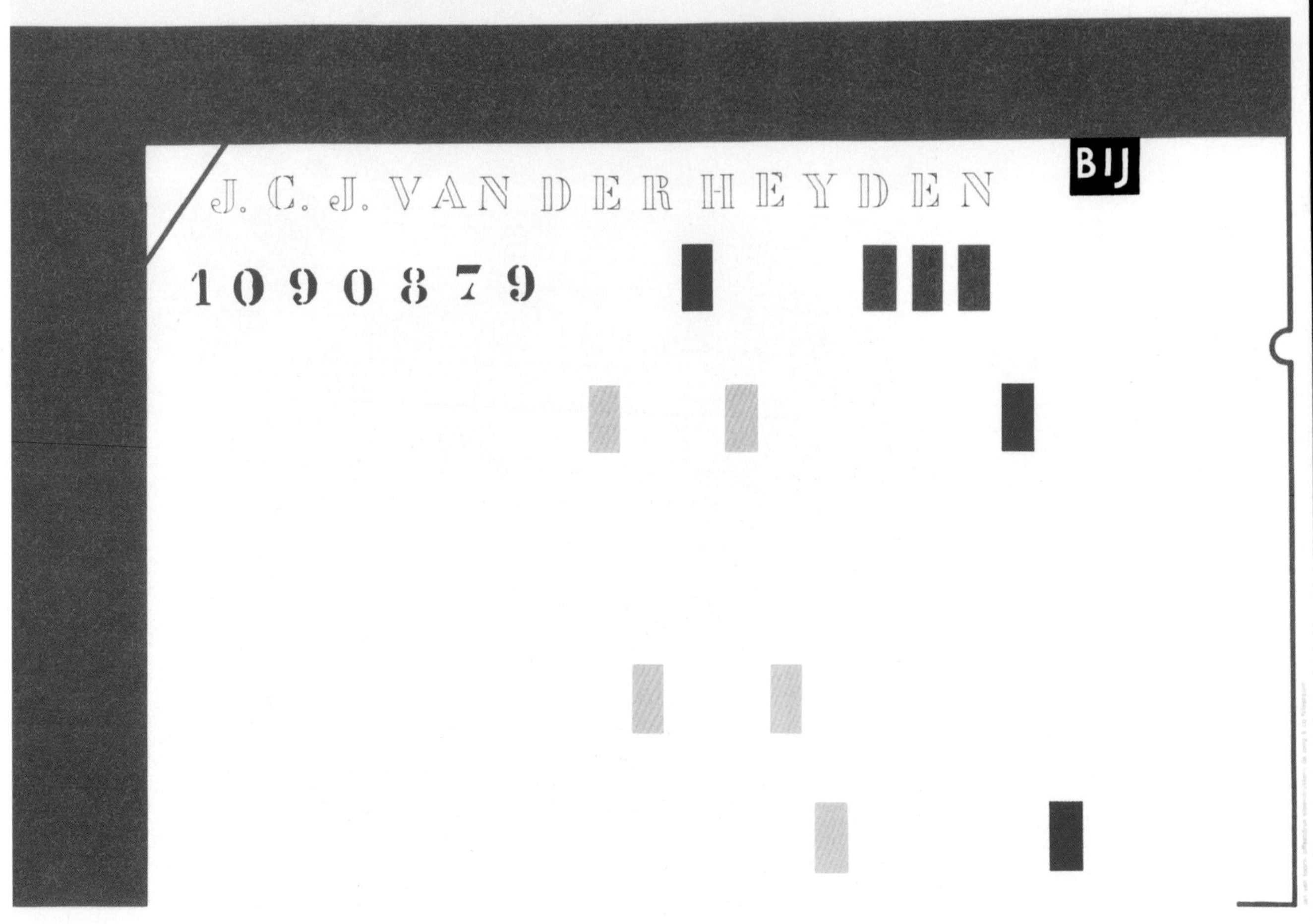

schilderingen grafiek

Stedelijk van Abbemuseum Eindhoven

PI

21 april tot en met 4 juni 1967

CA

BIA

FONTANA

Lucio Fontana
concetti spaziali
Stedelijk van Abbemuseum
Eindhoven
12 mei tot en met 18 juni 1967
openingstijden:
dagelijks van 10 tot 17 uur
zondag van 14 tot 18 uur

jan van toorn offsetdruk steendrukkerij de jong & co hilversum

Rijksmuseum Kröller-Müller Otterlo 15.7.tot 27.8.67
Stedelijk van Abbemuseum Eindhoven 8.9.tot 15.10.67

KOMPAS
schilderkunst uit New York na 1945
Stedelijk van Abbemuseum
Eindhoven
9 november tot en met
17 december 1967
peningstijden: dagelijks 10 tot 5 uur
zondag 2 tot 6 uur
dinsdag en donderdagavond
8 tot 10 uur
3
hommage Edwaerd Hopper
Jackson Pollock
Willem de Kooning
Franz Kline
Robert Motherwell
Arshile Gorky
Mark Rothko
Clifford Still
Ad Reinhardt
Barnett Newmann
Jasper Johns
Robert Rauschenberg
Andy Warhol
Roy Lichtenstein
James Rosenquist
Claes Oldenburg
Elsworth Kelly
Morris Louis
Kenneth Noland
Larry Poons
Frank Stella
Robbert Morris
Donald Judd
Dan Flavin

een fotografische dokumentatie
door Bernd en Hilla Becher
Stedelijk van Abbemuseum Eindhoven
5 januari tm 11 februari 1968

BOUWEN
VOOR DE
INDUSTRIE

in de 19e en 20e eeuw

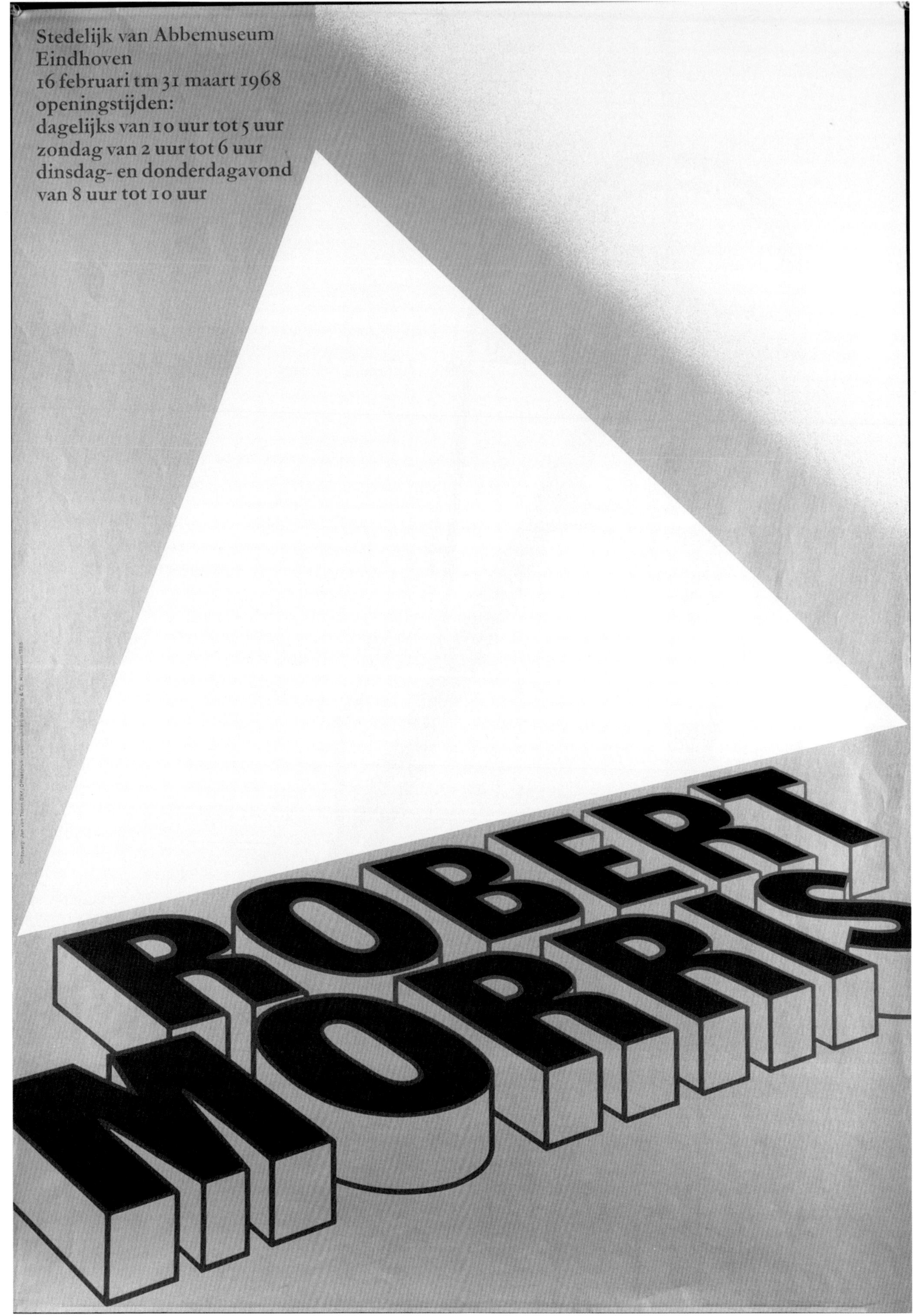
Stedelijk van Abbemuseum
Eindhoven
16 februari tm 31 maart 1968
openingstijden:
dagelijks van 10 uur tot 5 uur
zondag van 2 uur tot 6 uur
dinsdag- en donderdagavond
van 8 uur tot 10 uur
ROBERT
MORRIS

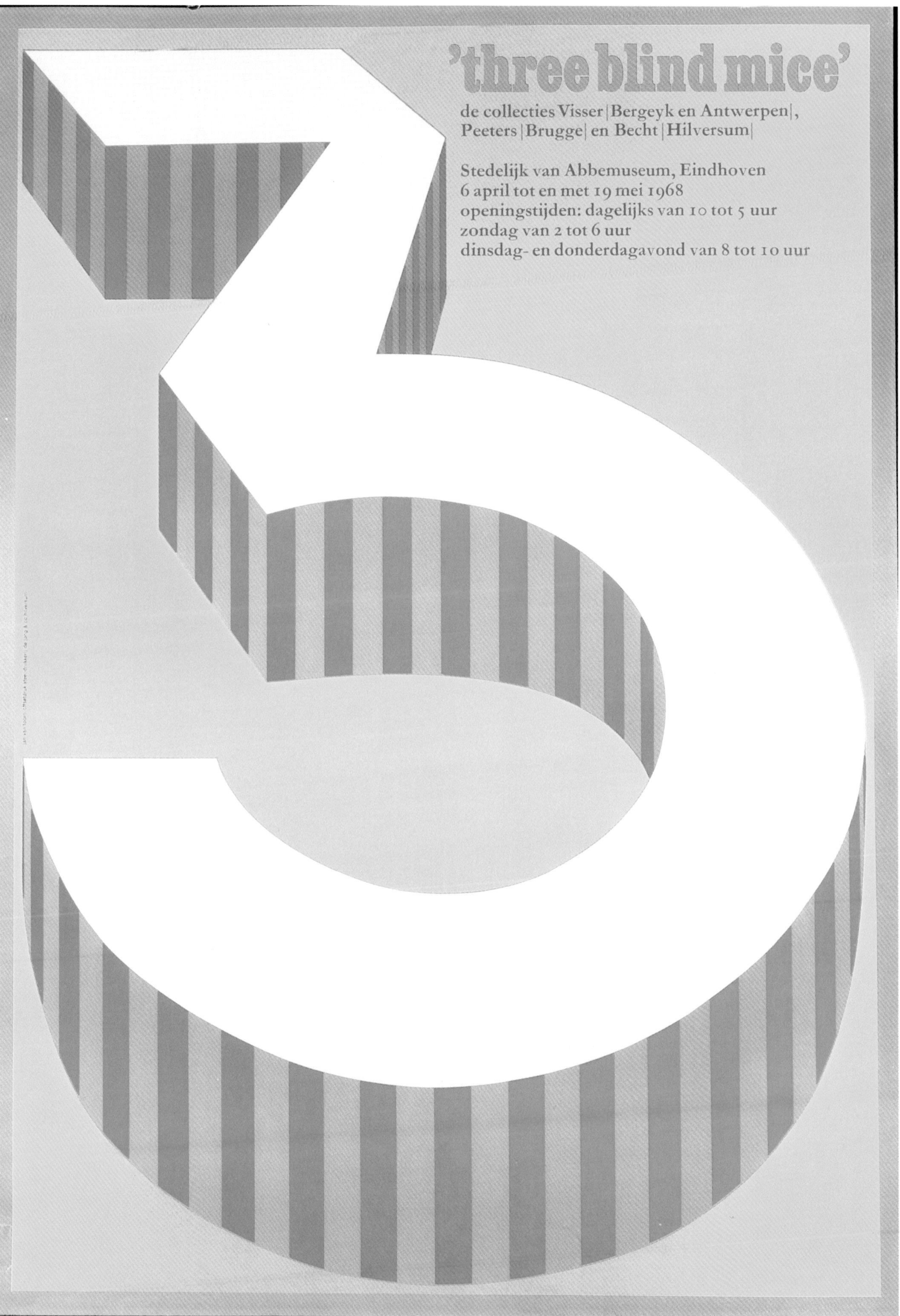
'three blind mice'
de collecties Visser|Bergeyk en Antwerpen|,
Peeters|Brugge| en Becht|Hilversum|
Stedelijk van Abbemuseum, Eindhoven
6 april tot en met 19 mei 1968
openingstijden: dagelijks van 10 tot 5 uur
zondag van 2 tot 6 uur
dinsdag- en donderdagavond van 8 tot 10 uur

openingstijden: dagelijks 10 tot 5 uur zondag 2 tot 6 uur
dinsdag- en donderdagavond 8 tot 10 uur
architect
HANS SCHAROUN
Stedelijk van Abbemuseum Eindhoven
13 september tot|met
13 oktober 1968
ontwerp: jan van toorn gkf/offsetdruk: steendrukkerij de jong & co. hilversum 1968

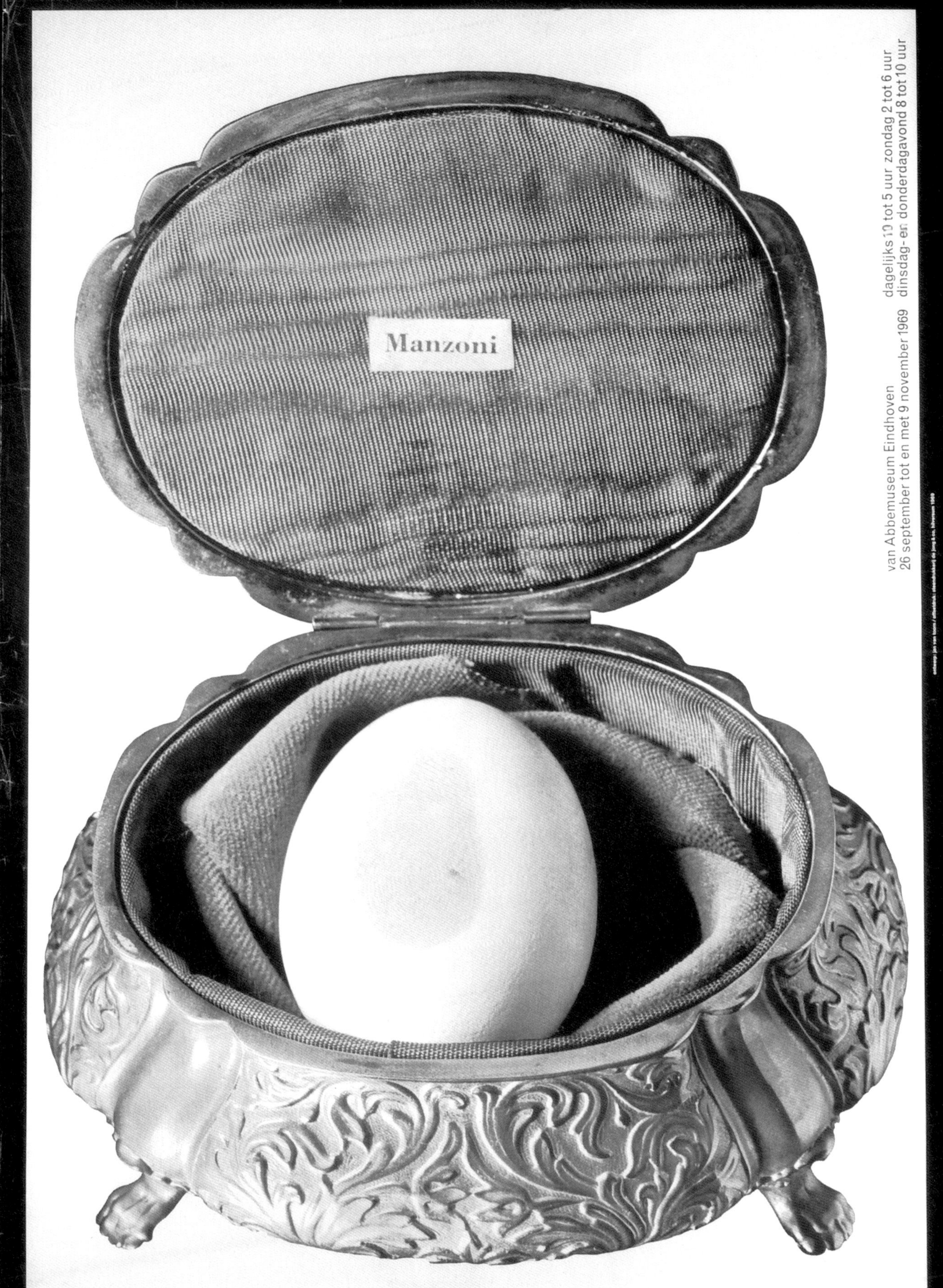
Manzoni
van Abbemuseum Eindhoven
26 september tot en met 9 november 1969
dagelijks 10 tot 5 uur zondag 2 tot 6 uur
dinsdag- en donderdagavond 8 tot 10 uur

DON

JUDD

VAN ABBEMUSEUM EINDHOVEN

16.1.1970 TM 1.3.1970

DAGELIJKS 10 TOT 5 UUR ZONDAG 2 TOT 6 UUR

DINSDAG-EN DONDERDAGAVOND 8 TOT 10 UUR

PROJEKTEN EN OBJEKTEN JOS MANDERS VAN ABBEMUSEUM

Eindhoven 13 maart tot en met 19 april 1970

dagelijks 10 tot 17 uur, zondag 14 tot 18 uur, dinsdagavond 20 tot 22 uur

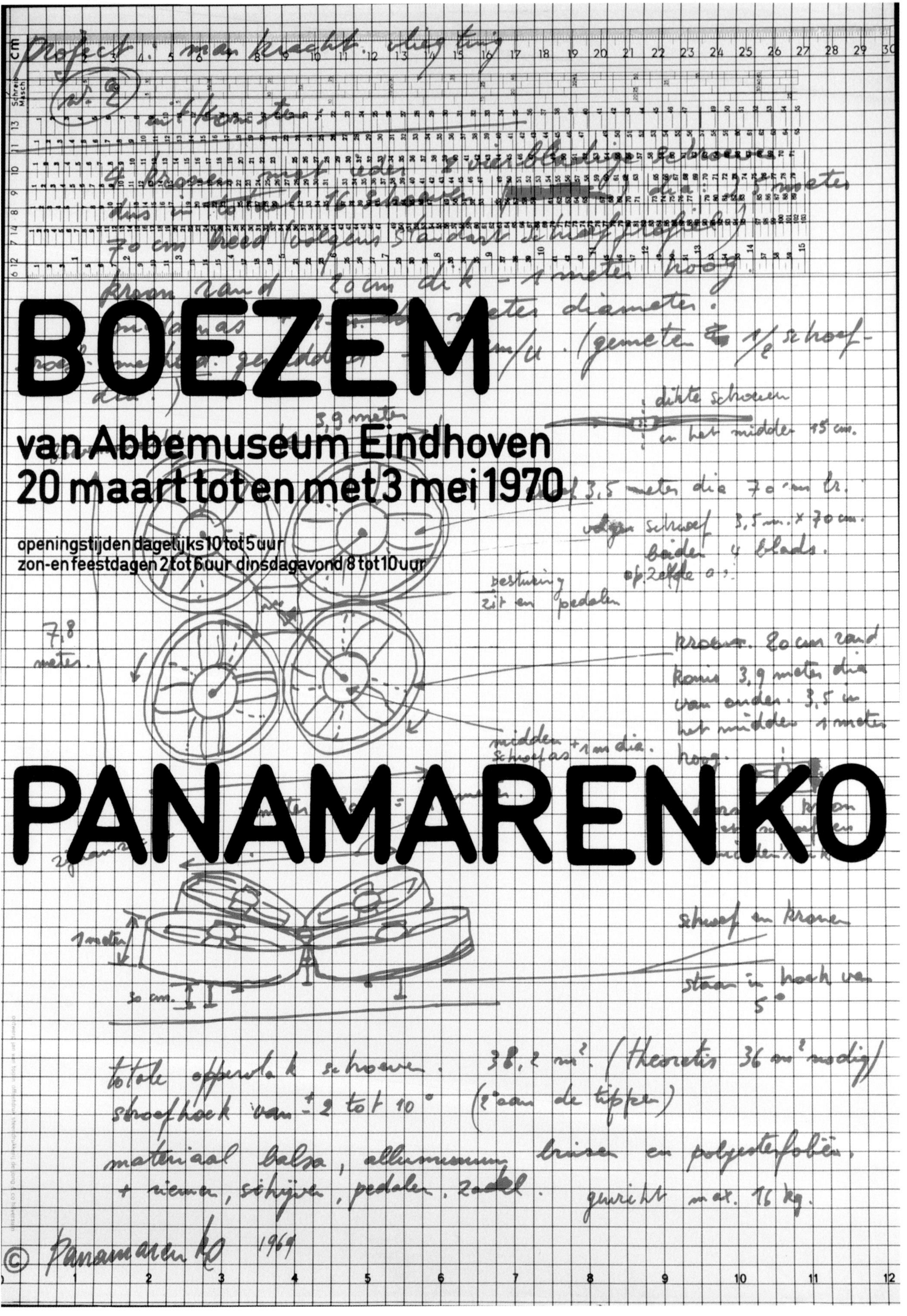
BOEZEM
van Abbemuseum Eindhoven
20 maart tot en met 3 mei 1970
openingstijden dagelijks 10 tot 5 uur
zon-en feestdagen 2 tot 6 uur dinsdagavond 8 tot 10 uur
PANAMARENKO
© Panamarenko 1969

JAN VAN MUNSTER

Van Abbemuseum Eindhoven

25 september tot en met 18 oktober 1970
openingstijden: dagelijks 10 tot 17 uur
zondag 14 tot 18 uur dinsdagavond 20 tot 22 uur

Deze tentoonstelling in het Van Abbemuseum is een vervolg van mijn expositie in het Stedelijk museum in Amsterdam december 1969.
In het Stedelijk bracht ik mijn thema 'bevruchting' in een open situatie naar voren. Wat binnen de dingen gebeurde, was duidelijk te zien. In het Van Abbemuseum doe ik hetzelfde, maar dan in een gesloten situatie. Wat in de dingen gebeurt, blijft binnen in, en komt maar zelden naar buiten.
Bijvoorbeeld 'Misstelling 6', is op het eerste gezicht een plaat ijzer; wie hem aanraakt krijgt een schok. De machine wordt dan agressief en in mentale zin plastisch.
De totale situatie is in Eindhoven geheimzinniger dan in Amsterdam, er is sprake van een vervolg op de stenen beelden die ik in 1959 maakte. Binnen in gebeurt er iets wat door iedereen anders geformuleerd kan worden.

ontwerp: jan van toorn offsetdruk steendrukkerij de jong & co. hilversum 1970

BERKELEY U.S.A.
PEOPLE'S PARK
Audio-visuele reportage over de gebeurtenissen in
Berkeley, mei 1969; Hoe mensen samen een park maakten
voor kinderen en hun moeders, bejaarden, verliefden; iedereen.
En hoe ingrijpen van politie en nationale garde een eind daar aan
maakte.
openingstijden
dagelijks 10 tot 5 uur
zondag 2 tot 6 uur
dinsdagavond 8 tot 10 uur
18 december 1970 tot 10 januari 1971
VAN ABBEMUSEUM EINDHOVEN

T A THOUSAND PARKS BLOOM

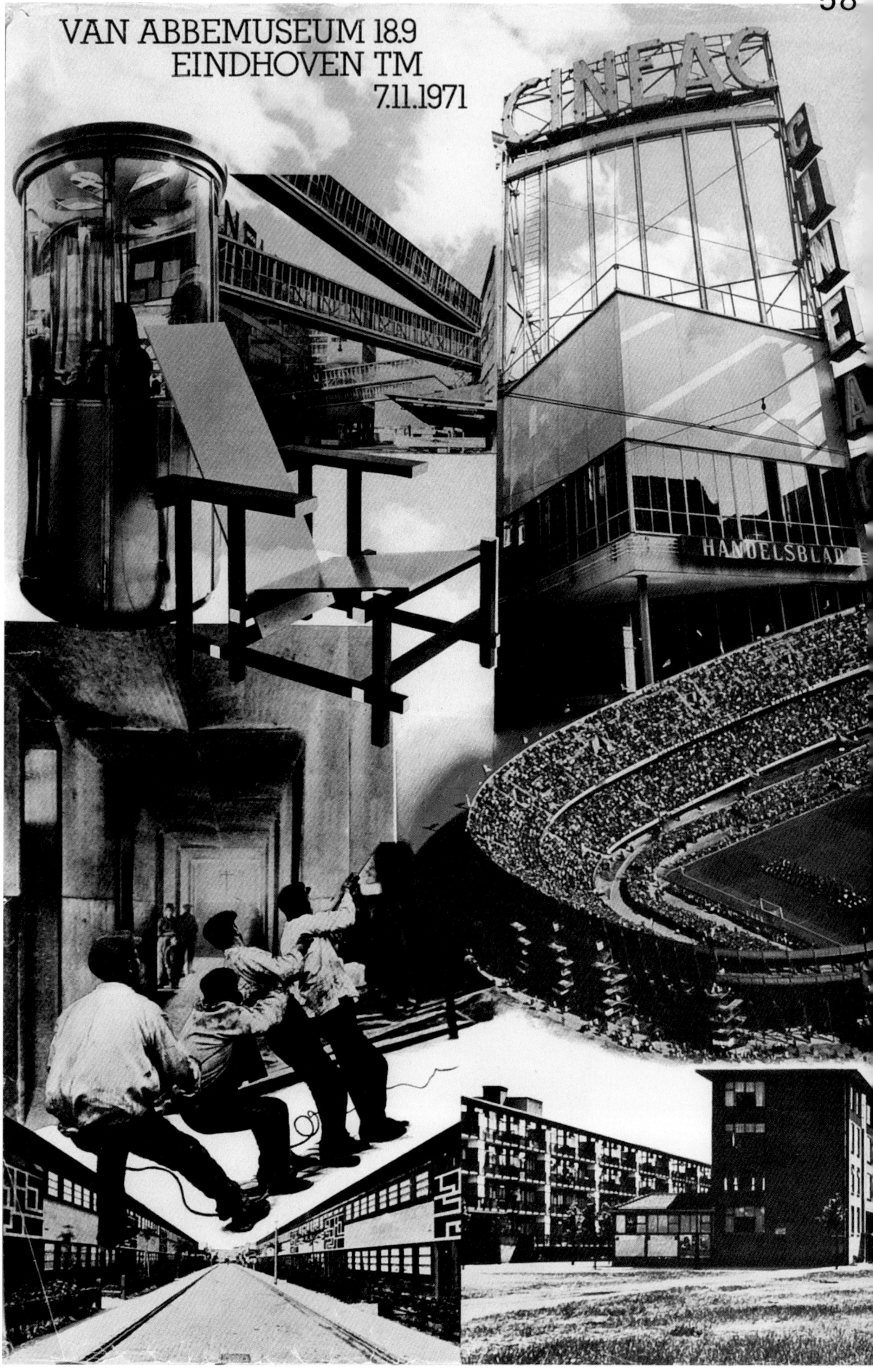

VAN ABBEMUSEUM 18.9
EINDHOVEN TM
7.11.1971

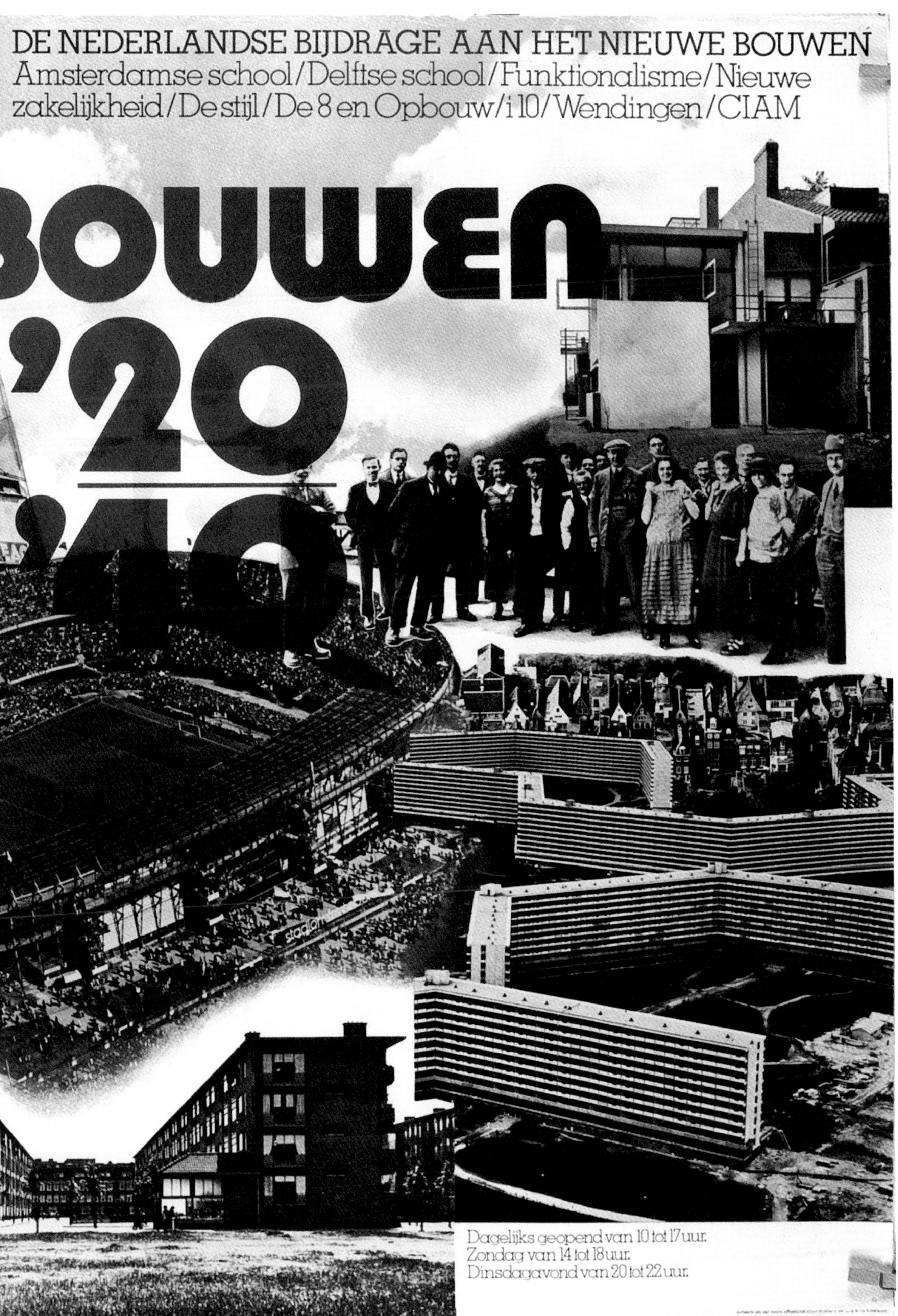
DE NEDERLANDSE BIJDRAGE AAN HET NIEUWE BOUWEN
Amsterdamse school / Delftse school / Funktionalisme / Nieuwe zakelijkheid / De stijl / De 8 en Opbouw / i 10 / Wendingen / CIAM
BOUWEN
'20
'40
Dagelijks geopend van 10 tot 17 uur.
Zondag van 14 tot 18 uur.
Dinsdagavond van 20 tot 22 uur.

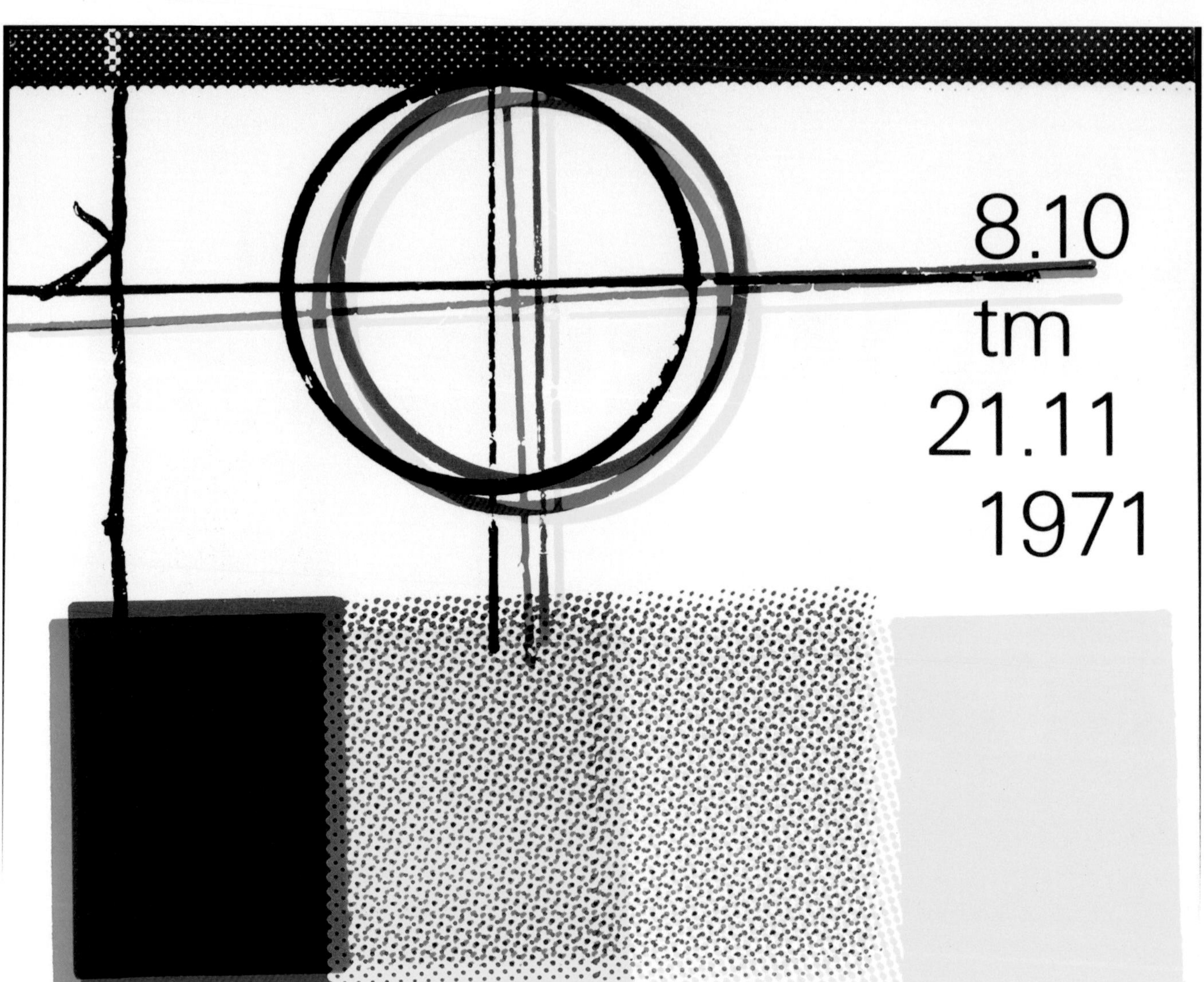

GEMINI G.E.

EXPERIMENT IN GRAFIEK

Van Abbemuseum
Eindhoven

3 december tm 16 januari 1972

Van Abbemuseum Eindhoven

JAN DIBBETS

Dagelijks geopend van 10 tot 17 uur
Zondag van 14 tot 18 uur
Dinsdagavond van 20 tot 22 uur

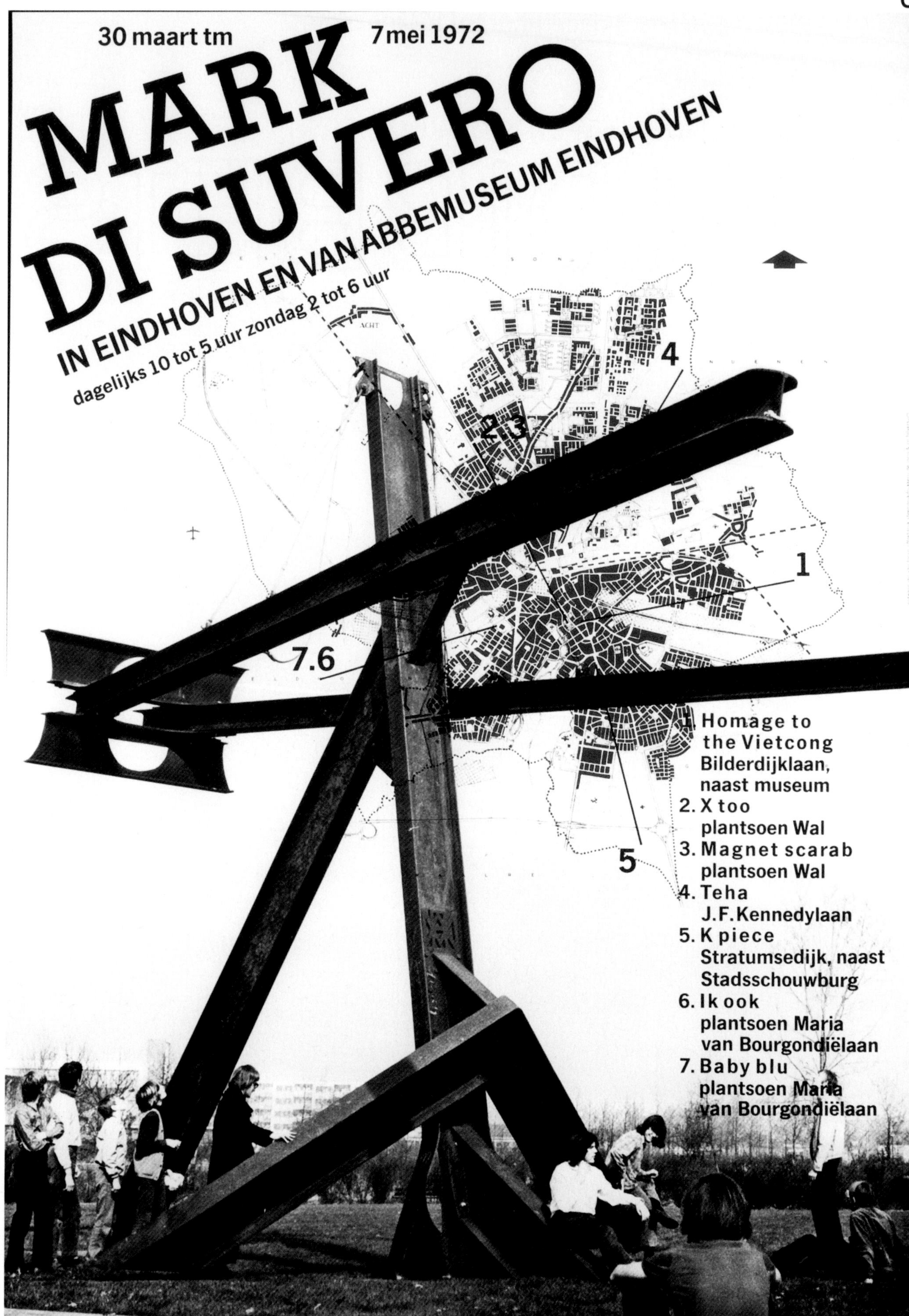
30 maart tm 7 mei 1972
MARK DI SUVERO
IN EINDHOVEN EN VAN ABBEMUSEUM EINDHOVEN
dagelijks 10 tot 5 uur zondag 2 tot 6 uur
4
2.3
1
7.6
5
1. Homage to the Vietcong Bilderdijklaan, naast museum
2. X too plantsoen Wal
3. Magnet scarab plantsoen Wal
4. Teha J.F.Kennedylaan
5. K piece Stratumsedijk, naast Stadsschouwburg
6. Ik ook plantsoen Maria van Bourgondiëlaan
7. Baby blu plantsoen Maria van Bourgondiëlaan

vehikel
materiaal
werk
kunstenaar
producent

Openingstijden:
dagelijks 10 tot 17 uur
zondag 14 tot 18 uur

21 en 28 oktober, 10 uur
(zaterdag)
Objekten voor gebruik

Franz Erhard
WALTHER

EINDHOVEN

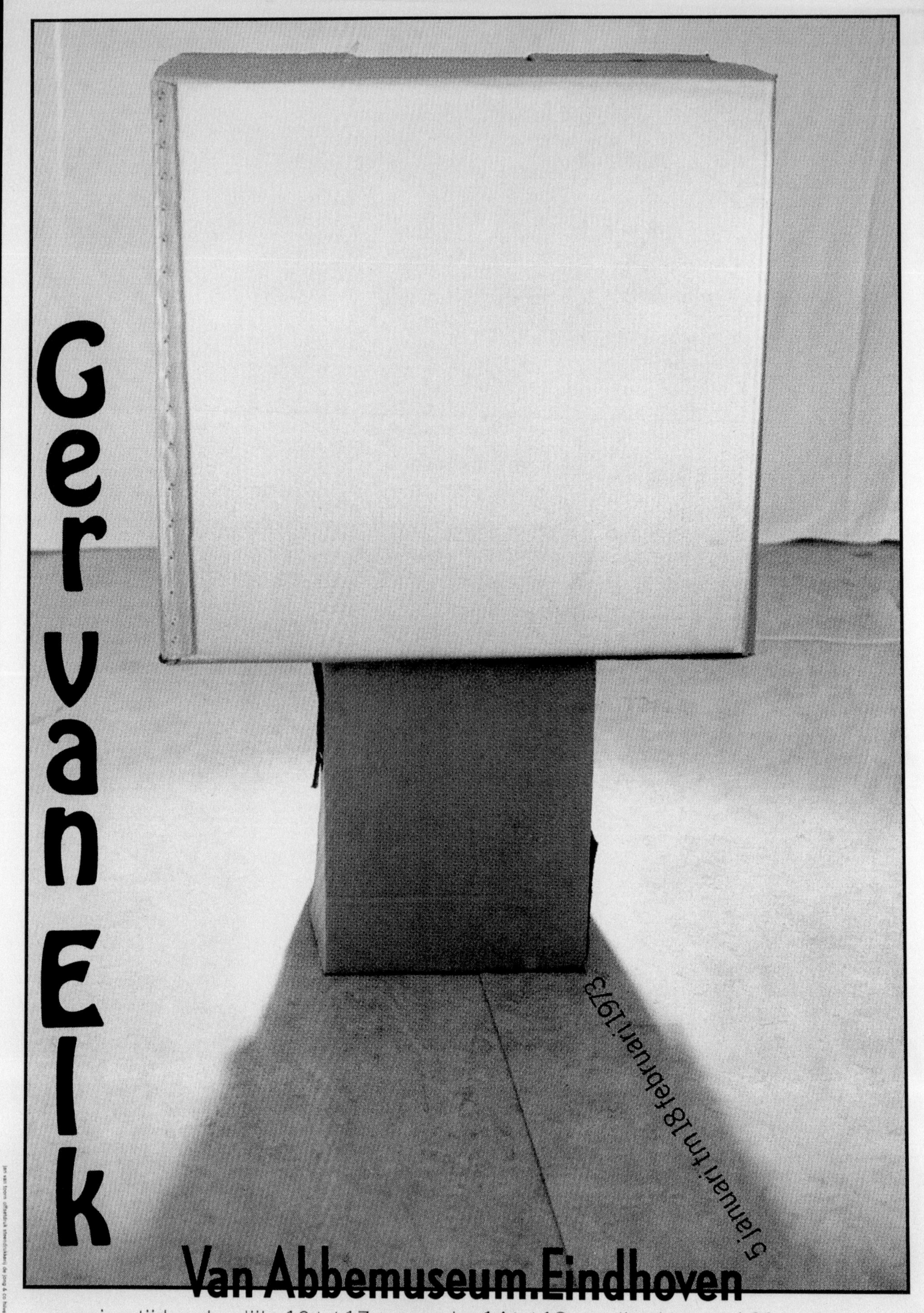
Ger van Elk
5 januari tm 18 februari 1973
Van Abbemuseum.Eindhoven
openingstijden: dagelijks 10 tot 17 uur zondag 14 tot 18 uur dinsdagavond 20 tot 22 uur

VAN ABBEMUSEUM EINDHOVEN

openingstijden: dagelijks 10 tot 17 uur zondag 14 tot 18 uur woensdagavond 20 tot 22 uur

10.2.tm 15.4.1973

een kollektie is ook

Een keuze

maar

uit de kollektie

een

door een gast:

mens

Wim Beeren

jan van toorn offsetdruk steendrukkerij de jong & co hilversum

12 oktober tm 25 november 1973

Van Abbemuseum Eindhoven

bruce nauman

openingstijden: dagelijks 10 tot 17 uur zondag 14 tot 18 uur dinsdagavond 20 tot 22 uur

5jaarlijkse

jonge kunst uit Zuid-Nederland

van Abbemuseum Eindhoven

van 8 december 1973 tot en met 20 januari 1974

openingstijden: dagelijks 10 tot 17 uur zondag 14 tot 18 uur dinsdagavond 20 tot 22 uur

PERSLUCHTMACHINES
Ray Staakman
EINDHOVEN
VAN ABBEMUSEUM
12.4 T/M 26.5.74
openingstijden: dagelijks 10 tot 17
14 tot 18 uur dinsdagavond 20

KunstLichtKunst. Catalogue cover and spread, 1966.
Publisher: Van Abbemuseum

Man Ray

is 27 Augustus 1890 in Philadelphia (VS) geboren; studeert tot 1907 architektuur en voor ingenieur, gaat daarna schilderen en bezoekt de kunstschool in New York. De 'Armory show' van 1913 wekt zijn belangstelling voor de abstrakte kunst. In 1915 heeft hij zijn eerste tentoonstelling in New York. In 1917 richt hij samen met Marcel Duchamp en Francis Picabia de Dadaisten-groep van New York op, in 1920 samen met Kathrin Dreier en Marcel Duchamp de 'société anonyme'. Van 1916 tot 1920 exposeert hij schilderijen, kollages, met de verfspuit vervaardigde werken en gevonden voorwerpen (ready mades).
In deze tijd ontstaat de in de Edition MAT uitgegeven 'Spirale', een van de eerste kinetische kunstwerken van deze eeuw. In 1921 verhuist hij naar Parijs. Hij werkt mee aan de tijdschriften 'Der Sturm' en 'de Stijl' en neemt deel aan de eerste Dada-tentoonstelling in de boekhandel '6'. Omstreeks 1922 ontwikkelt hij een nieuwe fotografische techniek, de 'rayographie', waarbij voorwerpen als fotogram direkt op het afdruk papier belicht worden. Sinds 1924 is hij aangesloten bij de surrealistische beweging, neemt hij aan alle surrealistische tentoonstellingen en manifestaties deel en werkt hij mee aan de surrealistische publikaties. Hij draait surrealistische films en verblijft van 1940 tot 1951 in Hollywood. Sinds 1939 heeft hij in Californië, Parijs, Londen en New York geëxposeerd. Hij woont in Parijs.

In this age, like all ages, when the problem of the perpetuation of a race or class and the destruction of its enemies, is the all-absorbing motive of civilized society, it seems irrelevant and wasteful still to create works whose only inspirations are individual human emotion and desire. The attitude seems to be that one may be permitted a return to the idyllic occupations only after meriting this return by solving the more vital problems of existence. Still, we know that the incapacity of race or class to improve itself is as great as its incapacity to learn from previous errors in history. All progress results from an intense individual desire to improve the immediate present, from an all-conscious sense of material insufficiency. In this exalted state, material action imposes itself and takes the form of revolution in one form or another.
Race and class, like styles, then become irrelevant, while the emotion of the human individual becomes universal. For what can be more binding amongst beings than the discovery of a common desire? And what can be more inspiring to action than the confidence aroused by a lyric expression of this desire? From the first gesture of a child pointing to an object and simply naming it, but with a world of intended meaning, to the developed mind that creates an image whose strangeness and reality stirs our subconscious to its inmost depths, the awakening of desire is the first step to participation and experience. It is in the spirit of an experience and not of experiment that the following autobiographical images are presented. Seized in moments of visual detachment during periods of emotional contact, these images are oxidized residues, fixed by light and chemical elements, of living organisms. No plastic expression can ever be more than a residue of an experience. The recognition of an image that has tragically survived an experience, recalling the event more or less clearly, like the undisturbed ashes of an object consumed by flames, the recognition of this object so little representative and so fragile, and its simple indentification on the part of the spectator with a similar personal experience, precludes all psycho-analytical classification or assimilation into an arbitrary decorative system. Questions of merit and execution can always be taken care of by those who hold themselves aloof from even the frontiers of such experiences. For, whether a painter, emphasizing the importance of the idea he wishes to convey introduces bits of ready-made chromos alongside his handiwork, or wether another, working directly with light and chemistry, so deforms the subject as almost to hide the identity of the original, and creates a new form, the ensuing violation of the medium employed is the most perfect assurance of the author's convictions. A certain amount of contempt for the material employed to express an idea is indispensable to the purest realization of this idea. Each one of us, in his timidity, has a limit beyond which he is outraged. It is inevitable that he who by concentrated application has extended this limit for himself, should arouse the resentment of those who have accepted conventions which, since accepted by all, require no initiative of application. And this resentment generally takes the form of meaningless laughter or of criticism, if not of persecution. But this apparant violation is preferable to the monstrous habits condoned by etiquette and estheticism. An effort impelled by desire must also have an automatic or subconscious energy to aid its realization. The reserves of this energy within us are limitless if we will draw on them without a sense of shame or of propriety. Like the scientist who is merely a prestidigitator manipulating the abundant phenomena of nature and profiting by every so called hazard or law, the creator dealing in human values allows the subconscious forces to filter through him, colored by his own selectivity, which is universal human desire, and exposes to the light motives and instincts long repressed, which should form the basis of a confident fraternity. The intensity of this message can be disturbing only in proportion to the freedom that has been given to automatism or the subconscious self. The removal of inculcated modes of presentation, resulting in apparent artificiality or strangeness, is a confirmation of the free functioning of this automatism and is to be welcomed. Open confidences are being made every day, and it remains for the eye to train itself to see them without prejudice or restraint.
Man Ray

- 2 Zonder titel 1921 rayogram
- 3 Zonder titel 1922 rayogram
- 4 Zonder titel 1923 rayogram
- 5 Zonder titel 1928 rayogram

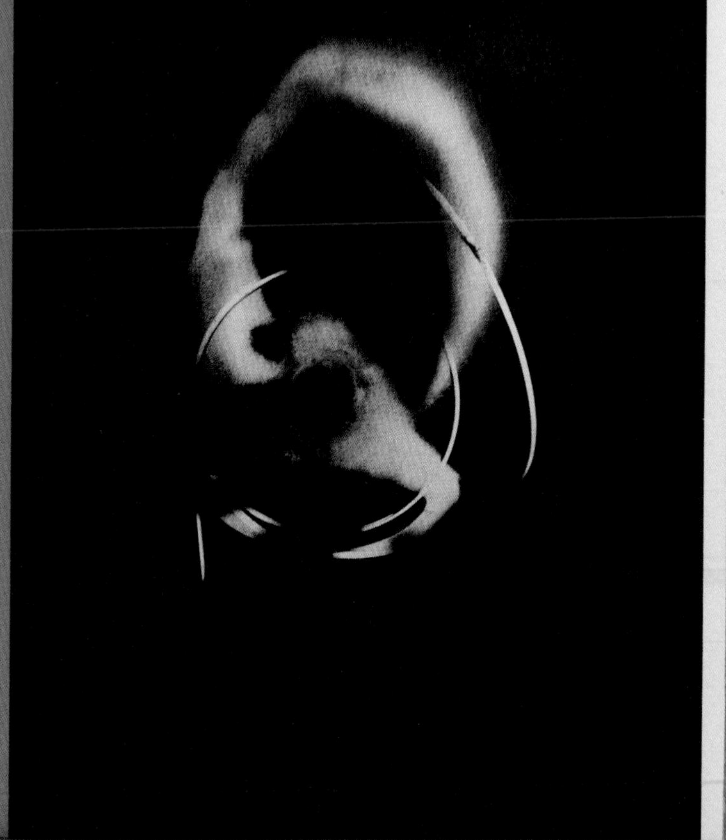

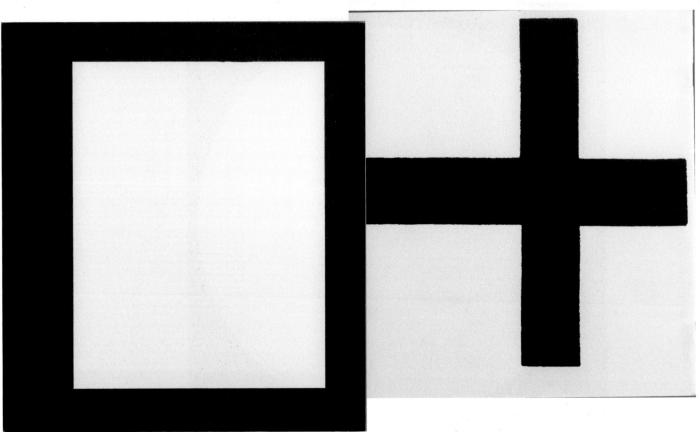

J.C.J. van der Heyden. Catalogue cover, front and back, and spreads, 1967. Publisher: Van Abbemuseum

1

Jacques van der Heyden signeert zijn schilderijen niet. Zou hij op verzoek van een koper bereid zijn een handtekening te plaatsen als getuigenis dat hij het was, die met penseel en verf op dit doek is bezig geweest, dan zou dat in zijn oog een getuigenis zijn betreffende een niet-eigenlijke gang van zaken. Niet dat hij weigert achter eigen werk te staan. Als daarmee iets goed te maken was, zou hij zijn naam op de achterkant van het doek kunnen schrijven. Zonder twijfel wil hij voor de gevolgen van zijn schilderen opdraaien, zowel wat aangaat de zonnigheden van de roem, als de schande van de spot, als de baten van de verkoop. Rijk worden van zijn kunst wil hij zelfs met genoegen. Hij doet overigens allang niet anders. Dat is juist de reden waarom hij niet signeert: als hij schildert, geeft hij niets, maar geeft het iets. Hij is een maker die zich ontvanger weet.

Aan deze situatie viel een mythisch klinkende term te verbinden door erover te spreken als over de manifestatie van een Kosmische Maker. Iets mystieks is aan Van der Heydens opvatting niet vreemd, maar in verband met kunst zegt zo'n opmerking niet veel: in die streek is men al sedert mensenheugenis haastig met de aanvoer van muzen, geesten, goden, gevleugelden en gewiekten, zo haastig, dat de gewieksten zonder kloppen dagelijks bij de goden in en uit schijnen te kunnen. Men zal zich intussen hoeden voor de vergissing, dat het bescheidenheid is als Van der Heyden niet signeert. Zijn overgang naar de anonimiteit keert óm wat in de renaissance gebeurde, toen artiesten hun werken begonnen te signeren en hun hoofden lieten lauweren. De overgang houdt in een totaal ander, een omgekeerd, maar geen geringer zelfbewustzijn als de overgang destijds. Toen introduceerde de kunstenaar met nadruk zijn signatuur, hij begon prijs te stellen op vestiging van de eigen naam, hij presenteerde door het werk zichzelf. De anonimiteit van Van der Heydens stukken betekent uiteraard op de een of andere manier juist de uitwissing van de eigen naam en daardoor van de eigen persoonlijkheid. Ze betekent vaagweg, maar toch beslist, dat het gemaakte op naam van een godheid wordt geschreven. Waarbij het proces misschien aan redelijkheid en waarschijnlijkheid wint, als gedacht wordt niet zozeer aan een kosmische maker, een persoon, als wel aan een kosmisch maken, een verbum op weg naar nominaliteit - en met nog voldoende afstand tot numinaliteit. In kosmisch maken zegt kosmisch van het maken, dat het een geordend en ordenend maken is, het tegengestelde van een chaotisch maken. Het chaotisch maken kan dan door het individu voltrokken worden op willekeurige wijze, het kosmisch maken openbaart de altijd geldende wetten van het maken. Dan doet het er minder toe wie dat maken in het werk stelt. Wat ertoe doet is, dat in het enkele werk zich algemene wetten manifesteren, dat het werk zoveel mogelijk slechts de manifestatie van die wetten is.

J.C.J. van der Heyden, op zoek naar zulke algemene wetten, kan die uitsluitend vinden in het afzonderlijke werk. Er bestaat voor het schilderen niet een soort wetskennis, die vervolgens was toe te passen. Dat zou de figuur van het altijd dreigende academisme zijn. Vrij van academisme is het werk dat in en door het gemaakt worden zelf de wetten openbaart waaraan het heeft te beantwoorden. Het is ook niet de schilder die optreedt als wetgever, alsof door hem de wet persoonlijk en willekeurig kan worden geponeerd. Dat is de figuur van een misbegrepen romantiek, waarin het persoonlijk willen en grillen van de kunstenaar als een supreem geschenk van het genie wordt gerespecteerd. De schilder volgens Van der Heyden is wetvinder, en de wetten die hij vindt, eerbiedigt hij als de natuurwetten van de schilderkunst. Die term 'natuurwet' suggereert een pathos van wetenschapsimitatie, dat niet is bedoeld. Was de natuurwet van de schilderkunst een natuurwet als bijvoorbeeld een wet in de fysica, dan zou vervolgens de schilder maître et possesseur de l'art kunnen worden op

15

2

precies dezelfde manier als sinds Descartes de fysici dankzij de formuleringen van hun wetten maîtres et possesseurs de la nature (Discours de la méthode, vi) werden. De schilder wordt nooit meester en bezitter van de kunst, hoogstens van een werk. Juist om aan te geven, dat hij nooit zelf dit werk waarvan hij meester en bezitter wordt, zo kan bewerken, dat het kunstwerk wordt, valt te zeggen, dat hij in het werk 'de natuurwetten van de schilderkunst' treft. Het zijn vreemde wetten, tegelijk algemeen en volkomen individueel: bij Jan van Eijck, Botticelli, Rembrandt, Vermeer telkens zich volmaakt presenterend, zodat niemand stip of streep van Van Eijck zou willen wijzigen, en desondanks volkomen anders als het later Rembrandt is die schildert. Zodat er ruimte komt voor het denkbeeld, dat het mogelijk moest zijn van het scheppingsproces al het persoonlijke (het typische van Van Eijck en Rembrandt) af te strippen en het puur artistieke over te houden. In alle artistieke bewegingen van de twintigste eeuw is dit min of meer bedoeld. In de koelste en de heftigste kunstrichtingen wordt deze uitschakeling van het biografisch individuele beoogd. Het koele is geen psychologische koelheid en het heftige geen psychologische heftigheid, maar koel en heftig en alles daartussen worden bereikt in een puur artistieke keuze van de plastische middelen. (Wat zo'n keuze betekent, wil ik aan de hand van Van der Heydens werk verderop toelichten). Er is niet méér expressiedrang (als expressie is de expressie van de biografische persoon) bij Pollock dan bij Elsworth Kelly. Er is bij beiden een afstrippen van de eigen persoon ten gunste van de pure plastiek. Beiden hebben, deelnemend aan wat nog altijd het meest revolutionaire en discutabele is in de twintigste-eeuwse beeldende kunst, afgezien van de figuratie. De verwijzing van beeld naar verbeelde, altijd beschouwd als het eigenlijke van de beeldende kunst, is opgeheven. Men zou dit ook aldus kunnen formuleren, dat het taalkarakter van het beeld is opgeheven. Daarvoor in de plaats kwam de samenval van beeld en verbeelde. Het verbeelde was het beeld zelf en het beeld was dit doek, deze verf, deze kleur. Misschien is de plastiek, nu ze is gezuiverd van literaire en dramatische elementen, puurder geworden, misschien is ze tegelijk ook komen te verkeren in het gevaar van een zekere semantische lichtheid. Een beeld zonder verbeelde is geen eigenlijk beeld meer, maar op zich een ding onder dingen. 'Beeldende kunst' - stel dat we die naam voor nonfiguratieve beeldende vormen mogen blijven gebruiken, ook als die non-figuratieve vormen niet de waarde wordt toegekend van psychogrammen van de maker - zo'n beeldende kunst kan dan vervolgens alleen nog betekenen, dat een ding dit ding is, en dat kan bij gelegenheid schokkend werken. De ogen kunnen ervan opengaan. De herhaalde aandrang op de identiteit van de dingen wordt daarentegen snel zouteloos: een geschilderd vlak als geschilderd vlak zien, de kleur als object behandelen (Léger), doek is doek en een gegeven maat een gegeven maat - dit extreme realisme dus, dat een tijdlang overrompelend is geweest in de na-oorlogse abstracte kunst, sneller dan alle trompe l'oeil is het gaan verraden, dat het de geleefde werkelijkheid tussen haakjes zet, de werkelijkheid van al de mogelijke betekenissen, om uitsluitend de handtastelijke betekenis van de materialiteit der dingen toe te laten. Gepretendeerd wordt af te rekenen met een te zwaar belaste ideologie van het kunstenaarschap en met de hinderlijk oncontroleerbare metafysische bedoelingen van het kunstwerk, met de waarheidsaanspraken van de kunst en de eis om respect te betuigen aan de grote K. De nieuwe pretentie lijkt simpeler. Men wil alles in kleine letters schrijven. De kunst krijgt een kleine letter en het leven en de mens. De kleine letter is de eigenlijke reikwijdte van het menselijk bestaan. Dat moet toch simpel zijn? Het enige dat deze kleine-lettersschrijver, die uit New-York en die uit Amsterdam, met grote letters overeind houden, is juist wat bij de oude kunst-met-metafysische-pretenties het verdachte en pijnlijke was: de musea, de kunsthandel, de toeter van de reclame. De oude kunst beschouwde

dat alles als een helaas onvermijdelijk kwaad. Het stond het eigenlijke in de weg. En het moet bekend: dat eigenlijke schreven ze met hoofdletters, en van puur respect werd buiten de toewijding van het makend bezigzijn, met minachting voor alle commerciële gevolgen van dien, over het eigenlijke vaak alleen maar gedróómd - gesproken werd en dan onder artiesten over techniek, verf, kwasten, soorten linnen en atelierlicht.

Het is zaak het werk van Van der Heyden goed te onderscheiden van de nieuwe tendenties, waarin kunst met een kleine letter wordt geschreven. Voor Van der Heyden verloopt het menselijk bestaan niet binnen het hek van de kleine letters. Op grond van zijn ervaringen in het atelier ontmaskert hij die willekeurige beperking en hij introduceert daarmee een nieuwe skepsis. De skepsis die 'de etische hogeborstzetterij' (Paul van Ostaijen) van de kunst ontmaskerde, is in een bepaalde constellatie nodig geweest; nu is met dezelfde kracht de tegengesteld werkende skepsis nodig die de ruimte voorbij de horizon weer bevrijdt uit het alles-al-weten van de het-ding-is-het-ding-beweerders. De retinale beperking van het kijken was een tijdelijk heilzaam antidotum tegen lichtgelovigheid, bijgeloof, ijdelheid, maar is in de tyrannieke gestalte van het moment een anti-humane dwang. Kijken voert bij mensen tot zien, en zien tot gezicht en vergezicht: het vergezicht is een reeks van onuitputtelijke betekenissen. In deze werkelijkheid leven mensen en er is geen reden een deel ervan, als het toch eenmaal geleefd en geloofd wordt, tussen haakjes te zetten.

Bij J.C.J. van der Heyden is een dubbele skepsis. Eerst: het antidotum tegen lichtgelovigheid, twee: het datum van het geloof.

Als een schilder tot zoiets als een eigen stijl is gekomen, wekt de weg waarlangs hij is gegaan, interesse. Men verwacht, dat de weg-waarlangs mogelijke verklaringen, redenen en oorzaken kan wijzen voor het voltooide werk. Breuken in de ontwikkeling wekken wantrouwen, maar als in het begin de hele latere ontwikkeling al aanwezig was, schenken wij geloof. Bij kunstbeoordeling heerst blijkbaar de prereflexieve overtuiging, dat alleen het als organisch gegroeide echt en de voluntaire beslissing dubieus is. De betekenis van deze overal bestaande critische vooronderstelling verdient overweging. Ze schenkt geloof aan iets dat niet de biografische persoon van deze kunstenaar is. Ze is precies zo revolutionair als het huidige kunstcritische verzet tegen het monopoliestreven van kunst- en literatuurhistorici. De grond daarvoor is feitelijk deze overtuiging: niet de historie met zijn vrij beslissende persoonlijkheden is het terrein waarop over kunst en onkunst wordt beslist, dat gebeurt in termen van worteling en groei, van de persoon en zijn beslissingen overstijgende processen. De theorie van de pure kunst (poésie pure en pure plastiek) poneert een ideaal en een geloof. Als de oorsprong van de theorie moet gezocht worden, dan schijnt het deze confuse en onbewuste vooronderstelling. Het is daarom de moeite waard er de aandacht op te vestigen. Ze is historisch te verklaren als een uit de romantische esthetiek neergeslagen substraat, dat niet langer rationeel wordt gecontroleerd. Belangrijk is, dat het substraat vruchtbaar blijft. In feite blijkt het zelfs een ons allen gemeenschappelijke idee omtrent kunst. Er is geen

4

andere kunst als de gegroeide. Wat niet is gegroeid - en eventueel toch mooi en zelfs betekenisrijk is - krijgt niet de naam van kunst. Het gaat in kunst niet alleen om mooi (veel is mooi dat geen kunst is), het gaat ook niet alleen om betekenis (betekenis heeft veel dat toch geen kunst is), het gaat om die twee, om een schoonheid en een zin voorzover verworven in een maken dat tevens groeien is, een aan de wil van het maken onttrokken proces.

Het groeiproces van J.C.J. van der Heyden. Om mee te beginnen: zoete groene landschappen. Daarna grijze polders uit de buurt van Den Bosch. Toen vernevelde het gezicht van de polders en liet alleen een nabije horizon achter, een dampige wolk, een water. En toen werden horizon, wolk en water verwisselbaar met de penseelstreek die er, retinaal gesproken, op doek of papier stond. Vervolgens brak die penseelstreek geheel uit de betekenissen van horizon, wolk en water. En de analyse ging verder. Het grijs splitste zich in zwart en wit, het horizontaal vroeg om het antwoord van een verticaal en het witte vlak vroeg om het zwarte, de zwarte penseelstreek om de witte.

Van der Heyden was toe aan (voorlopig) zijn stijl en zijn natuurwet van de schilderkunst. Hij was bezig met de pure penseelstreek en de pure vlakken - wat nog iets anders is als 'pure kunst'. De systematiek van pure penseelstreek en pure vlakken kan hoogst eigenzinnig door de schilder worden gewild. Ik geloof, dat Van der Heyden ogenblikkelijk dit eigen willen heeft doorgehad, het te licht heeft bevonden en verworpen. Met een onthutsende, bijna woedende onverschilligheid kladdert hij zwarte doeken slordig vol wit, op een manier die zo weinig mogelijk met het resultaat van doen wil hebben. Dan neemt hij zeer kleine doekjes, die hij samenvoegt om te zien of in die samenvoeging dat meerdere is, dat hij wensen, maar met willen niet afdwingen kan. Hij verdeelt grotere doeken in kleine vierkanten. Een zeer groot doek wordt van onder tot boven zwart geschilderd en plotseling ontstaat er -
- maar het is eigenlijk het beste daar niet over te spreken. Kan men in ernst beweren, dat een volkomen zwart geschilderd doek, op een zaterdagmiddag gezien, plotseling zoiets begint als te vibreren, dat is: begint iets anders te zijn als wat het is? Het is een boom in de ruimte. Het is licht dat het duister verdeelt. Een grote stilte midden in de stad. Een eiland van vertrouwen. Het stromen van ongevormde metalen. Een scheppingsdag van de morgen tot de avond. Waarom niet zeggen: het was alles? Bijbelse psalmisten gevraagd om woorden te vinden voor het deinen van de godheid.

Tevoren, namelijk vóór de mystieke verklaring overweldigend wordt, nogmaals zo technisch mogelijk het proces vertaald in geschiedenis. Het jarenlange werken met zwart en wit. Dat was niet zomaar een gestreng ascetisme, het was de gestrengheid van de wet. Het gebruik van elke kleur is een persoonlijke keus ergens tussen zwart en wit. Zwart en wit kiezen is als het kiezen van de grenzen. Daar valt individuele kleur samen met de algemene wet en met juist de uitschakeling van het persoonlijke. Zoals wie zich kleedt in het wit of het zwart wel zijn persoon demonstreert, maar vooral het algemene van droefheid of geluk dat zich aan hem voltrekt. Een bruid in het wit, een rouwende in het zwart betekenen wel het individuele optreden van een bruid of een rouwer, maar vooral het deelkrijgen van de enkeling aan het algemene. De niet-kleuren zwart en wit zijn het niet-individuele menselijke lotgeval, het alle mensen gemeenschappelijke lot. Zo schildert Van der Heyden, zwart op wit of wit op zwart, het vierkant, de horizontale, de verticale, de diagonale lijn. Geen lijnen, vlakken, kleuren van persoonlijk gevoel of lotgeval, maar de eeuwen vóór Van der Heyden bestaande, voor iedereen geldende mogelijkheden van kleuren en lijnen in een vlak. Alle andere als deze lijnen, vlakken,

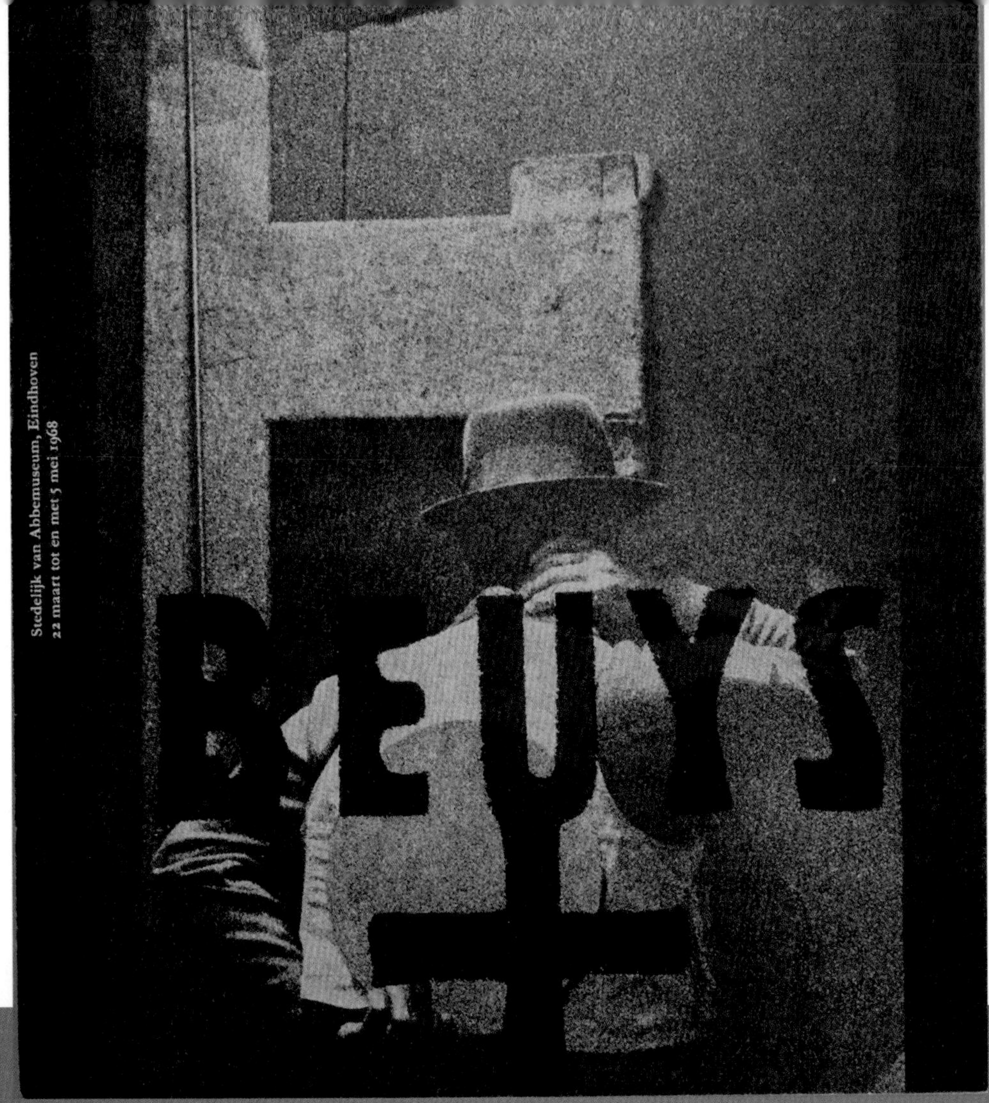

Beuys. Catalogue cover and folding pages, 1968. Publisher: Van Abbemuseum. Photographs: Ute Klophaus, Walter Vogel and Bernard Becher

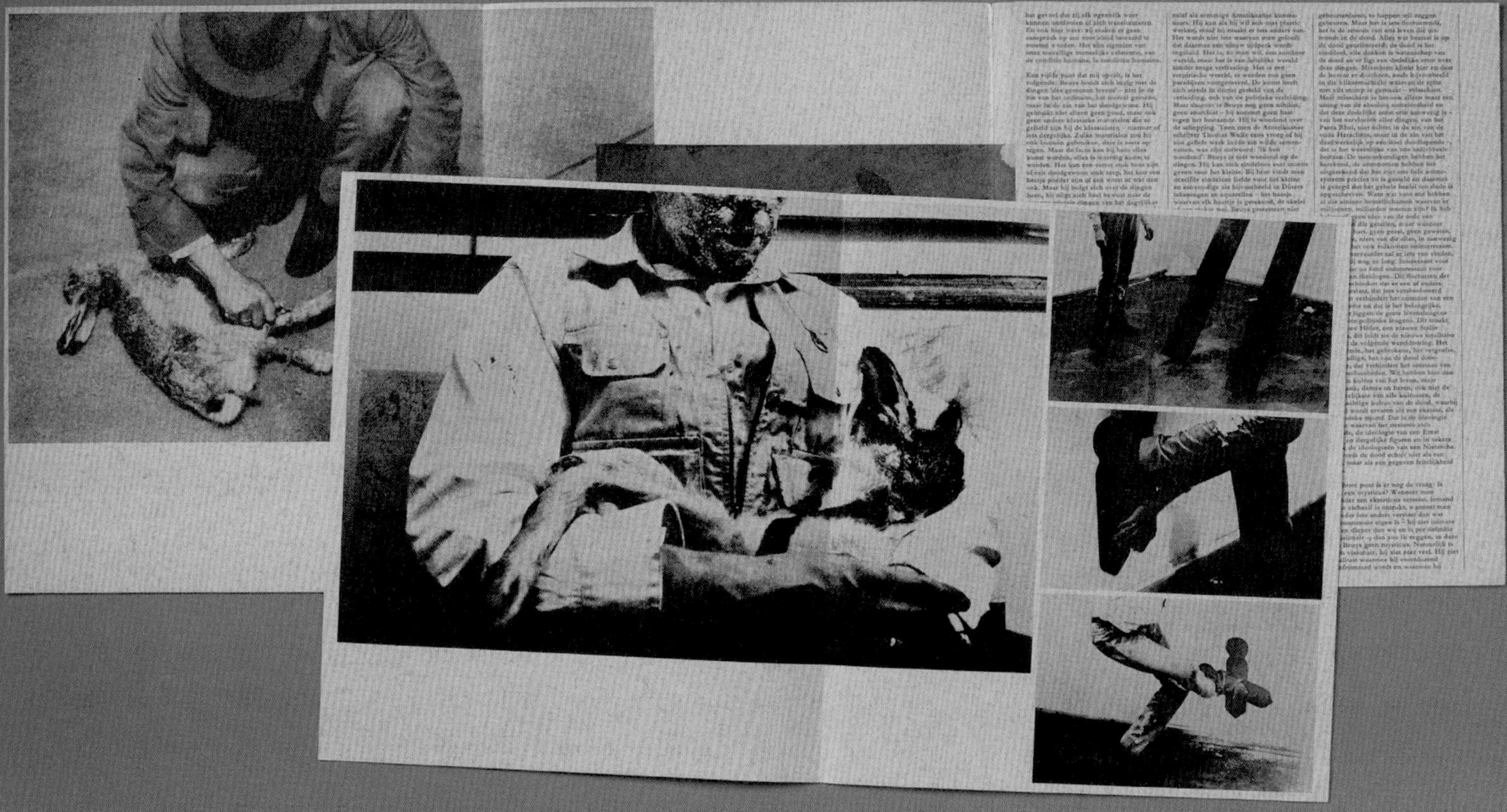

Abakanowicz. Catalogue with folding pages, 1969. Publisher: Van Abbemuseum. Photographs: Jan Michlewski and Marek Holzman

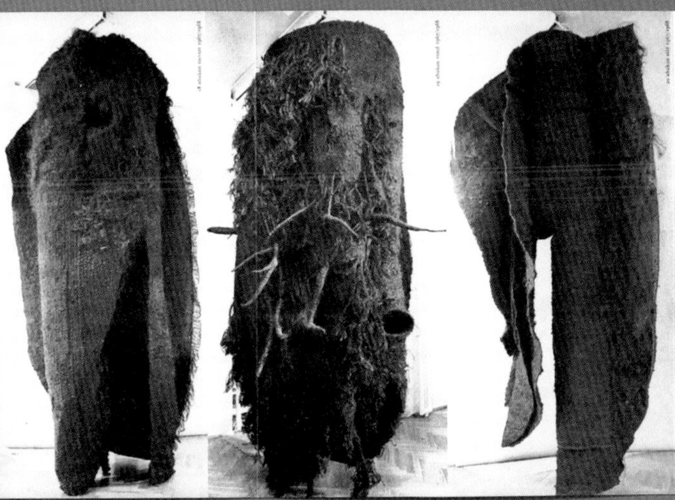

Abakanowicz. Catalogue cover, 1969. Publisher: Van Abbemuseum

Boezem / Panamarenko. Double-sided catalogue cover and spreads, 1970. Publisher: Van Abbemuseum

BOEZEM

Voor toezending van deel twee van deze katalogus, hieronder naam en adres invullen en inleveren aan de balie of opsturen aan de administratie van het museum.

aanvulling katalogus

BOEZEM/PANAMARENKO

aan (naam)

straat

stad

land

PANAMARENKO

Het projekt 'Maatervaring' van Boezem in deze tentoonstelling is er op gericht de betrokkene vanuit een nultoestand – gezeten in een stoel – bewust te maken van het verschijnsel maat. Die ervaring van afstand en maat doet zich in de werkelijkheid nog op talloze andere manieren voor. Hiervan geeft de katalogus enkele voorbeelden.
Tentoonstelling en katalogus beogen bij de bezoeker paralelle ervaringen op te roepen en bewust te maken. Om deze uitwisseling van ideeën vorm te geven zouden de samenstellers het op prijs stellen, als zij van u soortgelijke ervaringen van maat, afstand en tijd zouden mogen ontvangen.
Het zou plezierig zijn als u naast een beschrijving van deze ervaringen ook een illustratie zou kunnen leveren (foto's, tekeningen e.d.).

Boezem zou met een dergelijke uitwisseling zeer ingenomen zijn. Ook Panamarenko zou reacties van technische en aerodynamische aard bijzonder op prijs stellen.
Het is de bedoeling dat alle ingekomen reacties gebundeld worden en u als tweede deel van de katalogus worden toegezonden.

Om toezending van deel twee mogelijk te maken kunt u naam en adres in vullen op het etiket aan de omslag van deze katalogus, het etiket afscheuren en inleveren aan de balie van het museum of opsturen aan de Administratie van het Stedelijk van Abbemuseum, Bilderdijklaan 10, Eindhoven.

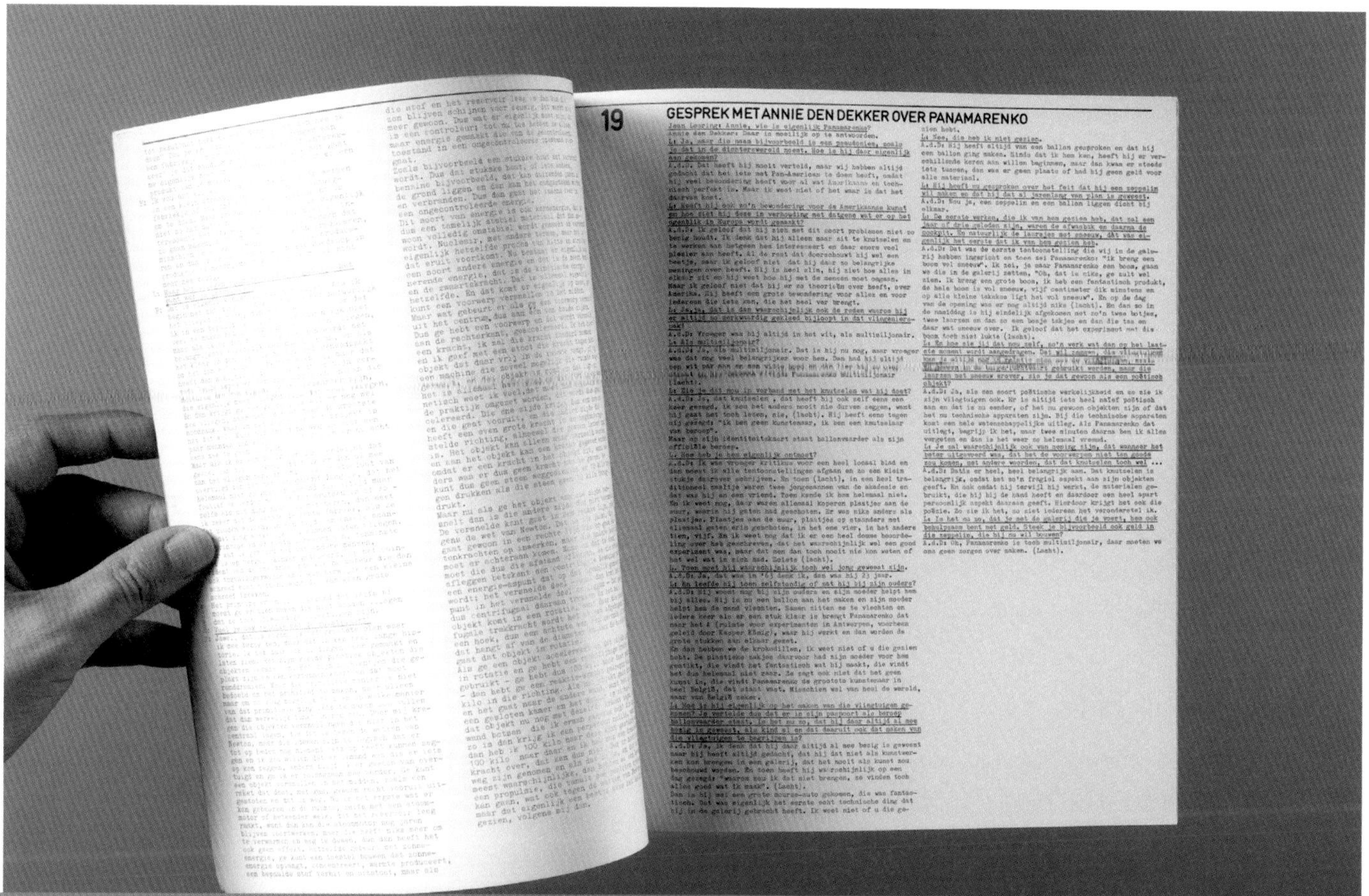

19

GESPREK MET ANNIE DEN DEKKER OVER PANAMARENKO

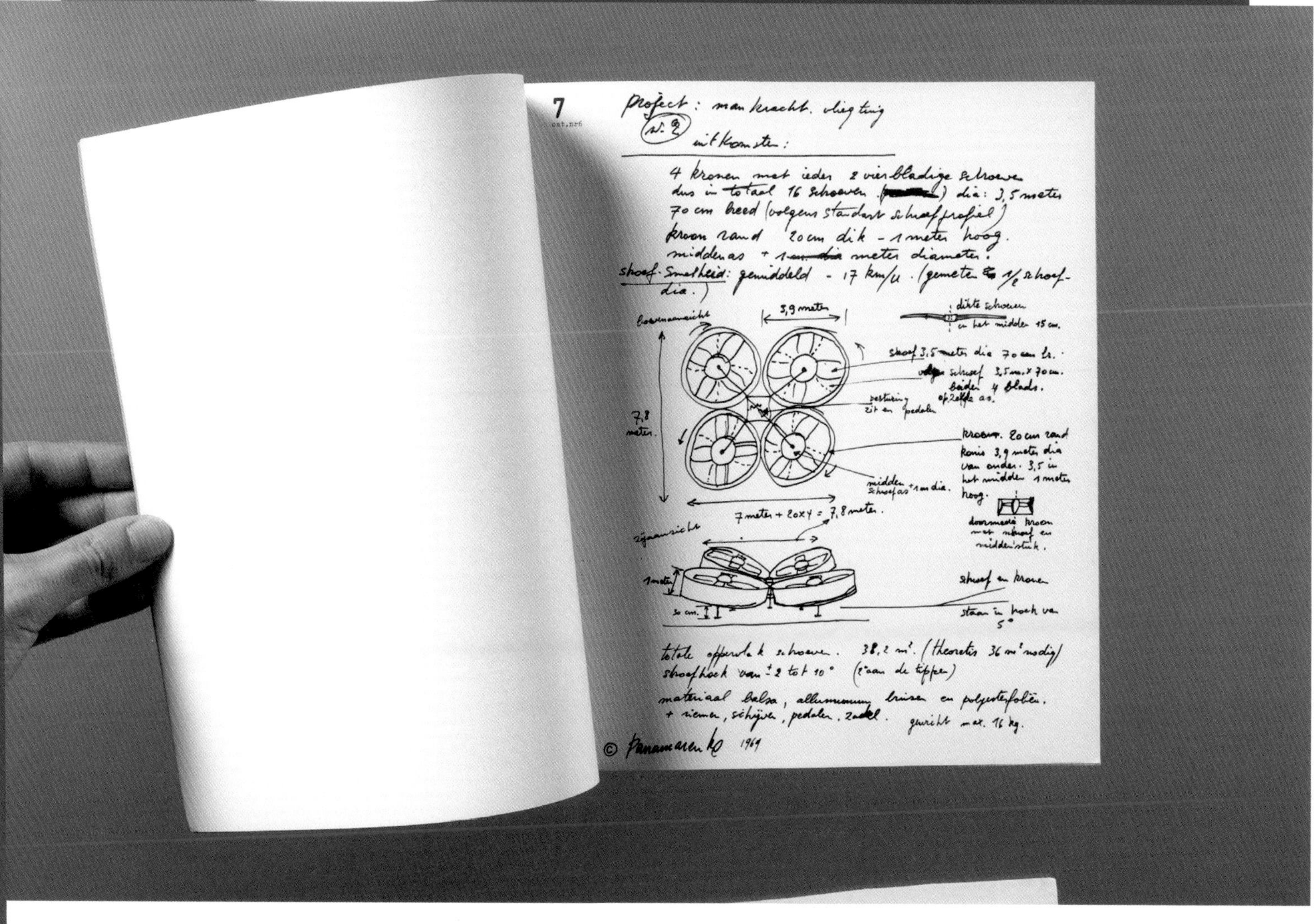

7

cat.nr6

project: man kracht. vlieg tuig

uitkomsten:

4 kronen met ieder 2 vierbladige schroeven
dus in totaal 16 schroeven ( ) dia: 3,5 meter
70 cm breed (volgens standart schroefprofiel)
kroon rand 20 cm dik - 1 meter hoog.
middenas + 1 meter diameter.
schroef Snelheid: gemiddeld - 17 km/u. (gemeten op 1/2 schroef-dia.)

totale oppervlak schroeven. 38,2 m². (theoretis 36 m² nodig)
schroefhoek van ± 2 tot 10° (aan de tippen)
materiaal balsa, allumunium buizen en polyesterfolien.
+ riemen, schijven, pedalen. zadel. gewicht max. 16 kg.

© Panamarenko 1969

"LESS THAN AT ANY TİME DOES A SİMPLE REPRODUCTİON OF REALİTY TELL US ANYTHİNG ABOUT REALİTY."

Bertolt Brecht

Critical practice

"ART İS NOT THE REFLECTİON OF REALİTY, İT İS THE REALİTY OF THAT REFLECTİON."

Jean-Luc Godard

Photograph: Michel Boesveld, 1986

Graphic design is a peculiar mix of pragmatism and idealism. Individuals who choose to enter the field often take it for granted that the visual aspect of things can make a significant difference to the quality of life. In the 1920s, the Modernists believed that design had a fundamental task to perform as an agent of social and political transformation. In the decades after the Second World War, as graphic design took shape as an organized business activity and as a would-be profession throughout the industrialized world, design's visual motivations and social purposes did not require much soul-searching. "After the war you had to stand for something," said Otto Treumann, designer in 1947 of *Rayon Revue*, house magazine of the artificial silk manufacturer Enka. "Whatever happened, you wanted to do your bit for the reconstruction of culture."[1] For the most part, it was enough to persuade clients that benefit would flow from projects that communicated effectively because they were visually inventive. In a period of rapid industrial, economic and media growth, it could seem entirely positive to supply the business world with logos, liveries and literature to help ensure high visibility, a competitive presence, and climbing levels of profit. We have come a long way since then. The idea of design, preached with conviction by so many design missionaries from the 1950s to the 1980s, fell on receptive ears – and eyes – and almost everyone is a design convert of some kind now. Design is everywhere; its possibilities have been so thoroughly itemized, assimilated and applied that it shapes almost everything we see and touch. Design is a means by which contemporary reality is structured, packaged, delivered to our doors, and imbued with an exciting air of rightness and normality.

So where does that leave the designer who takes the view that design, as a means of public communication, should be about more than merely providing promotional endorsement for our current version of reality? While many designers envy the freedom of artists to follow their own agendas, designers are required, by contrast, to focus their skills and commitment on the transmission of their clients' messages. Leaving aside overt forms of graphic protest, is it possible (was it ever possible?) to embed an alternative or contrary way of thinking in the everyday commercial practice of design? If graphic design is defined – as some still define it – as a service provider and "problem solver" pure and simple, with no content of its own, then this would appear to allow no place for a personal perspective, let alone for the "autonomy" that some designers desire.[2] Nevertheless, in the last 20 years, the case has been made many times for a model of practice that would allow room for designers to express their own points of view.[3] So this is hardly an outrageous new idea, especially when one considers the roots of Dutch graphic design in highly idiosyncratic work by the likes of Piet Zwart and Paul Schuitema. Yet the old unease that graphic design is in danger of mistaking itself for art and irresponsibly reneging on its duty to clients and audiences persists in some quarters. For those inclined to think that it should be possible to bring an individual point of view to practice, and even to adopt an actively questioning stance, there is still a need to demonstrate how a designer's personal agenda might be reconciled with the requirements and priorities of the client who pays the bill.

Poster, c. 1928. Design: Paul Schuitema

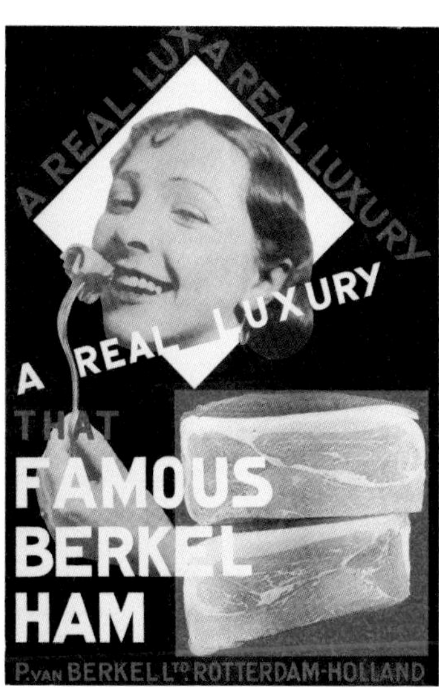

In this respect, Jan van Toorn provides an unusually rich example of a designer who has built a long career, and achieved an international reputation, by questioning the limitations of the graphic designer's role, as some continue to see it. Van Toorn is a design intellectual and practical thinker, an indefatigable auto-didact who describes himself as a "late starter". He was in his late 30s, with a substantial body of work behind him, before his ideas about design were fully formulated and he began to create pieces that we would recognize today as embodying his mature concerns. The work he has produced since 1970 is often striking for its formal daring, but it could rarely be described as beautiful. Van Toorn's focus is on meaning rather than on the stylistic and aesthetic expression that preoccupies many graphic designers. Instead of smoothness, wholeness, good taste and perfection, he offers discontinuity and disruption. Sometimes this can be described as informality, though just as often it is a calculated awkwardness. His designs persistently call attention to their status as visual contrivances, obliging the viewer to remain at a distance, requiring an effort to negotiate them. They tend to have an astringent, cerebral appearance that is quite different from the more sensual, seductive and spectacular norms of everyday commercial design. It is immediately obvious, even before you attempt to engage with his visual constructions, that they represent a set of concerns utterly opposed to routine professional ways of thinking, and that they are themselves the product of deep conviction and thought.

Van Toorn is known for his outspoken commitment to theoretical reflection and this is still rare among practitioners of graphic design, though decades of involvement in education have clearly helped to focus his intellectual interests. His public discussion with Wim Crouwel in 1972, which will be discussed later, can be seen as one of the landmark debates in Dutch graphic design history, a moment when two irreconcilable approaches to design – two value systems – were revealed more clearly by the clash. For the best part of a decade, until around 1980, Crouwel functioned (quite usefully in retrospect) as Van Toorn's "other", goaded by the radical designer's apparently insufferable transgressions into publicly challenging his thinking and even, on one occasion, going so far as to "correct" one of his designs. Since the early 1970s, Van Toorn has immersed himself in political and cultural theory. His library bears testimony to the weightiness of his reading, with books on politics, war, anarchism, Chinese history, the Third Reich, Modernism, the Situationists, 1960s radicalism, semiotics, communication and media. Authors well represented on his shelves include Gramsci, Habermas, Marcuse, Foucault, Bourdieu, Deleuze and Guattari, Debord, Eco, Illich, Mattelart, Chomsky, and Said. In the 1970s and 1980s, Van Toorn read in German, as well as Dutch; since the early 1990s, he has tended to read more in English. Pull down a book and you will often find pages marked with slips of paper and significant passages underlined in pencil.

Van Toorn's reflections on the aims that underpin his work can be tough going. While he is open to discussion and relishes debate, he seems prepared to make few concessions when it comes to defining his position and explaining his ideas to those who lack his extensive grounding in cultural theory. His occasional writing can be over-supplied with abstractions that are more persuasive for regular readers of theory who already share his intellectual assumptions than for less bookish fellow designers. I first met Van Toorn in 1992, in the culminating phase of his career, when he had recently been appointed director of the Jan van Eyck Academy, a postgraduate art school in Maastricht. The Dutch Ministry of Culture had accepted his proposal to extend the traditional combination of art and design with a new department of theory. "**Everything is mediated nowadays,**" he told me. "**Real experience no longer exists – it's all intertextual. At the same time, there are dominant forces establishing the way we deal with things. The combination of design and fine art in the traditional sense was not enough. My idea was to combine them with theory, and that tension should be explored and made productive by looking at their role in the public sphere.**"[4]

There is much to agree with here, but bringing about a marriage of design and theory proved no easier at the Jan van Eyck Academy than it has done elsewhere. The more urgent the issue, one might conclude, the more vital it is to frame arguments as clearly as possible. One of the challenges when addressing Van Toorn's body of work lies in establishing the relationship between his thinking and practice in particular projects. "Sometimes I would say to him: 'Why, Jan, the product isn't as far-reaching as the theory,'" noted museum director Jean Leering, who worked with Van Toorn for many years at the Van Abbemuseum in Eindhoven.[5] Van Toorn acknowledges that his output does not always match up to the expectations aroused by the high-sounding ideas that lie behind it. Yet his work has left a mark and, in the course of the last fifteen years, there have been many instances of new design that seem to relate to Van Toorn's way of looking at things. Sometimes the connections are obvious, as with the editorial and design direction of *Dot Dot Dot* magazine, co-edited by Peter Bilak, a Slovakian designer who studied at the Jan van Eyck Academy (although the relationship in this case lies more in a preference for concept over form, and obliqueness over a too-obvious directness, than in any overlap in political motivation and aims). Often it is less a matter of directly traceable influence than an observation that some young designers have come round to favouring visual devices and strategies that Van Toorn introduced, against the grain, in the 1970s. This makes his early pieces look all the more notable for their foresight.

Selling grey boxes

Van Toorn was born in the small town of Tiel in the Netherlands in 1932. His father, Wim van Toorn, was a tailor and, in 1935, Wim and his wife, Anna, moved to the Postjesweg in Amsterdam, in a newly built neighbourhood west of the centre. There they owned a green grocer's shop before Wim resumed being a tailor. Van Toorn was thirteen when the Second World War ended and he recalls the enormous feeling of hope when Amsterdam was liberated, and the conviction everyone shared that society could be renewed. At secondary school he learned German, French and English. After failing his final exam at the age of seventeen, he decided not to return to school to repeat the year – going to university was not, in any case, an option for someone from his lower middle-class background. He thought he would like to be a lithographer and his father took advice from other members of the family and found an offset printing firm, Mulder & Zoon. They offered Van Toorn a job in the studio cleaning the floor and he soon moved on to do hand-lettering in children's books. In the winter of 1949–50, he attended a school for the graphic industry to learn how to draw lettering and space type. At work he created illustrations for books, packaging and ceramic transfers. Everyone employed by the printer had to belong to one of the unions – social democratic, communist, and so on – and this was his first exposure to socialist politics.

Magnolia. Ceramic transfer for Mulder & Zoon, 1950s. New edition 2004

From 1950 to 1953, Van Toorn attended evening classes at the Instituut voor Kunstnijverheidsonderwijs (IvKNO – later named the Gerrit Rietveld Academy), where his teachers included Tom de Heus, Charles Jongejans, head of the typographic workshop, Lex Metz, a strongly leftwing illustrator, and Ab Sok, a graphic artist. It was a period of restoration and these were idealistic Modernists who talked about their dreams of a better society. "**Charles Jongejans and Lex Metz, who were students of Piet Zwart, Paul Schuitema and also Willem Sandberg, were great examples after the Second World War of designers trying to tell us that critical reflection on the social conditions creates the distance necessary for cultural renewal,**" Van Toorn recalled.[6] He found them inspiring, but he could not yet see how to apply this thinking to design practice, and he concluded several years later that their strategies were too closely bound to the aesthetic norms of mass production and consumption.

Game for Jumbo, c. 1960

Game with three toys to assemble for Jumbo, 1960s. Toy design: Van Toorn

In 1957, Van Toorn left Mulder & Zoon to go freelance; he spent much of his time designing packaging for Hausemann & Hötte, manufacturer of Jumbo board games. In 1959, Frans Spruijt asked Van Toorn to create a calendar for his printing company, Mart.Spruijt, because he liked the look of some of Van Toorn's board game instructions. Van Toorn's first calendar had no particular theme – it was simply designed to show off different printing techniques. He got on well with Spruijt, who was just a year older, and the calendar became an annual collaboration. In 1961, the theme was navigation, in 1962 musical instruments, and in subsequent years, Van Toorn based the calendars on letterforms, numbers, games and toys, trees and wood, and festivities. The designs were entirely conventional in appearance and approach: routine, professional exercises in visual research and description, where the graphic interest comes from the elegant, classical typography and the play of attractively diverse forms (pp. 28–31). Van Toorn became something of a calendar specialist, crafting similarly refined designs for organizations such as the Technisch Handelsbureau Junior (1961) and the city printer, Stadsdrukkerij van Amsterdam (1967). A calendar for the printer Drukkerij Sigfried (1963) demonstrates his considerable delicacy of touch as an illustrator, with a series of characterful animal portraits created using woodcuts, drawings and paper collage.

By the mid-1960s, Van Toorn had become involved in projects that would give him a grounding in editorial design and lead him towards the work he is known for today. In 1964, he received a call from Philips' Telecommunicatie Industrie in Hilversum asking him to attend a meeting to discuss the possibility of designing *Range*, the company's quarterly journal about telecommunications. He had been recommended by Dr G.W. Ovink, professor of the history and aesthetics of the art of printing at the University of Amsterdam. The first 24 issues of the journal, founded in 1955, were designed by Alexander Verberne (with Ton Raateland for the first seven years) and Van Toorn inherited the older designer's capitalized headings and open, classical pages based on Baskerville in two justified columns. The dry, technical nature of the subject matter posed some obvious challenges for a designer hoping to engage the reader with lively spreads. As Ovink notes in an article about *Range*'s design approach in issue 25 (Van Toorn's first as designer): "There is, graphically, not much difference between one transmitter and another, packed as they are in grey rectangular cabinets; nor between different switchboards or bundles of wires. All of these look clean and orderly."[7]

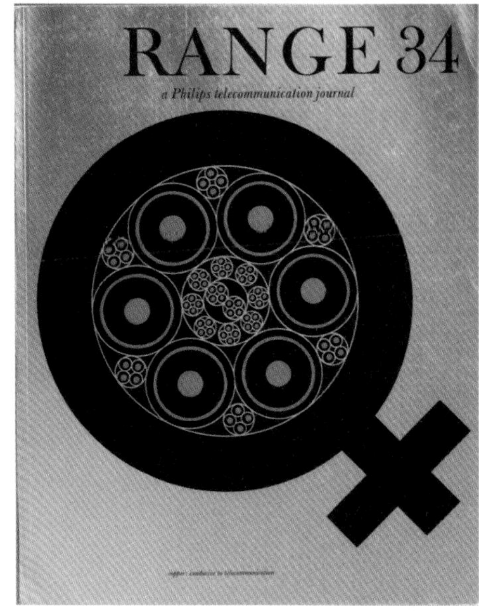

Range no. 34. Magazine cover, 1969. Publisher: Philips' Telecommunicatie Industrie

Verberne had nevertheless succeeded in animating this subject matter and the design of *Range* was regarded, Ovink remarks, as "one of the most interesting features of contemporary Dutch typography".[8] For Van Toorn, working on *Range* (pp. 23–6) provided an education in selecting photographs and operating as a visual editor and he gained much from his working relationship with *Range*'s editor, Niels Douwes Dekker, and the journal's technical contributors. "**Dekker was always saying that the magazine was selling grey boxes,**" remembers Van Toorn, "**and that it was intended for postmaster generals, ministers and people in charge of these enormous projects in developing countries, and all over the world, who would invest in these systems. So we had to represent this in a cultural and intellectual way, but also visually.**"

Van Toorn was well served by his background as an illustrator and proved adept at winkling out visual clues from the text and other sources and devising images to represent invisible technological processes and concepts that look sophisticated even today. He combined black and white photographs of equipment with diagrams and drawings printed in a second and third colour, sometimes overlapping these elements to form an intriguing photo/graphic montage. In one full-page illustration, for instance, he juxtaposes three kinds of image: a photo of an experimental electronic telephone exchange; a diagram indicating a telephone connection: and a photo-illustration showing two communicating receivers (they bracket the diagram) with rows of chess pawns to represent the telephone network's users. There is a clear relationship here with a well established visual tradition in Dutch corporate literature. Piet Zwart's *Het Boek van PTT* (1938) for the national post office fused

Range no. 27. Magazine spread, 1965. Publisher: Philips' Telecommunicatie Industrie

Artwork for *Range*, 1965

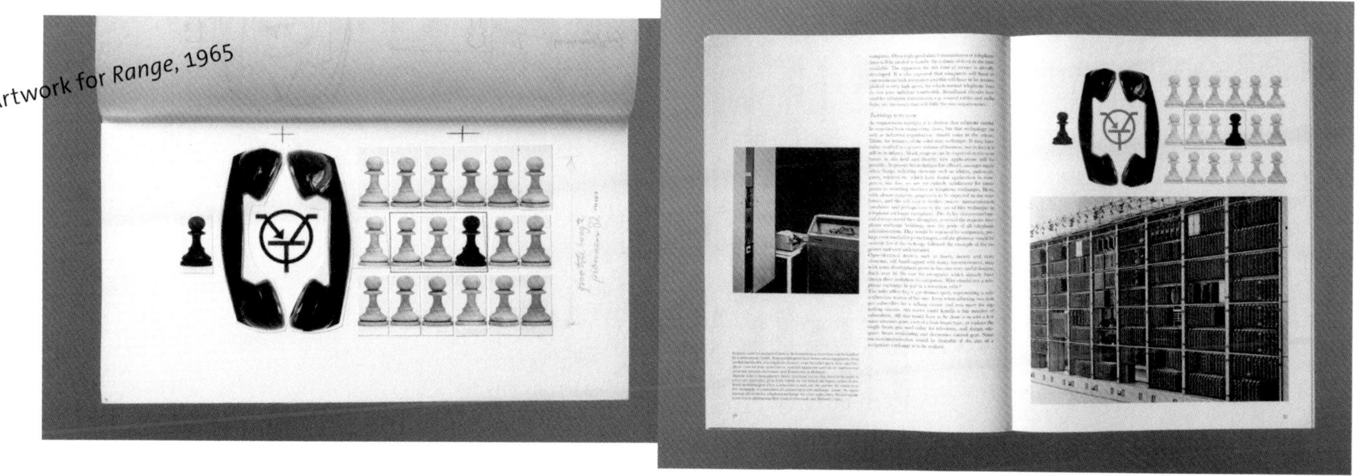

illustration and photomontage in page layouts as gracefully composed as they were dynamic, and Paul Schuitema made equally uninhibited use of photographic cut-outs and patches of spot colour to animate and accentuate designs dealing with building materials and construction. In the 1950s, Dick Elffers continued to challenge readers' expectations about the potential dryness of industrial subject matter by applying layers of vibrant colour over photos of power stations, pylons and electronic machinery in publications for Philips, Provinciale Limburgse Electriciteits Maatschappij, and other manufacturers.[9]

The inherent difficulty of the technical subject matter provided Van Toorn with an intensive course in visual narrative and structure. Under his direction, *Range*'s pages united a finely balanced, objective distillation of imagery with more subjective touches of artfulness that expressed Philips' creative spirit as a technological enterprise. It wasn't possible, as Van Toorn at first hoped, to develop the journal's typography along less classical lines, but *Range* marked a significant step forward for him when it came to organizing picture material.

Pictures on a page

By 1966, the question of photography and how to handle it as a visual editor had become central to Van Toorn's concerns as a designer. He was groping for a purpose and method, but lacked the intellectual tools at this point to establish exactly what he wanted to do with the medium. He had, however, discovered the writing of Jan Romein, a Marxist historian, essayist and professor at the University of Amsterdam, and had begun to read more seriously. "**He made me understand for the first time a more dialectical approach to history, instead of a descriptive, traditional, classic way,**" says Van Toorn. "**He called that 'integral historiography'.**"

The Sunday Times. Magazine spreads, 24 March 1968. Art direction: Michael Rand. Design: David King. Photographs Don McCullin

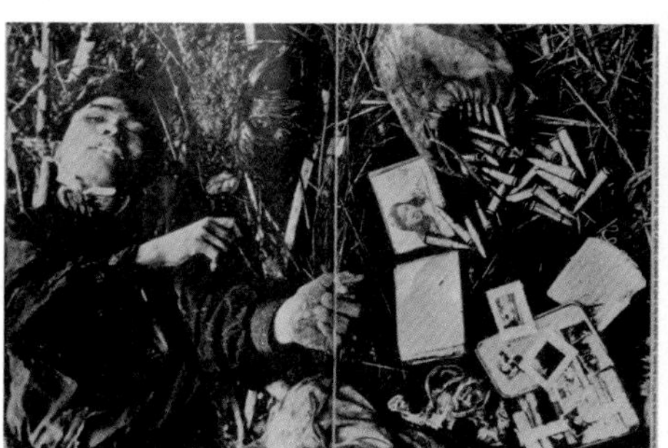

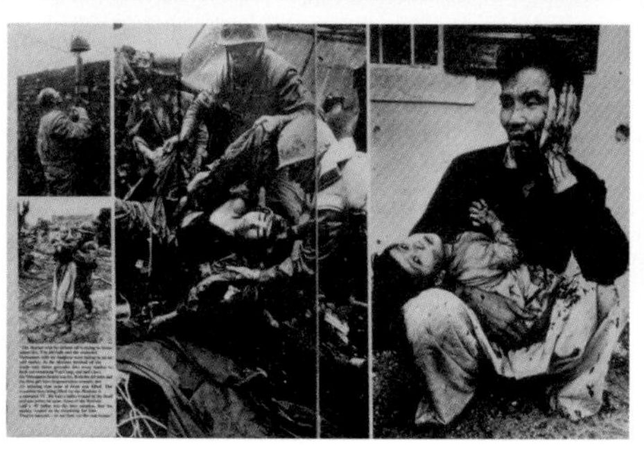

Van Toorn had also started to assemble his own library of photographs, culled from magazines and papers with the help of Monique van Stapele, a picture researcher who owned a photo-agency in Paris.[10] Every Sunday at 8 o'clock in the evening Van Toorn would head for Amsterdam's Central Station to pick up an imported copy of *The Sunday Times Magazine*. Under British art director Michael Rand and art editor David King, the colour supplement had developed a dramatically filmic approach to the use of photos and the construction of visual stories. "**There one can see what editing is all about,**" Van Toorn said later, "**whether of texts, imagery, or, especially, of the relationship between them. Likewise, you'll see what is meant by the narrative nature of information.**"[11] Later, too, he cited as a significant text former *Sunday Times* editor Harold Evans's *Pictures on a Page: Photo-journalism, Graphics and Picture Editing* (1978), a definitive study of the craft of newspaper picture editing. He also admired the incisive handling of news photos in *Paris Match* and *Der Spiegel*. The final influence on Van Toorn's developing interest in visual editing was the Dutch photobook and, in particular, the work of Jurriaan Schrofer. Van Toorn was familiar with Schrofer's highly cinematic designs for books such as Ed van der Elsken's *Een Liefdesgeschiedenis in Saint Germain des Prés* (1956, translated as *Love on the Left Bank*) and *Vuur aan Zee* (1958, Fire beside the sea), with its powerful sequence of factory shots, furnaces, flying sparks and workers' faces. In the late 1960s, as teachers at the Rietveld Academy, Schrofer and Van Toorn jointly developed a course in editorial design.

The mid-1960s was a period of social unrest in Amsterdam, as well as in other Dutch cities. The disturbances, involving students, artists and beatniks, who came to be known as *provos* (rebels) – after the title of a radical monthly magazine – began in spring 1965 with "happenings" in public places. These events were initially peaceful, but in August the police intervened violently during a gathering on the Spui in Amsterdam and made several arrests. The relationship between the rebels and police became tense, the protests turned political and provocation of the authorities became a deliberate aim. In a pattern seen in protest movements around the world during the 1960s, students occupied university buildings and there were demonstrations and riots for the rest of the decade. The loose coalition of protesters included pacifists, anarchists and members of "ban the bomb" groups. The rebels rejected the dullness and "greyness" of everyday life, the lack of adventure and limits placed on imagination by wage slavery, and the repressiveness and joylessness of the political process as it was conducted by a self-interested Establishment. They were opposed to nuclear weapons, militarism, war, political and economic exploitation, and the "system" responsible for these iniquities. In Amsterdam, the *provos* introduced the famous idea of the white bicycles, which anyone was free to climb on and ride, as a response to the clogged streets and pollution caused by cars. Demonstrations against the American military presence in Vietnam took place every month. In 1966, the *provos* entered the local elections and won a seat on the city's municipal council.[12]

Van Toorn, Grafisch Lyceum, Utrecht, late 1960s

Van Toorn, by then in his mid-30s, with a wife, Wil, and a family, did not take part in these protests; nor did he belong to, or work for, any radical political groups, either then or later. He was, however, receptive to the *provos*' playful revival of anarchism and he admired the way their games and campaigns exposed the authoritarian nature of the so-called "tolerant" society. "**Wil and I supported many of the movement's critiques, views and actions,**" he recalls. "**We bought the *provo* journal regularly.**"

His sympathies are clear in his photo-editing and design work for the *Stedelijk Jaarverslag Amsterdam* (city annual report) for 1966. Here, he was able to work as a visual journalist, using a set of photographs of the year's events in Amsterdam taken by Paul van den Bos, who had been an assistant of Ed van der Elsken, and Cor Jaring (pp. 32–3). While the aim of an official document that records the life of a city must ultimately be celebratory, the grainy pictures have the visual texture and engaged, urgent viewpoint of hard-hitting news photos, and Van Toorn emphasizes this by setting the 136-page book in a bold weight of Univers, with display numerals picked out in Bodoni Bold (which he sometimes used in calendars at this time). He devotes a sequence of ten pages to the protests and riots: protesters lift a white bicycle above their heads; young people stand in a line, chanting their message of defiance; and a man puts up a makeshift street sign saying "Provo-plein". In one picture, the designer Anthon Beeke, Van Toorn's assistant, lies on his back in

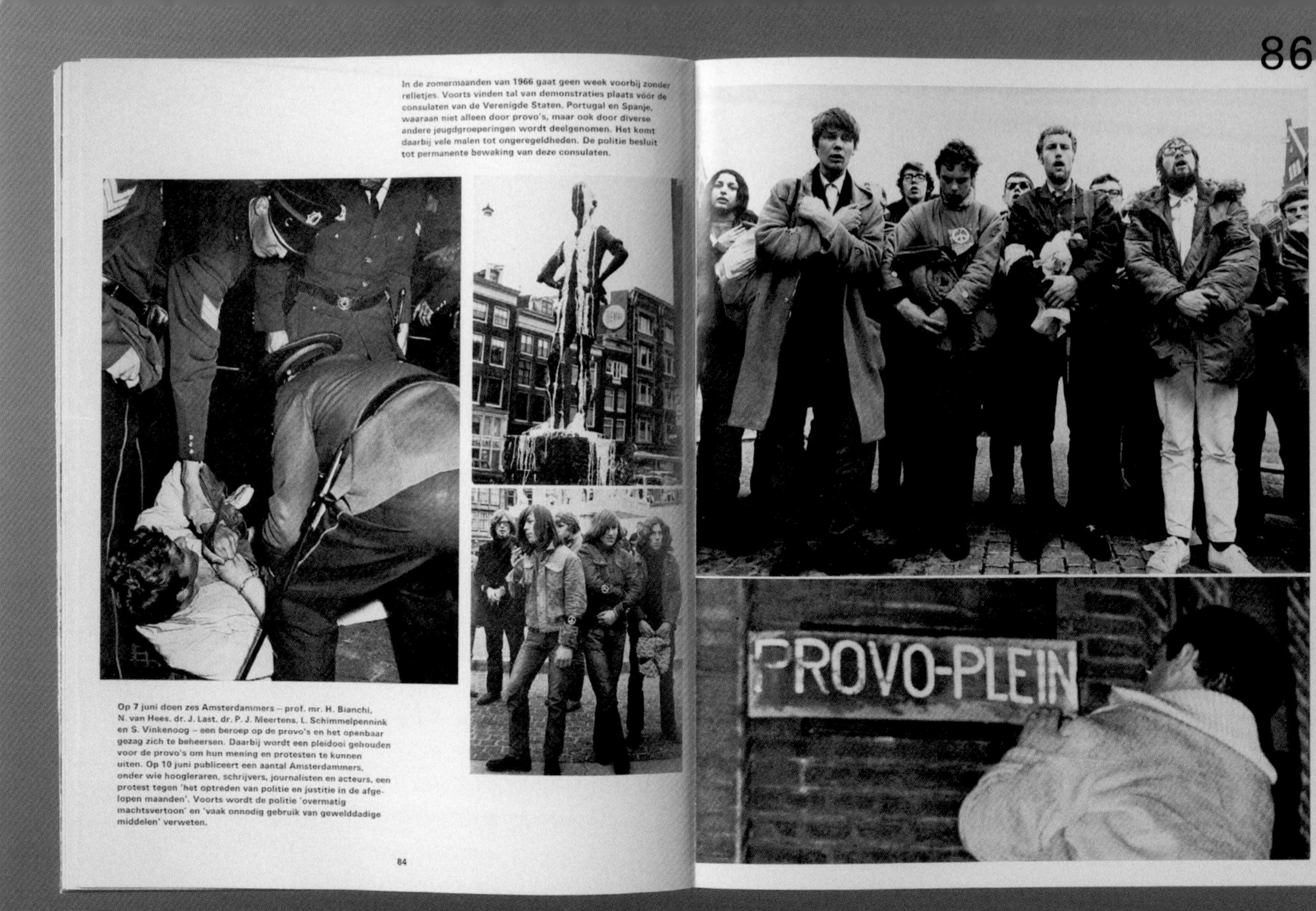

In de zomermaanden van 1966 gaat geen week voorbij zonder relletjes. Voorts vinden tal van demonstraties plaats vóór de consulaten van de Verenigde Staten, Portugal en Spanje, waaraan niet alleen door provo's, maar ook door diverse andere jeugdgroeperingen wordt deelgenomen. Het komt daarbij vele malen tot ongeregeldheden. De politie besluit tot permanente bewaking van deze consulaten.

Op 7 juni doen zes Amsterdammers – prof. mr. H. Bianchi, N. van Hees, dr. J. Last, dr. P. J. Meertens, L. Schimmelpennink en S. Vinkenoog – een beroep op de provo's en het openbaar gezag zich te beheersen. Daarbij wordt een pleidooi gehouden voor de provo's om hun mening en protesten te kunnen uiten. Op 10 juni publiceert een aantal Amsterdammers, onder wie hoogleraren, schrijvers, journalisten en acteurs, een protest tegen 'het optreden van politie en justitie in de afgelopen maanden'. Voorts wordt de politie 'overmatig machtsvertoon' en 'vaak onnodig gebruik van gewelddadige middelen' verweten.

84

Stedelijk Jaarverslag Amsterdam 1966. Annual report spread, 1967. Photographs: Paul van den Bos

the street, as several police officers attempt to arrest him.[13] Van Toorn resisted official attempts to get him to remove photos from the pages that might allow people to identify the policemen involved. He succeeds in devising an engaging visual narrative that shows the influence of picture editing in *The Sunday Times Magazine* and other similar publications, yet the annual report's transparency as a visual document keeps it firmly located within the conventions of editorial design. No aspect of the layout calls attention to the way it has been constructed through acts of selection on the picture editor's part.

In 1968, in an issue of *Sikkens Varia*, a journal produced by the Sikkens paint company, Van Toorn attempted for the first time to construct a visual essay using images. The publication also features a text by his brother, the poet and author Willem van Toorn, but this is most definitely a secondary element, turned sideways along the bottom of the page and occupying just a fraction of the space allotted to pictures. "**Our proposal was to offer the reader a picture of the time, the moment, and then, of course, to point to the use of colour,**" recalls Van Toorn. He composed the pages using images from photo-agencies, museums and his own photo library, pressed up close together to form intricate photo-patchworks (p. 37). A spread about art features fourteen pictures, including a Paul Delvaux painting, a sculpture by Niki de Saint Phalle, and a Parisian street blocked by Christo with barrels; another spread shows, among other things, scenes from Vietnam, a sky diver, a trio who could be Dutch protesters, and a scene from Samuel Beckett's play *Happy Days*. The viewer is left to determine the connections between these images. The problem for Van Toorn was that

Chronique Sikkens Varia no. 56. Journal spread, 1968. Publisher: Sikkens Groep

it was still an essentially "liberal" approach to describing the world. *Sikkens Varia* had a higher degree of complexity than the *Stedelijk Jaarverslag* because it connected all kinds of fields – art, science, technology, urban design, politics – but the tension between a personal stance, a critical point of view and the facts themselves was not dealt with rigorously enough for his liking. The publication failed, he felt, because it was insufficiently sceptical and lacked a position: "**It takes the world as it is and in all the different ways it appears.**"

Van Toorn came closer to achieving the ideal of a critical point of view in another project completed in 1968, a Christmas issue of *Drukkersweekblad en Autolijn* devoted to "De Nederlandse Museums" (Museums in the Netherlands), jointly produced by the Federation of Master Printers and the Netherlands Photo-engravers Association (pp. 34–6). Since the 1930s, the visual editing of this annual publication had been entrusted to its designer, and high standards of production had made it a coveted commission. The plan was to divide the book into sections devoted to Dutch museums that dealt with history, art, domestic crafts and culture, sound and gesture, science and technology, ethnology, and natural history. Van Toorn proposed to the editors that they treat all the museums, encompassing an estimated twelve million objects, as a single, vast, national collection. Accompanied by Wil he travelled the Netherlands, visiting museums chosen for inclusion, where he took Polaroids of objects he wanted to show. He had learned from the *Sikkens Varia* project that there could be a more informal way of

Drukkersweekblad en Autolijn, Christmas issue. Journal spread, 1968. Publishers: Federation of Master Printers and the Netherlands Photo-Engravers Association. Photographs: Joost Guntenaar, Aart Klein and Hans Samson

organizing the visual material and he wanted the images to represent the range of the museums' abundant holdings, while at the same time leaving the presentation open enough for the reader's imagination to be given play. Three photographers armed with his Polaroid references photographed all the objects. Even by today's frenetic visual standards, Van Toorn crams a huge amount of material on to the pages. He shows paintings in their frames with as little space between them as possible. He allows artefacts to overlap and, on black and white spreads, he singles out one or two items in a second colour – usually purple. He leaves only the smallest of margins around the images and text, amplifying the sensation of unchecked, storage-room profusion. Even the typography – Garamond Bold, ranged left and framed, like a picture in its own right, by a heavy purple box – cultivates an air of informality.

The client liked the project and a phone call from fellow designer Pieter Brattinga confirmed Van Toorn's view that he had succeeded in breaking free from the restraint and reverence with which art has traditionally been treated. According to Brattinga, it just wasn't acceptable to deal with art in this casual manner.

Disrupting the surface

By this stage, Van Toorn had already begun to work with a figure who would prove to be one of the most important collaborators of his career: Jean Leering, director of the Van Abbemuseum in Eindhoven from 1964 to 1973. Leering wanted to broaden the art museum's remit by encouraging public awareness of social change, and by repeatedly questioning the idea that a museum was merely a neutral display space for art, with no agenda of its own. He discovered in Van Toorn a designer who came to share these aims with a passion and he invested a great deal of trust in him. Van Toorn designed posters and catalogues for the museum from 1965, and throughout Leering's time as director, as well as contributing to the museum's policy on the presentation of information to the public (pp. 39–75).

While both men rejected the idea of a single, limiting "house style" to express the Van Abbemuseum's public identity, in the mid- to late 1960s Van Toorn's designs were still recognisably the work of the same designer who had created the "De Nederlandse Museums" publication.[14] Van Toorn used Garamond Bold for most of his projects and his ambitions were still constrained by the visual norms and expectations of "good design", much as he wanted to find critical alternatives to these design world conventions. Many of his 1960s museum posters and catalogues have an "American" quality of boldness and high definition; like so much international graphic design created at the time, they reflect the brashness, brightness and market-consciousness of Pop Art. A typical example is the "*Three Blind Mice*" catalogue (1968) for an exhibition about the collections of three wealthy Dutch art collectors. The unusual documentary approach, showing photographs of the collectors in meetings, looking at art works and chatting with colleagues over dinner, goes some way towards demystifying this influential group's normally concealed activities, but the catalogue's revelatory (and perhaps critical) intention is softened by the reassuringly inviting yellow, blue and silver Pop Art numerals that fill both cover and poster.

A year or two later, Van Toorn's Van Abbemuseum catalogues look like the work of a different designer. In 1969, he clad the pages of a Piero Manzoni catalogue in a piece of white, fluffy, floppy fabric that makes the experience of holding it curiously unnerving. In 1970, he bound a catalogue for Franz Erhard Walther in a cloth bag, printed with the artist's name and heavily stapled at the top, which doubled as an

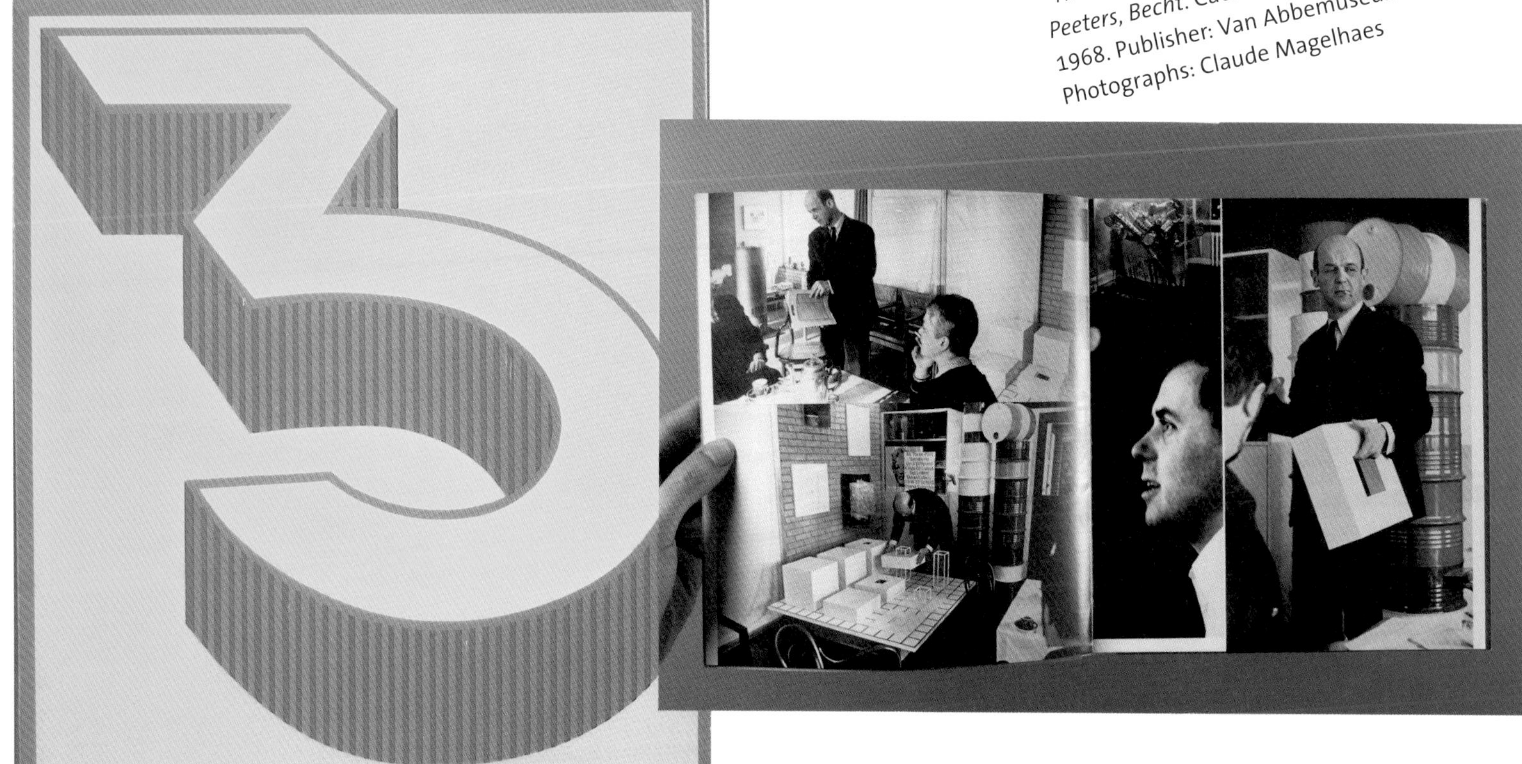

"Three Blind Mice" / De Collecties: Visser, Peeters, Becht. Catalogue cover and spread, 1968. Publisher: Van Abbemuseum. Photographs: Claude Magelhaes

envelope. A catalogue for Jan van Munster, produced in the same year, had to be extracted from inside a sealed, close-fitting, plastic sheath that gave no sign that it contained anything at all. These objects communicated both the physical reality and difficulty of the art experiences they represented, while reminding the viewer that the catalogue too had come about through someone's – the designer's – conceptual and aesthetic choices. Finally, Van Toorn had managed to resist his natural tendency as a designer to opt for graphic and typographic "stability", in the classical sense, and he had succeeded in disrupting the usually smooth and seamless surface of the designed object.

Something similar can be seen in the publication he designed for Sikkens in 1970, when the company awarded its annual prize for colour not to an individual (previous laureates included Le Corbusier, Johannes Itten and Theo van Doesburg) but to "hippies" in general for their extravagantly colourful contribution to society – the judges, on this occasion, included Willem Sandberg and Jean Leering. Van Toorn's design consists of two posters and eight pages scattered with typewriter-generated texts selected by the poet Simon Vinkenoog, stapled between folded linen (pp. 132–3). The wit of the project – an official communication from a long-established national institution – is that it ended up looking like a

Manzoni. Catalogue cover made of cloth, inside cover and spreads, 1969. Publisher: Van Abbemuseum

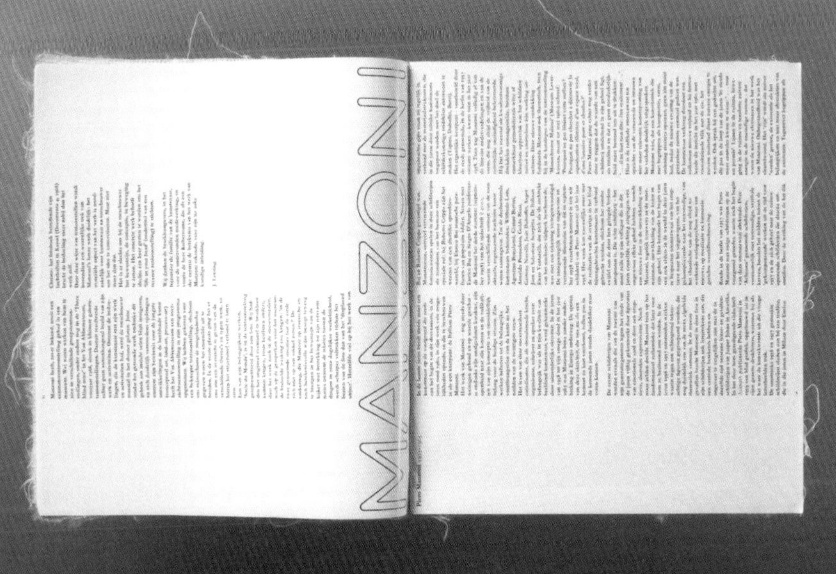

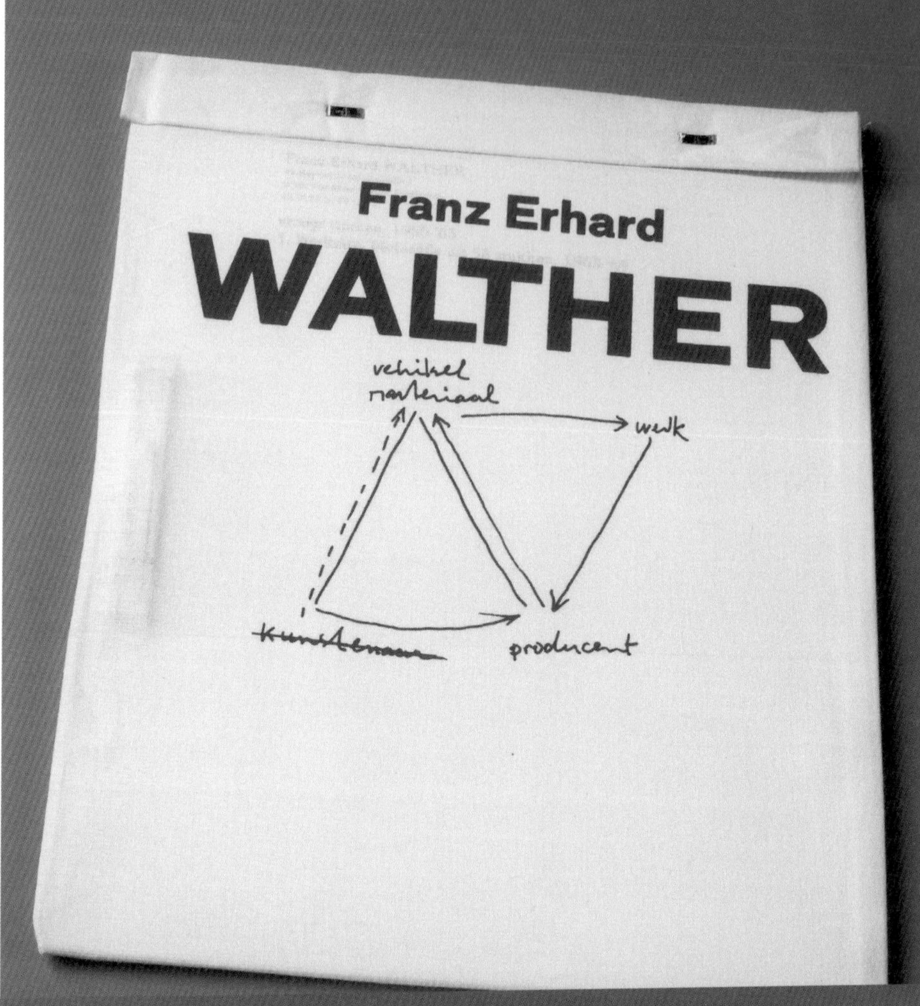

een proces in de tijd, in de handeling en deze ervaringen of deze ontwikkelingen kan ik dan een werk noemen. Maar het begrip werk duikt pas helemaal aan het einde op, in het verrichten van een handeling die ik moet doen. Maar die is niet aanwezig, alleen daarvoor bestemde voertuigen zijn beschikbaar. En dat is nog geen werk. Voor mij is dit het wezenlijke verschil met een of andere historiese kunstvorm. In de grond moet men mij dus toestaan iets van het publiek te vergen waarbij niets gezegd wordt. Ik moet ze dus eerst iets geven om tot handelen in staat te zijn. Het is hen ten volle toegestaan hun ervaringen ook op zeer veel eenvoudigere en naïevere vlakken op te doen.

V. U spreekt over een ontwikkeling in de tijd, in de werkelijke tijd, maar als het publiek deze objecten gebruikt krijgt het ook bepaalde subjectieve ervaringen, die het proces natuurlijk heel anders maken.

W. Ja, maar het moet eerst de ervaring opdoen, het moet werkelijke ervaring daarmee krijgen en dan kan men pas van een eerste begrijpen spreken, dan weet het waarover ik spreek.

V. Het woord is dus eigenlijk niet toereikend om deze ervaring met elkaar uit te wisselen. Maar aan de andere kant, hoe kan men anders te werk gaan om de motivering zo te stimuleren dat men werkelijk met een object gaat werken?

W. Ik zou dit probleem, bijvoorbeeld, kunnen verduidelijken tegen de achtergrond van de historiese kunst. Op histories vlak ligt de verklaring steeds weer bij mij alleen. Het object bevindt zich hier voor mij, tegen de muur of op de vloer. Er is een soort tweespraak, een dialoog, waar de andere deelnemer nooit bij betrokken is, het is altijd iets tussen mij en het object. Hier doen er zich configuraties voor waarbij twee of vier of nog meer personen samen een proces doormaken. Het proces dat uit dit werk voortvloeit is dan feitelijk verdeeld over bijvoorbeeld vier personen. Objectief kan ik spreken over één proces, maar dat is dan verdeeld over vier personen, zodat er noodzakelijkerwijs een tegenspraak is, maar dat is niet te vermijden. Nu kan ik natuurlijk trachten te ontleden wat er objectief aan de hand is, bijvoorbeeld het proces is objectief en vier processen zijn subjectief als er bijvoorbeeld vier personen aan deelnemen. Als ik dit tot een enkel proces wil comprimeren, dan moet het theoreties mogelijk zijn dat het totaal wordt uitgewisseld, dus de door de vier personen opgedane ervaringen. Dat gaat natuurlijk niet. Waarmee kan ik dit eigenlijk overdragen? Als ik alleen van een samenhang van gevoelens uitga kan ik gebruik maken van woorden en tekens, maar er zijn werkelijk zeer veel ervaringen. Ik ken zeer veel voorbeelden waarin zelfs de taal vaak niet voldoende is om dit over te dragen. In feite is er een soort gemoedservaring die in mijn binnenste werkzaam is, maar die ik niet op de anderen kan overdragen. Zelfs de vier personen, als het een project voor vier personen betreft, die samen iets hebben ontwikkeld, dus een proces tot stand gebracht, mogen daar gedeeltelijk niet over spreken, omdat het dan verstoord wordt.

V. En later?

W. Het kan zijn dat ik weken of maanden later, dat heb ik wel eens meegemaakt, daar weer over kan spreken in een heel andere samenhang; dan is het plotseling mogelijk dat de ervaring werkzaam wordt. Dan pas wordt hij bruikbaar en benut. Een voor mij zeer belangrijke faktor is ook dat de ervaring die tijdens het proces wordt opgedaan, dus de doorgemaakte ontwikkeling, geen gesloten, geen afgesloten systeem is, maar dat deze ervaringen kunnen worden overgedragen op andere levensgebieden, op andere ervaringsgebieden, en dat zij daar werkzaam worden. En pas als ze daar werkzaam worden zie ik het effect of maken zij het mij mogelijk daarover te spreken.

... En er is nog iets. Wij hebben het gehad over het proces en de ervaring, het feitelijke gebruik, de benutting van het proces in de tijd. Ik kan niet zo maar zonder meer zeggen dat dit een fragment in de tijd is. Er is een voorveld en een naveld. Welnu, met betrekking tot het voorveld vraag ik mij af wat mij motiveert, hoe kom ik er toe met dit object te gaan werken. Er moet werkelijk een innerlijke beweegreden zijn, als ik het niet gewoon willekeurig wil doen. Er is een grotere samenhang, ik sta met zeer veel dingen in verbinding. Op een of andere manier word ik ertoe gebracht met dit object te gaan werken. En dan komen alle velden die ik heb, al mijn verbondenheden, te voorschijn uit het dagelijkse leven, uit mijn denkpatronen. Die komen daar bij elkaar en dan begint het proces. Het proces vindt plaats en als ik het nu beëindig zeg ik: 'nu ga ik naar huis', maar dan houdt het niet op; het blijft werkzaam, er is een naveld. Het wordt voortgezet in het leven van elke dag, de ervaringen uiten zich in alle situaties. Ik kan niet zeggen: 'Het proces begint hier en daar houdt het op'. Dat kan niet, het gaat door. Het proces vangt ergens aan en leidt dan tot een gebruik, tot ervaringen, het sterft weg maar blijft toch werkzaam. Ik kan niet zeggen dat het ophoudt. Ik heb processen meegemaakt, zes, zeven of acht jaar geleden, die mij nog zo plasties voor ogen staan, waarvan de opgedane ervaring zo belangrijk was, dat ik ze in mijn denkwereld steeds weer gebruik op heel andere gebieden, in andere levensomstandigheden, bij wetenschappelijke kwesties, bij filosofiese overwegingen, enz. Ik kan dus zeggen dat een proces dat acht jaar geleden plaats vond zo nu en dan nog steeds werkzaam is.

Franz Erhard Walther. Catalogue in stapled cloth bag, inside cover and spreads, 1972. Publisher: Van Abbemuseum

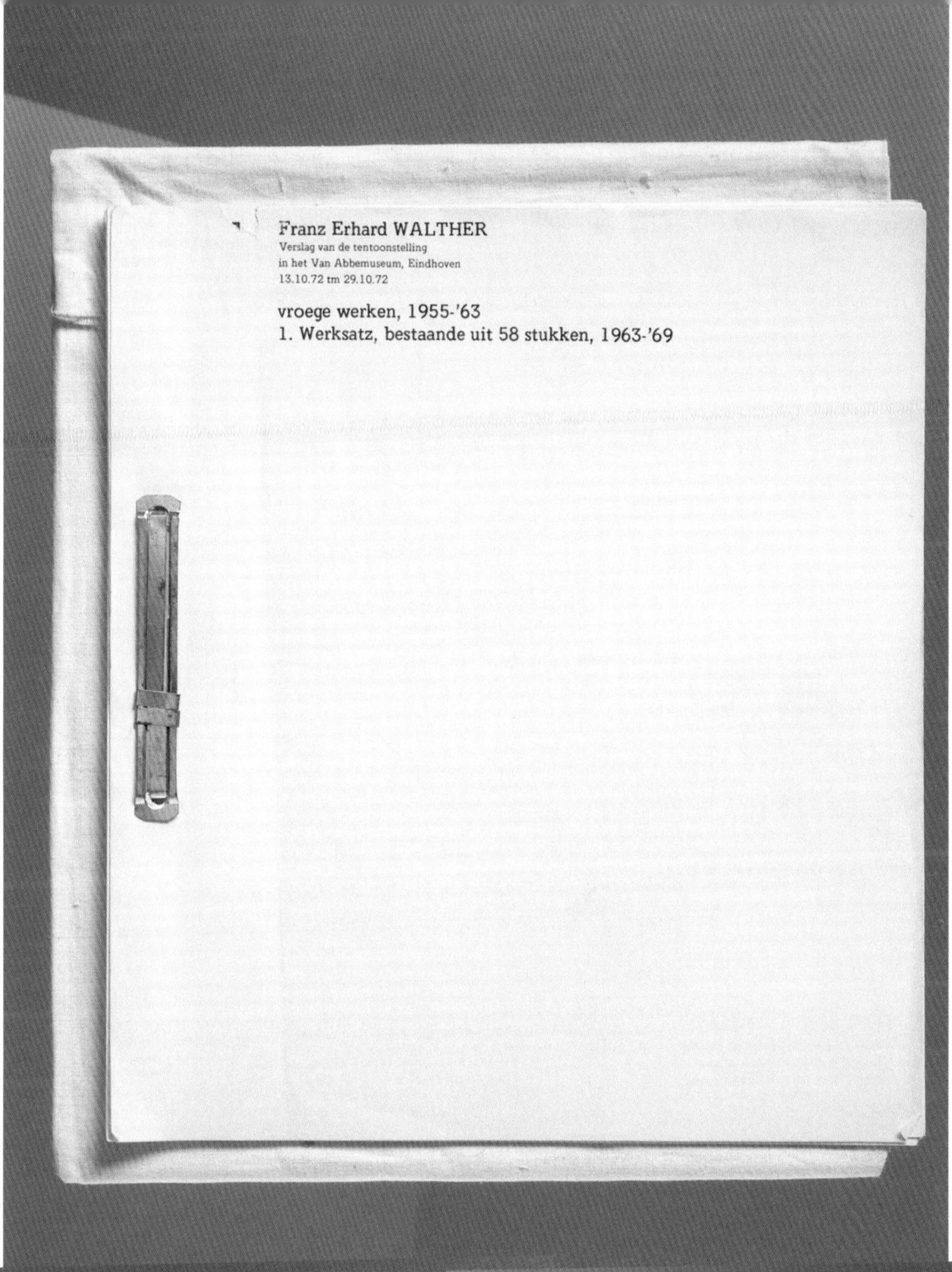

Franz Erhard WALTHER
Verslag van de tentoonstelling
in het Van Abbemuseum, Eindhoven
13.10.72 tm 29.10.72

vroege werken, 1955-'63
1. Werksatz, bestaande uit 58 stukken, 1963-'69

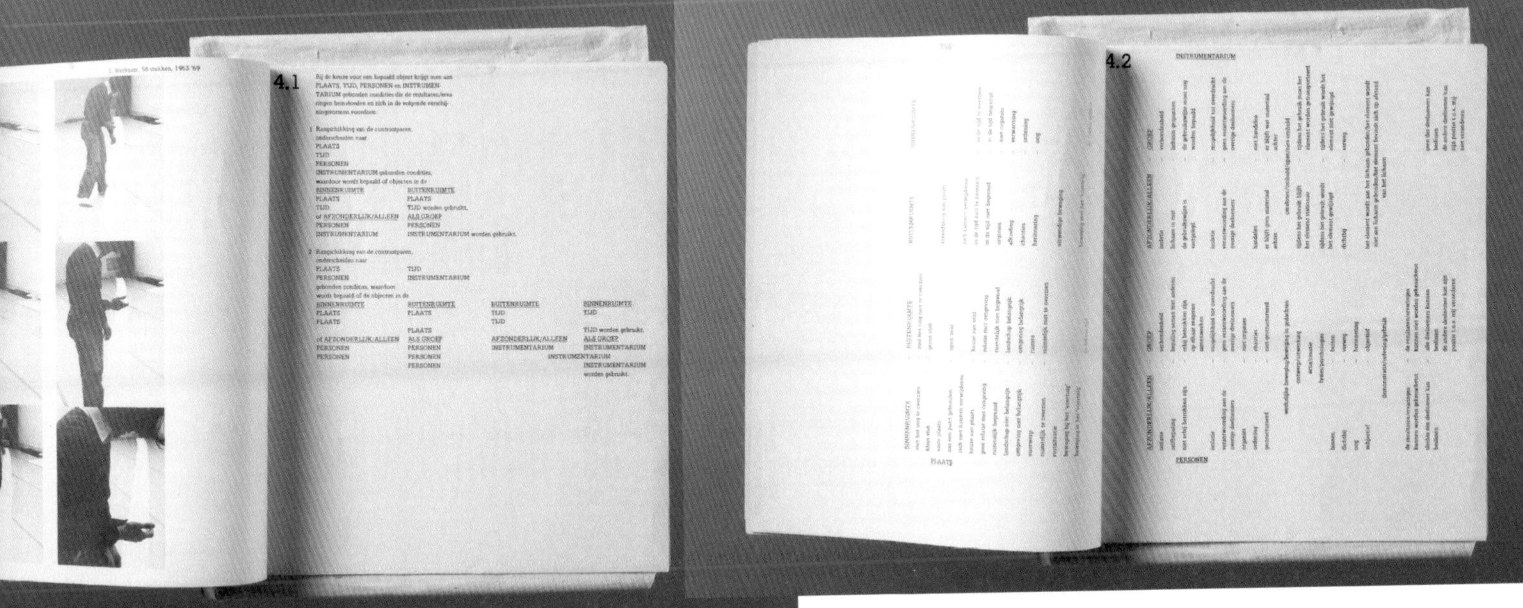

Jan van Munster. Catalogue in sealed plastic wallet, inside cover and spreads, 1970. Publisher: Van Abbemuseum, Eindhoven

group of hippie amateurs had cobbled it together. Van Toorn's professional skills as a designer had been hard won. Now, to say what he wanted to say, he needed to dismantle them.

The reflexive tradition

In the 1970s, Van Toorn's reading became more significant in the development of his thinking about design. He was particularly taken by the German poet and cultural critic Hans Magnus Enzensberger's ideas about media, which he first encountered in an issue of the German journal *Kursbuch*. Enzensberger distinguishes between repressive and emancipatory forms of media.[15] Repressive media, he explains, has a centralized programme, a single sender and many receivers, and acts to immobilize the isolated individual. Emancipatory media, on the other hand, is decentralized, treats every receiver as a potential sender, and acts to mobilize the population. Repressive media encourages passive consumption and depoliticization, and is produced by specialists and kept under bureaucratic control. Emancipatory media encourages interaction and feedback, contributes to the political learning process, and is collectively produced and autonomous. "All use of the media demands manipulation," writes Enzensberger. "The most elementary actions in (media) production, from the choice of the medium via recording, editing, synchronization and mixing, up to and including distribution, are all interventions in the given material. There is no such thing as unmanipulated writing, filming and broadcasting. The question, then, is not whether the media are manipulated or not, but who manipulates them. A revolutionary design need not cause the manipulators to vanish; indeed, it ought to turn everybody into manipulators."[16]

In 1917, in an essay titled "Art as Technique", the Russian Formalist critic Victor Shklovsky demonstrated the need to break with ordinary perception and the "habitualization" that leads people not to question their surroundings. Shklovsky wanted to recover the sensation of life through the experience of literature as art, and he called this process *ostranenie* – defamiliarization or "making strange". "The purpose of art is to impart the sensation of things as they are perceived and not as they are known," he writes. "The technique of art is to make objects 'unfamiliar,' to make forms difficult, to increase the difficulty and length of perception because the process of perception is an aesthetic end in itself and must be prolonged."[17] Shklovsky's concept of *ostranenie* was, in turn, an important influence on the German Marxist writer Bertolt Brecht, who wanted the audience to view his plays critically, with emotional detachment, and not to lose themselves in the experience as entertainment. The theatrical event should be perceived as a representation, rather than as an unproblematic transcription of "reality", which is in any case also a construction that can take many forms and be remade. To create a sense of distance, Brecht employed devices such as explanatory placards, the speaking out loud of stage directions, the direct address of the audience by the actors, and the use of song. He called this the *Verfremdungseffekt*, which is usually translated as "alienation effect" or A-effect for short. Brecht writes: "The A-effect consists in turning the object of which one is to be made aware, to which one's attention is to be drawn, from something ordinary, familiar, immediately accessible, into something peculiar, striking and unexpected. What is obvious is in a certain sense made incomprehensible, but this is only in order that it may then be made all the easier to comprehend. Before familiarity can turn into awareness the familiar must be stripped of its inconspicuousness; we must give up assuming that the object in question needs no explanation."[18]

Driestuiversroman (The Threepenny Opera). By Bertolt Brecht, 1960. Publisher: Allert de Lange. Woodcuts: Van Toorn

As a young man, Van Toorn was fascinated by Brecht. In 1960, he bought a book of Brecht's theoretical writings on theatre and he illustrated the Dutch translation of *The Threepenny Opera* in the same year. Over the years he has seen many of Brecht's plays, in Amsterdam and Hamburg, including *Baal, Rise and Fall of the City of Mahagonny, Mother Courage and her Children, The Life of Galileo, The Resistible Rise of Arturo Ui,* and *The Caucasian Chalk Circle*. In 1973, he received twenty paperback volumes of Brecht's collected writings in payment for a job instead of a fee.[19] On a page for the month of October, in the Mart.Spruijt calendar for 1976/77, Van Toorn quotes a lengthy comparison from Brecht's essay "The Modern Theatre is the Epic Theatre" between traditional theatre and his own epic theatre. Where dramatic theatre implicates the spectator in the events happening on stage, wears down his capacity for action, and provides him with sensations, writes Brecht, epic theatre turns the spectator into an observer, while arousing his capacity for action and forcing him to take decisions. Where dramatic theatre is about suggestion, feeling and growth, and takes the human being for granted, epic theatre is about argument, reason and montage, and treats the human being as an object of inquiry.[20] References to Brecht and to the idea of the epic narrative have continued to make appearances in Van Toorn's writing and personal projects, up to his book *Design's Delight* (2006).[21]

Another key influence on Van Toorn's development of techniques of graphic estrangement, equivalent to epic theatre, was French film-maker Jean-Luc Godard, who was similarly indebted to Brecht. If Van Toorn can be seen as the "Brecht of graphic design", as one writer dubbed him, then he can perhaps just as legitimately be described as the discipline's Godard.[22] Van Toorn saw early Godard films such as *Une Femme est une Femme* (1961), *Pierrot le Fou* (1965) and *La Chinoise* (1967) and continued to follow his work into the 1970s, 1980s and beyond. In *Vivre sa Vie* (1962) – often described as a Brechtian film – Godard divides the story into twelve chapters, each with its own title, and interrupts the narrative with playful digressions, a documentary interlude, and literary and filmic quotations. He frames shots and moves the camera unconventionally and sometimes films the actors from behind. Other breaks with the seamless conventions of "classical" cinema include jump cuts, unusually long takes and passages when all the sound cuts out.

Devices such as these make Godard a key figure in the evolution of reflexive forms of film-making and literature. "Reflexivity subverts the assumption that art can be a transparent medium of communication, a window on the world, a mirror promenading down a highway," writes film critic Robert Stam in a study of the reflexive tradition that Van Toorn read in the early 1990s.[23] According to Stam, strategies employed by reflexive artists such as Godard (and we might add by Van Toorn) include narrative discontinuities, authorial intrusions, essayistic digressions and stylistic virtuosities. The purpose of these discontinuities and disruptions, as with Brecht's use of the alienation effect, is to demystify aspects of reality that we are inclined to take for granted and to break "the charm of the spectacle in order to awaken the spectator's critical intelligence."[24] It is the very normality of ideology, notes Stam, that makes necessary an art which renders things strange. In an essay published in 1994, Van Toorn makes an explicit connection between Stam's lineage of reflexive artists and his own intentions as a designer: "**through the critical orientation of its products,**" he writes, "**the reflexive mentality raises questions among the public which stimulate a more active way of dealing with reality.**"[25]

In his work since around 1970, Van Toorn has attempted wherever possible – and not always with complete success, as he admits – to make viewers of his designs aware of the mechanics of manipulation. He has often returned to this idea, sometimes modifying his terminology and adding new detail and shading, but always insisting on this aim as a basic condition of honest, open, democratic communication. "**In our culture, the tradition is to strive for a closed product: a kind of statement composed of form and content that is somehow complete in itself**," he explains. "**Graphic designers find themselves in a situation which supports the institution and that becomes part of the product. If you strive for a closed message, both in form and in content, then you are not being true to the communicative character of the message, to the real aim of the communication. Producers of information try to hide their real aims and motives. Information becomes a commodity. Design is the ultimate answer to that.**"[26] It is the designer's role and responsibility as a mediator, Van Toorn argues, to find ways to break open and demystify the message, to make its provenance and manipulatory character visible in its form, so that the receiver can engage fully in the communication's argument. "**In one way or another,**" he says, "**the public must remain in a position where they can also measure the motives of the producer and mediator that lie behind the product, against their own experience of the world.**"[27]

Constructing a counter-reality

Van Toorn's reorientation as a designer was most marked in the series of calendars he designed for Mart.Spruijt from 1970 to 1977, which stand out as some of the most Brechtian, reflexive and outspoken of this designs. A printer's calendar might seem to be a relatively free space for a designer, but the aim of these items, as a rule, is simply promotion. Disturbing viewers with unexpected, inexplicable or shocking images, as they turn to a new page in search of the date, is not the gentlest or most persuasive way to advertise a company's services. Van Toorn does more in his calendars than simply reveal to viewers that these examples of fine printing are out to cajole them into giving Mart.Spruijt their business. He treats the pieces in the manner of an essay, as an opportunity to investigate aspects of the contemporary world that he finds revealing, or a source of concern, and attempts to provoke viewers of this otherwise quotidian print genre into giving these matters their attention and thought.

The 1970 calendar's theme broadly concerns representation, though to many viewers it must have come as a complete enigma (pp. 138–43). The only continuity with the previous year's circular design lies in the use of graph paper on the cover, but where before this was just a pleasant graphic texture, now even this motif takes on an air of strangeness. As a visual entity, the 1970 calendar has few unifying elements apart from the peculiar choice of the typeface Gill Sans Shadow for the dates. Van Toorn includes montages of the seventeenth-century City Hall (now Royal Palace) in Amsterdam, creating a view of the building that it was impossible to see from the street, and shows framed photographs of lorries hanging on a wall in a drivers' café. In one sequence of four pages, a weather balloon, shown upside down, gradually disappears from view, for no obvious reason. There are shots of empty meadows north of Amsterdam – "**photographs of nothing**", notes Van Toorn – while elsewhere right angles and straight lines appear to cast shadows: the shadows indicate the line's apparent presence, but in reality there is nothing there. In light of the remarkable series of calendars for Mart. Spruijt that followed, it is easy to overlook how original the marriage of art and design in this breakthrough project still appears 35 years later. Van Toorn's visual conundrums have more in common with the conceptual art of the time, in their austere mentality and relative indifference to matters of form, than with the expressive formal tendencies and unambiguous message-making of graphic design.[28]

1980. Photograph: Pieter Boersma

The most complex calendar in visual terms is 1972/73, where almost every page is a crowded photomontage of people, in most cases headshots (pp. 1–17). Van Toorn themes the pages around men and women, children, couples, shoppers, underwear models, marching soldiers, celebrities such as Frank Sinatra, John Lennon and Elizabeth Taylor, and politicians such as Richard Nixon and Golda Meir. He devotes one page to news photos of American radical activist and Black Panther Party associate Angela Davis, while French actress Jeanne Moreau receives two. The photos are cut out, often with deliberate clumsiness, and overlapped to produce informal compositions, much like a scrapbook. The montages move without immediately apparent connection between pictures of ordinary people, noteworthy only because such snapshots do not normally fill promotional calendars, and extraordinary news events of the day. In August, a page showing eleven unknown men is followed by a shocking and controversial photo by Horst Faas and Michel Laurent, documenting Bengali guerrillas bayoneting and killing three Bihari prisoners on a racetrack in Dacca, Bangladesh, in 1971, while a crowd looks on – the picture appeared on the front page of *The New York Times* and won a Pulitzer prize. It is not an image that many people would choose for their kitchen or office walls. A week later, Van Toorn assaults viewers with two bound figures being executed by firing squad and a man holding aloft a severed head. Van Toorn has taken the idea of the visual "collection", seen in so many of his 1960s projects, and reused it for a much more confrontational purpose. While there are no captions to explain anything, most of the news images would have been familiar at the time. By mixing these usually separated categories of photograph together on equal terms, Van Toorn violently intrudes the political into everyday reality (and nothing could be more "everyday" than a calendar) and implies connections between the public, the power of entertainment and advertising to distract the public, and alarming events that take place elsewhere in the world – sometimes "in our name", but not necessarily in accordance with our wishes.

The 1972/73 calendar revealed a designer who, at the age of 40, had truly found his voice. Van Toorn used a similar montage of raw, everyday photographs of post office workers on a poster for the Dutch PTT's 1972 annual report (p. 193), and he reworked images from the calendar on a poster for the catalogue of his exhibition at the Museum Fodor, also in 1972. Yet the calendar is a project that is clearly, in retrospect, very much a product of its time. It arrived during a highly politicized period, in which the political process and the way that the news media covered it were subjected to continuous scrutiny by those on the left. The calendar's sceptical sensibility has much in common with John Berger's *Ways of Seeing*, published in 1972 (a Dutch translation appeared in 1974). "Publicity turns consumption into a substitute for democracy. The choice of what one eats (or wears or drives) takes the place of significant political choice," writes Berger. "Publicity helps to mask and compensate for all that is undemocratic within society. And it also masks what is happening in the rest of the world."[29] Even so, public fatigue with the endless flow of images of conflict, cruelty, death and disaster on the TV news had yet to set in and it was still possible to believe that if only people's eyes could be opened and the public will mobilized, change might come. Subsequent calendars, showing portraits of Van Toorn's friends, neighbours and other members of the public, comparative shots of the flat, empty Dutch landscape, and images of duplicitous politicians from the media, are more detached and cerebral, still challenging, but without plunging the viewer so roughly into the cold water of contemporary visual reality. In today's cautious commercial climate, in which PR calls the shots, it seems remarkable that Frans Spruijt tolerated Van Toorn's brutally direct attempts to construct a "counter-reality" for so long.[30] Finally, after a long, unexplained delay in printing the completed 1977/78 calendar, the series came to an end. "We became friends, but slightly drifted apart later on," Spruijt explained in 1986. "I couldn't follow him any longer in his anarchistic and Marxist thinking."[31]

What is the information for?

Since Van Toorn had gone out of his way to challenge the limitations of "classical" design and was doing this from a socio-political point of view, it was hardly surprising that some took exception. His designs were subjective – he sought to express his own feelings about the world – and deliberately flouted standards of graphic correctness and decorum. As one observer noted later, his output could be seen as "wilfully anti-aesthetic, irrational and routine-avoiding".[32] No sooner had Van Toorn discovered his direction, than he also found his principal critic and ideological adversary: Wim Crouwel, co-founder, in 1963, of the Amsterdam design firm Total Design.[33]

Crouwel presented himself as an avatar of objectivity and neutrality: as a system-builder and functionalist. The designer had no business, he claimed, trying to insert himself and his personal opinions into a client's message. The difference in intention between two art museum posters produced by Crouwel and Van Toorn in 1971 could hardly be greater. Crouwel's *Hedendaagse Kunst* (Contemporary art) poster for the Stedelijk Museum in Amsterdam, constructed around the letters "SM", is an entirely formal expression of institutional identity, which puts all the emphasis on beautifully controlled typography that alludes – if it alludes to anything at all – to minimalist abstraction. The design exudes aesthetic authority, suggesting that the museum is highly modern. Van Toorn's acquisition poster for the Van Abbemuseum, by contrast, is a piece of graphic polemic that may be one of the frankest street communications ever sanctioned by a nationally-owned art gallery. The names of Chagall, Duchamp, Kandinsky, Yves Klein, Mondrian, Moholy-Nagy and Picasso are scrawled like items on a shopping list and a figure at the bottom tells us what these purchases cost the museum: 273,969 guilders. The poster is highly effective and memorable – more so, arguably, than Crouwel's – but it shows no interest in typographic harmony. Its purpose is both to confront and inform.

The pair's first public exchange of views occurred on 9 November 1972, at a discussion in Amsterdam on the occasion of Van Toorn's exhibition at the Museum Fodor. (Curiously, Crouwel designed the catalogue cover: Fodor was an institutional part of the Stedelijk Museum, for which he was the regular designer.) "To design subjectively," said Crouwel, during the much-cited debate, "means in its ultimate consequence that you only design that, which you support totally. That enlarges the chance of only having a very small work terrain [. . .] I believe in the maintenance of specialisms. Let everyone keep their hands off the specialism of others. You must not try, as intermediary, to get the message across better than the one who is emitting the message."[34] For his part, Van Toorn

Hedendaagse Kunst. Poster, 1971. Client: Stedelijk Museum. Design: Wim Crouwel

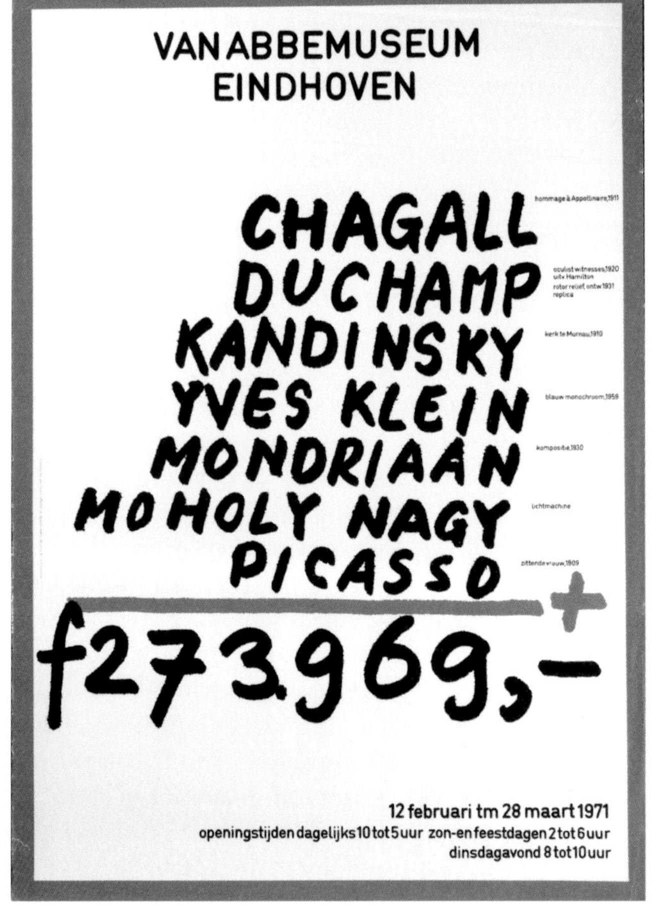

A Selection from the Collection of the Van Abbemuseum by Marinus Boezem. Exhibition poster, 1971. Client: Van Abbemuseum

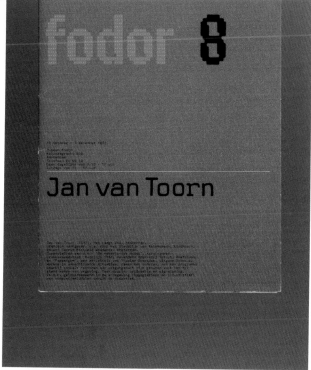

Fodor no. 8. Catalogue cover and poster, 1972. Cover: Wim Crouwel. Poster: Van Toorn

argued that, contrary to Crouwel's view, the designer did indeed have a dual role as a transmitter of information: "**his task is on the one hand conveyance of content, without interfering in it, on the other hand, he certainly does have an inescapably private contribution. Crouwel's fear of subjective interference leads to uniformity, causing a distinct identity to disappear.**"[35]

Crouwel and Van Toorn at a public discussion at the Museum Fodor, Amsterdam, 1972. Photographs: Wilco Geursen

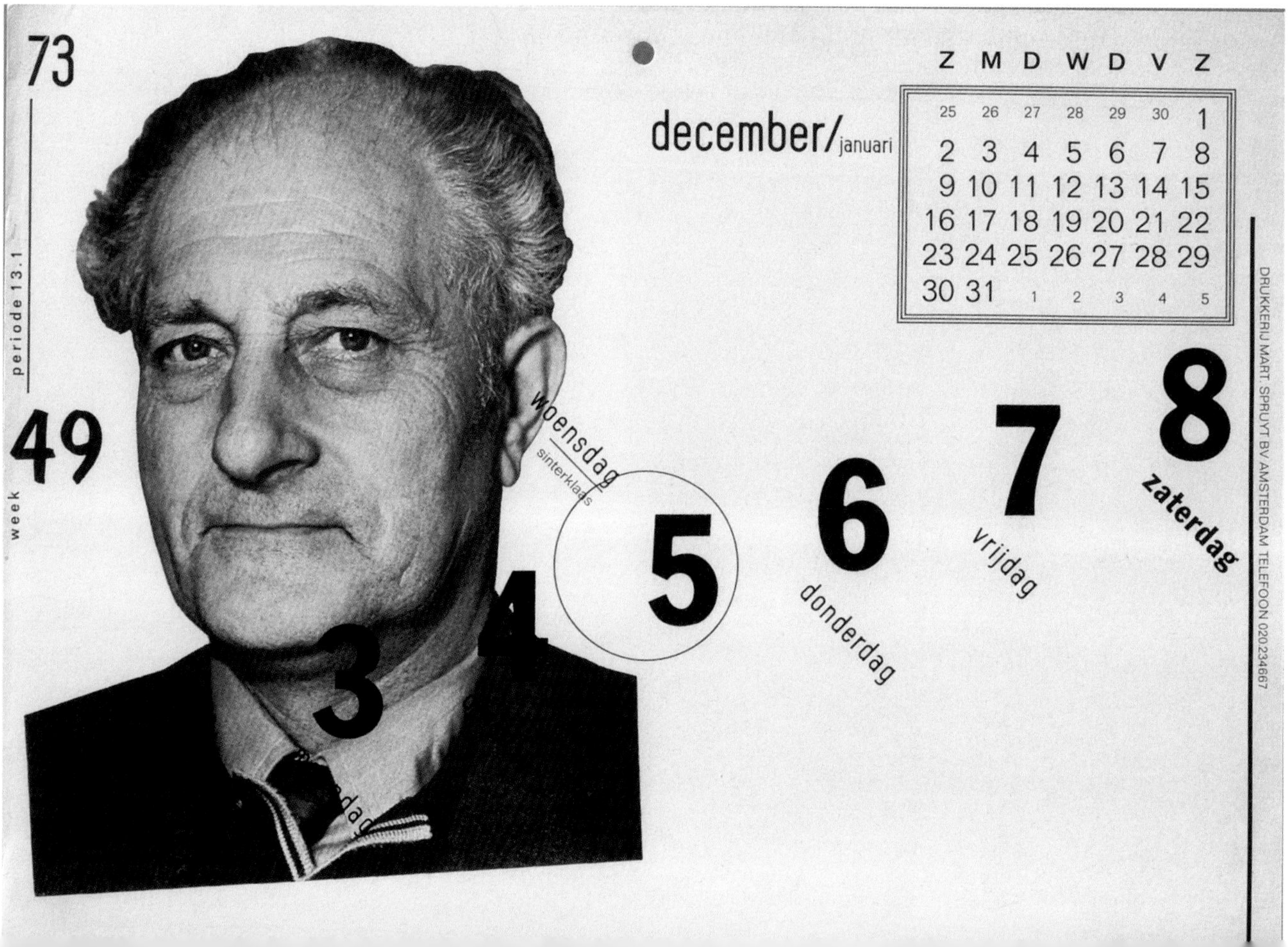

Crouwel was evidently not prepared to let the matter rest there, as an unresolvable difference of outlook and method. In 1974, apparently infuriated by Van Toorn's 1973/74 calendar for Mart.Spruijt, he produced an entire replacement calendar, featuring a picture of Van Toorn. "I embarked on my quest for answers because your work is too fascinating to be simply dismissed," Crouwel writes in an open letter to his wayward colleague, issued with the calendar.[36] Like a concerned teacher conducting a critique of an awkward student's project, he questions every aspect of Van Toorn's design: the direction of the dates, his use of a box for the monthly overview, and his choice of seven fonts. Ever the simplifier, Crouwel favoured a single font.

In 1978, Jean Leering and Van Toorn published a 32-page issue of *Documentaires*, an occasional publication from the printer Lecturis, with the title "Vormgeving in Functie van Museale Overdracht" (Design as a means of museological communication), presenting an illustrated dialogue in which they set out their ideas about design's role in the museum. The following year they contributed texts to *Museum in Motion?*, a substantial publication about the way forward for the contemporary art museum. By this time, Leering had become director of the Tropenmuseum in Amsterdam and they had many joint projects

1973/74 calendar. Publisher: Mart.Spruijt, 1973. Photograph: Mirjam de Vries

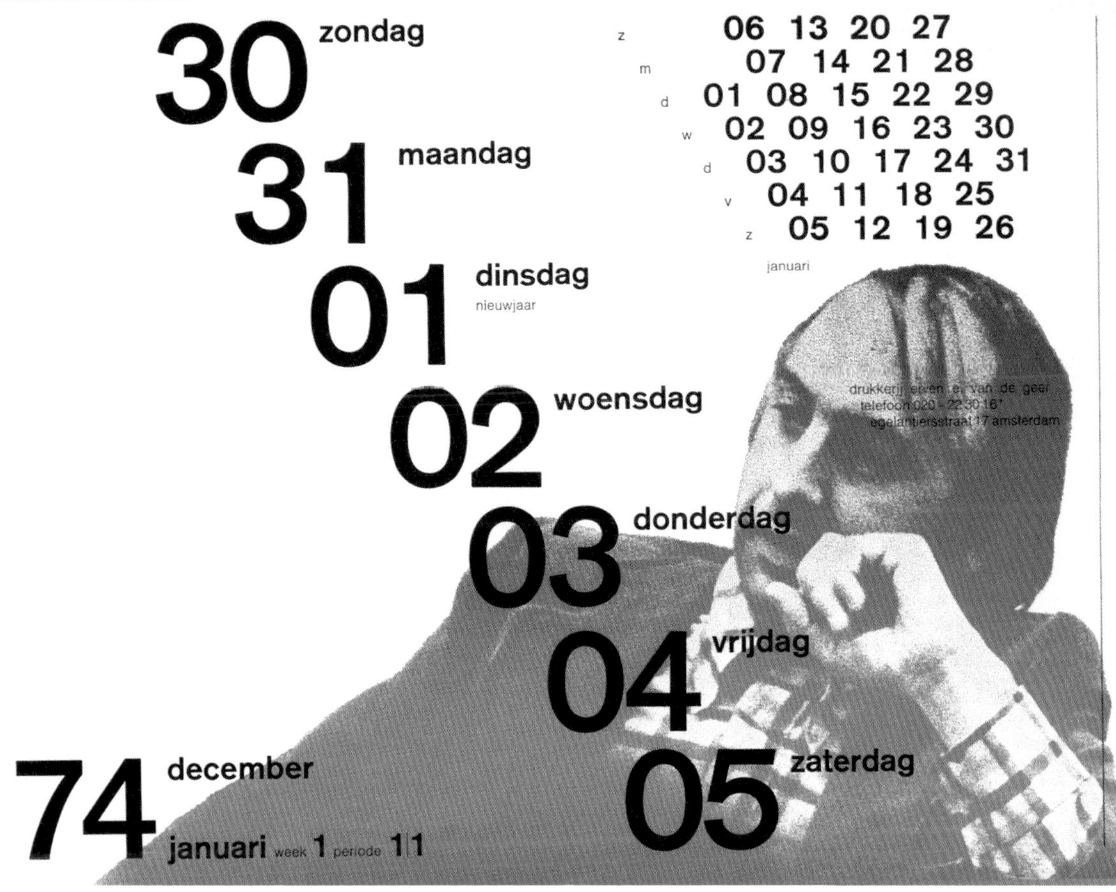

1974 calendar. Publisher and printer: Erven E. van de Geer. Design: Wim Crouwel. Photograph: Wilco Geursen

behind them, including *De Straat: Vorm van Samenleven* (The street: form of community), held at the Van Abbemuseum in 1972, an exhibition that, unusually for an art museum, featured no works of art. Instead, it plunged the visitor into a sea of photographic blow-ups showing life in the city, some of them panoramic. As Leering explained, "In choosing a theme of this nature, the Van Abbemuseum has proceeded from the ideal that the activities of a museum can be a means of encouraging public awareness of and participation in socially significant developments."[37] In their Lecturis dialogue, Leering and Van Toorn repeatedly challenge the idea that a museum and its publications should amount to little more than neutral frames for the art they display. "**As a museum, do you intend to act as a means for the public to forge its own independent opinions,**" asks Van Toorn, "**or does the museum position itself with respect to the public as an unquestionable authority to whom this task of choice and selection has been relegated on the grounds of its expertise?**"[38] He contends that the museum should relate to the public as a partner in dialogue, rather than as a teacher. According to Van Toorn, the key questions to address are: "**What kind of information? For whom? With what intentions? And, subsequently, designed in what way?**"[39]

The following issue of Lecturis' *Documentaires*, titled "Om de Kunst" (For art's sake), ran Crouwel's article "De Vormgeving en het Museum" (Graphic design and the museum) in reply. Van Toorn's key questions are false ones, Crouwel argues, comparing them dismissively to advertisers' jargon. "What we're talking about here is information that should be as objective as possible, for the benefit of all people interested, without

De Straat: Vorm van Samenleven (The street: form of community). Exhibition at the Van Abbemuseum, Eindhoven, 1972. Co-curator: Van Toorn

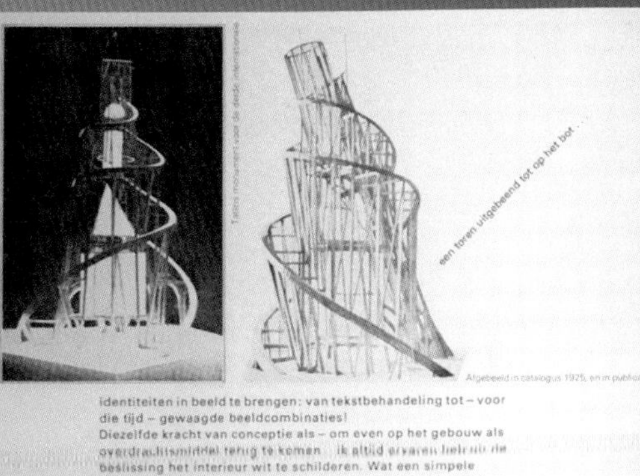

Afgebeeld in catalogus 1925, en in publicatie 1964

identiteiten in beeld te brengen: van tekstbehandeling tot – voor die tijd – gewaagde beeldcombinaties!
Diezelfde kracht van conceptie als – om even op het gebouw als overdrachtsmiddel terug te komen – ik altijd ervaren heb uit de beslissing het interieur wit te schilderen. Wat een simpele ingreep om het oude gebouw ineens bij de tijd te laten zijn! Zonder dat het verleden totaal weggemoffeld wordt, is er een nieuwe conditie in aangebracht die een aan de eigen tijd adequaat reageren voor de bezoeker mogelijk maakte. Precies diezelfde kwaliteit hadden de affiches, catalogi, maar ook de inrichting van de tentoonstellingen, die onder de hand van Sandberg, al of niet in samenwerking met anderen, vandaan kwamen.

Ja, daarmede vergeleken is er een ontstellende éénduidigheid betreffende het gebruik van de grafische middelen ontstaan, zoals ook op die andere gebieden, die je noemde. Ik moet daarbij ook denken aan de wijze, waarop musea hun verworven schilderijen op de wijze van een huisstijl inlijsten. Daarbij gebeurt hetzelfde. Kijk maar eens naar de Mondrians! Daar worden hele kasten omheen gebouwd, die qua vormgeving totaal indruisen tegen de opvatting, die Mondrian daarover zelf had. Hijzelf bracht eenvoudige latjes er omheen aan, maar zaagde die expres niet in verstek, maar liet ze 'koud op elkaar' – zoals men dat in het timmervak noemt – aansluiten. Heel bewust, en in aansluiting op zijn schilderkunstige visie, betreffende de spanning horizontaal-verticaal. Maar in de kasten, die het museum – terecht – om conservatorische redenen eromheen zet, houdt men met dat inzicht van Mondrian geen rekening. Daar wordt de hoek, zonder erbij na te denken, rustig in verstek gezaagd en weggeschilderd!

een schilderij uitgekleed tot op z'n hemd

Dat brengt mij de wijze in herinnering, waarop gebruikelijk met de afbeelding van schilderijen en dergelijke in de catalogus omgesprongen wordt. Niet alleen haalt men er nagenoeg altijd de lijsten vanaf, maar ook is het algemeen gebruik, dat je alle afbeeldingen haaks maakt, of de schilderijen zelf nu scheef zijn of niet, of zij doorzakken of niet of wat dan ook, ze worden bij de lithograaf haaks gemaakt. Cliches en litho's moeten haaks zijn, en daarmee ...

De typografie speelt daarmede een eigen spel, los van het object-karakter van het kunstwerk, dat daarmede volkomen opzij gezet wordt, en genegeerd. Zwart-wit afbeeldingen van schilderijen, zoals ook alle andere zaken, in de catalogus worden behandeld als grijze vlakken in de typografische compositie. Aan een ordening naar hun inhoudelijke betekenis komt de typograaf binnen een dergelijke, puur esthetische visie niet toe. Deze laatste ordening vraagt namelijk om **beeldredactie**, die in de gebruikelijke catalogi, zoals we die uit de internationale museale wereld ontvangen, bijna altijd ontlopen wordt. De ontkenning van het object-karakter van het af te beelden voorwerp vormt ook een van de meest sprekende voorbeelden, hoe het specialisme – hier dat van de typografie – een normstelling ontwikkelt die zover is doorgevoerd, dat alle mensen die met dat specialisme te maken hebben, ja zelfs de ontvangers, niet meer anders weten of verwachten! Het rechtmaken is tot een objectieve norm verheven, maar mijn vraag is, wat die norm – gemeten aan de eigenlijk bestaande realiteit, waarvan die reprodukties een afbeelding zouden moeten zijn – te maken heeft met die maar al te graag door diezelfde ontwerpers gehanteerde term objectiviteit.

Ja, en bovendien, wat de hoedanigheid van een dergelijke opvatting over typografie is met betrekking tot de communicatieve functie? Want door zo'n uitgewogen compositie loop je natuurlijk dik de kans, dat het typografische eindresultaat geheel en al op zichzelf geapprecieerd wordt, en niet meer verwijst naar die oorspronkelijke toestand van de werken zelf. Dan krijg je wederom de situatie, dat datgene wat als middellijk bedoeld is, de plaats in gaat nemen van het onmiddellijke contact met de werkelijkheid, en dus weer aanleiding geeft tot **consumptief gedrag.**
Toch kan ik mij een bepaalde zelfstandigheid – maar dan heel anders opgevat – van een catalogus heel goed voorstellen. En dan denk ik aan de catalogi die bijvoorbeeld de Neue Gesellschaft für bildende Kunst voor zijn tentoonstellingen te Berlijn als 'Kunst aus der Revolution', 'Kunst in die Produktion' en 'Wem gehört die Welt' geproduceerd heeft. Daarbij fungeert de catalogus als een complement op de tentoonstelling: omdat een tentoonstelling als **beeldmatig** overdrachtsmiddel zich moeilijk bezig kan houden met **begripsmatige** overdracht, vrij zelfstandig aan de catalogus overgelaten. In zulk een vorm fungeren de afbeeldingen niet – zoals bij Sandbergs catalogi het geval

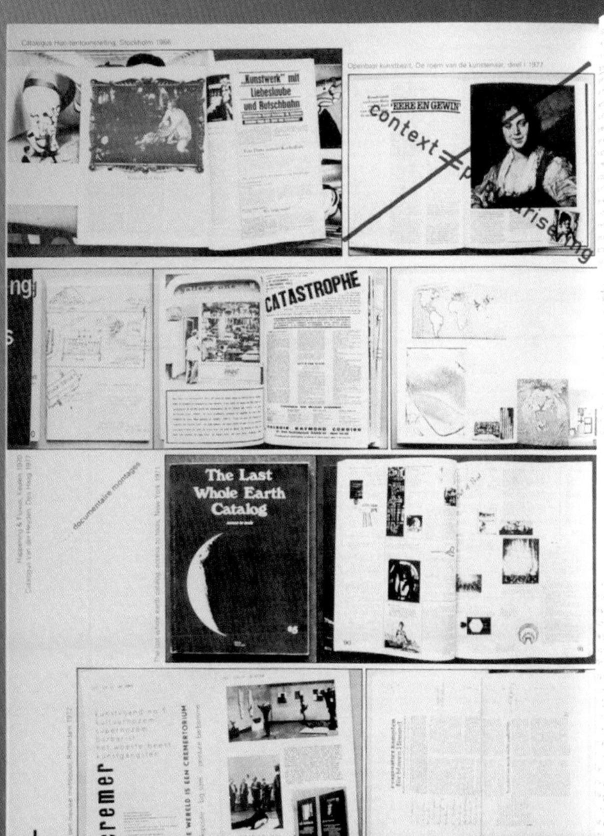

Nee maar Jan, daartoe verwaardigen de meeste kunstcatalogi zich toch niet! En als ze het doen dan vaak eerder om de stunt dan om inhoudelijke redenen.
Neem bijvoorbeeld de krant – een dagelijks ding dus –, die het Haags Gemeentemuseum in 1964 uitgaf bij de tentoonstelling 'Nieuwe Realisten'. De vorm was van de krant overgenomen – en zeker, dat was een **daad** voor dat deftige museum –, maar met de noodzakelijkheden waarom een krant er uitziet zoals hij er uitziet, had die catalogus natuurlijk weinig van doen. En dat proef je toch ook uit de lay-out ervan: de kolommen zijn voor een krant te netjes en te ruim geplaatst.

Vormgeving in Functie van Museale Overdracht (Design as a means of museological communication). Booklet spreads, 1978. Publisher: Lecturis

museum
Het museum voor moderne kunst ter diskussie
National Gallery, Washington 1978 'Highest quality and pink marble'
in
¿motion?

Museum in Motion? / Museum in Beweging? Book cover and spreads, 1979. Publisher: Government Publishing Office

1. Conversations with Andy Warhol are usually taped. The material thus collected is used among other places in his books.
2. Sleep, 1963. Film, 6 hours, black & white, silent.
3. Empire, 1964. Film, 8 hours, black & white, silent.
4. Album cover. In 1966 the Velvet Underground performed in Andy Warhols environmental show The Exploding Plastic Inevitable. For the first time dancers, music, film, light shows, art and the public were included in one show.

4A. Inflatable structure with Heliumgas, 1966.

Andy Warhol

1 4 4A
2 3

superstarshine vol.20
THE VELVET UNDERGROUND

The modern art museum at issue

Het museum voor moderne kunst ter diskussie

Editors/redaktie Carel Blotkamp, Marjon van Caspel, Frans Haks, Frank van der Schoor, Jan van Toorn, Martin Visser

Government Publishing Office/Staatsuitgeverij, 's-Gravenhage 1979

Museum in ¿motion?
Museum in ¿beweging?

.13.

Since most of his published material appeared in the specialized literature, his views understandably mainly reached the art world only. In its catalogue De Heide koerier, published for the exhibition Tot lering en vermaak (For instruction and entertainment (10), the Van Abbemuseum tried to make its aim clear to a wider public. The catalogue, presented in the form of a regional magazine – 60,000 copies were distributed to homes in Eindhoven – sought to inform the public about the problems facing a museum of modern art. It was explained that the Van Abbemuseum did not have any absolute answers: art remained essentially intangible, and even museums were not always able fully to understand or explain it. The Museum was seeking new ways of effectively reaching various sections of the public. Improvements would also have to be made to the museum's policies. Here there was room for innovation. 'Looking beyond the appearance of things (previously almost exclusively a religious practice), the cultivation of awareness has come to play a major role in our society, which is no longer conceivable without it. Today's artists – in their own way, of course – also look beyond'. (11) The museum should also seek to move in this direction, and the public was therefore invited to enter a dialogue with the Van Abbemuseum.

The staff of the Van Abbemuseum had come to realize that it was no easy task for a museum of avant-garde art to attract a broad public but the desire nonetheless existed to bring larger sections of the population into contact with the museum. The question, then, was how interested the public was in contemporary art and what the forms and functions of art were in our society. Leering deals with this topic in his discussion of museums in general. The article 'De kunst in een moeilijke situatie' (Art in a difficult situation) (12), published in 1971, deals with the question of whether art and thus perhaps museums too can perform a socially relevant function. Since about 1800, art had been increasingly excluded from the group of disciplines which determined the direction taken by society, its links with actuality were weakening it was no longer functioning in a context of immediate reality. This was in contrast to contemporary science and technology, with their direct impact on society. Art too had once had such a direct impact on society – in the Middle Ages, for example, it had enjoyed something of a primary social function. At the beginning of the present century constructivism had for a short time filled a similar role.

The time had come for art once again to fill a primary role. Leering believed that this could be achieved by means of a process of politization. For the sake of clarity and to avoid misunderstanding he states: 'The politization of art does not mean making art the servant of a political ideology or a means of propaganda'. (13) The artist must try to relate his work to social realities and to the environment: 'general environmental planning, townplanning, architecture and the design of our surroundings, whose projects and particularly their visual dimension, must ensure that the users – those who have to live with them – have ways and means of orientating and identifying themselves'. (14) If this were not to happen we would be threatened with a one-dimensioned culture dominated by a 'one-dimensional man'. Leering assigns to art the truly epic task of defeating the material and spiritual uniformity of our western culture. 'Art, while remaining orientated towards the visual, can by virtue of its polyvalent character break through such one-dimensional cultures'. (15) In Leering's view there was much valuable potential in art. In another context, the formulation of the objectives of the Van Abbemuseum, he attributes a didactic and therapeutic value to art. 'Together with its equivalent disciplines such as philosophy, science, technology, ethics etc., art plays a major role in the formation of lexical and visual concepts and the concrete shapes based on them, in which man can find ways of orientating himself in relation to his past and future and identifying himself with the present. Without such landmarks man is alienated from his own reality, and in this sense cultural activity, including the work of the museum, should be seen as one aspect of preventive mental health care'. (16)

These ideas relate in the first instance to art in general, but they naturally do not lose any of their validity when applied to museums. The 'politization' of art has its counterpart in the museums' social involvement.

From this point on, the beliefs and principles of the Van Abbemuseum were regularly set down on paper, not only in articles but also in prefaces and guiding notes in various exhibition catalogues. The Van Abbemuseum opted for social involvement. At this stage a definite line began to emerge in exhibition policy. This culminated in the exhibition Bouwen 20-40 (Building, 1920-1940) held in September/November 1971, which was put together by a team of experts from different fields, an approach which Leering had earlier advocated in his article on the function of the museum.

While the ideas for this exhibition were being evolved the accent shifted from the architectural highlights of the 1920s and 1930s to the ordinary homes of the period. The particular problems connected with building between 1920 and 1940 were also looked at in relation to the present time. With its various exhibitions of the art of the 1920s and 1930s, including the work of Duchamp, Picabia, Lissitzky, Moholy-Nagy, van Doesburg and Tatlin, the Van Abbemuseum has regularly turned its attention to artists who have endeavoured to create a more concrete relationship between art and society. These efforts are now more relevant than ever, since their example can stimulate efforts to restore to art the primary impact it once had.

Bouwen 20-40 was the last in the series of retrospective

(10) Exhibition catalogue De Heidekoerier, tot lering en vermaak (The Heidekoerier, for information and entertainment), Van Abbemuseum, Eindhoven, September 1970.
(11) op. cit. page 3.
(12) Jean Leering, 'De kunst in een moeilijke situatie' (Art in a difficult situation), Museumjournaal, 16 (1971), 2, 57-65.

(13) op. cit. page 58.
(14) op. cit. page 64.
(15) op. cit. page 64.
(16) Jean Leering, 'Doelstelling Van Abbemuseum' (Van Abbemuseum objectives), February 1971 (stencil).

bovenstaand citaat blijkt, gebruikte hij in april 1970 nog de formulering 'voorbereidende aktiviteiten'. Allengs evolueerden zijn inzichten over de kwaliteit van de bijdrage van de kunstenaar, zodat hij een jaar later zich uitte in termen van gelijkwaardig samenwerkingsverband. Het is zinvoller 'de artistieke reflexie omtrent ruimtelijke relaties niet naast de in de dagelijkse maatschappelijke situatie plaatsvindende technieken (o.a. planologie en ecologie) te laten gebeuren, maar deze twee benaderingswijzen zo veel mogelijk in elkaars verlengde te leggen'. (9)

Leering heeft zich beijverd organisatie en beleid van het museum om te buigen, en als verlengstuk daarvan, ervoor gepleit dat kunst en samenleving dichter bij elkaar zouden komen te staan. Omdat zijn publicatiemogelijkheden goeddeels in de vakliteratuur lagen, bleef de informatieoverdracht begrijpelijkerwijs voornamelijk beperkt tot de kunstwereld. Met de catalogus De Heidekoerier, behorende bij de tentoonstelling Tot lering en vermaak (10), trachtte het Van Abbemuseum ook buiten die kring duidelijk te maken wat het beoogde. De koerier die is opgemaakt in de trant van een regionale periodiek, en in Eindhoven in een oplage van 60.000 huis aan huis is verspreid, geeft informatie over de problemen waarvoor het museum voor moderne kunst zich geplaatst ziet. Er wordt in verduidelijkt dat het Van Abbemuseum geen waterdicht concept heeft; kunst blijft een moeilijk grijpbare zaak, waar het museum ook niet altijd raad mee weet. Het Eindhovense museum zoekt naar nieuwe methodes om de verschillende publieksgroepen effectief te bereiken. Er zal ook gesleuteld moeten worden aan de beleidsopvattingen van het museum. Hier biedt zich wel een nieuw perspektief aan. 'Dat kijken 'achter' de dingen (zoals dat vroeger bijna uitsluitend in godsdienstige zin bestond), dat bewust-maken, is een enorme rol gaan spelen in onze samenleving, is er niet meer uit weg te denken. De kunstenaar van nu doet dat ook, natuurlijk op zijn eigen wijze'. (11) Zo ook in die richting moet het museum zijn weg trachten te vinden. Het publiek wordt uitgenodigd met het Van Abbemuseum een dialoog aan te gaan.

De staf van het Van Abbemuseum was tot het inzicht gekomen, dat het voor een museum dat avantgardistische kunst brengt, geen gemakkelijke opgave is een breed publiek op te bouwen. Toch wilde men graag grotere groepen van de bevolking met het museum in contact brengen. Vragen als hoe staat het bij het publiek met de interesse voor hedendaagse kunst, en wat zijn de mogelijkheden van de kunst in onze samenleving, worden dan aktueel. Leering betrekt dit facet bij de discussie over het museumwezen. Of de kunst en daarmee wellicht ook het museum mogelijk maatschappelijk relevant bezig kan zijn, daarover gaan het in 1971 gepubliceerde artikel 'De kunst in een moeilijke situatie'. (12) Sedert ca. 1800 is de kunst meer en meer buiten de kring van disciplines komen te staan, die richting geven aan de samenleving. Het realiteitsbesef in de kunst is aan het vervagen. De kunst werkt niet meer met de direkte werkelijkheid. Dit in tegenstelling tot de huidige wetenschap en techniek, die primair ingrijpen in het maatschappelijk bestel. Ook de kunst heeft die primaire gerichtheid geruime tijd gekend. In de middeleeuwen bijvoorbeeld had de kunst iets van een primaire maatschappelijke werking. Het constructivisme heeft in het begin van deze eeuw die lijn gedurende korte tijd weer opgenomen.

Tegenwoordig zou de kunst opnieuw gediend zijn met een primaire werkzaamheid. De verwezenlijking hiervan ziet Leering verlopen via een politiseringsproces. Voor de duidelijkheid, om misverstanden te voorkomen, stelt hij: ''Politisering' van de kunst betekent niet haar in dienst stellen van een politieke ideologie, waardoor zij verwordt tot een (propaganda-)middel'. (13) Kunst moet proberen aansluiting te vinden bij de sociaal relevante werkelijkheid, bij het leefmilieu: 'planologie, stedebouw, architectuur en de vormgeving van onze omgeving, in wier projecten de oriënterings- en identificatiemogelijkheden van de gebruikers bij uitstek (door de visuele hoedanigheden) gegarandeerd moeten worden'. (14) Gebeurt dit niet dan dreigt een mono-cultuur te ontstaan, de 'eendimensionale mens' zal de boventoon gaan voeren. Leering ziet voor de kunst een waarlijk heroïsche taak om de materiële en geestelijke eenvormigheid van onze westerse cultuur te doorkruisen. 'De kunst, haar gerichtheid op visualiteit continuerend, kan door haar polyvalent karakter deze mono-cultures doorbreken'. (15) In de kunst liggen naar Leerings idee vele waardevolle mogelijkheden besloten. In een ander verband, namelijk daar waar hij een doelstelling formuleert voor het Van Abbemuseum, kent hij aan de kunst een didaktische en therapeutische waarde toe. 'Met haar aequivalenten als filosofie, wetenschap, techniek, gedragsethiek etc. speelt de kunst een belangrijke rol in de vorming van woord- en beeldbegrippen en daarop gebaseerde konkrete gestalten, waarin de mens de mogelijkheid vindt zich t.o.v. zijn verleden en toekomst te oriënteren en zich met het heden te identificeren. Tekorten hieraan doen de mens vervreemden van zijn werkelijkheid, en in deze zin is cultureel werk, waaronder het museumwerk, te zien als een onderdeel van actieve geestelijke gezondheidszorg'. (16)

Deze perspectieven zijn in eerste instantie gesteld voor de kunst. Natuurlijk verliezen zij echter niet hun geldigheid als het museum ter sprake komt. Het proces van 'verpolitisering' van de kunst vindt in de 'vermaatschappelijking' van het museum zijn complement.

Van nu af aan worden geregeld de overtuigingen en uitgangspunten van het Van Abbemuseum aan het papier

(9) Brabantprojekten in het kader van Sonsbeek 71, Amsterdam 1971, 3.
(10) Cat. tent. De Heidekoerier, tot lering en vermaak, Van Abbemuseum Eindhoven, september 1970.
(11) o.c. p. 3.
(12) Jean Leering, 'De kunst in een moeilijke situatie', Museumjournaal 16 (1971), 2, 57-65.

(13) o.c. p. 58.
(14) o.c. p. 64.
(15) o.c. p. 64.
(16) Jean Leering, Doelstelling Van Abbemuseum, febr. 1971 (stencil).

1.2

any other aim than to inform."[40] This is a reiteration of Crouwel's usual position, but there is a more telling criticism later in the essay of Van Toorn's conception of visual editing. It is one thing to call, as Van Toorn does, for design to allow freedom of interpretation and to reveal within itself its own point of view so that the reader can challenge it, as a partner in dialogue, but how will this be accomplished on the page without confusing the reader? Crouwel takes issue with the visual examples provided by Van Toorn and Leering: "having to plough through repetitive imagery and additional slide shows," he argues, "the reader is forced to rescue his own story from these meaningless and fashionable compilations of images."[41] It is quite possible to enjoy a wonderful meal, Crouwel suggests, without being aware of all the cooking activities going on in the kitchen. Neat as this metaphor might appear at first sight, it inadvertently serves to underline Van Toorn's position. While diners can enjoy a meal as a seamless and pleasurable experience, without further information they will be none the wiser about the many hidden factors involved in assembling the food and delivering it to their table. Crouwel wants the diner to sit back and let the experts (such as him) take care of everything. Van Toorn questions the paternalistic assumptions that lie behind this "expertise" and demands that the diner be allowed a more active role in the meal than just consuming it without question. We can only gain, he believes, from knowing what we are eating.

Crouwel's last significant published response to Van Toorn came in the early 1980s and it amplifies, on both sides, some crucial points. In a brief text surrounded by ambiguous images and a collage of quotations from Illich, Eco and William Burroughs, published in the art bulletin *Quad*, Van Toorn proposes that a critical designer should make recipients aware of the manipulations of design by basing the work "**on references to existing visual codes and by employing recognizable traces of redundancy**" – this sounds like the "noise" that Crouwel had previously rejected.[42] The designer, Van Toorn continues, "**should make the code visible by re-structuring it with the intention of making the aesthetic message open up something for the recipient which is not part of what the public expects.**"[43] Hard on Van Toorn's heels as ever, Crouwel used the next issue of *Quad* to reply. He suggests, echoing his earlier arguments, that the associative approach that Van Toorn appears to favour (as seen in *Quad*) runs the risk of failing to communicate anything at all. "Making associations by means of pictures and texts supposes a certain knowledge of that specific picture material and its meaning, and a certain training in interpreting texts; this method is therefore a rather intellectual one. The result will be that the message has a relatively limited range."[44]

This remains a fundamental point. Although it is often said that there has been a growth in visual literacy in recent decades, as audiences became familiar with increasingly elaborate imagery and spectacular visual effects in film, TV and advertising (as well as design), much of the visual material issuing from the realms of commercial promotion and entertainment operates within narrowly defined intellectual limits. At the same time, while anyone might chance upon a challenging exhibition poster in the street, specialized communications of this type are targeted at minority audiences – in this case, gallery-goers – that already possess

All art publications (exhibitions) are subjected to the terror of an international codified lay-out (disciplined printed matter)

Quad no. 2. Journal spread, October 1980.
Text: Van Toorn

Van Toorn in his Amsterdam studio, 1980
Photograph: Pieter Boersma

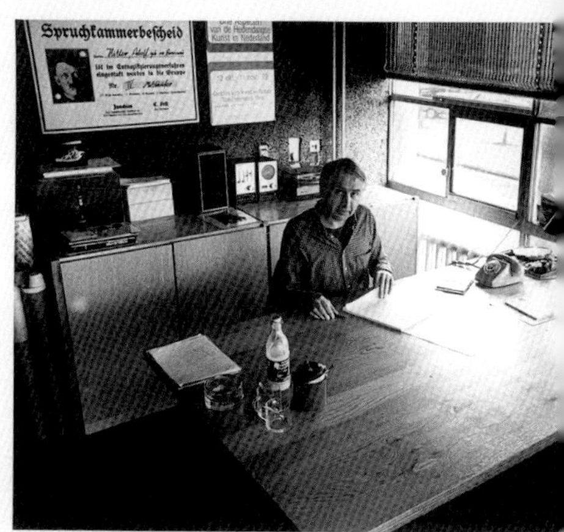

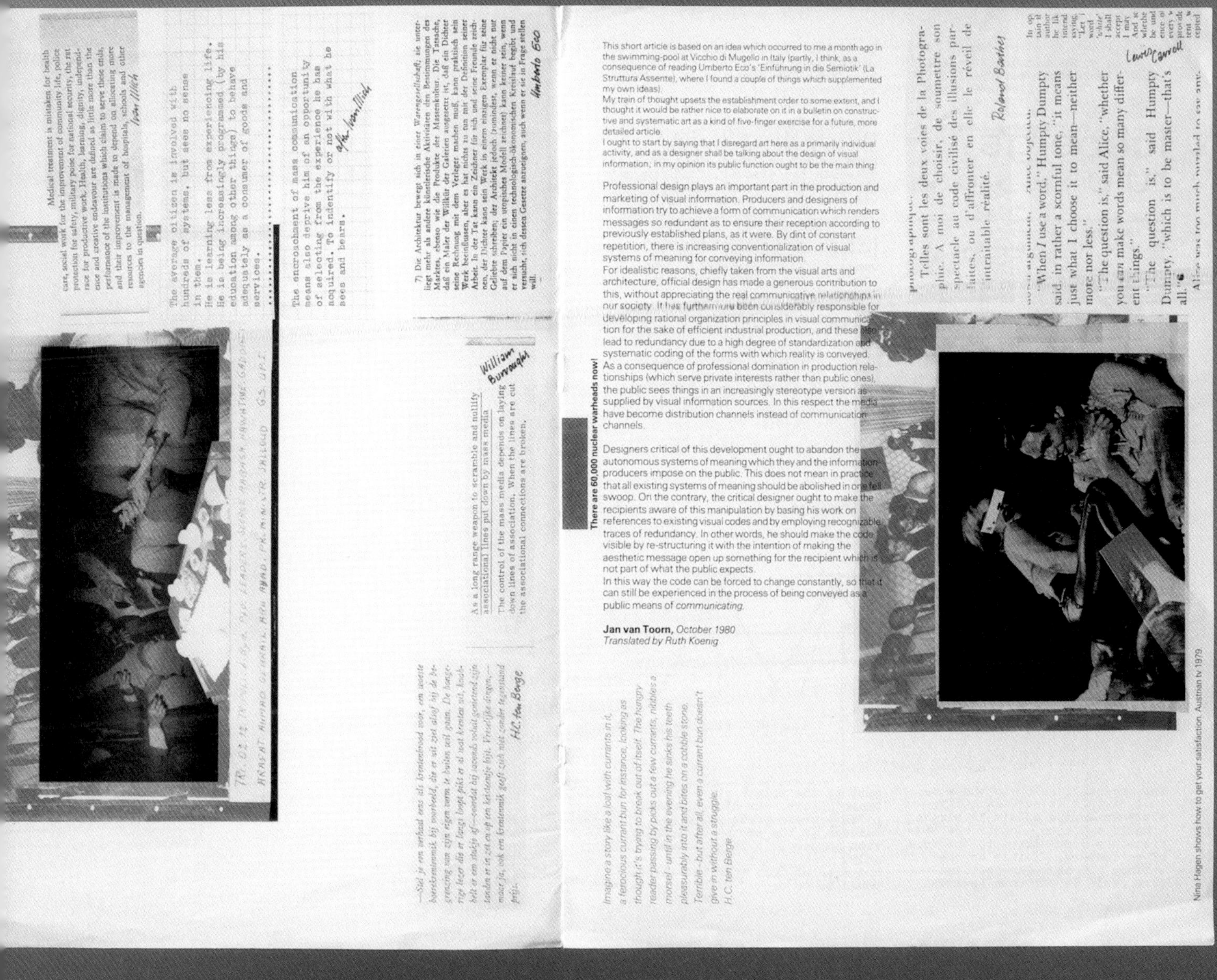

This short article is based on an idea which occurred to me a month ago in the swimming-pool at Vicchio di Mugello in Italy (partly, I think, as a consequence of reading Umberto Eco's 'Einführung in die Semiotik' (La Struttura Assente), where I found a couple of things which supplemented my own ideas).
My train of thought upsets the establishment order to some extent, and I thought it would be rather nice to elaborate on it in a bulletin on constructive and systematic art as a kind of five-finger exercise for a future, more detailed article.
I ought to start by saying that I disregard art here as a primarily individual activity, and as a designer shall be talking about the design of visual information; in my opinion its public function ought to be the main thing.

Professional design plays an important part in the production and marketing of visual information. Producers and designers of information try to achieve a form of communication which renders messages so redundant as to ensure their reception according to previously established plans, as it were. By dint of constant repetition, there is increasing conventionalization of visual systems of meaning for conveying information.
For idealistic reasons, chiefly taken from the visual arts and architecture, official design has made a generous contribution to this, without appreciating the real communicative relationships in our society. It has furthermore been considerably responsible for developing rational organization principles in visual communication for the sake of efficient industrial production, and these also lead to redundancy due to a high degree of standardization and systematic coding of the forms with which reality is conveyed.
As a consequence of professional domination in production relationships (which serve private interests rather than public ones), the public sees things in an increasingly stereotype version as supplied by visual information sources. In this respect the media have become distribution channels instead of communication channels.

Designers critical of this development ought to abandon the autonomous systems of meaning which they and the information-producers impose on the public. This does not mean in practice that all existing systems of meaning should be abolished in one fell swoop. On the contrary, the critical designer ought to make the recipients aware of this manipulation by basing his work on references to existing visual codes and by employing recognizable traces of redundancy. In other words, he should make the code visible by re-structuring it with the intention of making the aesthetic message open up something for the recipient which is not part of what the public expects.
In this way the code can be forced to change constantly, so that it can still be experienced in the process of being conveyed as a public means of *communicating*.

Jan van Toorn, *October 1980*
Translated by Ruth Koenig

There are 60,000 nuclear warheads now!

Imagine a story like a loaf with currants in it, a ferocious currant bun for instance, looking as though it's trying to break out of itself. The hungry reader passing by picks out a few currants, nibbles a morsel - until in the evening he sinks his teeth pleasurably into it and bites on a cobble stone. Terrible - but after all, even a currant bun doesn't give in without a struggle.
H.C. ten Berge

Nina Hagen shows how to get your satisfaction. Austrian tv 1979.

a sophisticated level of visual understanding. These audiences are not, in that sense, average viewers. Van Toorn's conception of reflexive design places a great deal of faith in people's willingness and ability to interpret complex graphic signals that might, in practice, baffle them or pass them by.

Art and ordinary life

This is one reason, no doubt, why Van Toorn's most characteristic projects have tended, since the 1970s, to find most favour with clients in the cultural sector. Occasionally, however, he was able to produce designs for a much wider audience, and the best opportunities tended to come from the Dutch post office, the PTT – a patron, over the decades, of many of the Netherlands' most distinguished designers. In a set of three stamps, designed in 1980, Van Toorn succeeded in packing the tiny rectangles with a symbolic commentary on three founding fathers of contemporary Dutch politics, which they were issued to celebrate: A.F. de Savornin Lohman (1837–1924), an advocate of conservative

Christian politics; P.J. Troelstra (1860–1930), a revolutionary and founder of the social democratic party; and P.J. Oud (1886–1968), co-founder and leader of the conservative liberal party.

Three Politicians. Stamps, 1980. Client: PTT

Each of the stamps is a miniature photomontage that shows an obvious kinship with Dutch Modernist design. The work of figures such as Piet Zwart and Paul Schuitema was a significant influence on Van Toorn, who admired the way its radical form embodied its meaning, and the stamps follow the same principle. The politicians' faces are seen in close-up and bleed off the perforations, intensifying their impact. Van Toorn organizes the trio of figures, both within each stamp and in their relationship to each other, according to their place on the political spectrum. Crucial, here, is the image of the chair of the Speaker of the House, seen in the background of each stamp. The chair is situated in relation to the politicians to reflect the positions occupied by the different parties in 1980 in the Dutch Parliament. The choice of colour likewise expresses the political orientation of the three men: red, white and blue (the national colours) for the liberal; light orange and blue for the Christian monarchist; red for the socialist. Van Toorn's typography is similarly "Modernist" and notably unconstrained for a set of official stamps. The size of type used for the denomination varies – the 50c is smaller and appears slightly heavier – and the "c" moves around to fit the space available. Van Toorn angles the lowercase, letter-spaced "nederland" to play against the other elements. It would be an overstatement to call these stamps a critique, but they certainly confirm that even the most elementary graphic communications can be invested with unexpected layers of meaning and a personal point of view.

For the most part, in the late 1970s and 1980s, Van Toorn continued to work on editorial and exhibition-related projects. In 1977, he designed the first issue of a new magazine, *Dutch Art + Architecture Today*, initiated by the Netherlands Ministry for Cultural Affairs, Recreation and Social Welfare (pp. 180–3). Published in English, *DA+AT*'s aim was to provide information about significant developments in painting, sculpture, drawing and graphics, architecture, film and video, and applied art and "intermedia". Van Toorn's format, which remained unchanged until the magazine's last issue in 1989, was a modest masterpiece of loose-fit accessibility and informality. *DA+AT*'s cover was also its postal container and the picture stuck to the front served as an address label. To read the magazine, it was necessary to tear off a perforated strip along the fore-edge, leaving a permanently rough edge. The idea of breaking open a design in some way to access its contents has been used by graphic designers (including Van Toorn) on countless occasions. Here, it seems entirely practical, rather than gratuitous, while setting the tone for both the content and design of the pages inside.

DA+AT displays all of the most characteristic elements of Van Toorn's mature style of typography. To achieve the informal appearance he sought, he letter-spaced the Univers 55 (roman) and 65 (bold) text type to open up the pages. He determined the degree of spacing by showing his neighbours trial settings and asking them which they preferred. The three text columns, on the other hand, are tightly spaced, requiring the use of rules to divide them; slightly heavier than they need to be to do

Dutch Art + Architecture Today no. 9. Magazine spread, September 1981. Publisher: Netherlands Ministry for Cultural Affairs, Recreation and Social Welfare. Design assistance: Piet van Meijl

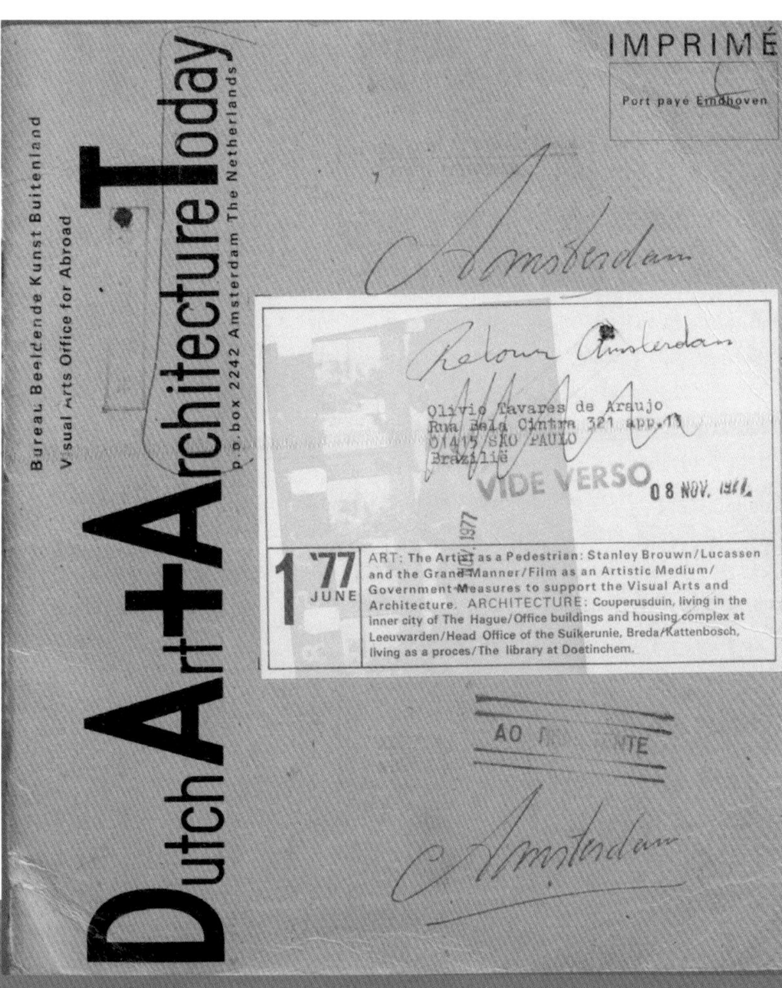

Dutch Art + Architecture Today no. 1. Magazine cover, June 1977. Publisher: Netherlands Ministry for Cultural Affairs, Recreation and Social Welfare

...g at the Lieverdje, Spui, ...am, 1960s

FRANK GRIBLING

Happening & Fluxus

The word *happening* has become an accepted expression in Dutch for any spontaneous, playful, unorganized group activity. The term was popularly used in the sixties to denote the humorous, subversive activities of the group of young anti-establishment enthusiasts who called themselves Provos. These happenings had nothing at all to do with the art world, they were manifestations of a sub-culture whose ideals were the free development of creative expression and the raising of consciousness on all levels.
The idea of the happening was introduced in the Netherlands by a small group of artistic figures who had heard of the emergence, in the United States, of a new art form, somewhere in between the theatre, visual art and music, which was practised by people like Jim Dine and Claes Oldenburg. Allan Kaprov was the first to use the word *happening* to describe this kind of activity, in 1958.
But the happenings that were held in Holland were, from the very start, essentially different from the happenings of the American artists, which, with their carefully planned structure, were the opposite of spontaneous audience participation.

The first manifestation in Holland to be announced as a happening took place in 1962 in Amsterdam. It was entitled **Open the Grave**, and was organized by Simon Vinkenoog together with Melvin Clay, who acted with the Living Theatre, and Frank Stern, a filmmaker. The title was a reflection on two events which exemplified mass manipulation at that time: a TV marathon show called *Open het dorp* (to collect money for a village specially designed for the handicapped), and the publicity surrounding the funeral of the old queen, Wilhelmina.
Among the participants in **Open the Grave** was Jean Jacques Lebel, a Frenchman; unlike most of the others, he had had some personal experience with the American happenings, notably through his participation in one of Jim Dine's happenings in New York. Shortly before the event in Amsterdam Lebel had mounted a spectacular happening in Paris: **Pour conjurer l'espirit de catastrophe**, in which the addictive effect of the mass media was put to the test. In Amsterdam, too, he manifested himself as a TV commentator gone haywire.
The other participants in **Open the Grave** were typical exponents of the Amsterdam sub-culture, such as Robert Jasper Grootveld, Johnny the Selfkicker and the flipped-out medical graduate Bart Huges, who later made te headlines with his self-conducted operation to drill a hole in his skull in order to secure a *permanent high*. These circles had their own conception of what a happening was: to them it was spontaneous action, rather like the free improvization practised by Jazz musicians. The Amsterdam *scene* had come into contact with the life-style and jargon of the American Beat Generation – largely through meetings on the Mediterranean island of Ibiza. As a result of these influences, the climate in Amsterdam soon became favourable for a young generation of rebels against the blessings of the consumer society.
In September 1961 Robert Jasper Grootveld launched his anti-smoke campaign against the **dope syndicates**

Translated by INA RIKE

12 13

Robert-Jasper Grootveld and Gerrit Lakmaaker in the Anti-Smoke temple, 1962

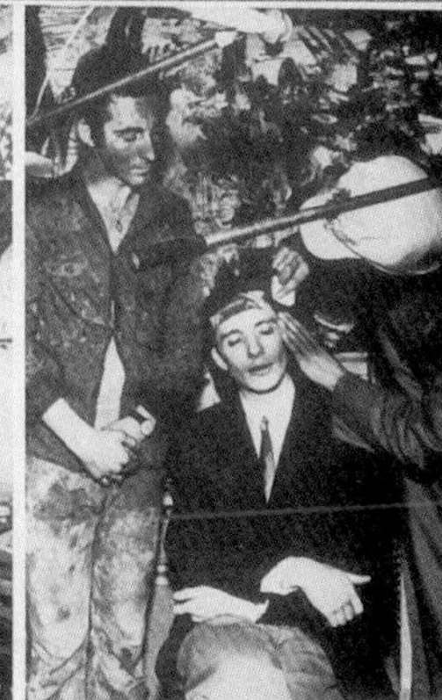

Stoned in the Streets, 1965. Bart Hughes drills a hole in his skull to obtain a permanent high

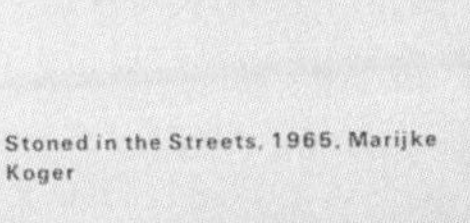

Open the Grave, 1962, with Robert-Jasper Grootveld and others

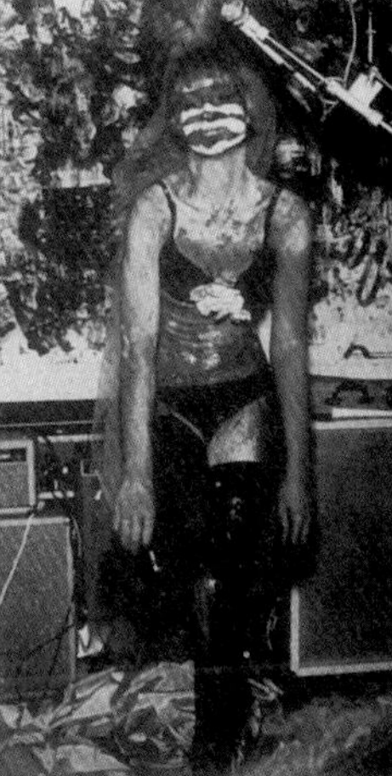

Stoned in the Streets, 1965, Marijke Koger

the job (although they match the Univers 65), the rules can run from the top to the bottom of the page. As vertical markers, they introduce a strong rhythmic movement to the spreads, as well as providing a sense of structure. Following Van Toorn's habit, the text is also pushed out to the edges of the page on all sides, while the headlines lock into a shallow panel above the text at the top. The sans serif headline typeface, Planschrift, with its large x-height and straight-sided appearance, is a genuine oddity. The highly patterned pages work especially well when the images are printed in black and white. Even so, the collective effect of all these decisions is to produce a feeling of disturbance. *DA+AT* looked completely different from other art magazines of the time, which tended to follow the same well-worn typographic conventions (and approach to cover binding) as any other kind of specialist magazine. Van Toorn rejected the usual way of handling type, seeing it as "harness" from which both designers and readers should be un-tethered. He wanted the magazine's pages to have a kind of "artificiality" to make the reader aware of the designer's intervention.

Van Toorn in his Amsterdam studio, c. 1982

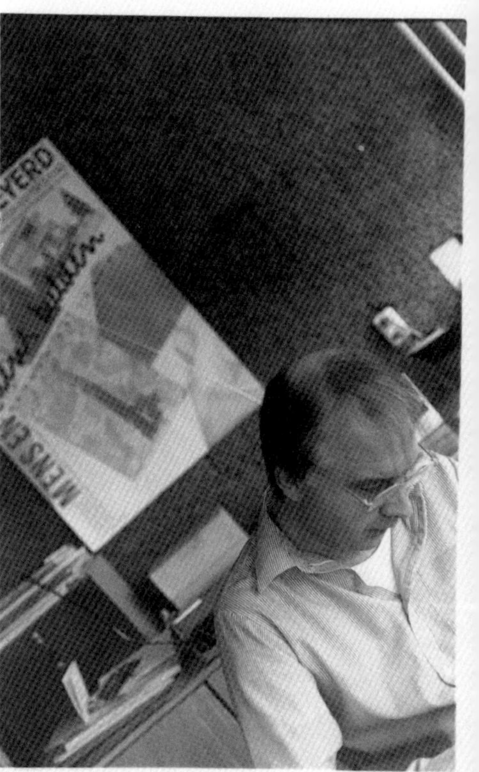

During this period, Van Toorn was also designing covers for the long-running *Museumjournaal* (the English edition's closure had led to the launch of *DA+AT*). For this scholarly journal written by art historians and museum curators, he created some of his most provocative images (pp. 175–9). An issue from 1979 confronts readers with a group of naked, middle-aged men taking a communal shower – a rude intrusion of ordinary life into the antiseptic, insulated domain of the art professional. This was a single image, wrapped around on to the back cover and overlaid with type, but more usually Van Toorn created a montage. For an issue dealing with violence in the arts, he forces three kinds of violent image into an unfamiliar dialectical exchange with each other. The dominant photo shows the hideously mutilated limbs of the victim of a bombing raid, displayed in a German anti-war exhibition in the 1920s. Inset is a 1973 press-kit band photo of the American glam-rockers The New York Dolls. Their singer, David Johansen, raises his fists in a gesture of cartoon-like aggression staged for the camera. On the back, Van Toorn lays out pictures of events staged by the Viennese actionist artists Hermann Nitsch and Rudolf Schwarzkogler, whose performances in the 1960s were orgies of blood, meat and ritualistic violence, sometimes focused on the performers themselves. In the context of so much art activity devoted to making gestures from the imagery of violence, the stomach-churning main picture of a broken body is a disturbing reminder of the physical truth of violent death. Van Toorn's montage, replete with torn edges, lashes out like a blow to the head. It is hard to imagine any art magazine, anywhere, publishing such a confrontational cover today.

By the early 1980s, the international mood was changing. In the course of the decade, the embrace by American president Ronald Reagan and British Prime Minister Margaret Thatcher of monetarism, deregulation, privatization and the free market would bring about a neo-liberal social and economic climate that was hostile to many of the politically progressive aims and values that had inspired left-inclined cultural producers in the 1970s. The Netherlands was not immune to these forces. Christian liberal governments compensated for the supposed "wastefulness" of earlier, socialist-inspired policies by implementing harsh cut-backs, while a growing number of avant-garde "business-artists", swiftly adapting to the mood of the times, took an obsessive interest in the economic conditions of their trade.

Van Toorn, who was by then in his 50s, found fewer opportunities for challenging work. One notable project in this period is the series of seven posters he designed, from 1981 to 1987, for a series of exhibitions titled *Mens en Omgeving* (Man and environment) at the De Beyerd visual arts centre in Breda (pp. 114–20). The posters, each one built upon the same graphic framework – triangular fragments of a television image of Italian actress Sophia Loren and her son – represent the final stage in the gradual development of Van Toorn's montage method of image-construction. Although he had yet to encounter the term, the series can be seen as a sustained exercise in reflexive design, with each poster pointing forwards or backwards to the sequence as a whole. By using Warholian repetition, Van Toorn draws attention to the designer's role as the shaper of public communications and to print as a medium based on the multiple reproduction of an image. He also reminds viewers of the media's power to create and sustain a global star such as Loren, though it is less clear, even in retrospect, whether his "restructuring of the code" of the contemporary art museum poster is meant to map on to the meaning of the individual exhibitions, to offer a parallel commentary, or just to provide an element of alienating "redundancy". In the most striking poster, the two shards of the original picture clasp a second image of Loren and her son – just as Loren clasps the boy – and the media icon acts as a frame for herself, while her enlarged eyes become a mask concealing her true identity. It is a curiously satisfying moment of fusion in a series built on layers of self-referentiality.

Pre-prints for the *Mens en Omgeving* (Man and environment) poster series for De Beyerd, 1981–7. Ten alternatives were produced from the same plates

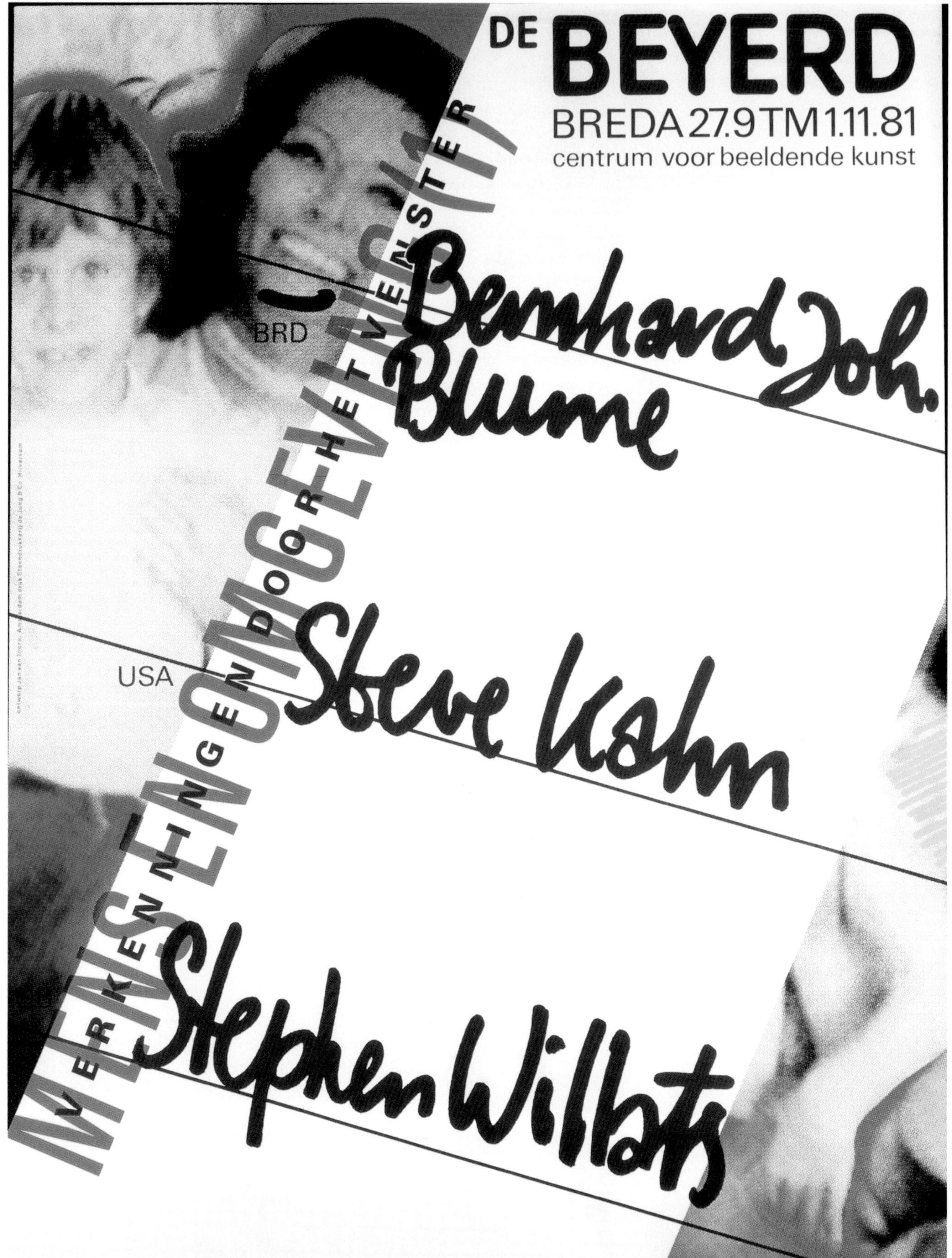
DE BEYERD
BREDA 27.9 TM 1.11.81
centrum voor beeldende kunst
MENS EN OMGEVING
VERKENNINGEN DOOR HET VENSTER
BRD
Bernhard Joh. Blume
USA
Steve Kahn
Stephen Willats
Boschstraat 22, 4811 GH Breda openingstijden:
dinsdag tot en met zaterdag 10-17 uur, zondag 13-17 uur, maandag gesloten

DE BEYERD
BREDA 9.1 TM 21.2.82
centrum voor beeldende kunst

ЛЕНГИЗ

КНИГИ

ЛЕНГИЗ

KONSTRUKTIES OP EEN WERKPLAATS
MENS EN OMGEVING

RUSLAND 1918-1928: STEPANOVA/
EXTER/EL LISSITZKY/MAYAKOVSKY/
KLUTSIS/MEYERHOLD/RODCHENKO/
TATLIN/VESNIN & VESNIN/
EN ANDEREN

Boschstraat 22, 4811 GH Breda openingstijden:
dinsdag tot en met zaterdag 10-17 uur, zondag 13-17 uur, maandag gesloten

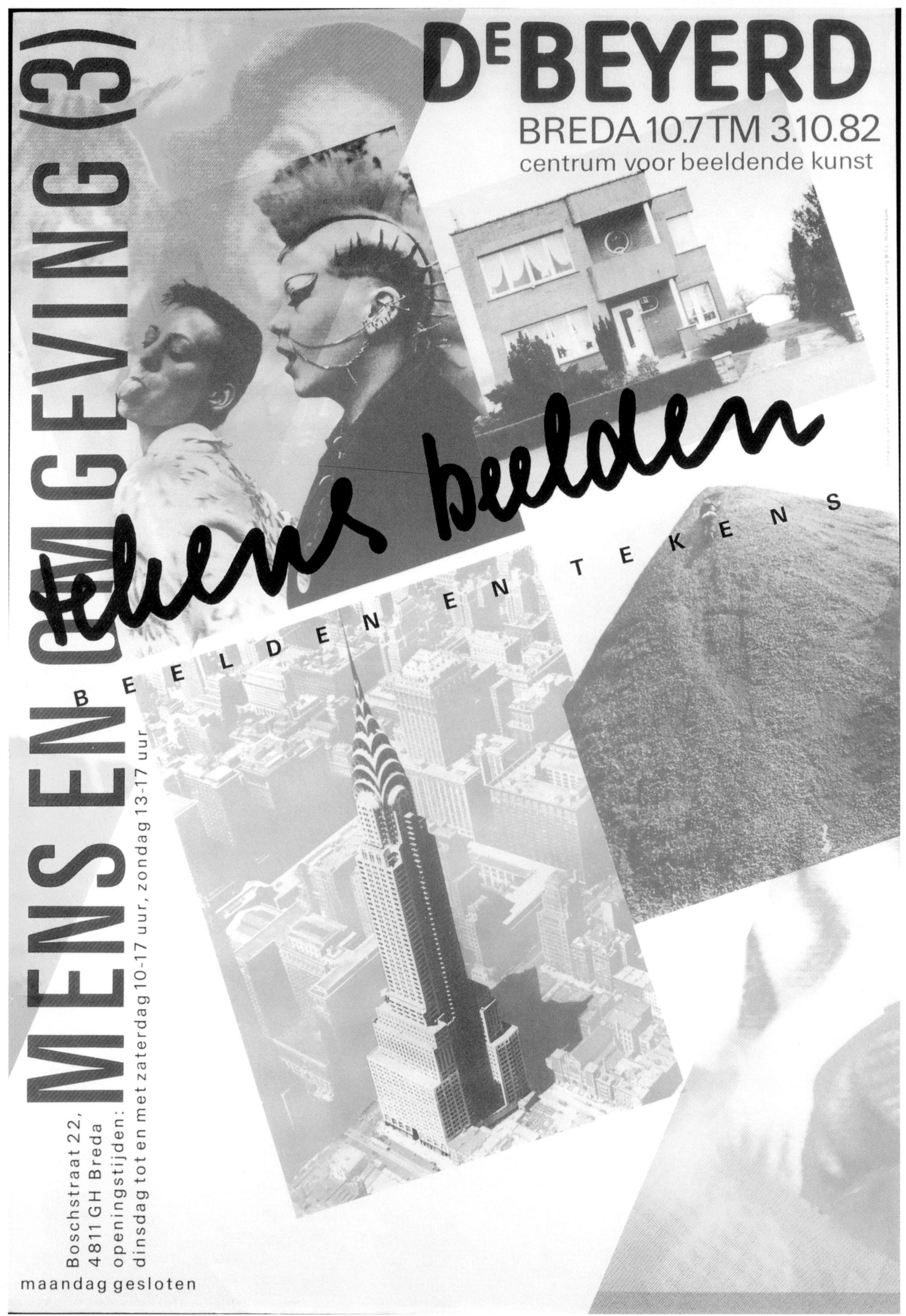
DeBEYERD
BREDA 10.7 TM 3.10.82
centrum voor beeldende kunst
tekens beelden
BEELDEN EN TEKENS
MENS EN OMGEVING (3)
Boschstraat 22,
4811 GH Breda
openingstijden:
dinsdag tot en met zaterdag 10-17 uur, zondag 13-17 uur
maandag gesloten

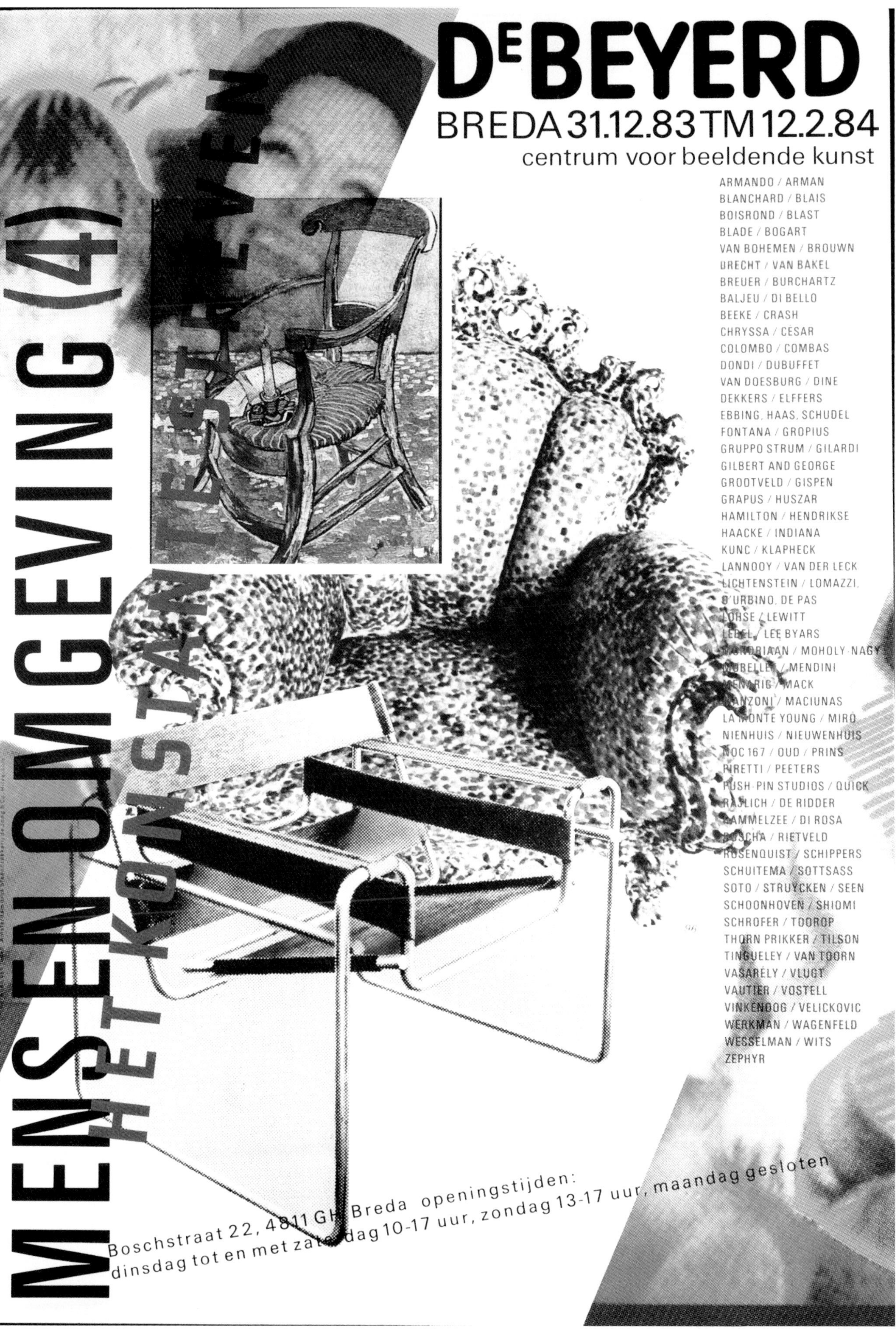

DeBEYERD
BREDA 31.12.83 TM 12.2.84
centrum voor beeldende kunst
MENSEN OMGEVING (4)
HET KONSTANTE STREVEN
ARMANDO / ARMAN
BLANCHARD / BLAIS
BOISROND / BLAST
BLADE / BOGART
VAN BOHEMEN / BROUWN
URECHT / VAN BAKEL
BREUER / BURCHARTZ
BALJEU / DI BELLO
BEEKE / CRASH
CHRYSSA / CESAR
COLOMBO / COMBAS
DONDI / DUBUFFET
VAN DOESBURG / DINE
DEKKERS / ELFFERS
EBBING, HAAS, SCHUDEL
FONTANA / GROPIUS
GRUPPO STRUM / GILARDI
GILBERT AND GEORGE
GROOTVELD / GISPEN
GRAPUS / HUSZAR
HAMILTON / HENDRIKSE
HAACKE / INDIANA
KUNC / KLAPHECK
LANNOOY / VAN DER LECK
LICHTENSTEIN / LOMAZZI,
D'URBINO, DE PAS
LOHSE / LEWITT
LEBEL / LEE BYARS
/ MOHOLY-NAGY
/ MENDINI
/ MACK
/ MACIUNAS
LA MONTE YOUNG / MIRO
NIENHUIS / NIEUWENHUIS
NOC 167 / OUD / PRINS
PIRETTI / PEETERS
PUSH PIN STUDIOS / QUICK
/ DE RIDDER
/ DI ROSA
/ RIETVELD
ROSENQUIST / SCHIPPERS
SCHUITEMA / SOTTSASS
SOTO / STRUYCKEN / SEEN
SCHOONHOVEN / SHIOMI
SCHROFER / TOOROP
THORN PRIKKER / TILSON
TINGUELEY / VAN TOORN
VASARELY / VLUGT
VAUTIER / VOSTELL
VINKENOOG / VELICKOVIC
WERKMAN / WAGENFELD
WESSELMAN / WITS
ZEPHYR
Boschstraat 22, 4811 GH Breda openingstijden:
dinsdag tot en met zaterdag 10-17 uur, zondag 13-17 uur, maandag gesloten

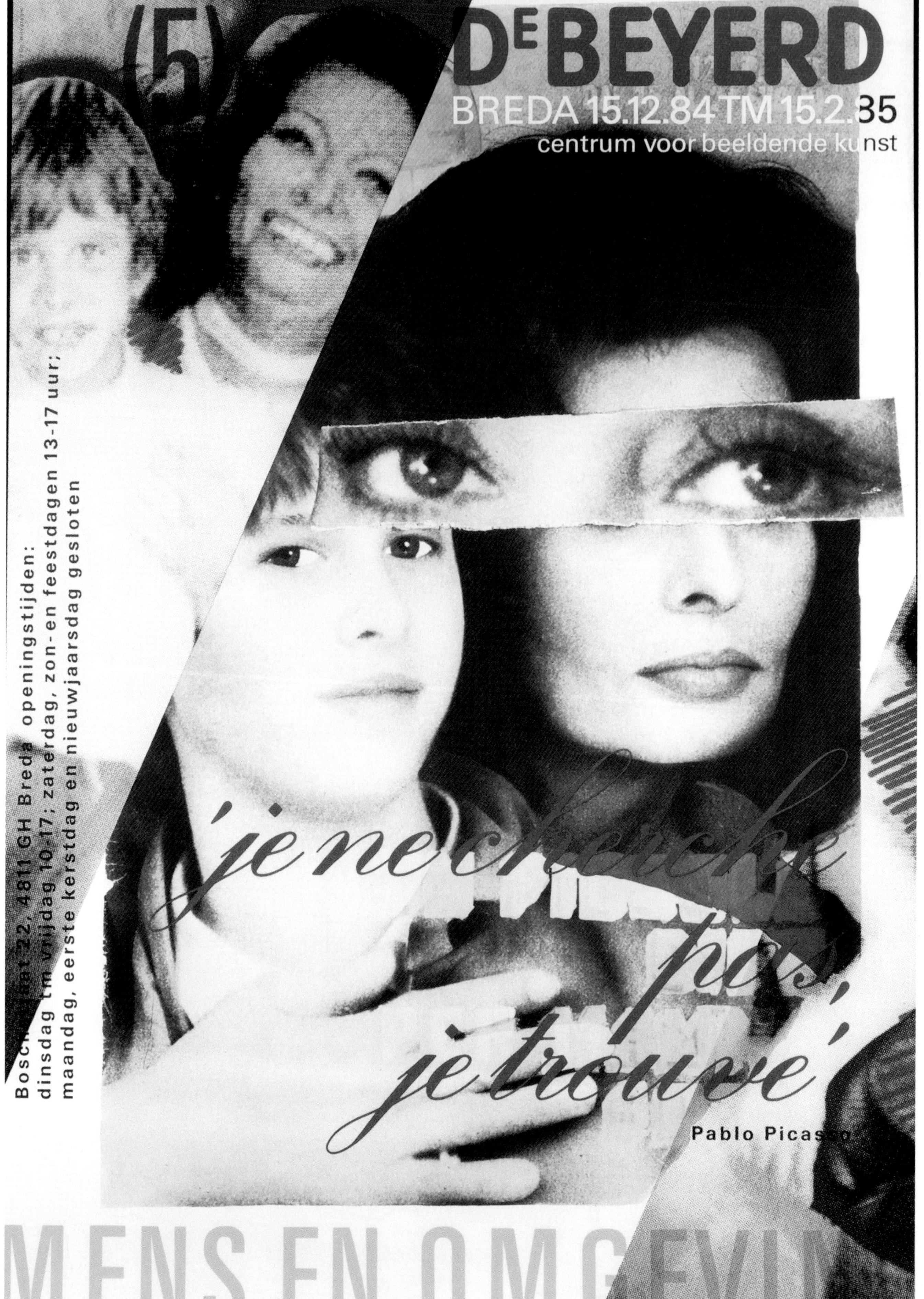
(5)
DeBEYERD
BREDA 15.12.84 TM 15.2.85
centrum voor beeldende kunst
Bosch aat 22, 4811 GH Breda openingstijden:
dinsdag tm vrijdag 10-17; zaterdag, zon- en feestdagen 13-17 uur;
maandag, eerste kerstdag en nieuwjaarsdag gesloten
'je ne cherche pas, je trouve'
Pablo Picasso
MENS EN OMGEVI

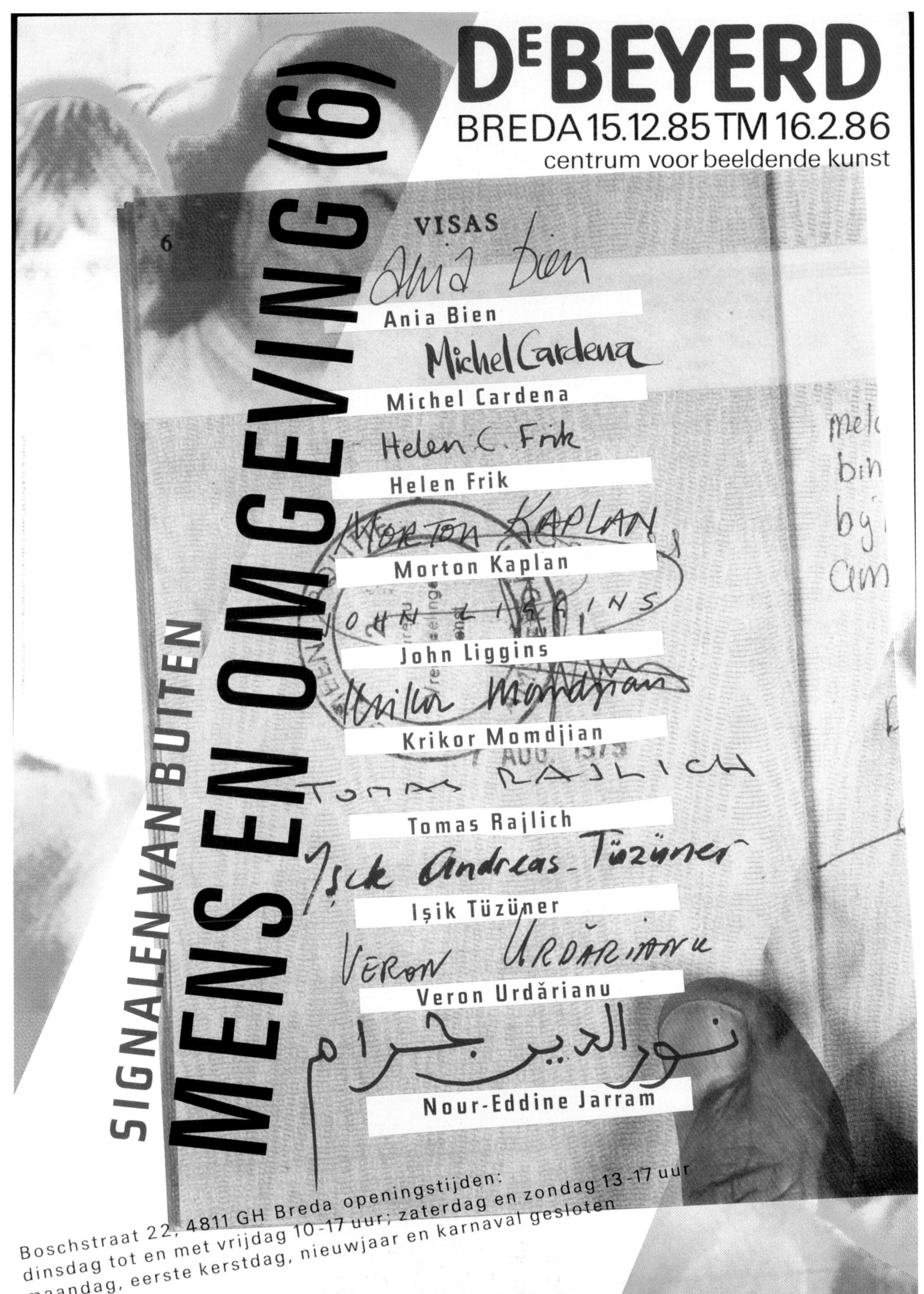
DE BEYERD
BREDA 15.12.85 TM 16.2.86
centrum voor beeldende kunst
SIGNALEN VAN BUITEN
MENS EN OMGEVING (6)
VISAS
Ania Bien
Michel Cardena
Helen Frik
Morton Kaplan
John Liggins
Krikor Momdjian
Tomas Rajlich
Işik Tüzüner
Veron Urdărianu
Nour-Eddine Jarram
Boschstraat 22, 4811 GH Breda openingstijden:
dinsdag tot en met vrijdag 10-17 uur; zaterdag en zondag 13-17 uur
maandag, eerste kerstdag, nieuwjaar en karnaval gesloten

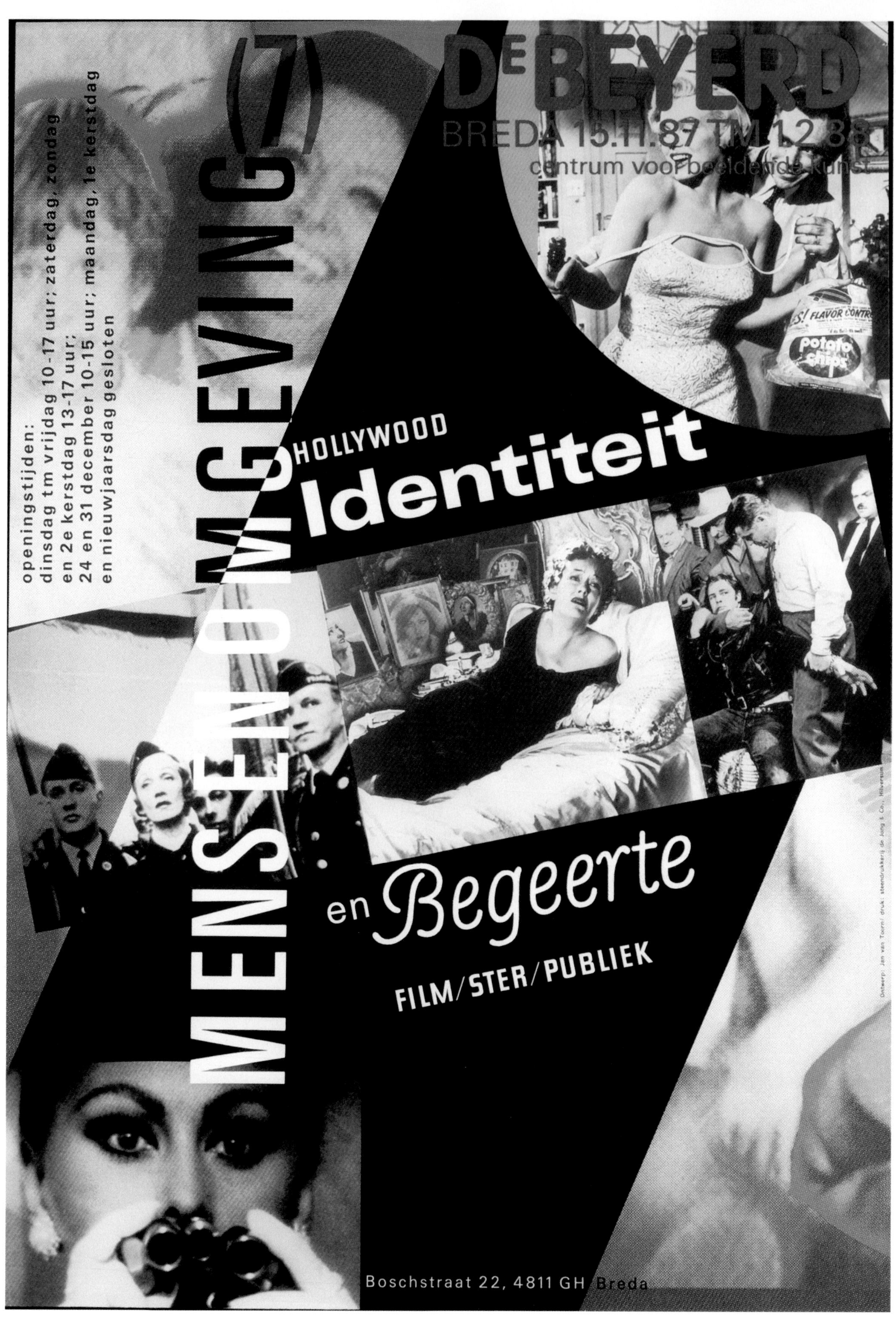
De BEYERD
BREDA 15.11.87 TM 12.88
centrum voor beeldende kunst
MENS EN OMGEVING (7)
openingstijden:
dinsdag tm vrijdag 10-17 uur; zaterdag, zondag
en 2e kerstdag 13-17 uur;
24 en 31 december 10-15 uur; maandag, 1e kerstdag
en nieuwjaarsdag gesloten
HOLLYWOOD
Identiteit
en Begeerte
FILM/STER/PUBLIEK
Boschstraat 22, 4811 GH Breda

Education and dialogic design

Van Toorn worked in education throughout most of his career and a considerable part of his influence on younger designers has come from his activities as a teacher. From 1968 to 1985, he taught at the Rietveld Academy and, in the early 1980s, he also taught at the Institute of Art History at Amsterdam University and in the department of architecture at the Technical University in Eindhoven. From 1987 to 1989, he was head of the multi-media department at the Rijksacademie (the postgraduate State Academy of Fine Arts) in Amsterdam. In 1987, one of Van Toorn's former students at the Rietveld Academy, Rob Schröder, co-founder of the radical design collective Wild Plakken, described the impact of his teaching. "In Van Toorn's classes you didn't do much more than engage in discussions," Schröder recalled. "You would bring along your work and then a discussion about it would follow [. . .] you would think you had mastered the craft of graphic design and that you knew what images mean, and you would be completely thrown off your feet by Jan van Toorn [. . .] he showed that the sectors of society that we opposed were actually using these platitudes to intimidate other groups into an inert state of mind in which they would be unable to consider their position."[45]

Van Toorn with Tom de Heus, standing, Rietveld Academy, Amsterdam, early 1970s

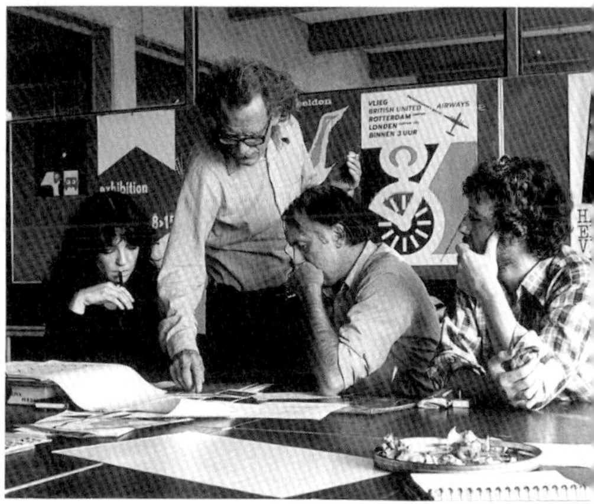

For Van Toorn, experiences gained as associate professor at the Rhode Island School of Design in Providence, where he was invited to teach in 1987 by the head of graphic design, Thomas Ockerse, would prove to be particularly significant. American design education was more systematic and Van Toorn was impressed by the standard of discourse, the thriving culture of research and the quality of exchange between staff and students. All of this helped to push his approach to teaching into a higher gear. His appointment, in 1991, as director of the postgraduate Jan van Eyck Academy in Maastricht gave him what seemed to be the perfect opportunity to create an environment where the critical thinking that underpinned his own body of work could be developed and disseminated by encouraging interaction between the academy's departments of art, design and theory. This was a direct challenge to the traditional distinction in Dutch higher education between universities devoted to academic study and institutions offering "professional training". In the 1970s and 1980s, for instance, Dutch design students were not required to write a thesis. Van Toorn's initiatives were also prescient: today, professional education courses routinely incorporate research programmes. The fact that it was a designer attempting such an ambitious cross-disciplinary synthesis, rather than someone with a background in art or theory, suggested that design's moment had come. It seemed that the field was at last receiving the recognition it deserved – at least in this corner of the Netherlands – as an intellectual undertaking with profound implications for culture and society. The new courses began in 1992 and Van Toorn's tenure as director, which lasted until his retirement in 1998, was remarkable for the assertive public profile that the academy achieved so rapidly. Within two or three years of his arrival, an institution with a small teaching staff and just 40 to 50 students – the academy's preferred term was "participants" – was staging regular conferences and turning their proceedings into a series of thoughtfully edited, well-designed books that put many much larger art and design schools to shame.[46]

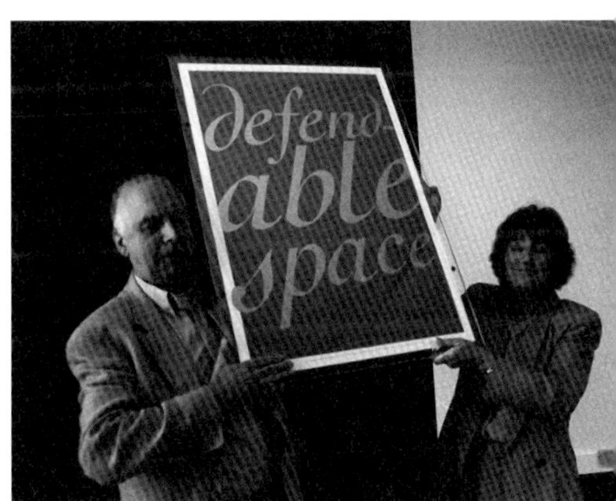

Opening of *"And justice for all . . .* at the Jan van Eyck Academy, Maastricht, 1993. Van Toorn presents a poster designed by Gerard Hadders to Hedy d'Ancona, Minister of Health, Welfare and Cultural Affairs

For Van Toorn, this phase of his career provided a period of intense reflection. Most of his theoretical writing, usually published in academic journals, dates from this time. In these essays, some of them presented as reflexive collages of text and image, he returns again and again to the ideas that have motivated his work. What has changed by this time is less the critical method he advocates than the instrumental conditions – cultural, political and economic – in which design now operates. In an essay published in *"And justice for all . . .* (1994), based on the academy's third conference, Van Toorn criticizes the design profession for succumbing to market forces. "**Because designers and intellectuals fail to reflect critically upon the conditions under which their own action comes about, their mediating role between private and public interest has been lost,**" he writes. "**In the media, problems of** [a] **public nature are veiled by a multiform spectacle, the public interest is increasingly formulated by marketing, and the visual language of graphic or other design – originally intended to act as a liberating force – has been replaced by the forms of expression of advertising and public relations.**"[47] Elsewhere in the same essay, invoking Guy Debord, he notes that, "**We have reached a point where reality is permeated by the spectacle.** [. . .] **Like most other public activities, design serves as a theatrical substitute for essential forms of social communication.**"[48]

Seminar about *Colors* magazine with Hugues Boekraad, Gerard Hadders, chair, and Tibor Kalman, speaking, Jan van Eyck Academy, 1994. Van Toorn watches from the audience

While it was apparent from Jan van Eyck publications such as *"And justice for all . . .* and *Towards a Theory of the Image* (1996) that visiting lecturers often shared Van Toorn's sense of crisis and his wish for a more critical mentality in design and image production, the inevitable question was whether the participants shared the same analysis and goals. What did it mean to the students, in terms of their early creative endeavours and future client relationships, when Van Toorn stated that, "**Our critical positions as professionals must be made visible in day-to-day practice**"?[49] I visited the academy towards the end of Van Toorn's time as director and at regular intervals in the two years after he left (I was appointed as a project tutor) when it was reasonable to expect that his socio-political agenda would be flourishing, if this were ever going to happen. In conversations with design participants during 1997 to 2000, I encountered only one student – from Britain – who could be said to share Van Toorn's socio-political agenda and aims for design in any fully articulated and unequivocal sense. "The Dutch students haven't appreciated the theoretical position of the Academie," notes Peter Bilak, an overseas design student at Jan van Eyck from 1997 to 1999; "quite on the contrary, they were turned off by it – [this] has to do with the pragmatism of the Dutch, as opposed to [the] idealism of Jan van Toorn."[50] The design students were naturally committed to their own sometimes idiosyncratic researches, but this was no different from postgraduates studying anywhere else. It was hard not to conclude that many of the young designers arriving at the academy during the 1990s had already found it necessary to make their own accommodations with a reality "permeated by the spectacle".

Workshop about the dialogic image with James Coulson, Sylvie Toux and Van Toorn, Jan van Eyck Academy, c. 1996

One gets a sense of the difficulty Van Toorn faced in fulfilling such an ambitious programme in remarks he made to the academy's staff and students at the start of the 1994–5 academic year. He begins by acknowledging that "**ideas must ultimately prove themselves in practice, although doing so is conceptually more difficult to manage than we imagined it would be**".[51] Then, clearly referring to the three departments that make up the academy – art, design and theory – he suggests that we all have a tendency "**to avoid the psychological discomfort which accompanies critical reorientation by reducing our discussions to familiar dualistic schemes and stereotypical concepts.**"[52] This was a tactful way of saying that the departments had been less willing to interact and forge productive relationships than he had hoped.

Yet a few Dutch Jan van Eyck graduates from the 1990s have certainly gone on to work in the same critical spirit as Van Toorn. One example is Felix Janssens, author in 1993 (with Mark Schalken) of the "Manifesto of the Sober Thinking Society" and designer of the *"And justice for all . . .* essay collection. "Perhaps graphic design is doing so well in the Netherlands because not a great deal of thinking is put into it," write Janssens and Schalken. "What is the sense of this ever-expanding stream of images? What is behind this ever-renewing language of forms? [. . .] The sunny image we get from graphic design is merely a façade."[53] Aiming to combat what he later described as the "powerlessness of visual culture", Janssens founded T(c)H&M – Office for Tele(communication), Historicity & Mobility – in Rotterdam to work on projects for city authorities and cultural institutions that involve diverse local communities in strategic and visual decision-making. "We wanted a dynamic environment, not a black box," Janssens explained about one public project by T(c)H&M, "in which information keeps circulating, everyone is sender and receiver, there is no hierarchical structure, the layer is horizontal and vertical, the information flows both ways."[54] Janssens' aims here bear an obvious similarity to Van Toorn's.

Some might be inclined to see Van Toorn as over-optimistic, yet his work provides a model – one of the most consistently challenging in recent decades – of what can be achieved with a fusion of design and theory for socially critical purposes. Those who share his political mentality and convictions will not find themselves disagreeing in any substantial way with his analysis, though questions of appropriate strategy are always open to debate. In a published dialogue, the American designer and educator Katherine McCoy, responding to Van Toorn's call for "dialogic" design, poses the question: "how do we invest everyday design practice for the typical commercial client with dialogic elements?"[55] (Van Toorn uses the word "dialogic" to describe the interaction with the viewer that he wants design to stimulate.) The question is so central to the development of critical design that it cannot be avoided, even if the answer might be that it is in practice rarely if ever possible to invest potentially subversive dialogic elements in projects that exist solely for commercial reasons.

The disparities of intention surrounding any hopes for dialogic design can be seen within the dialogue itself. McCoy answers her own question by suggesting that it is possible to invest even the most mainstream commercial projects with dialogic elements, and she goes on to say that

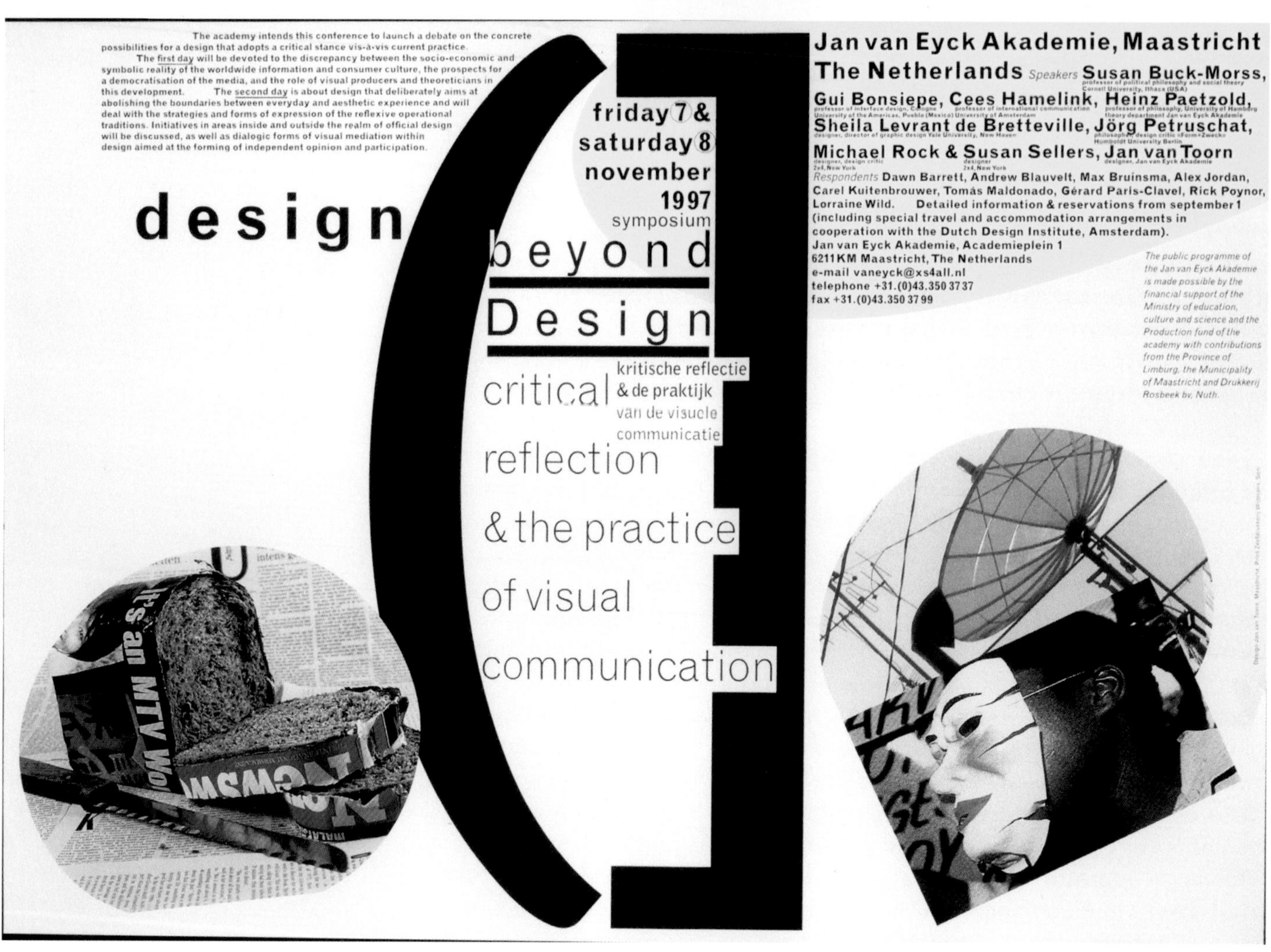

The academy intends this conference to launch a debate on the concrete possibilities for a design that adopts a critical stance vis-à-vis current practice.
The first day will be devoted to the discrepancy between the socio-economic and symbolic reality of the worldwide information and consumer culture, the prospects for a democratisation of the media, and the role of visual producers and theoreticians in this development. The second day is about design that deliberately aims at abolishing the boundaries between everyday and aesthetic experience and will deal with the strategies and forms of expression of the reflexive operational traditions. Initiatives in areas inside and outside the realm of official design will be discussed, as well as dialogic forms of visual mediation within design aimed at the forming of independent opinion and participation.
design
friday 7 & saturday 8 november 1997
symposium
beyond
Design
critical reflection & the practice of visual communication
kritische reflectie & de praktijk van de visuele communicatie
Jan van Eyck Akademie, Maastricht The Netherlands
Speakers Susan Buck-Morss, professor of political philosophy and social theory Cornell University, Ithaca (USA)
Gui Bonsiepe, professor of interface design, Cologne University of the Americas, Puebla (Mexico)
Cees Hamelink, professor of international communication University of Amsterdam
Heinz Paetzold, professor of philosophy, University of Hamburg theory department Jan van Eyck Akademie
Sheila Levrant de Bretteville, designer, director of graphic design Yale University, New Haven
Jörg Petruschat, philosopher, design critic «Form+Zweck» Humboldt University Berlin
Michael Rock, designer, design critic 2x4, New York
& Susan Sellers, designer 2x4, New York
Jan van Toorn designer, Jan van Eyck Akademie
Respondents Dawn Barrett, Andrew Blauvelt, Max Bruinsma, Alex Jordan, Carel Kuitenbrouwer, Tomás Maldonado, Gérard Paris-Clavel, Rick Poynor, Lorraine Wild.
Detailed information & reservations from september 1 (including special travel and accommodation arrangements in cooperation with the Dutch Design Institute, Amsterdam).
Jan van Eyck Akademie, Academieplein 1
6211KM Maastricht, The Netherlands
e-mail vaneyck@xs4all.nl
telephone +31.(0)43.350 37 37
fax +31.(0)43.350 37 99
The public programme of the Jan van Eyck Akademie is made possible by the financial support of the Ministry of education, culture and science and the Production fund of the academy with contributions from the Province of Limburg, the Municipality of Maastricht and Drukkerij Rosbeek bv, Nuth.

design beyond Design. Conference poster, 1997. Client: Jan van Eyck Academy

jaded audiences need "challenge, gaming and play for engagement with visual communications."[56] However, Van Toorn is talking about more complex and substantial forms of interactivity that go much further in challenging and opening up the content of communication than merely adding a dash of extra entertainment value to a message, as he points out to McCoy in his reply. Elsewhere, he notes that "**In the light of the economic and social relations of power in the world, it is not realistic, I believe, to hope for direct participation in the media by those who have no voice. That accounts for the incredible importance that practical intellectuals as designers should attach to an emancipatory view of their role as a contribution to the real democratisation of the media as public spaces.**"[57] Small-scale, open-ended cultural commissions – of the kind Van Toorn has favoured – seem rather more likely to provide opportunities for "emancipatory" dialogic design and public interaction than designing for corporate media and global brands. It is also the case, as admiring visitors to the Netherlands have often affirmed, that the Dutch have displayed an openness towards graphic design's potential as challenging personal expression that cannot always be assumed to exist in other countries, where designers operating in the commercial sector might find themselves far more heavily constrained.

During his time as director of the academy, and in the years since then, Van Toorn produced some of his most characteristic designs and projects. His final conference, *design beyond Design*, in November 1997, was his most ambitious public event. It set out to address what Van Toorn saw as the huge rift between the socio-economic and symbolic reality of the global information and consumer culture and the possibility of democratizing the media. In his introduction to the book of conference speeches and commentaries, Van Toorn observed, once again, that "**It is striking with how little political awareness designers think about the meaning of visual mediation in a socio-cultural sense at the present time. The discipline has abandoned the previous mental space in which it reflected on its social role and has therefore lost the critical distance that determined its relation vis-à-vis the client's brief**."[58]

It was a rather downbeat conclusion after seven years of hard work at the academy. Yet the conference, with all its provocative supporting materials – Van Toorn's typically disjunctive poster; the booklet of images and quotations that he put together; his design of the essay book (from the same DNA as *DA+AT*) – was an inspiring event to attend because of the way it managed to concentrate so much intelligent commitment in one place (pp. 226–9). *design beyond Design* suggested not that Van Toorn's hopes were pipedreams, but that the issues he has addressed with such vigour throughout his career are still crucially important and require even greater attention and effort by designers and design analysts who endorse his concerns. The director's final public communiqué can be seen as an early sign of a shift in thinking within some parts of design education and design practice. From the late 1990s, calls for graphic designers to take a more personally engaged and ethical view of their role as public communicators became increasingly frequent.[59] Van Toorn's unyielding scepticism and unfailing readiness to disturb and cloud the smooth waters of professional communication helped to prepare the ground for a more socially aware and critical form of design practice. Designers who share his deep commitment to the public interest are free to hack away the undergrowth of complacency that will always threaten to obscure the way forward and to extend the path that his body of work opened up.

1. Quoted in Leonie ten Duis and Annelies Haase, *De Wereld moe(s)t Anders: Grafisch Ontwerpen en Idealisme/The World must Change: Graphic Design and Idealism*, Amsterdam: Sandberg Instituut and Uitgeverij De Balie, 1999, p. 107. See also Toon Lauwen, *Otto Treumann*, Rotterdam: 010 Publishers, 2001.

2. See, for instance, Andrew Blauvelt, "Towards Critical Autonomy or Can Graphic Design Save Itself?", *Emigre* no. 64, winter 2003, pp. 35–43.

3. See *Eye* no. 20 vol. 5, "The Designer as Author", spring 1996; *Emigre* nos. 35 and 36, "Mouthpiece: Clamor over Writing and Design", summer and fall, 1995; and *Items* no. 5 vol. 16, August 1997, with a special supplement, "The Designer as Editor", documenting the eponymous two-day symposium at the Vormgevingsinstituut (Dutch Design Institute) in Amsterdam, November 1996.

4. Rick Poynor, "Why Foucault's Pendulum Swings over Maastricht", *Blueprint*, June 1992, p. 8.

5. Quoted in William Rothuizen, *Ontwerpen Jan van Toorn*, Breda: De Beyerd (catalogue), 1986, p. 22 (trans. Jan Wynsen).

6. Quoted in Elizabeth Pick, "Everything you always wanted to know about reflexivity but were afraid to ask", (interview with Van Toorn) in Paul Hefting and Karel Martens (eds.), *View to the Future*, Maastricht: Jan van Eyck Akademie Design Department, 1997, p. 41.

7. G.W. Ovink, "Talking Technics to Technicians", *Range* no. 25, 1964, p. 3.

8. Ibid., p. 2.

9. See Kees Broos, *Piet Zwart: Typotect*, New York: Princeton Architectural Press, 2004; Dick Mann, *Paul Schuitema: Visual Organizer*, Rotterdam: 010 Publishers, 2006; and Max Bruinsma, Lies Ros and Rob Schröder, *Een Leest Heeft Drie Voeten; Dick Elffers en de Kunsten*, Amsterdam: Uitgeverij De Balie, 1989.

10. Jetteke Bolten-Rempt, an art historian and former curator of the Van Abbemuseum, subsequently took on this task. Some of Van Toorn's photo archive survived until the late 1990s when he returned to Amsterdam from Maastricht.

11. Jean Leering and Jan van Toorn, "Vormgeving in Functie van Museale Overdracht" (Design as a means of museological communication), *Documentaires* no. 7, 1978, p. 29.

12. See Kees Schuyt and Ed Taverne, *Dutch Culture in a European Perspective Volume 4, 1950: Prosperity and Welfare*, Basingstoke: Palgrave Macmillan/Assen: Royal Van Gorcum, 2004, pp. 362–7.

13. Beeke worked with Van Toorn in 1965–6. "Because of my lack of formal training, I had little choice but to pursue the unconventional. Van Toorn taught me about typography, while my anarchic behaviour fanned the flame of his creativity. In short: a perfect symbiosis." Anthon Beeke, *Dutch Posters 1960–1996*, Amsterdam: BIS Publishers, 1997, p 45.

14. In "Mad Dutch Disease", a lecture delivered in 2004 to the Premsela Dutch Design Foundation in Amsterdam, Michael Rock argued that the elimination of house style at the Van Abbemuseum can be seen in retrospect as a house style in its own right – "no style as house style" – just as much as Wim Crouwel's work for the Stedelijk Museum. "Each institution used the figure of the designer, or his purported absence, as an aesthetic expression in itself," notes Rock. http://www.premsela.org/pdf/cultuur/co/premsela_lezing_01_en.pdf

15. Hans Magnus Enzensberger, "Baukasten zu einer Theorie der Medien" (Building blocks for a theory of media), *Kursbuch* no. 20, Frankfurt am Main: Suhrkamp, March 1970, pp. 159–86.

16. Ibid., p. 166. Quoted by Jan van Toorn in calendar for Drukkerij Mart.Spruijt, 1976/77. English translation in Jetteke Bolten-Rempt, "Jan van Toorn, Medium + Message", *Dutch Art + Architecture Today* no. 19, June 1986, p. 27.

17. Victor Shklovsky, "Art as Technique" in Lee T. Lemon and Marion J. Reis (trans.), *Russian Formalist Criticism: Four Essays*, Lincoln and London: University of Nebraska Press, 1965, p. 12.

18. Bertolt Brecht, "The A-Effect as a Procedure in Everyday Life" in John Willet (ed. and trans.), *Brecht on Theatre: The Development of an Aesthetic*, London: Methuen, 2001, pp. 143–4.

19. Bertolt Brecht, *Gesammeltes Werk*, Frankfurt am Main: Suhrkamp Verlag, 1967.

20. Willet, *Brecht on Theatre*, p. 37.

21. Jan van Toorn, *Design's Delight*, Rotterdam: 010 Publishers, p. 206.

22. Gerard Forde, "The Designer Unmasked", *Eye* no. 2 vol. 1, winter 1991. p. 68.

23. Robert Stam, *Reflexivity in Film and Literature from Don Quixote to Jean-Luc Godard*, New York: Columbia University Press, 1992, p. xi. On Godard see Richard Roud, *Godard*, London: Thames & Hudson, 1970; Colin MacCabe, *Godard: Images, Sounds, Politics.*, London: Macmillan Press, 1980; Michael Temple, James S. Williams and Michael Witt (eds.), *For Ever Godard*, London: Black Dog Publishing, 2007 (first edition 2003).

24. Ibid., p. 211.

25. Jan van Toorn, "Design and Reflexivity", in Andrew Blauvelt (ed.) *Visible Language*, "New Perspectives: Critical Histories of Graphic Design", vol. 28 no. 4, 1994, p. 324. See also: Pick, "Everything you always wanted to know about reflexivity but were afraid to ask", pp. 33–50.

26. Quoted in Natalia Ilyin and Katie Salen, "Jan van Toorn" (interview), *Spirals '91*, Providence: Rhode Island School of Design, 1991, p. 57.

27. Quoted in Els Kuijpers, "Pro and Con: Defining Design History, Correctly" (interview), *AIGA Journal of Graphic Design* vol. 12 no. 3, 1994, p. 47.

28. See, for instance, Tony Godfrey, *Conceptual Art*, London: Phaidon Press, 1998; Peter Osborne (ed.) *Conceptual Art*, London: Phaidon Press, 2002; and Michael Archer, *Art Since 1960*, London: Thames & Hudson, 1997.

29. John Berger, *Ways of Seeing*, London: British Broadcasting Corporation and Penguin, 1972, p. 149.

30. Forde, "The Designer Unmasked", p. 62.

31. Frans Spruijt quoted in Rothuizen, *Ontwerpen Jan van Toorn*, p. 20.

32. Rolf Mager (quotation from *Adformatie* no. 31, 1974). Ibid., p. 18.

33. See Kees Broos, *Ontwerp: Total Design*, Utrecht: Reflex, 1983; Frederike Huygen and Hugues C. Boekraad, *Wim Crouwel – Mode en Module*, Rotterdam: 010 Publishers, 1997; Kees Broos, *Wim Crouwel Alphabets*, Amsterdam: BIS Publishers, 2003; Wim Crouwel, Catherine de Smet and Emmanuel Bérard, *Wim Crouwel Architectures Typographiques/Typographic Architectures*, Paris: Galerie Anatome and Éditions F7, 2007.

34. Quoted in Broos, *Ontwerp: Total Design*, p. 91.

35. Ibid.

36. Printed and published by Drukkerij Erven E. van de Geer, Amsterdam, 1973.

37. Introduction to "The Street", quoted by Jean Leering in Carel Blotkamp, Marjon van Caspel, Frans Haks, Frank van der Schoor, Jan van Toorn and Martin Visser (eds.), *Museum in Motion? The Modern Art Museum at Issue/Museum in Beweging? Het Museum voor Moderne Kunst ter Diskussie*, The Hague: Government Publishing Office/Staatsuitgeverij, 1979, p. 80.

38. Leering and Van Toorn, "Vormgeving in Functie van Museale Overdracht", pp. 2–3.

39. Ibid., p. 1.

40. Wim Crouwel, "De Vormgeving en het Museum" (Graphic design and the museum) in "Om de Kunst" (For art's sake), *Documentaires* no. 8, 1978, p. 15. For an abridged version of Crouwel's text (2006), omitting references to Van Toorn, see Ben and Elly Bos, *AGI: Graphic Design since 1950*, London: Thames & Hudson, 2007, pp. 669–71. Crouwel adds his more recent thoughts on design for museums.

41. Ibid., p. 18.

42. Jan van Toorn, untitled article, *Quad* no. 2, October 1980, no page number.

43. Ibid.

44. Wim Crouwel, "Design", *Quad* no. 3, March 1981, no page number.

45. Rob Schröder quoted in Rothuizen, *Ontwerpen Jan Van Toorn*, p. 27.

46. The major events and publications produced during Van Toorn's time as director of the academy were: Ine Gevers (ed.), *Place Position Presentation Public*, Maastricht: Jan van Eyck Akademie, 1993 (symposium: "PPPP", April 1992); Hugues C. Boekraad and Paul Hefting (eds.), *The Boundaries of the Postage Stamp: Marketing, Management and Design*, Maastricht: Jan van Eyck Akademie Design Department, 1993 (symposium: March 1993); Ole Bouman (ed.), *"And justice for all . . .*, Maastricht: Jan van Eyck Akademie Editions, 1994 (symposium: April 1993); Jon Thompson (ed.), *Towards a Theory of the Image*, Maastricht: Jan van Eyck Akademie Editions, 1996 (symposium: March 1995); Heinz Paetzold (ed.), *City Life: Essays on Urban Culture*, Maastricht: Jan van Eyck Akademie Editions, 1997 (symposium: "The Politics of the Visual Culture of Contemporary Cities", April 1996); Jan van Toorn (ed.) *design beyond Design: Critical Reflection and the Practice of Visual Communication*, Maastricht: Jan van Eyck Akademie Editions, 1998 (symposium: November 1997).

47. Jan van Toorn, "Thinking the Visual; Essayistic Fragments on Communicative Action" in *"And justice for all . . .*, pp. 142–3.

48. Ibid., p. 147.

49. Ibid., p. 144.

50. Peter Bilak in response to Rick Poynor, "Jan van Toorn: Arguing with Visual Means", *Design Observer*, 21 March 2004. http://www.designobserver.com/archives/000120.html

51. Jan van Toorn, "Opening of the 1994–1995 academic year", unpublished notes for a speech to the staff and students at Jan van Eyck Academy, September 1994.

52. Ibid.

53. Quoted in Peter Bilak, "Contemporary Dutch Graphic Design: An Insider/Outsider's View", *HD: Holland Design New Graphics*, Barcelona: Actar, 2001, no page number.

54. See Timo de Rijk, "A Powerless Visual Culture" (interview with Felix Janssens), *Yearbook Dutch Design 03/04*, Rotterdam: Episode, 2004,

pp. 84–92. Other examples of Dutch graduates from Jan van Eyck during Van Toorn's period as director who went on to work in a critical spirit include Femke Snelting (design), Renee Turner and Riek Sijbring (both from the theory department), who in 1996 founded the activist collective De Geuzen: A Foundation for Multi-visual Research in Rotterdam; Daniël van der Velden, designer (with Maureen Mooren) of *Archis* magazine; and Jop van Bennekom, founder, editor and designer of *Re-Magazine* and *Butt* magazine. On De Geuzen, see http://www.geuzen.org. On Van der Velden, see Stuart Bailey, "File under ARCHIS", *Eye* no. 45 vol. 12, autumn 2002, pp. 48–53. On Van Bennekom, see Alice Twemlow, "No Muscles, No Tattoos", *Eye* no. 61 vol. 16, autumn 2006, pp. 34–41. Although *Re-Magazine* began life as a thesis project at the Jan van Eyck Academy, Van Bennekom has spoken critically of his experience there as a student: "It was a terrible institution at that time. It was all about the institute, not about the students. I was searching for a new language, one that was not about theory, but about the everyday. I got so sick of design that was all about design." http://www.designmuseum.org/design/jop-van-bennekom

55. Katherine McCoy, Teal Triggs and Jan van Toorn, "Undiscovered Delights", *Visual Communication* vol. 1 no. 3, 2002, p. 331.

56. Ibid.

57. Jan van Toorn, "Communication Design: A Social Practice" in *design beyond Design*, p. 166.

58. Jan van Toorn, introduction in *design beyond Design*, p. 11.

59. Van Toorn was one of 33 signatories of the controversial "First Things First 2000" manifesto, published internationally in 1999 by *Adbusters*, *Items* magazine in the Netherlands, and other magazines, though he expressed misgivings about what he regarded as an insufficiently penetrating critique. Books on socially aware design published since then include Steven Heller and Véronique Vienne (eds.), *Citizen Designer: Perspectives on Design Responsibility*, New York: Allworth Press, 2003; John Cranmer and Yolanda Zappaterra, *Conscientious Objectives: Designing for an Ethical Message*, Mies, Switzerland: RotoVision, 2003; Milton Glaser and Mirko Ilic, *The Design of Dissent*, New York: Rockport Publishers, 2005; Kalle Lasn, *Design Anarchy*, Vancouver: Adbusters Media Foundation, 2006; and Lucienne Roberts, *Good: An Introduction to Ethics in Graphic Design*, Lausanne, Switzerland: AVA Publishing, 2007.

"WE GREW UP WITH ONE SET OF SOCIAL CONVENTIONS AND SUDDENLY IT WAS ALL BROKEN UP. IMAGINE WHAT THAT MEANT ... CONVENTIONS COULD BE MANIPULATED. YOU COULD INFLUENCE SOMETHING. YOU COULD CHANGE SOMETHING."

Jan van Toorn

Poppetgom. Book in a tin, 1970. Publisher: Octopus Foundation

Poppetgom, an invented word that suggests puppets and pop, was an anarchic theatrical production created and performed by Theater Scarabee, a group of artists led by director Adri Boon. After its 1969 debut at their studio in The Hague, the show moved to the De Zonnehof arts centre in Amersfoort and the Het Venster theatre in Rotterdam, and it was also presented in Paris, Geneva and Milan. The 224-page book documenting the production consists of drawings and diagrams, photographs of the performances, and texts by Dutch poet and painter Lucebert, as well as the script, although the show – divided into tableaux with titles such as "Plucking Flowers", "The Painting of the Big Tiger" and "Airwick's Dream" – was a collage of imagery and music rather than a piece of conventional linear writing. Van Toorn proposed the idea of concealing the book inside an oil tin, which had to be opened at the bottom using a can opener. The bulky volume tended to fall apart when removed, an effect he intended, and it was held in place inside the can by a yellow plastic pillow. Van Toorn's interventions include a spread about the war in Vietnam, showing official portraits of dead soldiers, and a US flag where the stars are replaced by skulls. The hole through the pages seen in the copy shown here is not part of the design and was made at a later date.

Poppetgom. Book spreads, 1970. Publisher: Octopus Foundation

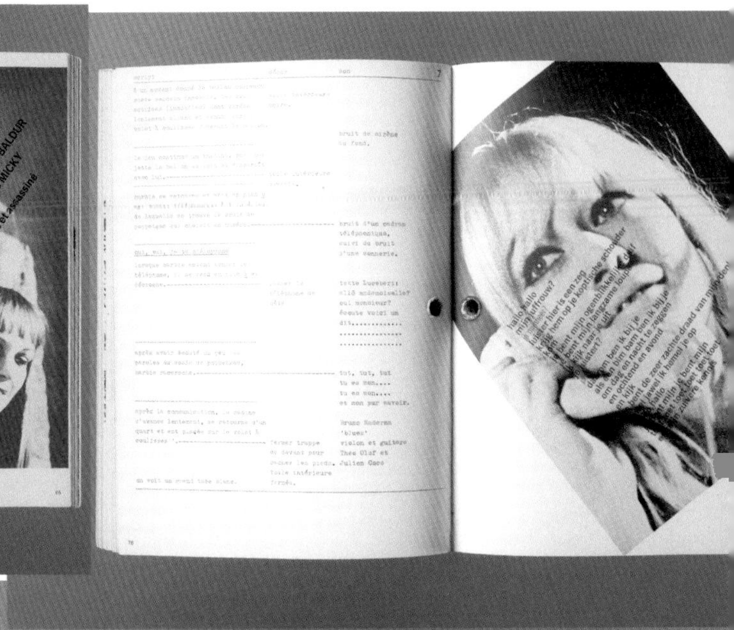

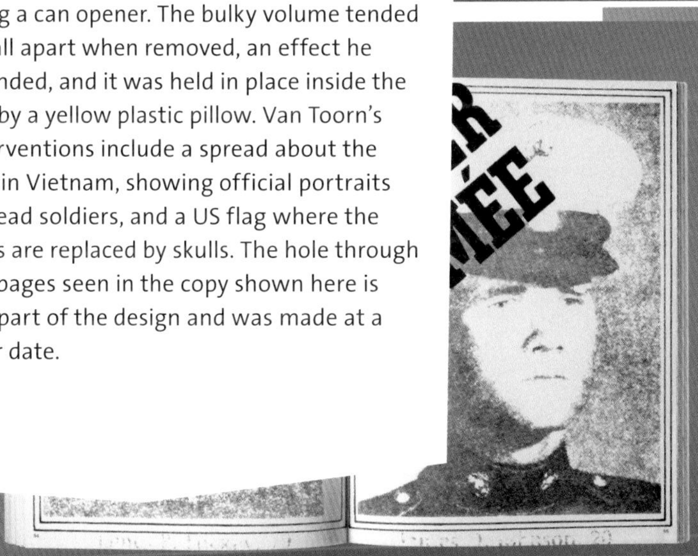

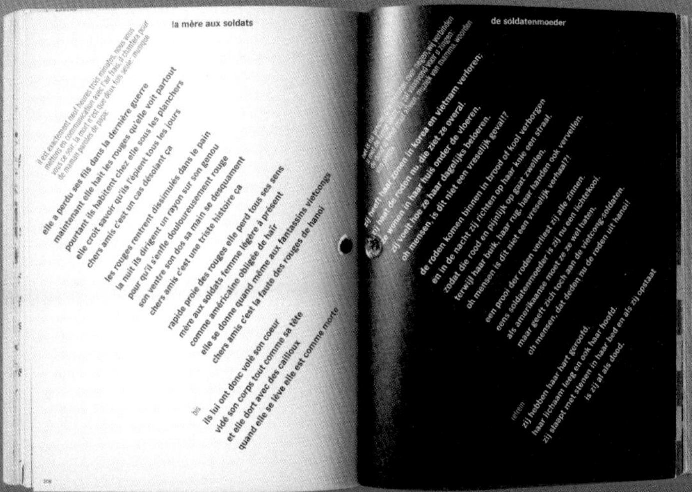

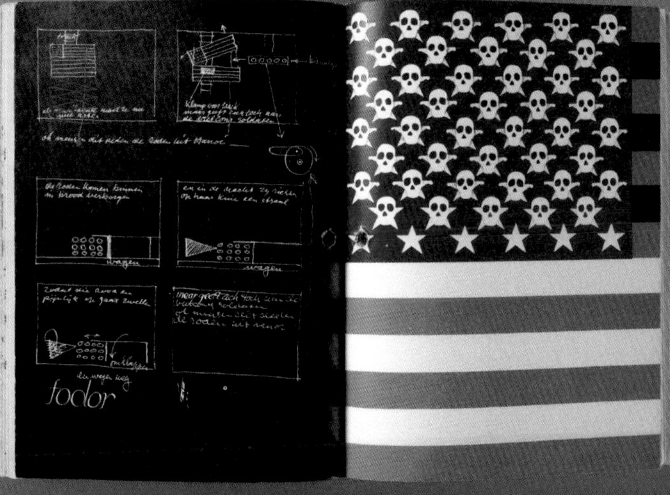

1970 Sikkens Prize for "Hippies". Stapled cover, spreads and poster, 1970. Publisher: Sikkens Groep. Photographs: Ed van der Elsken, Eva Besnyö, Koen Wessing, Geertjan Dusseljee, Bob Baarsma, Oscar van Alphen, Pieter Boersma, Simon Vinkenoog, and others

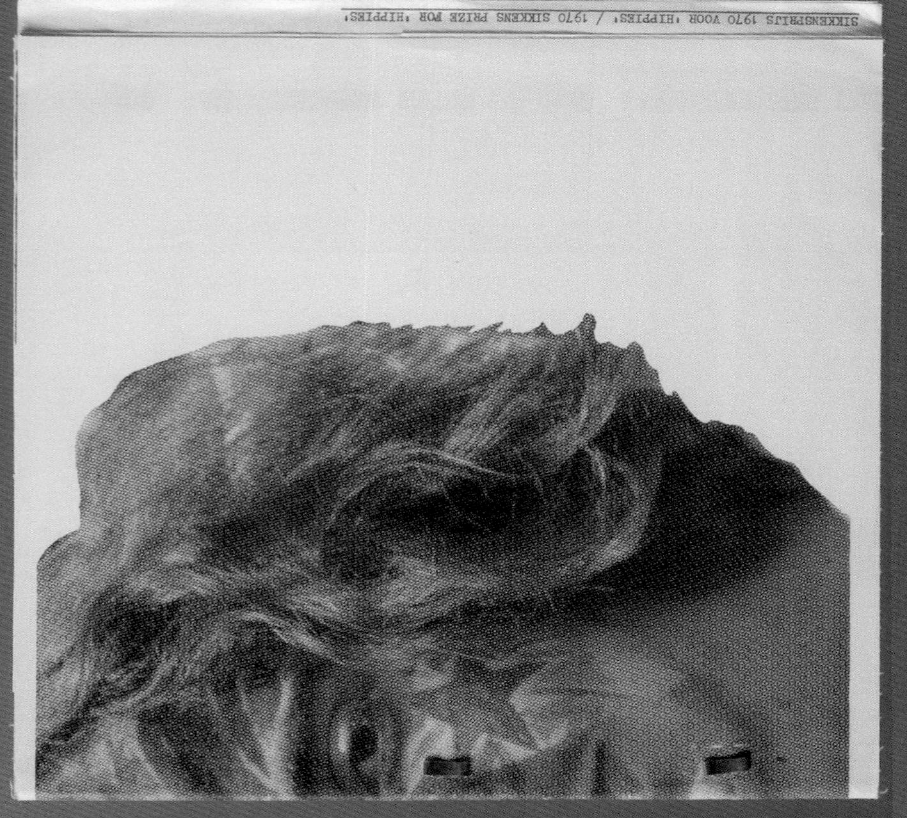

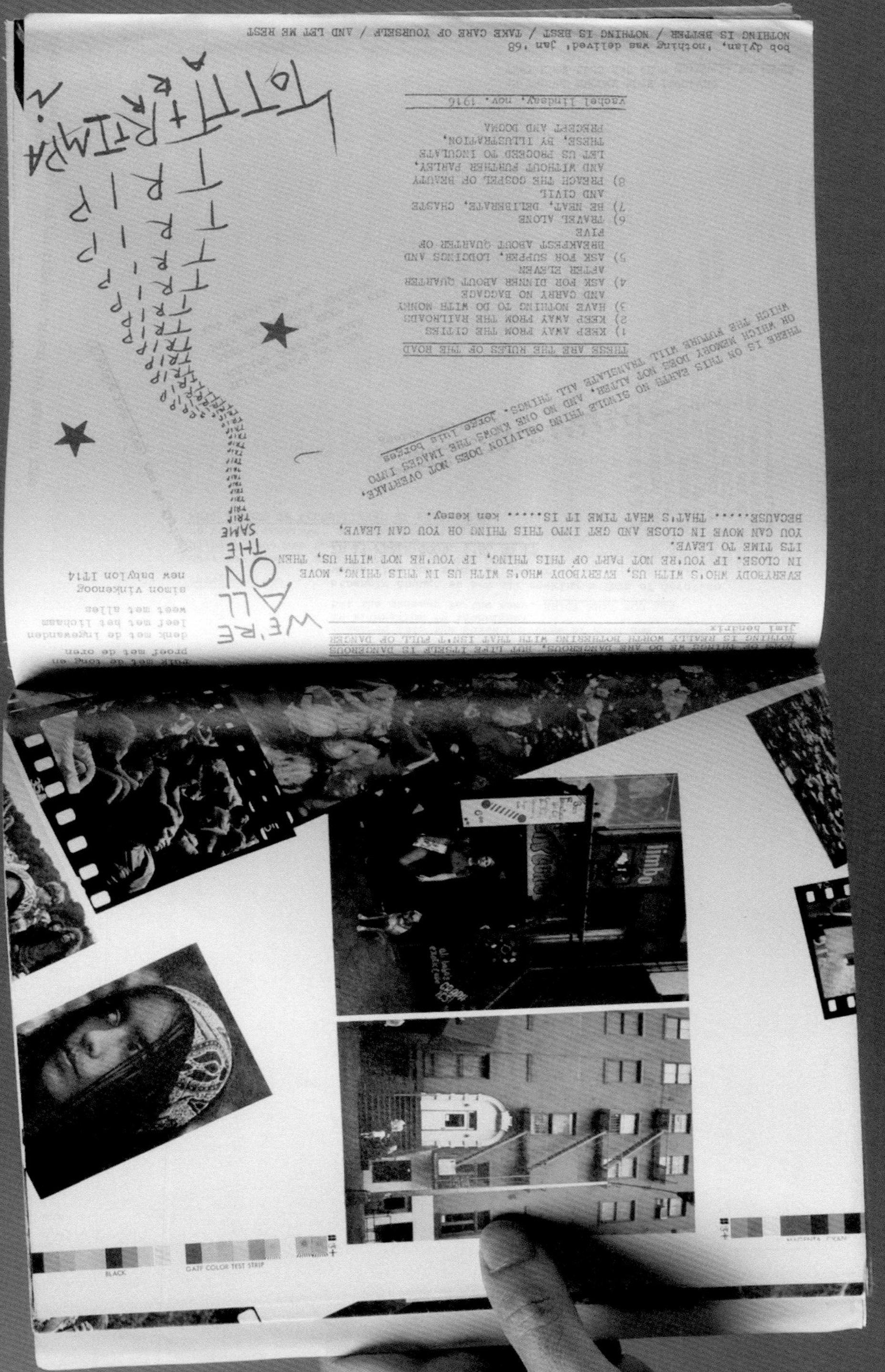

9
RAINBOW TRAIL
WALK ON A RAINBOW TRAIL;
WALK ON A TRAIL OF SONG,
AND ALL ABOUT YOU
WILL BE BEAUTY.
THERE IS A WAY OUT OF
EVERY DARK MIST,
OVER A RAINBOW TRAIL.
NAVAJO SONG
Liefde, 1965, p.222.
WIE IK O.M. BEN
MUNTJES IN 62 UITVERKOCHT!

KIJK|UIT!

kiezen is een keuze

Een tentoonstelling over het politieke affiche. Daaronder verstaan wij alle gedrukte of geschreven politieke propaganda die in het openbaar wordt aangeplakt en niet kleiner is dan 20 bij 30 cm. De politieke affiches die tentoongesteld worden zijn allemaal van de laatste vijf jaar en afkomstig uit ongeveer dertig landen. Wij hebben niet geprobeerd om zo veel mogelijk landen bijeen te brengen, wel zo veel mogelijk verschillende soorten landen: Westerse democratische staten, Oost-Europa, derde-wereld landen, landen in revolutionaire-of overgangs-situaties, landen die direkt betrokken zijn bij internationale spanningen enz.enz.

De bedoeling van de tentoonstelling is om bij de grote verscheidenheid van landen en affiches bepaalde overeenkomsten te laten zien, en ook bepaalde verschillen, die in alle landen tussen de verschillende soorten van affiches op te merken zijn. Je kunt globaal drie hoofdgroepen onderscheiden:

1) portretten van **politieke leiders, idolen en staatshoofden**

2) propaganda van **politieke partijen, en officiële instellingen**

3) propaganda van **niet-officiële organisaties, aktiegroepen, bevrijdingsbewegingen**

Wij hebben ook gelet op bepaalde thema's die steeds terugkeren. Voorbeelden zijn symbolen, nationale en ideologische, het realisme in de affiches uit Rusland, Oost-Europa en China, het reclamebureau-karakter van de verkiezingsaffiches in West-Europa, Noord-Amerika en Japan.
En natuurlijk hebben wij er actuele politieke kwesties in gebracht. De verkiezingsstrijd van vorig jaar in Duitsland en nu in Nederland. De tegenstellingen Israël, Arabische landen, Palestijnen.
Het politieke affiche is tenslotte in de eerste plaats een strijdmiddel.

De samenstellers

Kijk Uit! Kiezen is een Keuze (Look Out! Voting is a choice). Catalogue cover and spreads for an exhibition about political posters, 1977. Client: Rotterdamse Kunststichting. Co-curators: Rudolf de Jong and Van Toorn

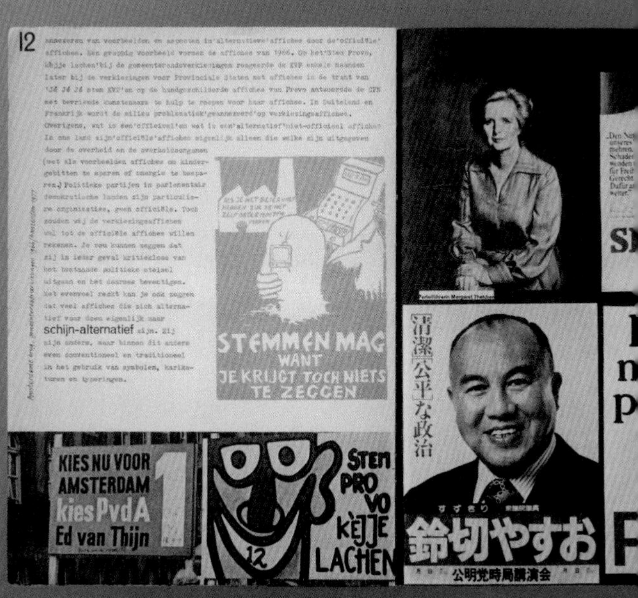

Kijk Uit! Kiezen is een Keuze (Look Out! Voting is a choice). Lijnbaancentrum, Rotterdam, 1977

"THE MAIN FOCUS SHOULD ALWAYS BE ON THE RECEIVER, WHO SHOULD BE CONTINUOUSLY ALLOWED TO BE THE EXPERT OF HIS OWN EXPERIENCE, HIS OWN HISTORY."

Jan van Toorn

1970/71 calendar. Cover and pages. Publisher and printer: Mart.Spruijt

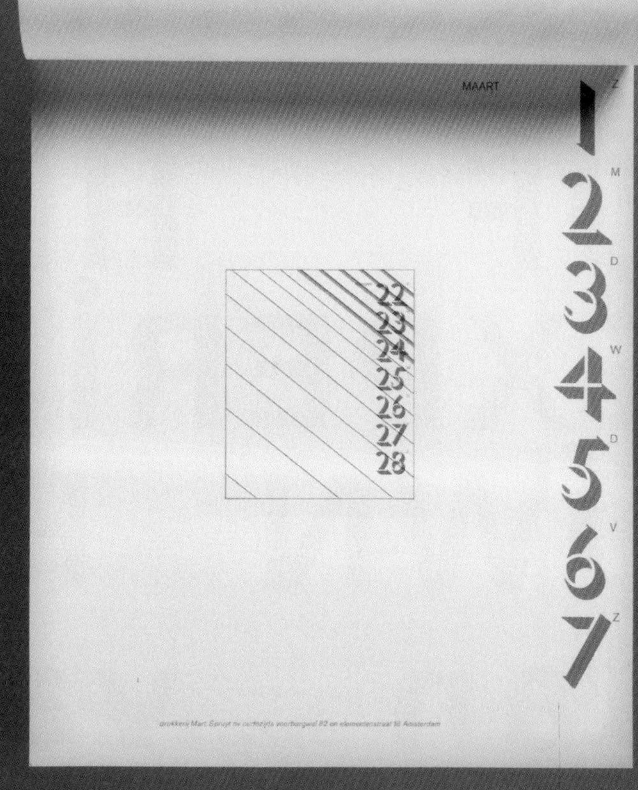

MAART

8 Z
9 M
10 D
11 W
12 D
13 V
14 Z

drukkerij Mart. Spruijt nv oudezijds voorburgwal 182 en elementenstraat 16 Amsterdam

APRIL

12 Z
13 M
14 D
15 W
16 D
17 V
18 Z

drukkerij Mart. Spruijt nv oudezijds voorburgwal 182 en elementenstraat 16 Amsterdam

MEI

3 Z
4 M DODENHERDENKING
5 D BEVRIJDING
6 W
7 D HEMELVAART
8 V
9 Z

Wij Nederlanders hebben ons eigen erfgoed, ook op het gebied van het volkslied. Van de twaalfde eeuw af tot vandaag. Een rijke schat waar in alle menselijke roerselen tot uitdrukking komen, sober en treffend, onvergetelijk en als bron van bezieling. Vele Europese liederen hebben in onze Lage Landen zelfs hun allerbeste vorm gevonden, zoals: Heer Halewijn, Ik zag Cecilia komen, ... En niet met banaliteiten als: 'En dat we toffe jongens zijn', maar met de pure schoonheid van: 'Die winter is vergangen' gaven wij Nederlanders eeuwenlang de toon aan, tot diep in Europa.

Uit de brochure Wenken voor de viering van 5 mei 1970

MEI 10 Z
11 M
12 D

WHITE MAN UNITE

JOIN THE
NATIONAL STATES RIGHTS PARTY
Write P.O. BOX 11018
CINCINNATI, OHIO 45211

THERE IS ONLY ONE ISSUE. THE DETERMINATION OF WHITE CHRISTIANS TO REMAIN FREE FROM CONTAMINATION AND FORCED MONGRELIZATION WITH BLACK AFRICAN JUNGLE NIGGERS, AND HIS SPONSORS, BROWN SKIN, ASIATIC, ANTI CHRIST, HOOKNOSED JEWS.

13 W
14 D
15 V
16 Z

Kaartje uitgedeeld onder de aanhangers van Wallace, amerikaans presidentskandidaat 1968

MEI 17 Z PINKSTEREN
18 M PINKSTEREN
19 D
20 W
21 D
22 V
23 Z

MEI 24 Z
25 M
26 D
27 W
28 D
29 V
30 Z
31 Z
JUNI 1 M
2 D
3 W

JUNI 21 Z 22 M 23 D
24 W
25 D
26 V
27 Z

5
M
6
D
7
W
8
D
9
V
10
Z
11

AUGUSTUS
Z
9
M
10
D
11
W
12
D
13
V
14
Z
15

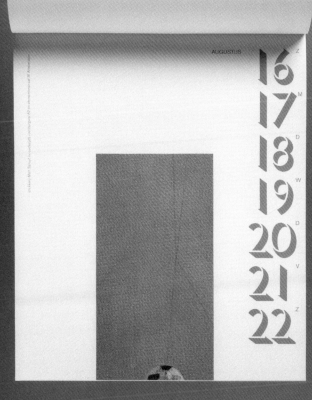

AUGUSTUS
Z
16
M
17
D
18
W
19
D
20
V
21
Z
22

SEPTEMBER
Z
6
M
7
D
8
W
9
D
10
V
11
Z
12

SEPTEMBER

13 20 Z
14 21 M
15 22 D
16 23 W
17 24 D
18 25 V
19 26 Z

drukkerij Mart. Spruyt nv oudezijds voorburgwal 62 en elementenstraat 18 Amsterdam

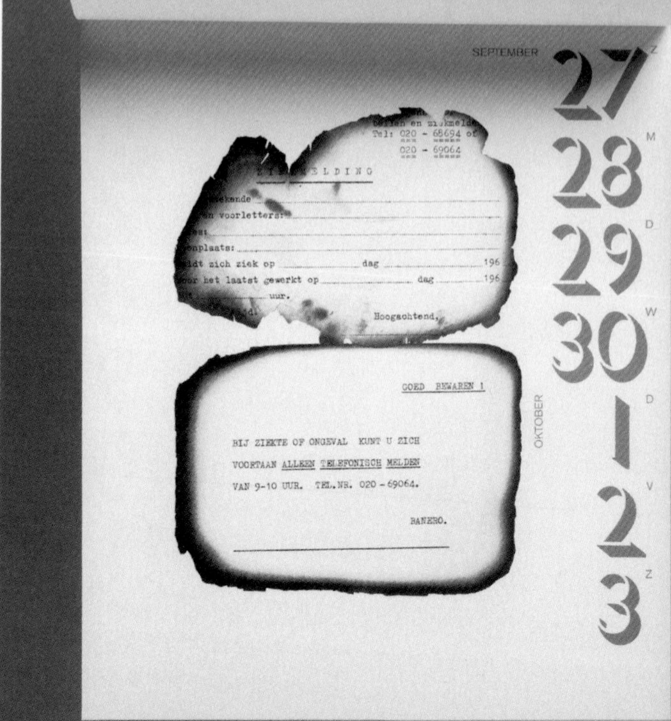

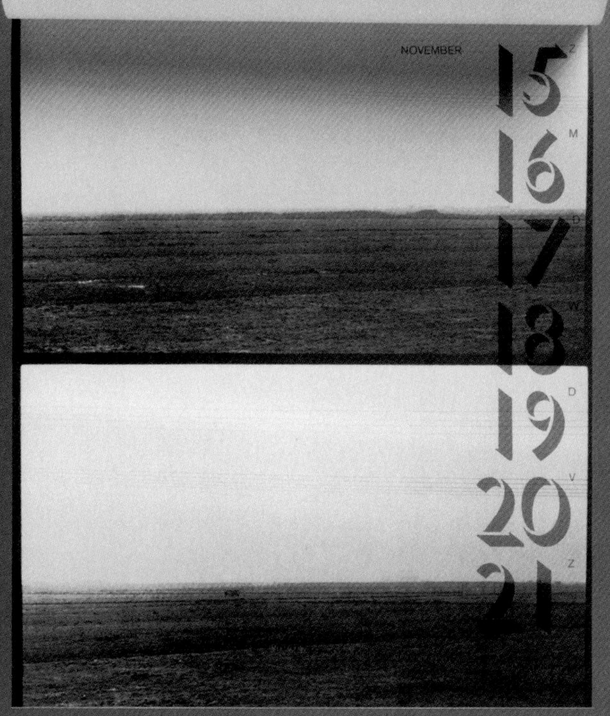

DECEMBER
27 Z
28 M
29 D
30 W
31 D
JANUARI
NIEUWJAAR
1 V
2 Z
DE NEDERLANDSCHE BANK
TIEN GULDEN

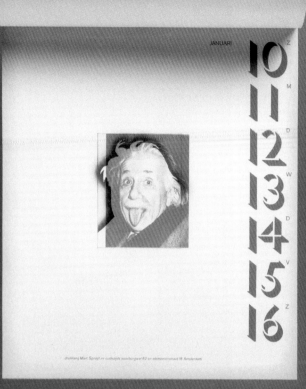
JANUARI
10 Z
11 M
12 D
13 W
14 D
15 V
16 Z

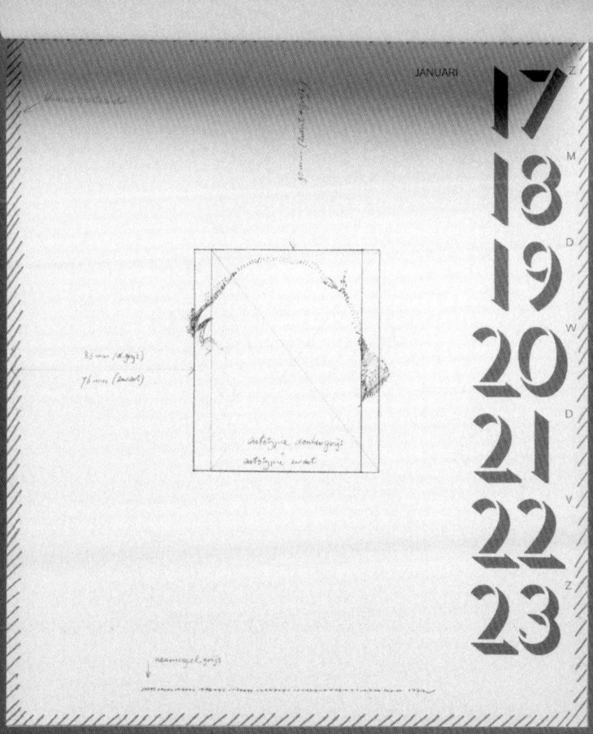
JANUARI
17 Z
18 M
19 D
20 W
21 D
22 V
23 Z

JANUARI
24 Z
25
26
27
28
29
30

drukkerij Mart. Spruyt nv oudezijds voorburgwal 82 en elementenstraat 18 Amsterdam
kalender voor negentieneenenzeventig-negentientweeënzeventig

1971/72 calendar cover and pages. Publisher and printer: Mart.Spruijt. Photographs: Geertjan Dusseljee

In the autumn of 1970, Van Toorn took a trip to the Ardennes, through the province of Limburg in Belgium, where he was struck by the remarkable variations in the design of Belgian houses, boasting styles ranging from rustic to modern. Dutch houses were, by contrast, much less individualistic and more likely to be designed in the same style as their neighbours, while detached houses were less prevalent. It took several trips to scout the best locations and complete the project, with Van Toorn's assistant, Geertjan Dusseljee, an accomplished photographer, shooting the pictures according to Van Toorn's directions. Van Toorn was familiar with the industrial photographs of Bernd and Hilla Becher, which had been exhibited at the Van Abbemuseum in 1968, and his Belgian house studies for Mart.Spruijt's 1971/72 calendar display a similar concern with typology and maintaining a consistent viewpoint. Each house is viewed frontally on a rectilinear grid to stress the formal quality and artificiality of the image, and each picture is based on a dominant vertical axis, which can be central or not; the visual information is flattened as though the viewer were looking at an architect's drawing. Van Toorn had the photos printed on thin, matt document paper rather than glossy paper to add to the flatness and, when it came to the layout, he juxtaposed the pictures carefully for comparative purposes.

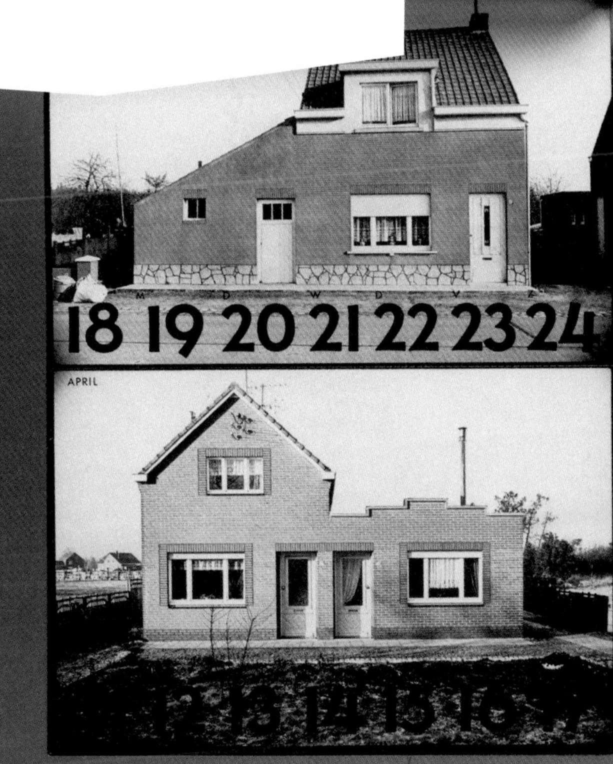

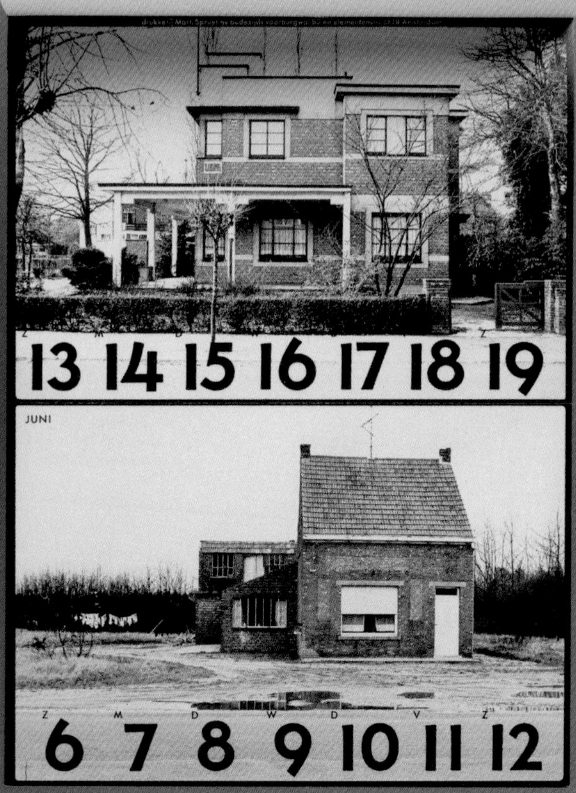
13 14 15 16 17 18 19
JUNI
Z M D W D V Z
6 7 8 9 10 11 12

JUNI
JULI
27 28 29 30 1 2 3
JUNI
Z M D W D V Z
20 21 22 23 24 25 26

JULI
25 26 27 28 29 30 31
JULI

AUGUSTUS
Z M D W D V Z
22 23 24 25 26 27 28
AUGUSTUS

drukkerij Mart. Spruyt nv oudezijds voorburgwal 82 en elementenstraat 18 Amsterdam
OKTOBER
Z M D W D V Z
3 4 5 6 7 8 9
SEPTEMBER
OKTOBER
W
26 27 28 29 30 1 2

drukkerij Mart. Spruyt nv oudezijds voorburgwal 82 en elementenstraat 18 Amsterdam
OKTOBER
W D V Z
19 20 21 22 23
OKTOBER
Z M D
10 11 12 13 14 15 16

DECEMBER
12 13 14 15 16 17 18
DECEMBER
W
5 6 7 8 9 10 11

drukkerij Mart. Spruyt nv oudezijds voorburgwal 82 en elementenstraat 18 Amsterdam
Jan van Toorn
Dusseljee en Jan van Toorn
l. van Leer & co nv. Amsterdam
Zwanenburg
MART. SPRUYT NV AMSTERDAM
oudezijds voorburgwal 82 en elementenstraat 18
FEBRUARI
Z M D
27 28 29

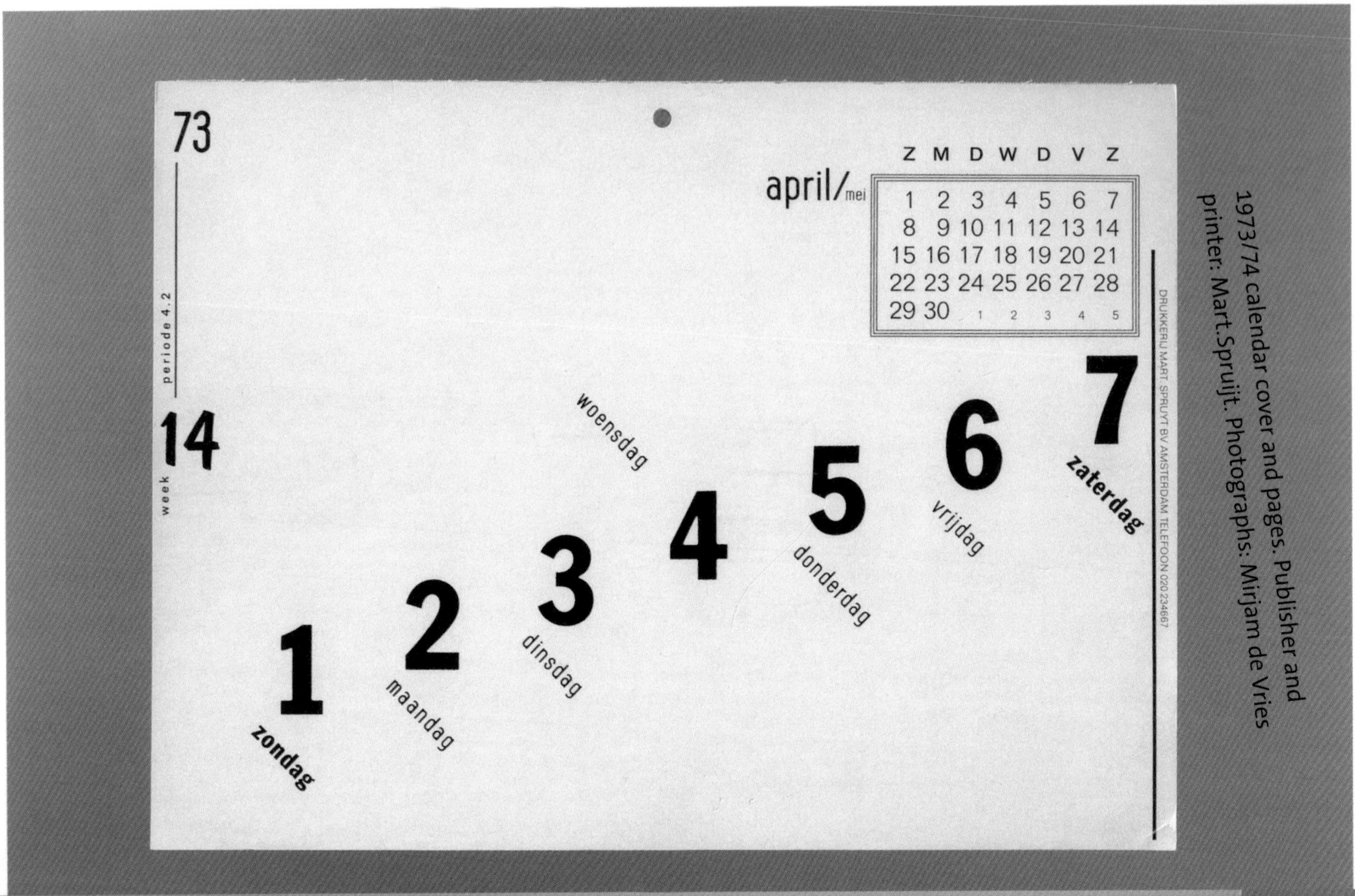

73
april/mei
Z M D W D V Z
1 2 3 4 5 6 7
8 9 10 11 12 13 14
15 16 17 18 19 20 21
22 23 24 25 26 27 28
29 30 1 2 3 4 5
week 14 periode 4.2
1 zondag
2 maandag
3 dinsdag
4
woensdag
5 donderdag
6 vrijdag
7 zaterdag
DRUKKERIJ MART. SPRUIJT BV AMSTERDAM TELEFOON 020 234667

73
mei/juni
Z M D W D V Z
29 30 1 2 3 4 5
6 7 8 9 10 11 12
13 14 15 16 17 18 19
20 21 22 23 24 25 26
27 28 29 30 31 1 2
week 19
8
9
10 donderdag
11 vrijdag
12 zaterdag
DRUKKERIJ MART. SPRUIJT BV AMSTERDAM TELEFOON 020 234667

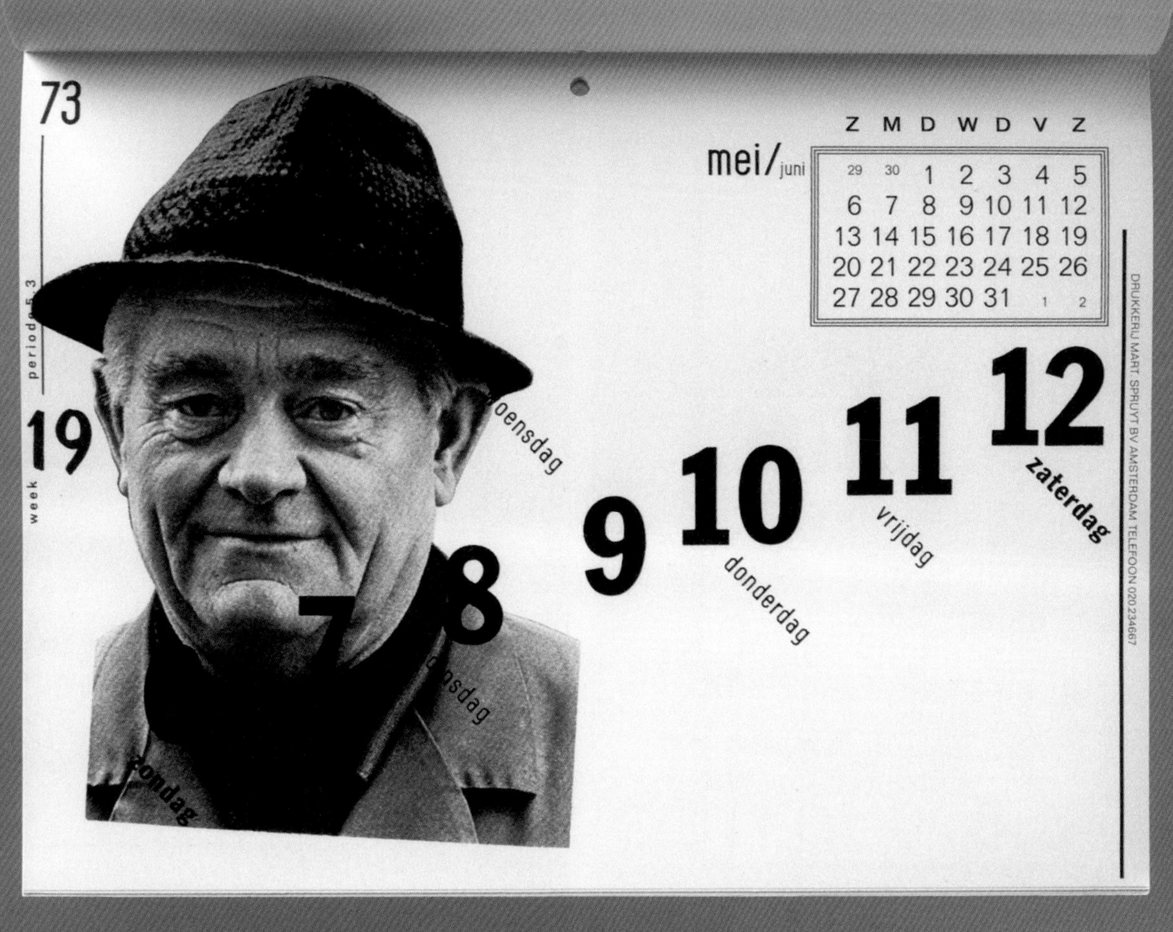

1973/74 calendar cover and pages. Publisher and printer: Mart.Spruijt. Photographs: Mirjam de Vries

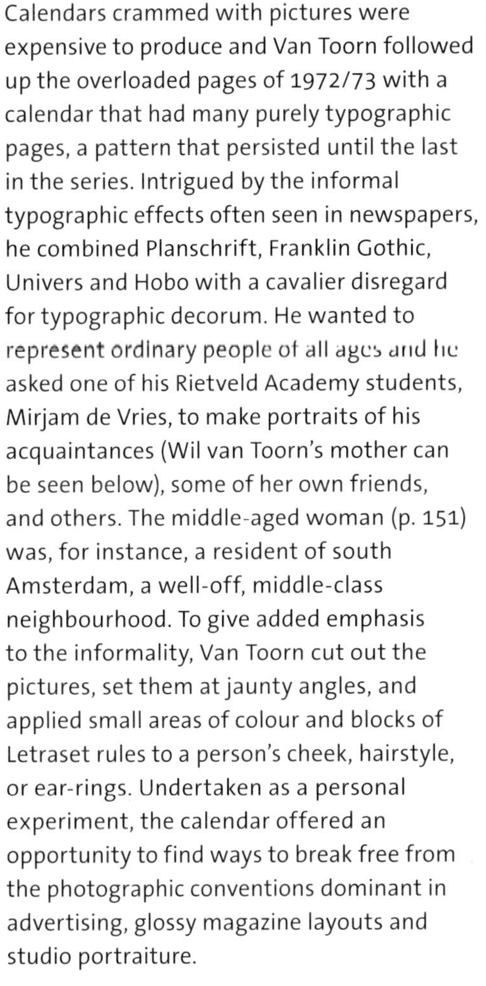

Calendars crammed with pictures were expensive to produce and Van Toorn followed up the overloaded pages of 1972/73 with a calendar that had many purely typographic pages, a pattern that persisted until the last in the series. Intrigued by the informal typographic effects often seen in newspapers, he combined Planschrift, Franklin Gothic, Univers and Hobo with a cavalier disregard for typographic decorum. He wanted to represent ordinary people of all ages and he asked one of his Rietveld Academy students, Mirjam de Vries, to make portraits of his acquaintances (Wil van Toorn's mother can be seen below), some of her own friends, and others. The middle-aged woman (p. 151) was, for instance, a resident of south Amsterdam, a well-off, middle-class neighbourhood. To give added emphasis to the informality, Van Toorn cut out the pictures, set them at jaunty angles, and applied small areas of colour and blocks of Letraset rules to a person's cheek, hairstyle, or ear-rings. Undertaken as a personal experiment, the calendar offered an opportunity to find ways to break free from the photographic conventions dominant in advertising, glossy magazine layouts and studio portraiture.

73
augustus/september
Z M D W D V Z
29 30 31 1 2 3 4
5 6 7 8 9 10 11
12 13 14 15 16 17 18
19 20 21 22 23 24 25
26 27 28 29 30 31 1
week 32 periode 8.4
5 zondag
6 maandag
7 dinsdag
8 woensdag
9 donderdag
10 vrijdag
11 zaterdag
DRUKKERIJ MART SPRUYT BV AMSTERDAM TELEFOON 020 234667

73
september/oktober
Z M D W D V Z
26 27 28 29 30 31 1
2 3 4 5 6 7 8
9 10 11 12 13 14 15
16 17 18 19 20 21 22
23 24 25 26 27 28 29
30 1 2 3 4 5 6
week 36 periode 9.4
2 zondag
3 maandag
4 dinsdag
5 woensdag
6 donderdag
7 vrijdag
8 zaterdag
DRUKKERIJ MART SPRUYT BV AMSTERDAM TELEFOON 020 234667

73
oktober/november
Z M D W D V Z
30 1 2 3 4 5 6
7 8 9 10 11 12 13
14 15 16 17 18 19 20
21 22 23 24 25 26 27
28 29 30 31 1 2 3
week 41 periode 11.1
7 zondag
8 maandag
9
10
11 donderdag loofhuttenfeest isr
12 vrijdag loofhuttenfeest isr
13 zaterdag
DRUKKERIJ MART SPRUIJT BV AMSTERDAM TELEFOON 020 234667

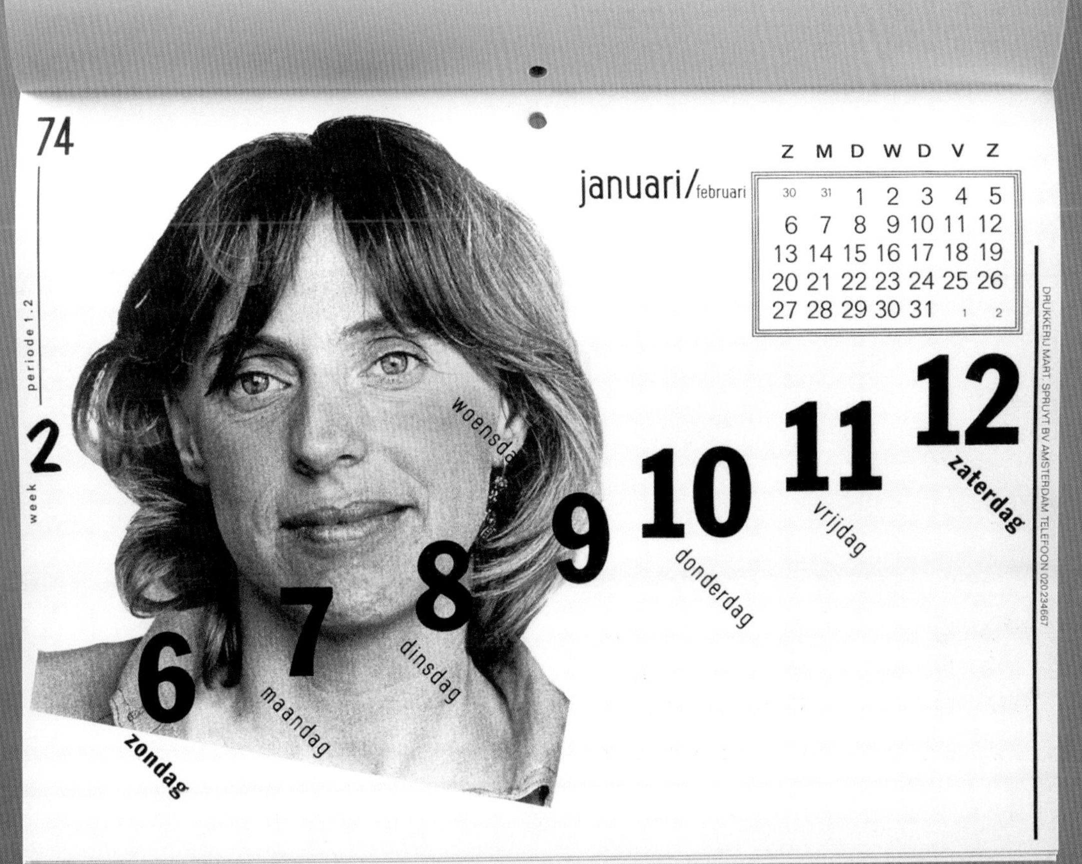
74
januari/februari
Z M D W D V Z
30 31 1 2 3 4 5
6 7 8 9 10 11 12
13 14 15 16 17 18 19
20 21 22 23 24 25 26
27 28 29 30 31 1 2
week 2 periode 1.2
6 zondag
7 maandag
8 dinsdag
9 woensdag
10 donderdag
11 vrijdag
12 zaterdag
DRUKKERIJ MART SPRUIJT BV AMSTERDAM TELEFOON 020 234667

1974/75 calendar cover and pages. Publisher and printer: Mart.Spruijt

[1974]

MAART	APRIL					
zondag	maandag	dinsdag	woensdag	donderdag	vrijdag	zaterdag
31	**1**	**2**	**3**	**4**	**5**	**6**

DRUKKERIJ MART SPRUIJT BV OUDEZIJDS VOORBURGWAL 82 AMSTERDAM 020.234667

For the 1974/75 calendar, Van Toorn returned to the political imagery that had formed a large part of the confrontational 1972/73 calendar. Drawing on photos from his own archive, he wanted to expose the ways that scenes from the theatre of contemporary politics are represented by the media. His cast of world figures, constantly in the news at the time, includes US president Richard Nixon and national security adviser Henry Kissinger, Chairman Mao, General Franco of Spain, Argentine president Juan Perón, Haile Selassie, emperor of Ethiopia, and Israeli military leader Moshe Dayan. Van Toorn was interested in political cartoons, though he wasn't himself a cartoonist, and a satirical cartooning impulse informs images such as Nixon transformed into a boxer (p. 154), or Kissinger grandly superimposed on a portrait of the 19th-century German-Austrian diplomat Von Metternich (p. 156), a figure Kissinger admired. It wasn't enough, Van Toorn believed, simply to show the photos without any signs of mediation. To make it clear that the calendar's subject was the content and codes of the pictures, signs of his own intervention had to be obvious to the viewer. He cut out images to strengthen them and made airbrush adjustments around people's outlines to stress aspects of their poses. He highlights Dutch politicians' tendency to represent themselves as ordinary workers by montaging a succession of heads on the same plain set of clothes (p. 159).

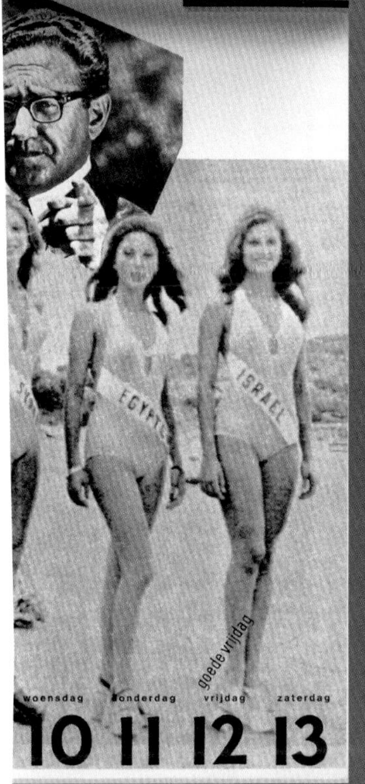

Zuid-vietnam, 1973. President Thieu legt de eerste steen van een monument ter herinnering aan de 12-jarige rol van de Verenigde staten in Vietnam
NXP/SGP496-3/28/73-SAIGON: South Vietnam's Pres. Nguyen Van Thieu ladd the cornerstone for a monument commemorating the role of the U.S. in the 12-year-old Indochina war. Looking on are U.S. Amb. Ellsworth Bunker (L) and Gen. Frederick Weyand, commander of U.S. forces in Vietnam, UPI
pasen pasen
APRIL
zondag maandag dinsdag woensdag donderdag vrijdag zaterdag
14 15 16 17 18 19 20

Met Ali Mac Graw [32]

Met Liv Ullman [?]

APRIL
zondag maandag dinsdag woensdag donderdag vrijdag zaterdag
21 22 23 24 25 26 27

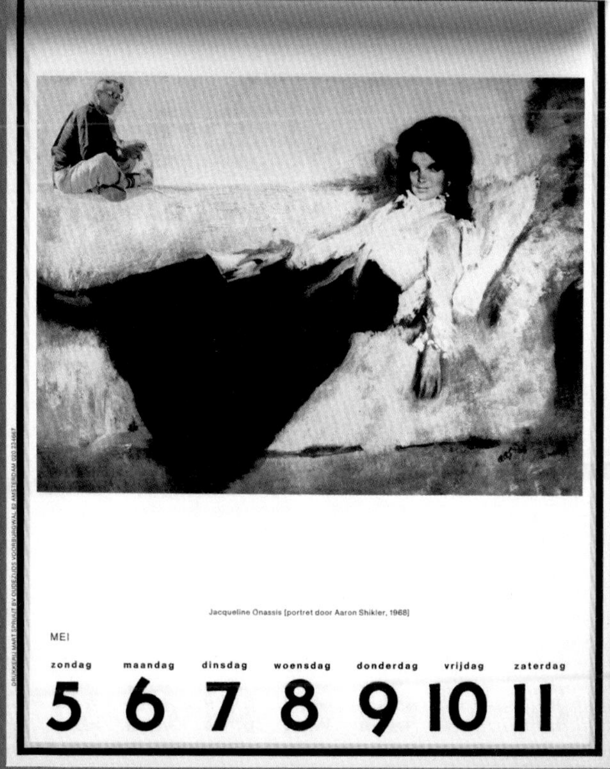

Jacqueline Onassis [portret door Aaron Shikler, 1968]

MEI
zondag maandag dinsdag woensdag donderdag vrijdag zaterdag
5 6 7 8 9 10 11

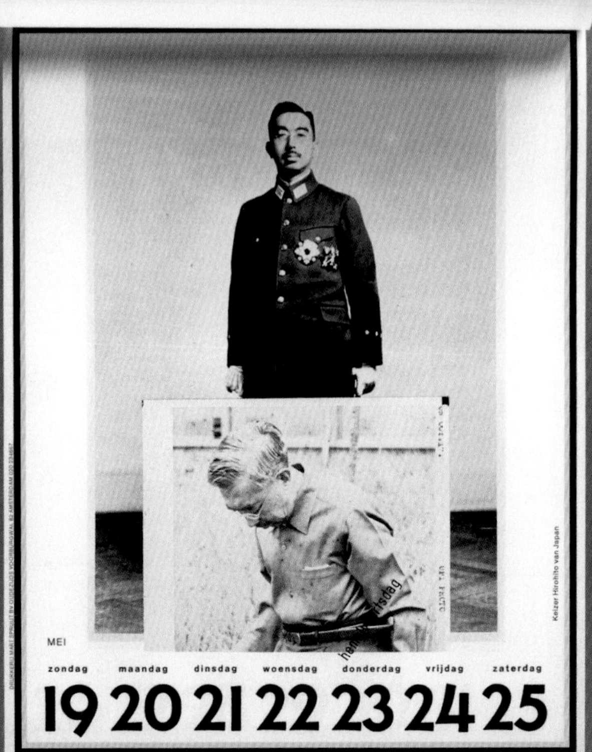
MEI
zondag maandag dinsdag woensdag donderdag vrijdag zaterdag
19 20 21 22 23 24 25
Keizer Hirohito van Japan

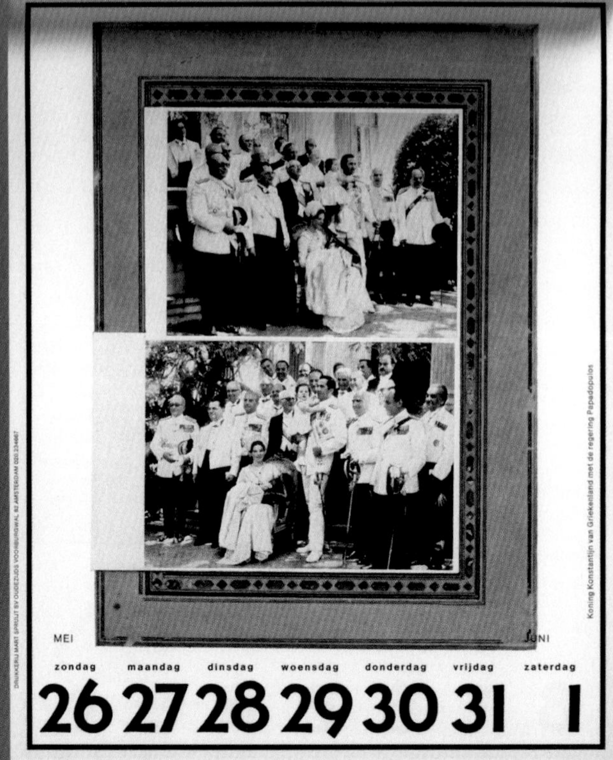
MEI
JUNI
zondag maandag dinsdag woensdag donderdag vrijdag zaterdag
26 27 28 29 30 31 1
Koning Konstantijn van Griekenland met de regering Papadopulos

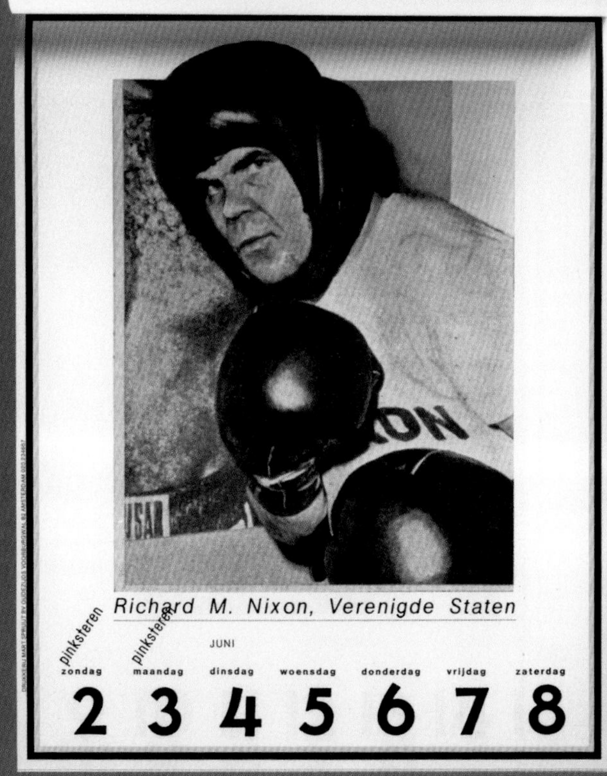
Richard M. Nixon, Verenigde Staten
pinksteren
pinksteren
JUNI
zondag maandag dinsdag woensdag donderdag vrijdag zaterdag
2 3 4 5 6 7 8

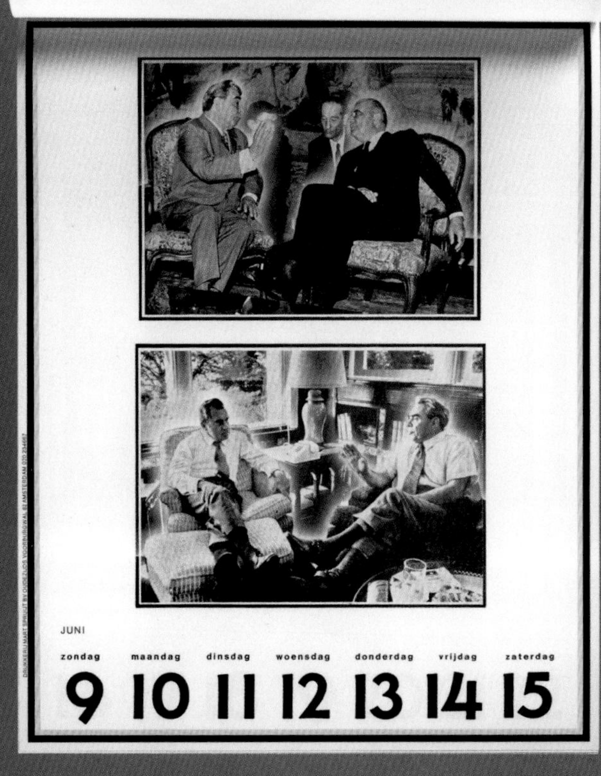
JUNI
zondag maandag dinsdag woensdag donderdag vrijdag zaterdag
9 10 11 12 13 14 15

JUNI	JULI					
zondag	maandag	dinsdag	woensdag	donderdag	vrijdag	zaterdag
30	1	2	3	4	5	6

DRUKKERIJ MART SPRUIJT BV OUDEZIJDS VOORBURGWAL 82 AMSTERDAM 020 234667

JULI
zondag maandag dinsdag woensdag donderdag vrijdag zaterdag
7 8 9 10 11 12 13

Met premier Tanaka van Japan
JULI
zondag maandag dinsdag woensdag donderdag vrijdag zaterdag
14 15 16 17 18 19 20

Kissinger à la Von Metternich
JULI
zondag maandag dinsdag woensdag donderdag vrijdag zaterdag
21 22 23 24 25 26 27

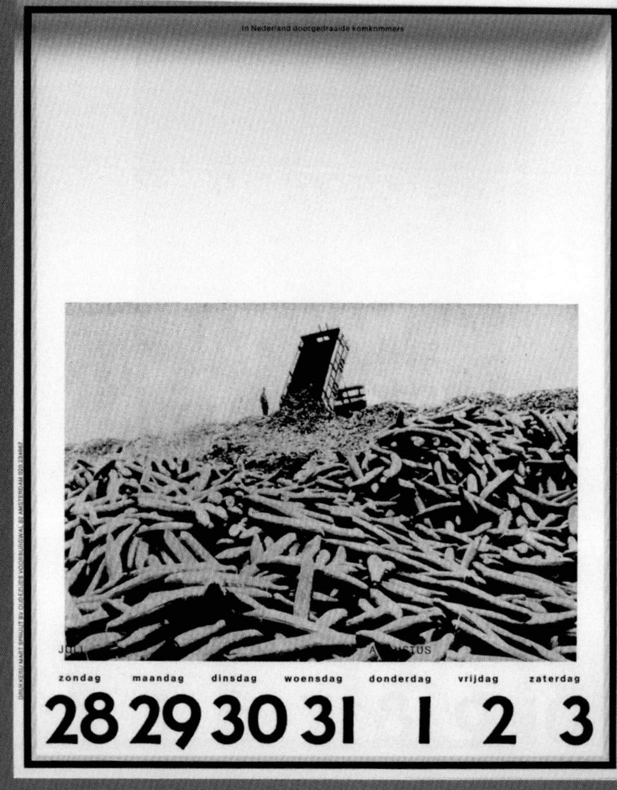
In Nederland doorgedraaide komkommers
zondag maandag dinsdag woensdag donderdag vrijdag zaterdag
28 29 30 31 1 2 3

Keizer Haile Selassie van Ethiopië
AUGUSTUS
zondag maandag dinsdag woensdag donderdag vrijdag zaterdag
11 12 13 14 15 16 17

Sjah Resa Pahlewi van Perzië
AUGUSTUS
zondag maandag dinsdag woensdag donderdag vrijdag zaterdag
18 19 20 21 22 23 24

M. Dayan, minister van oorlog van Israël
AUGUSTUS
zondag maandag dinsdag woensdag donderdag vrijdag zaterdag
25 26 27 28 29 30 31

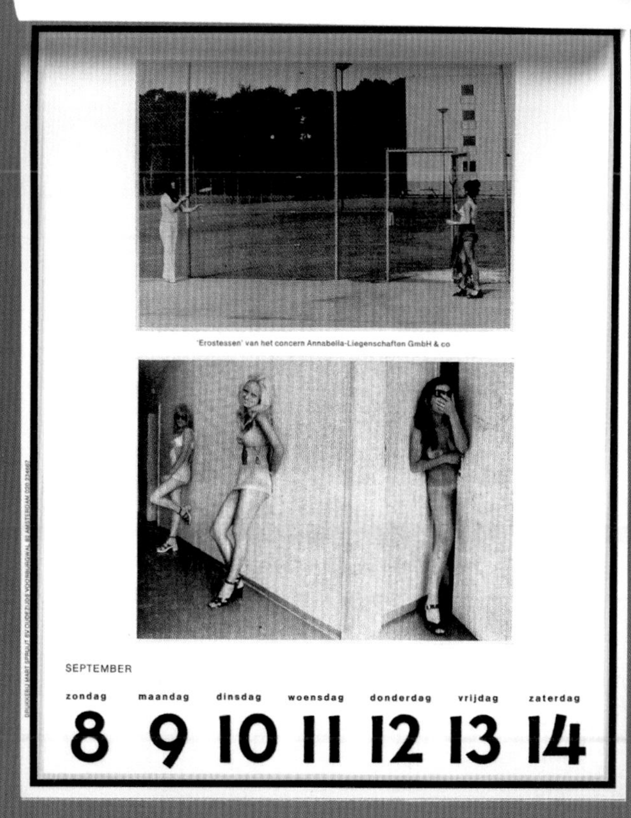
'Erostessen' van het concern Annabella-Liegenschaften GmbH & co
SEPTEMBER
zondag maandag dinsdag woensdag donderdag vrijdag zaterdag
8 9 10 11 12 13 14

Τό διακεκριμένον Phantom
הפנטום-המעולה שבמטוסים
Die berühmte Phantom
Phantom, El Modelo

Uit een advertentie van Douglas McDonnell en een stand in Israël, 1973

SEPTEMBER

zondag	maandag	dinsdag	woensdag	donderdag	vrijdag	zaterdag
15	16	17	18	19	20	21

DRUKKERIJ MART SPRUIJT BV OUDEZIJDS VOORBURGWAL 82 AMSTERDAM 020 234667

FLY THE DIFFERENCE
zondag
zaterdag
22
28

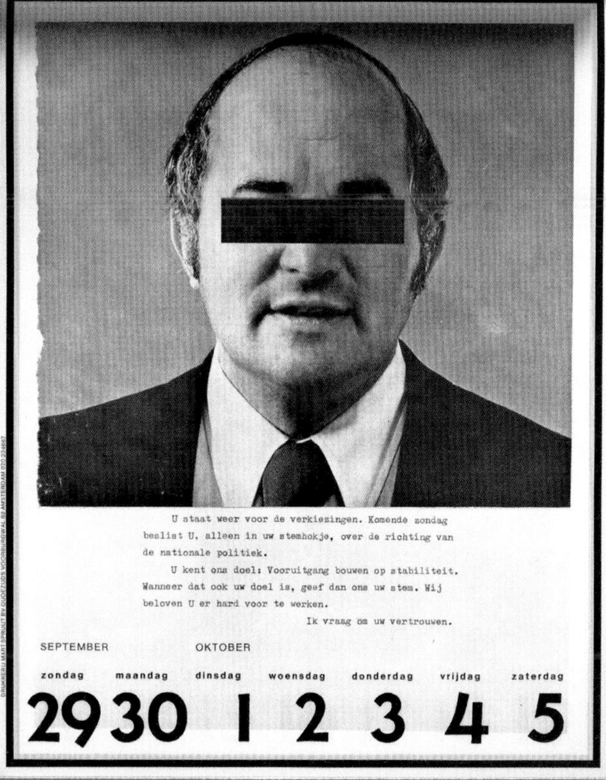

DRUKKERIJ MART SPRUIJT BV OUDEZIJDS VOORBURGWAL 82 AMSTERDAM 020 234687
U staat weer voor de verkiezingen. Komende zondag beslist U, alleen in uw stemhokje, over de richting van de nationale politiek.
U kent ons doel: Vooruitgang bouwen op stabiliteit. Wanneer dat ook uw doel is, geef dan ons uw stem. Wij beloven U er hard voor te werken.
Ik vraag om uw vertrouwen.
SEPTEMBER
OKTOBER
zondag maandag dinsdag woensdag donderdag vrijdag zaterdag
29 30 1 2 3 4 5

OKTOBER
zondag maandag dinsdag woensdag donderdag vrijdag zaterdag
13 14 15 16 17 18 19

OKTOBER
zondag maandag
zaterdag
27 28 29
1 2

april 1975
mei
ZO 27
MA 28
DI 29
WO 30
DO 1
VR 2
ZA 3
ZO 4
MA 5
DI 6
WO 7
DO 8
VR 9
ZA 10
hemelsvaartdag
DRUKKERIJ MART. SPRUIJT BV OUDEZIJDS VOORBURGWAL 82 AMSTERDAM

1975/76 calendar cover and pages. Publisher and printer: Mart.Spruijt. Photographs: Van Toorn

The 1975/76 calendar shows a series of pictures taken by Van Toorn in Austria, Italy, Belgium and the Netherlands. The sequence begins with images of the idealized natural environment and, as it develops, man's impact on the landscape becomes increasingly marked. While the selection of pages shown here gives a good idea of Van Toorn's intentions, in the published calendar some of the countryside images had to be moved out of the proposed sequence, into the later pages dealing with human intervention, when the job was printed a month later than planned. Each page offers slightly different views of the same location, encouraging the viewer to compare the two versions and acknowledge the arbitrariness of all points of view: where does the "truth" of a scene actually lie? Inspired by the artificial printed colour he had seen in photographs in a Chinese magazine, Van Toorn applied small amounts of red paint to some images as a subtle indication of his own presence as mediator. As with the earlier calendars, the style of both photography and printing has a calculated dullness.

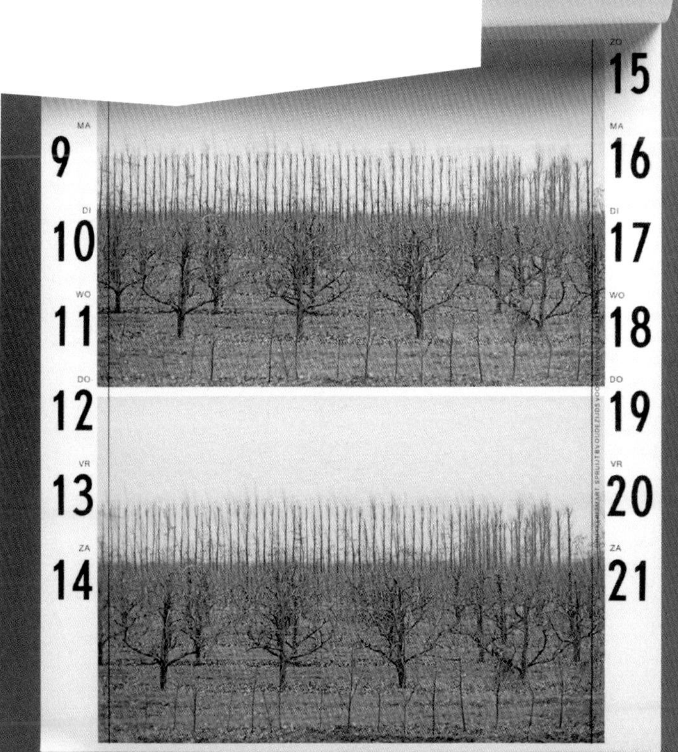

juli
augustus
ZO 20 MA 21 DI 22 WO 23 DO 24 VR 25 ZA 26
ZO 27 MA 28 DI 29 WO 30 DO 31 VR 1 ZA 2

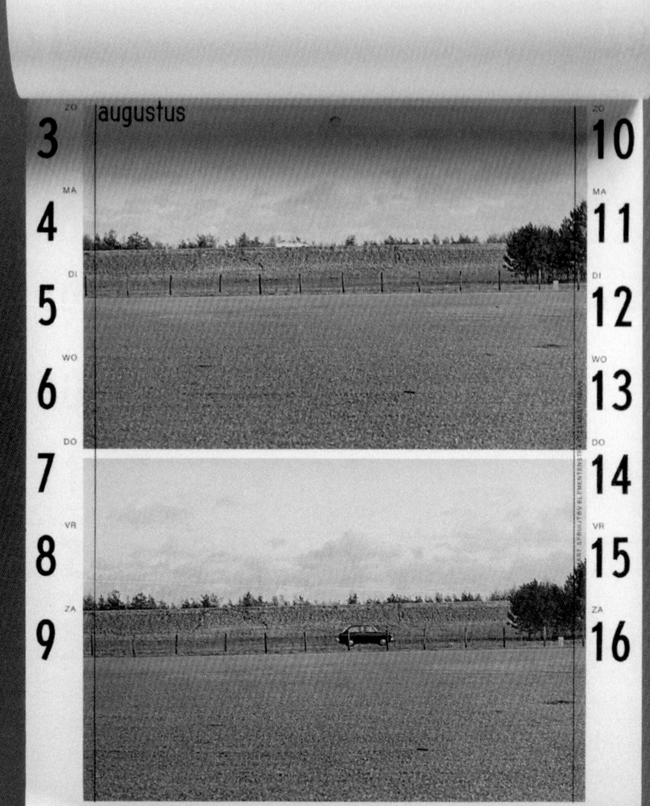
augustus
ZO 3 MA 4 DI 5 WO 6 DO 7 VR 8 ZA 9
ZO 10 MA 11 DI 12 WO 13 DO 14 VR 15 ZA 16

augustus
september
ZO 31 MA 1 DI 2 WO 3 DO 4 VR 5 ZA 6
ZO 7 MA 8 DI 9 WO 10 DO 11 VR 12 ZA 13

september
oktober
ZO 28 MA 29 DI 30 WO 1 DO 2 VR 3 ZA 4
ZO 5 MA 6 DI 7 WO 8 DO 9 VR 10 ZA 11

november
december
ZO
23
MA
24
DI
25
WO
26
DO
27
VR
28
ZA
29
ZO
30
MA
1
DI
2
WO
3
DO
4
VR
5
ZA
6
st nicolaas
DRUKKERIJ MART. SPRUIJT BV ELEMENTENSTRAAT 23 AMSTERDAM

december

ZO 7 · MA 8 · DI 9 · WO 10 · DO 11 · VR 12 · ZA 13

ZO 14 · MA 15 · DI 16 · WO 17 · DO 18 · VR 19 · ZA 20

december januari 1976

ZO 21 · MA 22 · DI 23 · WO 24 kerstmis · DO 25 kerstmis · VR 26 · ZA 27

ZO 28 · MA 29 · DI 30 · WO 31 · DO 1 nieuwjaar · VR 2 · ZA 3

februari
ZO 1
MA 2
DI 3
WO 4
DO 5
VR 6
ZA 7
ZO 8
MA 9
DI 10
WO 11
DO 12
VR 13
ZA 14

februari
ZO 15
MA 16
DI 17
WO 18
DO 19
VR 20
ZA 21
ZO 22
MA 23
DI 24
WO 25
DO 26
VR 27
ZA 28

maart
ZO 28
MA 29
DI 30
WO 31
DO 1
VR 2
ZA 3
ZO 4
MA 5
DI 6
WO 7
DO 8
VR 9
ZA 10

april
ZO 11
MA 12
DI 13
WO 14
DO 15
VR 16
ZA 17
ZO 18
pasen
MA 19
pasen
DI 20
WO 21
DO 22
VR 23
ZA 24
23
24

1976/77 calendar cover and pages. Publisher and printer: Mart.Spruijt

Drukkerij Mart.Spruijt bv Elementenstraat 23 Amsterdam telefoon 020-849495

kalender negentien zes en zeventig / negentien zeven en zeventig

notities

25 ZO

26 MA

27 DI

28 WO

29 DO

koninginnedag 30 VR

1 ZA

APRIL/MEI

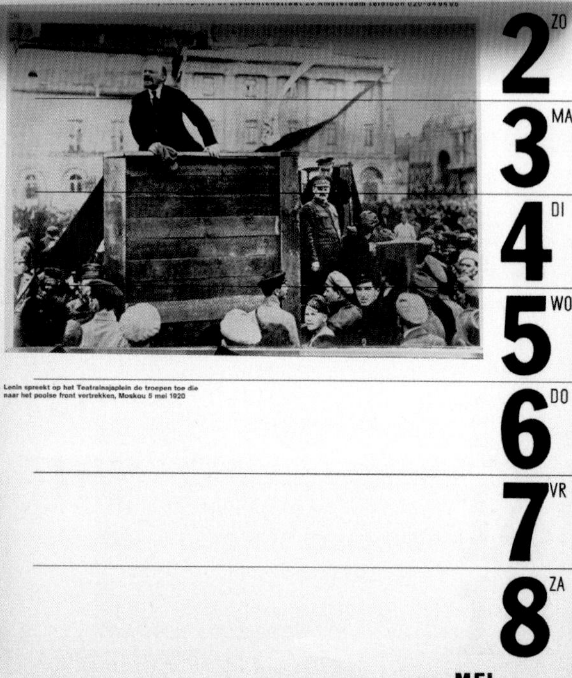

Drukkerij Mart.Spruijt bv Elementenstraat 23 Amsterdam telefoon 020-849495

9 ZO

10 MA

11 DI

12 WO

Lenin spreekt op het Teatralnajaplein de troepen toe die naar het poolse front vertrekken, Moskou 5 mei 1920 (na 1923)

13 DO

14 VR

15 ZA

MEI

Drukkerij Mart.Spruijt bv Elementenstraat 23 Amsterdam telefoon 020-849495

De ontdekking van het alfabet
zal vergeetachtigheid teweeg brengen
in de geest van de leerlingen,
omdat zij hun geheugen niet zullen gebruiken;
zij zullen vertrouwen op die buiten henzelf geschreven tekens
en niet zelf onthouden . . .

• •

Zij zullen de helden van veel dingen zijn
en niets hebben geleerd;
zij zullen alwetend lijken
en in het algemeen niets weten.
kennen

Socrates

16 ZO

17 MA

18 DI

19 WO

20 DO

21 VR

22 ZA

MEI

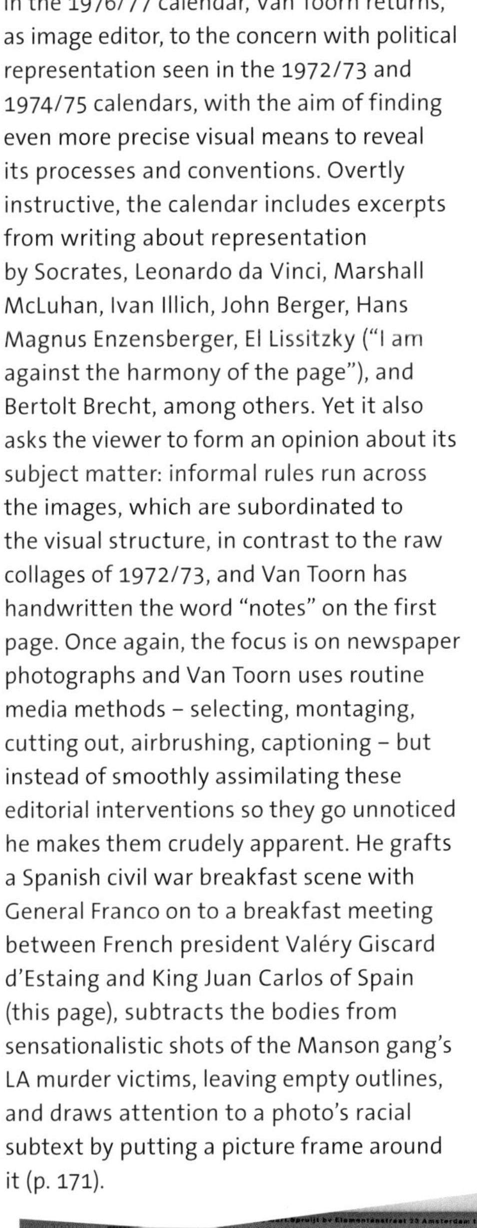

In the 1976/77 calendar, Van Toorn returns, as image editor, to the concern with political representation seen in the 1972/73 and 1974/75 calendars, with the aim of finding even more precise visual means to reveal its processes and conventions. Overtly instructive, the calendar includes excerpts from writing about representation by Socrates, Leonardo da Vinci, Marshall McLuhan, Ivan Illich, John Berger, Hans Magnus Enzensberger, El Lissitzky ("I am against the harmony of the page"), and Bertolt Brecht, among others. Yet it also asks the viewer to form an opinion about its subject matter: informal rules run across the images, which are subordinated to the visual structure, in contrast to the raw collages of 1972/73, and Van Toorn has handwritten the word "notes" on the first page. Once again, the focus is on newspaper photographs and Van Toorn uses routine media methods – selecting, montaging, cutting out, airbrushing, captioning – but instead of smoothly assimilating these editorial interventions so they go unnoticed he makes them crudely apparent. He grafts a Spanish civil war breakfast scene with General Franco on to a breakfast meeting between French president Valéry Giscard d'Estaing and King Juan Carlos of Spain (this page), subtracts the bodies from sensationalistic shots of the Manson gang's LA murder victims, leaving empty outlines, and draws attention to a photo's racial subtext by putting a picture frame around it (p. 171).

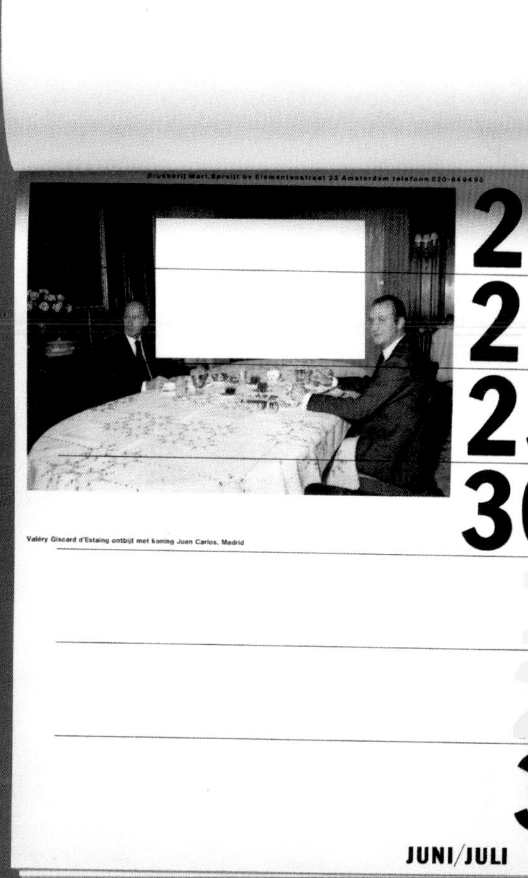

Drukkerij Mart.Spruijt bv Elementenstraat 23 Amsterdam telefoon 020-849495

Amerikaans radarstation Keflavik, IJsland

25 ZO
26 MA
27 DI
28 WO
29 DO
30 VR
31 ZA

JULI

Drukkerij Mart.Spruijt bv Elementenstraat 23 Amsterdam telefoon 020-849495

Witten in het zuiden van Afrika

8 ZO
9 MA
10 DI
11 WO
12 DO
13 VR
14 ZA

AUGUSTUS

Drukkerij Mart.Spruijt bv Elementenstraat 23 Amsterdam telefoon 020-849495

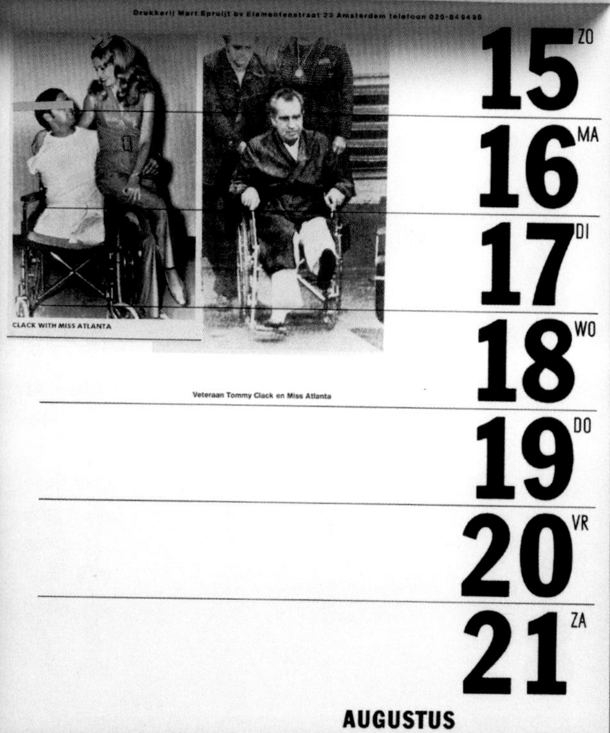

CLACK WITH MISS ATLANTA

Veteraan Tommy Clack en Miss Atlanta

15 ZO
16 MA
17 DI
18 WO
19 DO
20 VR
21 ZA

AUGUSTUS

Drukkerij Mart.Spruijt bv Elementenstraat 23 Amsterdam telefoon 020-849495

Saloon aan de Prudhoe bay, Alaska

22 ZO
23 MA
24 DI
25 WO
26 DO
27 VR
28 ZA

AUGUSTUS

Drukkerij Mart.Spruijt bv Elementenstraat 23 Amsterdam telefoon 020-849495

12 ZO

13 MA

14 DI

15 WO

16 DO

17 VR

18 ZA

Het neerschieten van een syrische Soechoj-7 door een israëlische jager

SEPTEMBER

Drukkerij Mart.Spruijt bv Elementenstraat 23 Amsterdam telefoon 020-849495
19 ZO
20 MA
21 DI
22 WO
23 DO
24 VR
Het neerschieten van een syrische Soechoj-7 door een israëlische jager
25 ZA
SEPTEMBER

Drukkerij Mart.Spruijt bv Elementenstraat 23 Amsterdam telefoon 020-849495
26 ZO
27 MA
28 DI
'Cruise missile'
29 WO
30 DO
1 VR
2 ZA
SEPTEMBER/OKTOBER

Drukkerij Mart.Spruijt bv Elementenstraat 23 Amsterdam telefoon 020-849495
10 ZO
11 MA
SCV 1
12 DI
13 WO
14 DO
Terugkeer op de zomer-residentie
15 VR
16 ZA
OKTOBER

Drukkerij Mart.Spruijt bv Elementenstraat 23 Amsterdam telefoon 020-849495
17 ZO
18 MA
19 DI
20 WO
21 DO
De Piëta gerestaureerd na de vernieling door een hongaars emigrant
22 VR
23 ZA
OKTOBER

Drukkerij Mart.Spruijt bv Elementenstraat 23 Amsterdam telefoon 020-849495

De luchtzak-test

①

②

③

28 ZO
29 MA
30 DI
1 WO
2 DO
3 VR
4 ZA

NOVEMBER/DECEMBER

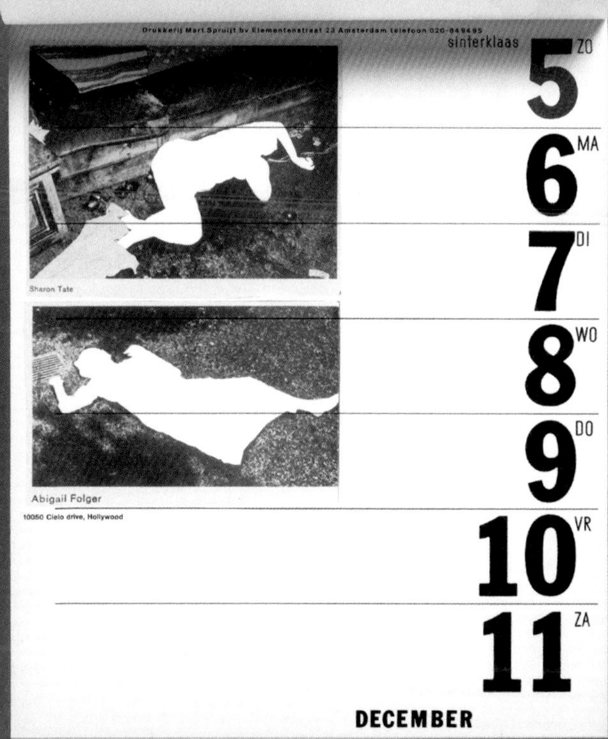

Sharon Tate

Abigail Folger

10050 Cielo drive, Hollywood

Drukkerij Mart.Spruijt bv Elementenstraat 23 Amsterdam telefoon 020-849495
kerstmis
26 ZO
DOW
27 MA
28 DI
29 WO
30 DO
31 VR
nieuwjaar
1 ZA
DECEMBER/JANUARI

Gerald Ford op ziekenbezoek bij zijn vrouw

Drukkerij Mart.Spruijt bv Elementenstraat 23 Amsterdam telefoon 020-849495
23 ZO
24 MA
25 DI
26 WO
27 DO
28 VR
29 ZA
Kenia, 1975, Alles is erg veranderd!
JANUARI

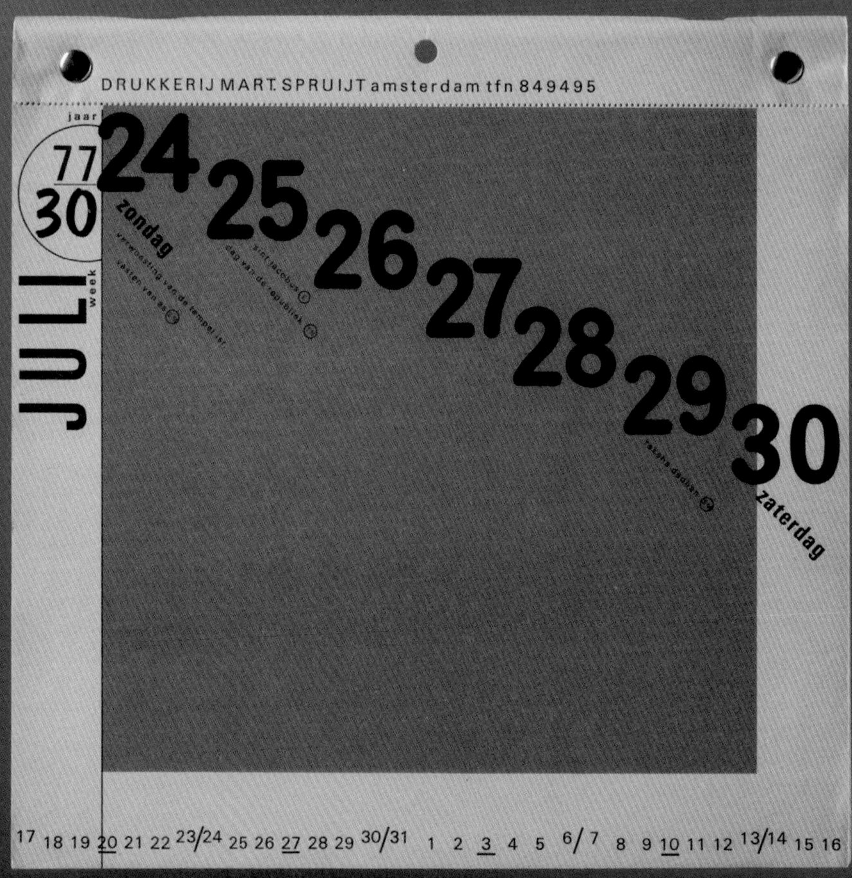

1977/78 calendar cover and pages. Publisher and printer: Mart.Spruijt

The publication of the Mart.Spruijt calendar, which usually took place in April or May, was delayed until July 1977. Changes of political thinking at the company and a growing mood of public conservatism in the Netherlands made it increasingly awkward to send politically provocative calendars to clients. Van Toorn's typographical solution, a belated response to Wim Crouwel's criticisms of the 1973/74 calendar's typography, combines Univers, an informal brush script, and a modified version of Din for the numbers. Avoiding overt social and political statements, the final calendar lists religious and national holidays – Turkish, Moroccan, Tunisian, Israeli, Portuguese, Spanish, Yugoslavian, and so on – for different communities in the Netherlands. The printer's clients received this early example of multiculturalism without complaint.

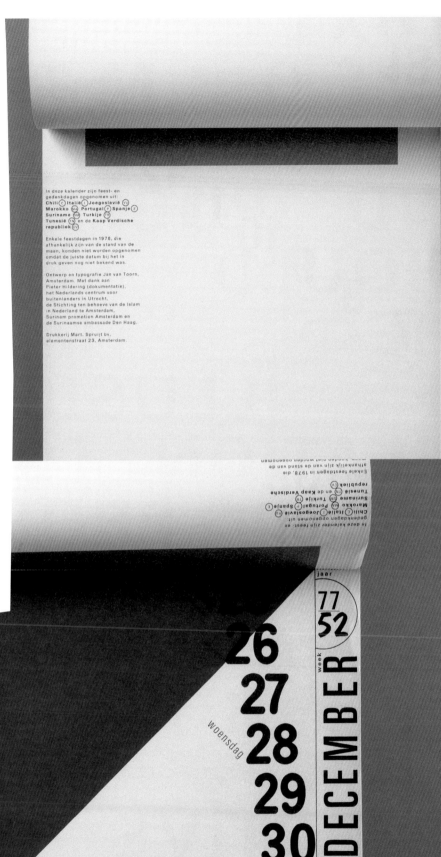

"TEXT AND INFORMATION ABOUT EXHIBITIONS AND PUBLICATIONS SHOULD PRESENT THE MINIMUM OF ILLUSION IN RELATION TO WHAT IS BEING PROFFERED. IT SHOULD BE NARRATIVE WITHOUT DETRACTING FROM THE OBJECTIVE VALUE."

Art and artifice

Jan van Toorn

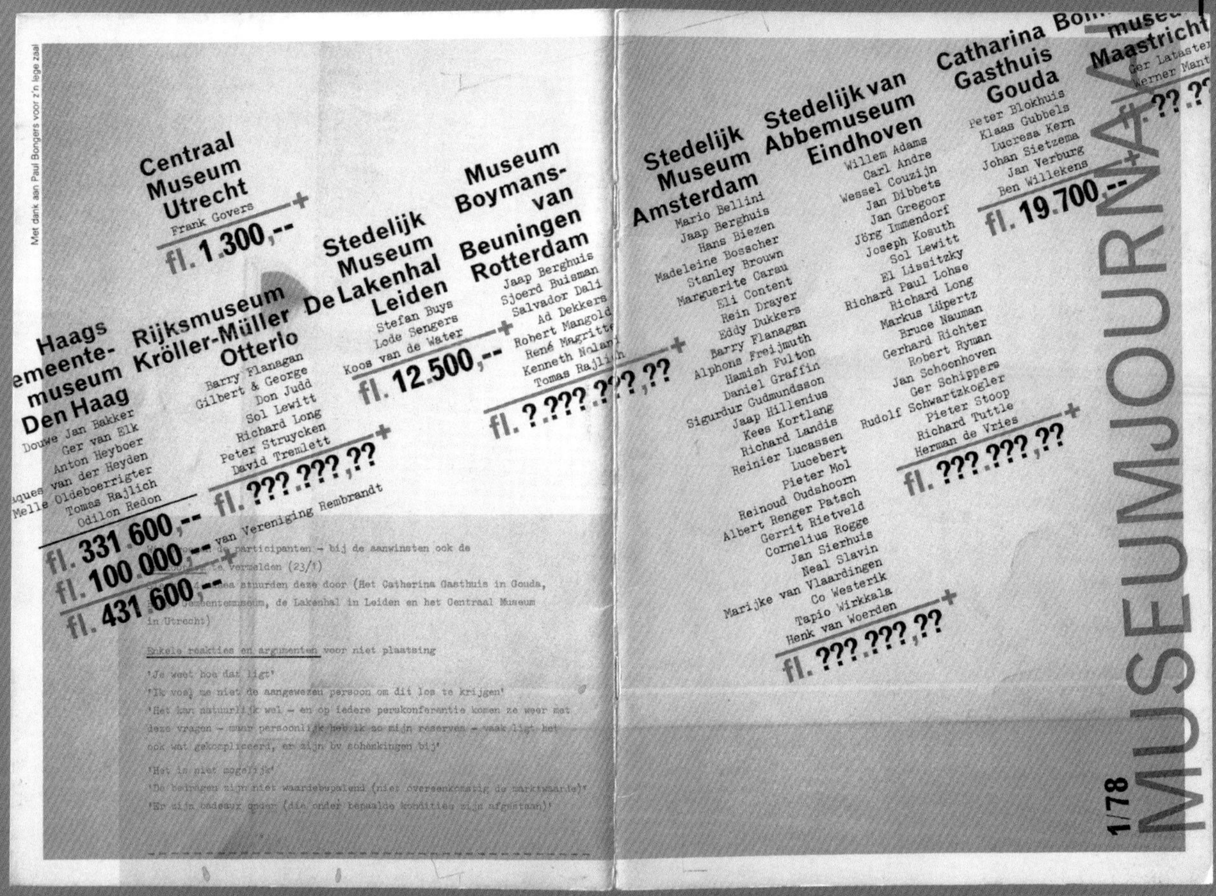

Museumjournaal vol. 23 no. 1. Cover, front and back, February 1978. Publisher: Stichting Kunstpublikaties. Design: Swip Stolk and Van Toorn

Museumjournaal vol. 23 no. 3. Cover, front and back, June 1978. Publisher: Stichting Kunstpublikaties

Museumjournaal vol. 23 no. 5. Cover, front and back, October 1978. Publisher: Stichting Kunstpublikaties

Museumjournaal vol. 23 no. 6. Cover, front and back, December 1978. Publisher: Stichting Kunstpublikaties

Museumjournaal vol. 24 no. 1. Cover, front and back, February 1979. Publisher: Stichting Kunstpublikaties

Museumjournaal vol. 24 no. 2. Cover, front and back, April 1979. Publisher: Stichting Kunstpublikaties

Cees Hamelink in De mythe van de vrije informatie [1978]:

De informatiemedia bieden vensters op een sterk gereduceerde en vertekende wereld.
Hun beelden van de wereld dragen weinig bij tot het verkrijgen van inzicht in de bestaande maatschappelijke verhoudingen en hoe deze met de eigen situatie van de mediaconsument verbonden zijn.

/.../Tenslotte lijkt het ook mogelijk binnen de bestaande structuren het gesprek te openen over de onaantastbaarheid van de professionele normen. De beroepswereld van de informatieproducenten is in dit opzicht nogal defensief en lichtgeraakt en heeft de neiging zich te verschuilen achter de autonomie en magie van de professie.

MUSEUMJOURNAAL
4
79

Museumjournaal vol. 24 no. 4. Cover, front and back, June 1979. Publisher: Stichting Kunstpublikaties

Museumjournaal vol. 24 no. 5. Cover, front and back, August 1979. Publisher: Stichting Kunstpublikaties

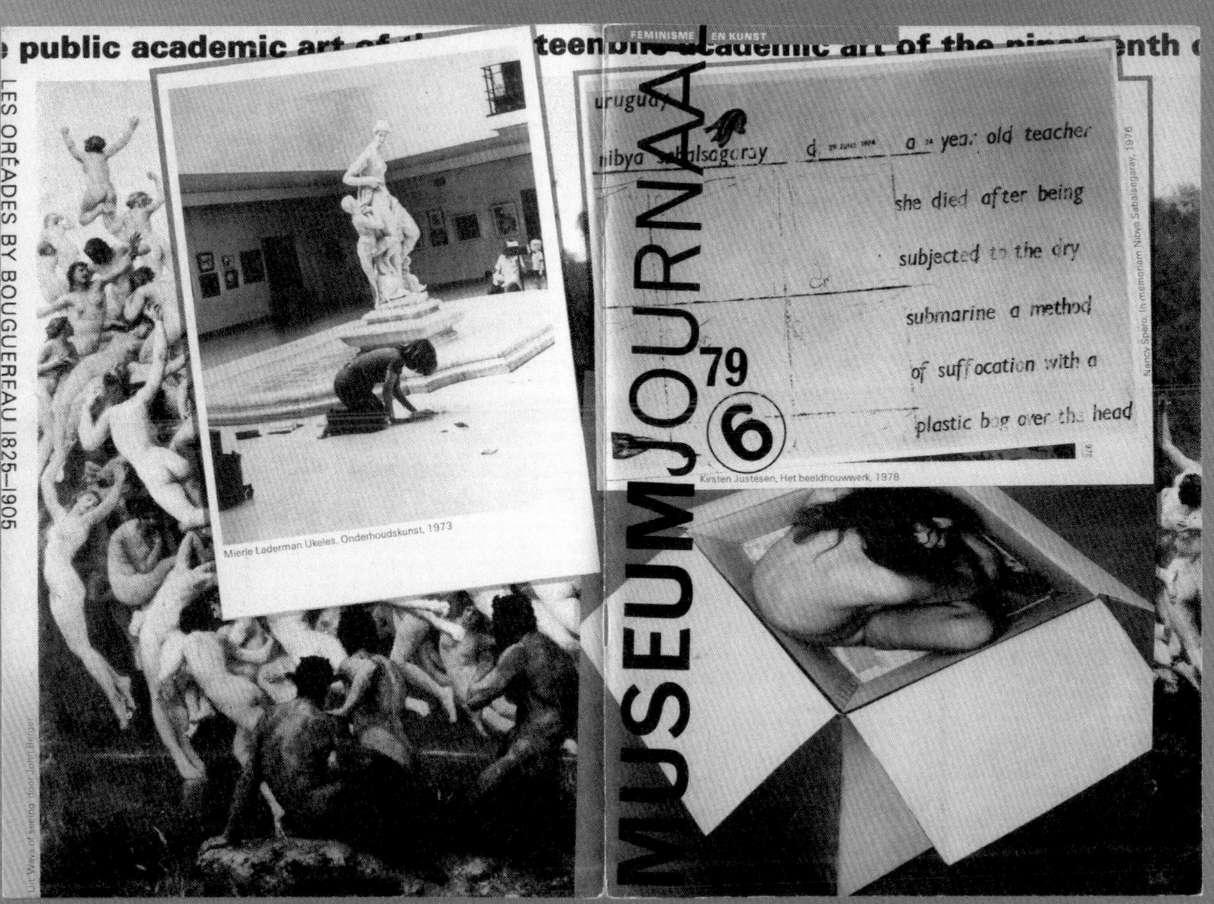

Museumjournaal vol. 24 no. 6. Cover, front and back, November 1979. Publisher: Stichting Kunstpublikaties

Museumjournaal series 25 no. 3. Cover, front and back, April 1980. Publisher: Stichting Kunstpublikaties

Dutch Art + Architecture Today no. 7. Cover, June 1980.
Publisher: Netherlands Ministry for Cultural Affairs, Recreation and Social Welfare

Bureau Beeldende Kunst Buitenland
Visual Arts Office for Abroad

Dutch Art+Architecture Today

p.o.box 2242 1000 CE Amsterdam The Netherlands

IMPRIMÉ

Port payé Eindhoven

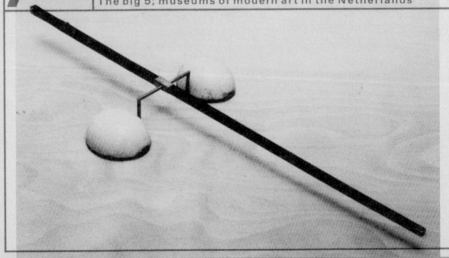

7 '80
JUNE

ART: Pieter Holstein, image-maker / A changing order; The constructive in Dutch sculpture / Carel Visser, recent sculptures / Abramović / Ulay / ARCHITECTURE: Labyrinth and square; the architectural story of Aldo van Eyck / A+A: The big 5; museums of modern art in the Netherlands

Dutch Art + Architecture Today no. 17. Cover sealed and torn open, May 1985. Publisher: Netherlands Ministry of Welfare, Health and Cultural Affairs

Dutch Art + Architecture Today no. 9. Magazine spreads, September 1981. Publisher: Netherlands Ministry for Cultural Affairs, Recreation and Social Welfare. Design assistance: Piet van Meijl

4. Circle developing towards a Square, 1970

AD DEKKERS
Nieuwpoort 1938 – Gorinchem 1974
Group exhibitions (a selection)
Documenta 1968
Amsterdam-Paris-Düsseldorf Guggenheim Museum, New York, 1972
One man exhibitions (a selection)
Gemeentemuseum, The Hague, 1972 (with catalogue)
Stedelijk van Abbemuseum, 1974 (with catalogue)

Fig. 1: J.P. Smid, Kunsthandel Monet, Amsterdam.
Fig. 2: Private Collection.
Fig. 3: Museum Boymans-van Beuningen, Rotterdam.
Fig. 5: Municipal Museum, The Hague.
Fig. 6: McCrory Corporation, New York.
Fig. 7: Collection Martin Visser, Bergeyk.
Fig. 8: Estate of the artist.

2

CAREL BLOTKAMP

About Ad Dekkers

Ad Dekkers has featured in DA+AT before. In no. 2 (December 1977), Paul Hefting wrote about the two relief walls which Dekkers designed for the new wing of the Kröller-Müller Museum in Otterlo a few years before his premature death in 1974. The same writer discussed constructive tendencies in Dutch sculpture in the sixties and seventies in no. 7 of June 1980, naming Dekkers as one of the most important exponents. In both cases only a fragmentary impression of his art could be given, understandably so due to the limited scope and specific context of the articles. The retrospective to be given in December 1981 in Amsterdam's Stedelijk Museum and subsequently in some museums abroad is a good reason for taking a fresh look at the work of this artist.

Dekkers' work used to be regarded as exemplifying systematic art, an offshoot – with highly rational features – of the typically European tradition of concrete art which originated with Van Doesburg and which in the fifties and sixties flourished to quite a degree, as in Switzerland in the work of artists such as Bill and Lohse.
To be sure, Dekkers' art cannot be considered separately from that tradition, but particularly in its mature phase it is far more complex, and strongly determined internally by personal, non-rationalistic considerations and externally by his reflection on the contemporary developments usually referred to as minimal art and conceptual art.
Indubitably, the sources of Dekkers' early work are in pre-war abstract art. Born in 1938 and trained in the mid-fifties as a graphic designer at the Rotterdam Art Academy, Dekkers embarked on a career as a free artist in 1960. That same year, two changes with far-reaching consequences occurred. First of all he proceeded from an accurate, naturalistic reproduction of visible reality via stylization towards an abstract design in which he used geometric shapes almost exclusively. Secondly, he started to make reliefs instead of paintings, due to his dissatisfaction with the illusory character of painting and to his need for concrete forms and materials – motivations which had been important to artists before him such as Biederman, Baljeu and other structuralists and were so at about the same time for Americans such as Judd, LeWitt and Morris.
Dekkers' first abstract work demonstrated his great admiration for the classical masters of the genre such as Mondrian, Arp and Nicholson. His preferences were chiefly intuitive and developed in a relative state of isolation. He had not received much encouragement in that direction at art-school, nor had he had much contact with similarly-minded artists who were carrying on the line of *De Stijl* and constructivism. That came later. This trend in Dutch art was in any case exiguous around 1960. Contrary to expectation, the influence of *De Stijl* was fairly marginal in its native country. Free, lyrical abstraction held sway in the Netherlands as it did everywhere else. Dekkers arrived at his contrariwise choice of models from visits to museums such as the Kröller-Müller with its rich collection of classical moderns, and from what he saw and read in books and journals; the reason, however, lay deeper. The work of artists such as Mondrian satisfied his ingrained need for clarity and order, a need which was

2. Transition from Circle to Square, 1967

Translated by RUTH KOENIG

3

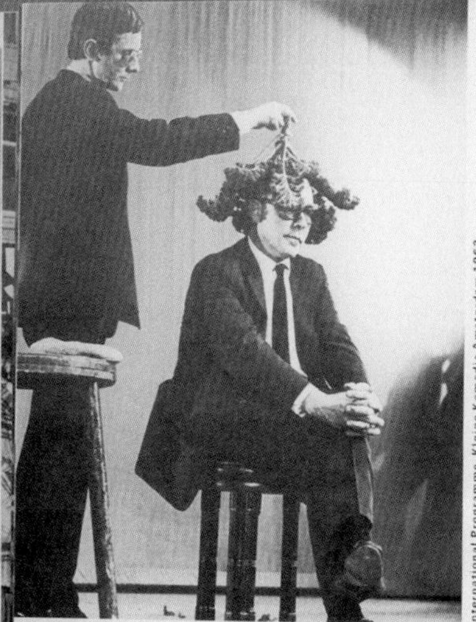

International Programme, Kleine Komedie Amsterdam 1963. 13 façons d'employer le crame de Emmett Williams (Robert Filliou), carried out by Willem de Ridder and Emmett Williams

Stanley Brouwn, Galerie Amstel 47, Amsterdam, 1964

programme for young people **Hoepla** (1967) for the VPRO broadcasting organization, he realized his adynamic ideas before an audience of millions of viewers. Simply showing a nude girl on the screen was at that time still considered so outrageous that the matter was raised in Parliament. It was the first step toward the mass popularization of ideas that had originated in a small Fluxus circle.
With his later TV shows Schippers made himself popular with a large public, which soo caught on to the humour of double-edged trivialities.
It is fair to say that in Holland, more than anywhere else, the Fluxus and Happening concepts succeeded in invading the mass culture of the sixties – nowhere have the limits of Art been stretched so far.

18

19

Translated by RUTH KÖNIG

Dick Raaijmakers
The electric method

THE PRINCIPLE OF THE METHOD
Most components in our modern electric apparatus can be reduced to superposed elementary archetypal shapes (plane, spheres, lines, loops and points). The kind of superposition and the choice of shape provides the component's purpose and name: transistor, inductor, capacitor, resistor, conductor and so forth.
Superposing archetypal shapes not only produces constructions with a particular electro-physical effect but also, albeit on a miniature scale, veritable edifices of quite considerable plastic-architectonic quality.

Especially in the early days of the development of electric apparatus this formal quality was in perfect balance with the effect and behaviour of the apparatus.

Not for long, though. Our modern technology has completely encapsulated the archetypal appearance of the modern electronic component. (Nowadays a chip consists in terms of plasticity of 99.9% case and 0.1% content. No wonder that the contents look more like printed matter than a three-dimensional plastic shape.)

My 'Electric Method' project aims at visualizing the original common roots of both qualities – technical and visual – of elementary superpositions. The use of R.W. Pohl's illustrations is an example.

Dutch Art + Architecture Today no. 19. Magazine spread, June 1986. Publisher: Netherlands Ministry of Welfare, Health and Cultural affairs. Design assistance: Piet van Meijl

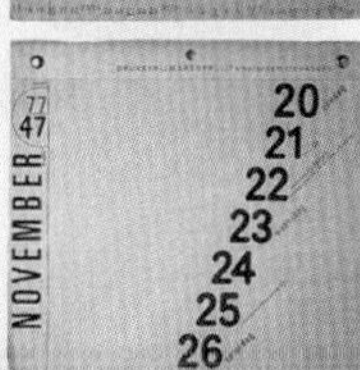

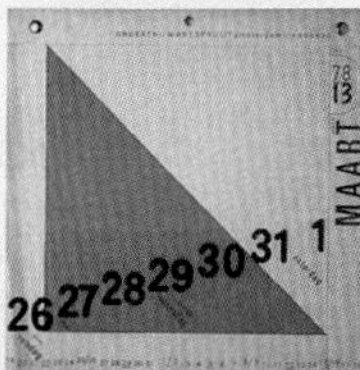

Three pages from the Mart. Spruyt calendar 1977-1978

Eight stills from the TV programme 'Macchiavelli, or the ways of the world', 1977-1978

Two pages from the Mart. Spruyt calendar 1974-1975

JETTEKE BOLTEN

Jan van Toorn medium + message

Communicare necesse est. . . vivere non est necesse. I came across this maxim in one of the handsome numbers of Range, the Philips telecommunications journal which Jan van Toorn (b. 1932) designed between 1964 and 1971.[1]
The remark of course refers to the survival of the firm behind the magazine, but may equally well be applied to the Amsterdam graphic designer himself.
Independent since 1957, Van Toorn has developed into one of the leading graphic designers of the Netherlands. In the spring of 1985 he received the Piet Zwart prize, established in 1983 by the Total Design Foundation and awarded every two years to a Dutch individual, group or institution for stimulating contribution towards the development of one or more areas in which designer Piet Zwart, who died in 1977, had been active.[2]
It was notably Piet Zwart who after World War I gave new meaning and content to Dutch design. He designed interiors and furniture, glass and tableware, exhibition stands, postage stamps, products and packaging. Together with avant-garde artists such as Moholoy-Nagy and Paul Schuitema, Zwart introduced modern photography to the Netherlands, combining it with printing and advertising (photo-typography). He took the new (re)production techniques as his point of departure in designing for a wide public.
Jan van Toorn is a worthy successor; not only has he endowed graphic design with aesthetic meaning, his approach to form and content is based on a critical attitude towards society. 'All use of the media demands manipulation. The most elementary actions in (media) production, from the choice of the medium via recording, editing, synchronization and mixing, up to and including distribution, are all interventions in the given material. There is no such thing as unmanipulated writing, filming and broadcasting.
The question, then, is not whether the media are manipulated or not, but who manipulates them. A revolutionary design need not cause the manipulators to vanish; indeed, it ought to turn everybody into manipulators'. This remark of Hans Magnus Enzensberger's is characteristic of the mentality at the basis of Jan van Toorn's work. It is a vision of commitment which has been gaining ground since the 1960s and has made it impossible to sit on the fence in matters of society.
Marshall McLuhan's The Medium is the Message became a byword. The two tracks converge in Van Toorn's own vision, in which medium and message reinforce each other.
In practice, Van Toorn's contribution covers a long series of typographically interesting designs for products such as magazines, posters, catalogues, books, postage stamps, exhibitions, annual reports, interior and exterior design, etc. Theoretically significant is Van Toorn's role in the entire process, ranging from the idea to the realization of what he prefers to call visual communication. Neither aspect can be regarded separately, and he stresses both when mentoring new generations of designers.[3]

Jan van Toorn was born in 1932 in Tiel, a small town in the centre of a region bounded by the major rivers. He attended evening classes in Illustration for three years at the Institute of Applied Art Education in Amsterdam (the present Gerrit Rietveld Academy), but did not complete the course. Basically, his training was practical. His contact with the printing firm of Mart Spruijt proved significant.
From 1960 to 1977 Van Toorn designed and edited the firm's annual calendar, a kind of printing tradition: a printer's visiting-card, as it were, meant to display to clients the perfection of form and printing of which a firm is capable.
The free hand Frans Spruijt gave Van Toorn when he entrusted him with the calendar was partly responsible for a new form of autonomous printing, even if that sounds like a contradiction in terms.
Van Toorn's development as a typographic designer can be clearly traced in this series of calendars. **Up to the end of the 1960s,** he says, **it was real *design:* later I slowly but surely started to do other things. Tackling form more from the aspect of content, experimenting with visual means for conveying all sorts of things, on a political basis too; that's when it became much more of a laboratory situation for me.**

The subject and artwork of the **1971-1972 calendar** are striking: each week has a picture of a typical Belgian house photographed (together with Geertjan Dusseljee) head-on. This frontal photography and the consequent absence of any perspective foreshortening creates an unnerving graphic image due to the contrast between the two-dimensional facade and the illusionistic character of the photograph. This is further enhanced by the quantity. The calendar is realy a monument to anonymus Belgian architecture
For the **1977 calendar** Van Toorn used solely typographic elements, different types of numbers, letters, words and lines, with an occasional patch of colour (red or blue). He placed the dates of the week diagonally on the page at regular intervals, shifting like the hands of a clock.
This unusual layout conveyed a visual impression of the passing of time.
There was method in his madness, though! The calendar lists the most obscure high days and holidays from Chile, Italy, Morocco, Portugal, Spain, Surinam, Tunisia, Turkey, the Cape Verdian Republic and Yugoslavia. A conceptual manner of broadening people's horizons in view of the large immigrant working population of the Netherlands – for whom the calendar was surely not intended. Political involvement is even more apparent in the calendars in which Van Toorn used pictures taken from newspapers and magazines: Miss Israel cheek-by-jowl with beauties from Saudi Arabia, Syria, Egypt in 1974 (first without, then combined with the head of Kissinger, pictured further on as The Middle-East Coachman and identified with Metternich); Japan's Emperor Hirohito then and now (1974), packed with meaning for the Netherlands with its – partly – Indonesian war history.
A calendar like this is not only a time-indicator but a document of (art) history

26

Dutch Art + Architecture Today no. 17. Magazine spread, May 1985. Publisher: Netherlands Ministry of Welfare, Health and Cultural Affairs. Design assistance: Piet van Meijl

KEES BROOS

Hard Werken

'But it's so ugly . . . if only they didn't make such ugly things at Hard Werken . . .!'
This was said to me by a middle-aged graphic designer on the staff of a respectable Dutch design studio of international repute. He seemed quite shaken.
A critic on one of the national dailies wrote that Gerard Hadders – a member of the Hard Werken association – deserved to be put in jail for several years because of his graphic design, plus '. . . an extra year for designing such a repulsive cover for De Naam van de Roos [the Dutch edition of Umberto Eco's book] that I refuse to buy or read the book'.
Such violent reactions make one curious about the work of a group of graphic designers whose aim is evidently not to delight the traditional eye.

In the autumn of 1984, the Boymans-van Beuningen Museum in Rotterdam organized a big exhibition entitled Art from Rotterdam. Forty painters, sculptors, architects, photographers, graphic and fashion designers of all ages participated, either individually or as groups.
Museum director Wim Beeren introduced the event under the motto of 'a momentary glimpse of a creative city', defending what without a doubt was a highly varied presentation. The exhibition was not to be seen as an inventory of everything currently being done on the city's art scene, but as a reflection of 'the creative moment that the city is experiencing in the eighties in the field of visual art and its fringe'. This accounts for the selection of different generations and various disciplines.
Fortunately, the organizers were not out to spotlight common 'Rotterdam' features. The main characteristic was the tremendous variety of means and ends, the highly varied forms in which Rotterdam artists are currently expressing themselves. In one part of the exhibition, the 'mixed media' section, some connection was apparent. And in that section it was the members of the Hard Werken association whose products – graphic design, stage decors, furniture – displayed extremely characteristic features, even if they did not appeal to everyone.

A brief historical survey shows that in the seventies there was another hive of artistic activity in Rotterdam besides the Boymans-van Beuningen Museum: the Rotterdam Art Foundation. This institution, funded by the municipal council, was spread over a number of different locations. There were various exhibition premises and a theatre, De Lantaren, which also housed a graphic design studio and a video workshop.
Reports on the numerous exhibitions and on theatre, music, film and literature appeared in a periodical issued by the Foundation and entitled Magazijn.
For many years the paper was designed by Willem Kars, of the Grafische Werkplaats (Graphic Workshop). Visual contributions were also invited from guest designers, among them Henk Elenga en Rick Vermeulen, who will crop up again later on in this article.
Magazijn provided a fair amount of scope for experimentation with graphic and typographic tools. In addition, because the Graphic Workshop was a meeting place for a mixed bunch of graphic designers, artists and theatre people – a constant stream of film, theatre and exhibition posters rolled off the presses – intensive cooperation developed.
Before long, they decided that they would like to publish their 'own' magazine, with literary contributions and informative articles on art, film, architecture and so forth. Whilst featuring Rotterdam activities, the editors also wanted to take a look at what was going on beyond the city limits. The design – including advertisements – was to be left entirely to the editors, and that's what happened.
Willem Kars thought up the semi-ironical title of **Hard Werken (hard work).** I say

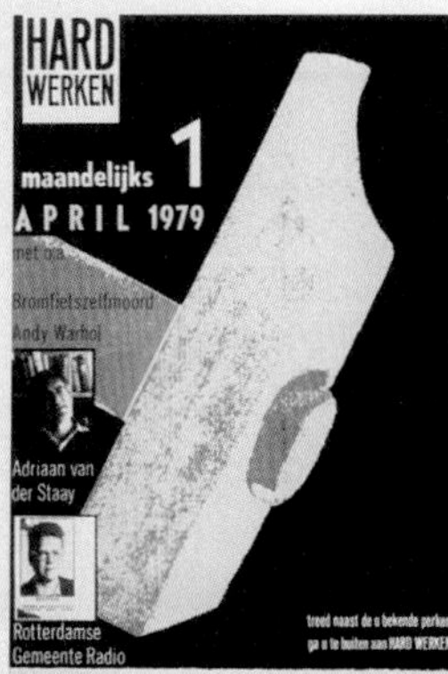

Hard Werken no. 1, April 1979

Gerard Hadders, poster 'Sauve Qui Peut', for Film International

Helen Howard, cover for catalogue 'De Kunst van het Moederschap', 1981

Translated by RUTH KOENIG

26 27

MIT NATUR ZU TUN
TO DO WITH NATURE
Visual Arts Office for Abroad / Amt Bildende Künste Ausland, Amsterdam 1979
1 Nature and Art 1967-1972
Natur und Kunst 1967-1972
Jan Dibbets, Ger van Elk, Marinus Boezem, Axel van der Kraan, Marit & Lex Wechgelaar, Sjoerd Buisman, Ger Dekkers, Anton Heyboer, Ben d'Armagnac, Gerrit Dekker, Hans de Vries
2 Nature as Process
Natur als Prozess
Hans de Vries, Krijn Giezen, Sjoerd Buisman
3 Nature as Metaphor
Natur als Metapher
Armando, Nikolaus Urban, Pieter Engels, Sigurdur Gudmundsson, Pieter Mol, Douwe Jan Bakker

NATUR ALS ARBEITSFELD / KUNST ENTSTEHT IN DER NATUR

NATURE AS A FIELD OF ACTIVITY / ART MADE IN NATURE

Mit Natur zu Tun / To Do with Nature. Catalogue cover and spreads, 1979. Publisher: Visual Arts Office for Abroad of the Ministry for Cultural Affairs

NIKOLAUS URBAN

(1942) Spijkerstraat 49, 6828 DB Arnhem
085-454.974

27 **Parrot Training**
Papageiendressur, 1976
a colour photograph / Farbfoto, 58.3 x 63.5 cm
b text / Text, 58.3 x 63.5 cm
c black-and-white photograph / Schwarzweissfoto, 58.3 x 63.5 cm
d black-and-white photograph / Schwarzweissfoto, 58.3 x 63.5 cm

28 **Meat Plan**
Fleisch-Plan, 1977
10 black-and-white photographs / 10 Schwarzweissfotos, 53.5 x 69.5 cm

Bibliography / Bibliographie: Personal Worlds, Visual Arts Office for Abroad, Amsterdam 1978

Papageiendressur
Ich habe versucht, einen Papagei einen Satz aus einem deutschsprachigen philosophischen Werk zu lehren. Es war eine achttägige Performance mit der Möglichkeit eines sofortigen Endes, falls der Vogel den Satz wiederholt hätte. Die Zuschauer wurden aufgefordert, sich auch am Unterricht zu beteiligen. Sie sprachen meist eine andere Sprache und gerieten ebenfalls in das mechanische Lernen. Normalerweise kann dieses Abrichten erst dann erfolgreich sein, wenn man das Vertrauen des Vogels gewonnen hat. Acht Tage waren eine sehr kurze Zeit. Die Erwartungen beruhten in unserem Fall auf der Tatsache, dass der Papagei ein Symbol der Wiederholung ist. 'Wovon man nicht sprechen kann, darüber muss man schweigen' ist der letzte Satz von Wittgensteins Tractatus. Er formuliert das, worüber wir schweigen müssen, das Zitat schliesst sich selbst aus.
Einer meiner Träume vor dem Abrichten: Ich war in einem Garten und fand einen Papagei. Ich erzählte ihm den Satz. Er wiederholte ihn sofort. Ein anderer Traum: Jemand bat mich, den vorletzten Satz des Buches aufzusagen.

Fleisch-Plan war eine Performance für fünf Hunde. Dieses Ereignis wurde von einer Reihe von Zuschauern beobachtet. Fleischstücke wurden in der Form von Kontinenten geschnitten und den Hunden zugeworfen. Der Rest des Fleisches wurde in kleinere Stücke geschnitten, die dann die Inseln darstellten. Diese wurden den Tieren ebenfalls zugeworfen. Einige der Hunde lehnten ihre Portionen ab, weil der Künstler ein Fremder war oder weil sie kurz zuvor gefüttert worden waren.
Die Performance fand 1977 während des Wiener Kunstmarktes am Stand der Amsterdamer Stiftung 'De Appel' statt.

Nikolaus Urban

Parrot Training
I have attempted to teach a parrot a sentence from a philosophical work in German. It was an eight-day performance, with the possibility of an immediate end if the bird should repeate the phrase. The public was invited to participate in the lesson too. They usually had another language and became involved in the mechanical learning as well. Ordinarily this training can only be succesful after one has gained the trust of the bird. Eight days was a very short time.
The expectations in our case were based on the fact that the parrot is a symbol of repetition.
'Wovon man nicht sprechen kann, darüber muss man schweigen' is the last sentence of Wittgenstein's Tractatus'. It is formulation of that of which we must be silent, the quotation excepted. 'What we cannot speak of, we must be silent about.'
One of my dreams before the training: I was in a garden and found a parrot. I told him the sentence. He repeated it immediately. Another dream: Somebody asked me to say the sentence before the last one in the book.

Meat Plan was performed for five dogs. This event was witnessed by a number of onlookers. Pieces of meat were cut into the shapes of continents and thrown to the dogs. The remainder of the meat was cut into smaller pieces which then represented the islands. These were also thrown to the animals. Some of the dogs refused their portions due to the artist being a stranger or as a result of recent feeding.
The event took place at the stand of Foundation 'De Appel', Amsterdam, during the Art Fair in Vienna, 1977.

Nikolaus Urban

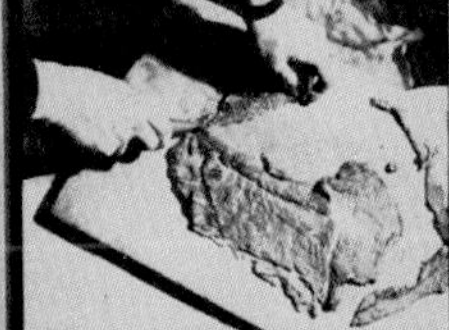

28

projekt K
KUNST KERNENERGIE
voorzichtige, vaak pijnlijke
zal hij proberen de materie waar
an is, in beelden te reorganiseren
wachting meer uitzicht te geven
komst, inzicht in het nu, over-
het verleden. Noodzakelijk in
zijn de soms gevaarlijke en
besluiten in de tijd en de reali-
et moment.
zoek van de kunstenaar zal zich
beperken tot wat hem als
wordt aangedragen uit de
verworvenheden, die op voor-
evolutie meer in zich dragen of
aten, ook al zou dat menigeen
vallig zijn en nuttig schijnen als
plezierig oponthoud!
THEO BESEMER
DE BEYERD BREDA
K
K
projekt K
KUNST KERNENERGIE
Voor de kultuurpolitiek geldt op dit moment
hetzelfde: liever een kritiek die hout snijdt
dan een vlucht naar voren in alternatieven.
Politiek strijdbare kunstenaars en gelijk met
hen opwerkende intellektuelen kunnen beter
horzels zijn op de nek van de burgerlijke
kultuur dan vrolijke cirkusartiesten in de tros
van de proletariese legers.
(een citaat van J.F. Vogelaar uit projekt K)
centrum voor beeldende
20 december 1980 t/m
openingstijden:

Projekt K. Exhibition poster, 1980. Client: De Beyerd

Theo Besemer's exhibition at the De Beyerd cultural centre in Breda, curated by Sonja Herst and Willem Oomens, dealt with the issue of nuclear power. Oomens was interested in Van Toorn's ideas and approach and asked him to design the catalogue, which can be seen as a continuation of his methods for the Van Abbemuseum. In the 1970s, the Netherlands had two nuclear power stations at Borssele and Dodewaard and *Projekt K*, short for *kernenergie* (nuclear energy), took a critical view of their presence. Van Toorn wanted the document to have some of the qualities of a handout, without completely denying its institutional origins, and the plastic plate clamped in place by two rivets toughens up the "Sandbergian informality" – seen in the lack of a conventional binding and the different reading directions – with a degree of authority. The blue text assembled by Besemer and Oomens includes documents such as press articles and statements about nuclear power from Dutch political parties. The black text discusses the relationship between science and art and the responsibility of art when it comes to nuclear power. A third discursive layer takes the form of quotations from Lenin, Brecht, Gramsci, Marcuse, Berger and others about science's role in society.

'Als een probleem te moeilijk is om op te lossen, dan kun je niet zeggen dat je het hebt opgelost door verwijzing naar alle inspanningen die je hebt gedaan om tot een oplossing te komen'.
Dit is een citaat van de Nobelprijswinnaar H. Alfven. Hij zei dit naar aanleiding van de redenering van een aantal voorstanders van kernenergie. Deze redenering kwam erop neer dat het met kernenergie wel goed zou zitten omdat er zoveel zorg is besteed aan de veiligheid in de atoomindustrie. En hij prikte die redenering vervolgens door: 'het werkelijke probleem is of de blauwdrukken van de technici zullen werken in de echte wereld, en niet slechts in een technologisch paradijs'.

Bij kunst bijvoorbeeld ligt het eenvoudig: een kunstwerk wordt nooit beoordeeld naar de inspanning die de kunstenaar heeft moeten leveren, maar altijd naar het eindprodukt.
Uiteindelijk gaat het steeds om de mate waarin wij de verschijnselen om ons heen kunnen beheersen. Niemand kan echter alles beheersen. Wij leven op dit moment in een gespecialiseerde wereld. Iedereen hoeft ook niet alles te kunnen beheersen, zolang de samenleving maar voldoende instrumenten heeft om de specialismen op elkaar af te stemmen en te voorkomen dat een specialisme de mensen (van die samenleving) gaat beheersen. Door de steeds verdergaande ontwikkeling van specialismen doen zich in de samenleving kontinu veranderingen voor. Soms zijn die veranderingen zo belangrijk dat zij de hele samenleving op zijn kop zetten; namelijk in die zin dat zo'n verandering op alle gebieden konse-

Het uit zijn boeien bevrijde geweld van het atoom heeft alles veranderd, behalve onze denkgewoonten, en we gaan een katastrofe tegemoet als er nooit geweest is.(Einstein)

Projekt K. Catalogue cover and spreads, 1980.
Publisher: De Beyerd

10

Als de nieuwe beeldentaal op een andere manier gebruikt zou worden, dan zou zij daardoor mensen een nieuw soort macht kunnen geven. Op gebieden waar woorden ontoereikend zijn, zouden wij nauwkeuriger uitdrukking kunnen gaan geven aan onze ervaringen. (Zien gaat aan woorden vooraf.) Niet alleen aan onze persoonlijke ervaringen, maar ook aan de wezenlijke historiese ervaring van onze verhouding tot het verleden: dat wil zeggen de ervaring van het trachten zin te geven aan ons leven, het proberen de geschiedenis te begrijpen, die wijzelf bewust in eigen handen kunnen nemen.

John Berger
Ways of seeing

Signaal voor kernenergie-ontwikkeling.
'Teken voor het afzeggen van de tijd', 1976

11

"Een nieuwe kultuur komt niet alleen tot stand door middel van individuele "originele" ontdekkingen maar ook en vooral door de kritiese verbreiding van reeds ontdekte waarheden; men moet deze, om het zo maar eens te zeggen "socialiseren" zodat ze de basis kunnen worden voor daadwerkelijk handelen, element van koördinatie en van intellektuele en morele discipline. Als het lukt een massa mensen ertoe te brengen de bestaande werkelijkheid koherent als een eenheid te beschouwen, dan is dat een veel belangrijker "filosofies" en "origineel" feit dan de ontdekking door een filosofies "genie" van een nieuwe waarheid die het geestelijk erfdeel van kleine groepjes intellektuelen blijft."

Gramsci

Gevaarsignaalborden bij kerncentrales, 1976

12

Het steeds weer opnieuw proberen nieuwe beelden vrij te maken, te ordenen en te visualiseren: de kunstenaar zal niet ophouden de chemie van al het visuele in zijn laboratorium te onderzoeken en er zijn produkten uit te destilleren. Gebonden aan zijn noodzakelijke vrijheid zal hij onderzoek plegen naar wat hem fascineert en uitdaagt vanuit het onzekere, toch in de zekerheid verbanden in beeld te brengen die anderen wellicht niet zien.

Zo, met voorzichtige, vaak pijnlijke ingrepen zal hij proberen de materie waar hij deel van is, in beelden te reorganiseren in de verwachting meer uitzicht te geven op de toekomst, inzicht in het nu, overzicht over het verleden. Noodzakelijk in dit proces zijn de soms gevaarlijke en gedurfde besluiten in de tijd en de realiteit van het moment.
Het onderzoek van de kunstenaar zal zich niet mogen beperken tot wat hem als materiaal wordt aangedragen uit de burgerlijke verworvenheden, die op voorhand geen evolutie meer in zich dragen of zullen toelaten, ook al zou dat menigeen zeer wel gevallig zijn en nuttig schijnen als tijdelijk en plezierig oponthoud!

Op dit moment, meen ik, wordt het maar al te zeer aantoonbaar dat de kunstenaar zelf degene zal moeten zijn, die zijn kunstenaar-zijn, de evoluerende kracht van zijn werkzaamheden en het wezenlijke aan zijn produktieve arbeid zal moeten onderzoeken in het licht van een groot aantal maatschappelijke ontwikkelingen, die hem openlijk en versluierd ommantelen.
In dat licht zullen kunst, kunstenaar, kunstprodukt

. Overigens neemt dat niet weg dat een kunstwerk onmogelijk artistiek waar kan zijn als het maatschappelijk onwaar is. Geen werk laat onafhankelijk van elkaar twee oordelen toe, een artistiek en een politiek.

Kunst kan de maatschappelijke tegenstellingen alleen in haar vormgeving uitdrukken.

De irrationaliteit van de kunstwerken wordt in het algemeen door leken op kunstgebied veel hoger aangeslagen dan door diegenen, die zich in de discipline van de werken zelf verdiepen en er iets van begrijpen."

Adorno. Kritische modellen.

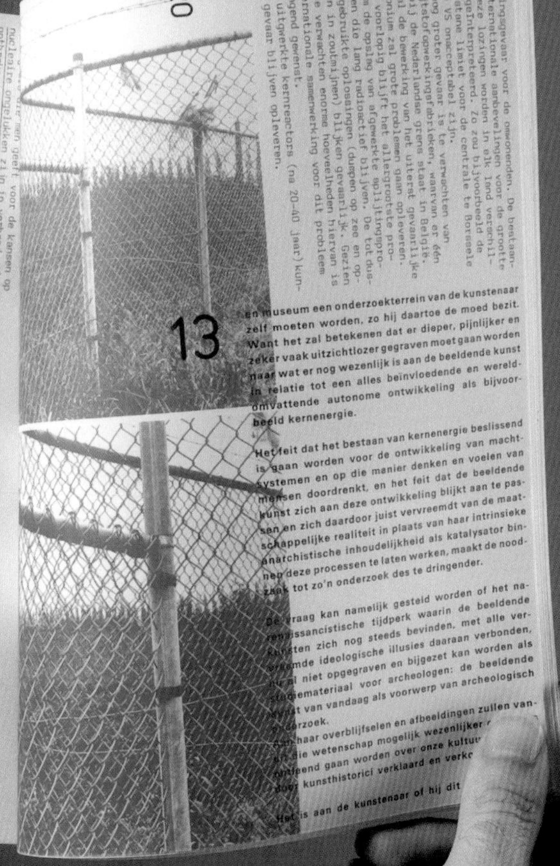

1) *Vrijheid*. Ik heb lang nagedacht over dit geheimzinnige woord, totdat ik tot het inzicht kwam dat het uiteindelijk, alles welbeschouwd, niets anders betekent dan 'vrijheid om de dood te verkiezen'. En dat is zonder enige twijfel een opzienbarende ontdekking, omdat leven een plicht is. Daarover zijn de katholieken (het leven is heilig omdat God het ons heeft geschonken) en de communisten (men moet leven om zijn plicht jegens de maatschappij te vervullen) het toch roerend met elkaar eens? Ook de natuur is het met deze stelling eens; om ons te helpen hartstochtelijk aan het leven gehecht te zijn schenkt ze ons het 'instinct tot zelfbehoud'. Ware het niet dat de natuur — dit in tegenstelling tot de katholieken en de communisten — dubbelzinnig is: ze schenkt ons namelijk tegelijkertijd een hiermee strijdig instinct — het verlangen naar de dood. Dit conflict — dat niet op een tegenspraak duidt, zoals onze rationele en dialectische geest maar al te graag zou willen, maar alleen op een tegenstelling (het conflict is dus niet progressief en leidt niet tot optimistische synthesen) — voltrekt zich diep in onze ziel, in het gebied waar het bewustzijn nooit doordringt zoals men wel weet. Maar de 'auteurs' hebben de taak dit conflict zo veel mogelijk manifest en expliciet te maken. Zij missen namelijk de tact en het vermogen om *niet* tot op zekere hoogte het 'verlangen naar de dood' te onthullen en *niet* tekort te schieten in de door het instinct tot zelfbehoud opgelegde normen, of — simpeler gezegd — *niet* tekort te schieten in ZELFBEHOUD. *De vrijheid is dus een vrijwillige aanslag op het eigen zelfbehoud.* De vrijheid kan slechts worden geuit door een groot of klein martelaarschap. En elke martelaar martelt zichzelf met behulp van het zelfbehoud, dat als beul optreedt.
Om op het ons vertrouwde terrein van de stijl — van de poëzie, van de cinema — te

22

Tellus III, 1980

23

blijven kunnen we derhalve constateren dat elke inbreuk op het codesysteem — een noodzakelijke handeling om creatief te zijn — tegelijkertijd een inbreuk op het Zelfbehoud is. En dus ook de demonstratie van een daad van zelfbeschadiging is, waarbij iets tragisch en onbekends in de plaats komt voor iets banaals en bekends (het leven).

P. Pasolini. Skrien 1979.

DE JUISTHEID VAN EINSTEINS THEORIE IS NOOIT ZO DUIDELIJK AANGETOOND ALS BIJ HET ONTPLOFFEN VAN DE EERSTE ATOOMBOM IN 1945

A.J. KOX

28

Omdat kunstwerken reproduceerbaar zijn, kunnen zij in theorie door iedereen gebruikt worden. Toch worden reprodukties—in kunstboeken, tijdschriften, films; of in huiskamers, in vergulde lijsten—meestal gebruikt om de illusie in stand te houden, dat er nog steeds niets veranderd is, dat kunst, met zijn unieke, onverminderde gezag, de meeste andere vormen van gezag rechtvaardigt; dat kunst ongelijkheid adelt en autoritaire gezagsverhoudingen opwindend maakt. Het hele idee van een Nationaal Kultureel Erfgoed bijvoorbeeld misbruikt het gezag van de kunst om het huidige maatschappelijke stelsel en zijn prioriteiten te verheerlijken.

John Berger. 'Ways of seeing'

Esterno, 1980

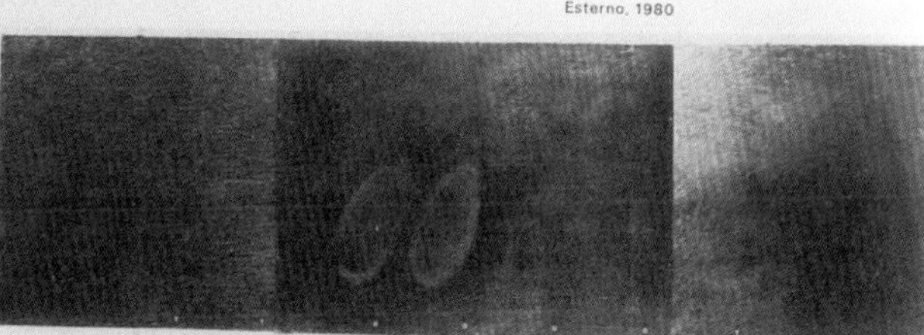

29

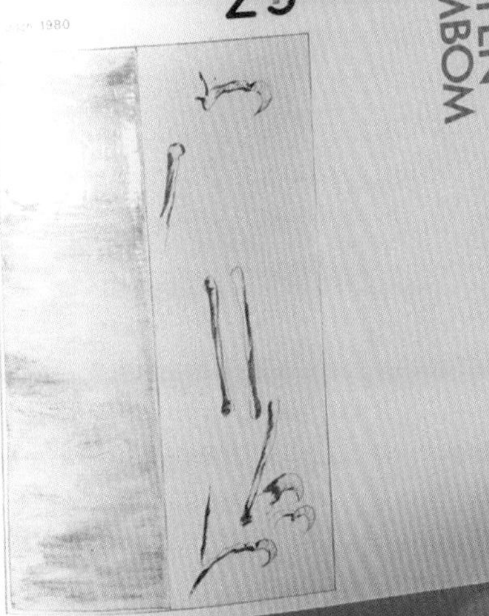

“WORKİNG WİTHİN THİS REALİTY, WE WİLL CONSTANTLY FİND OURSELVES CAUGHT İN A FİELD OF TENSİON BETWEEN İNDİVİDUAL, CORPORATE AND PUBLİC İNTERESTS; OBLİGED TO POSİTİON OURSELVES AND MAKE THAT CLEAR İN OUR PRODUCT.” Jan van Toorn

Ootje Oxenaar and Paul Hefting of the PTT's art and design department selected Van Toorn to work on the three PTT reports for 1972. Responding to the widespread relaxation of social conventions, Oxenaar requested an unpretentious, down-to-earth publication printed on ordinary paper – Sandberg's reports for 1970 and 1971 had been similarly informal. Van Toorn chose a newspaper typeface, Cheltenham Bold Condensed, for headings and Univers for the text. He had just completed the 1972/73 calendar for Mart.Spruijt and he applied the same unvarnished style to the photography of staff members – shown on a folding sheet included in both the financial and social reports – to remind readers that thousands of ordinary workers made up the company (p. 193).

Annual report. Cover, spreads and poster, 1972.
Client: PTT

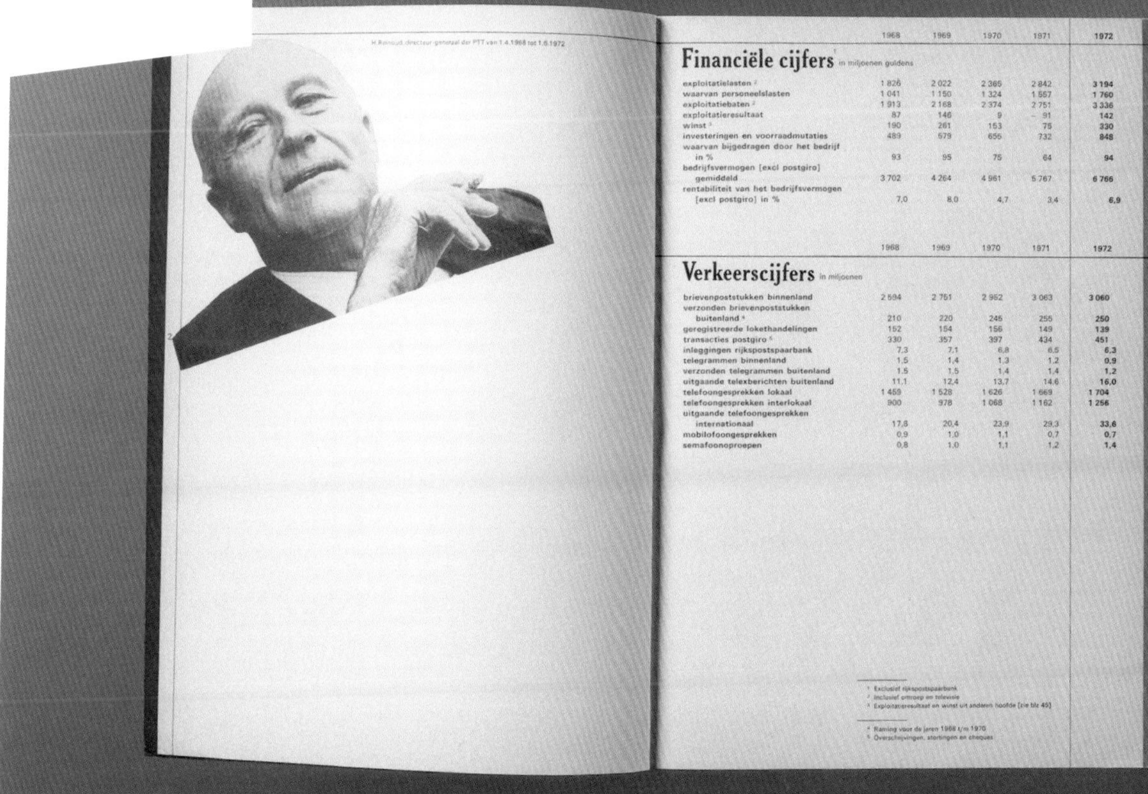

Financiële cijfers[1] in miljoenen guldens

	1968	1969	1970	1971	1972
exploitatielasten [2]	1 826	2 022	2 365	2 842	3 194
waarvan personeelslasten	1 041	1 150	1 324	1 557	1 760
exploitatiebaten [2]	1 913	2 168	2 374	2 751	3 336
exploitatieresultaat	87	146	9	– 91	142
winst [3]	190	261	153	75	330
investeringen en voorraadmutaties	489	579	655	732	848
waarvan bijgedragen door het bedrijf in %	93	95	75	64	94
bedrijfsvermogen [excl postgiro] gemiddeld	3 702	4 264	4 961	5 767	6 766
rentabiliteit van het bedrijfsvermogen [excl postgiro] in %	7,0	8,0	4,7	3,4	6,9

Verkeerscijfers in miljoenen

	1968	1969	1970	1971	1972
brievenpoststukken binnenland	2 594	2 751	2 952	3 063	3 060
verzonden brievenpoststukken buitenland [4]	210	220	245	255	250
geregistreerde lokethandelingen	152	154	156	149	139
transacties postgiro [5]	330	357	397	434	451
inleggingen rijkspostspaarbank	7,3	7,1	6,8	6,5	6,3
telegrammen binnenland	1,5	1,4	1,3	1,2	0,9
verzonden telegrammen buitenland	1,5	1,5	1,4	1,4	1,2
uitgaande telexberichten buitenland	11,1	12,4	13,7	14,6	16,0
telefoongesprekken lokaal	1 459	1 528	1 626	1 669	1 704
telefoongesprekken interlokaal	900	978	1 068	1 162	1 256
uitgaande telefoongesprekken internationaal	17,8	20,4	23,9	29,3	33,6
mobilofoongesprekken	0,9	1,0	1,1	0,7	0,7
semafoonoproepen	0,8	1,0	1,1	1,2	1,4

1 Exclusief rijkspostspaarbank
2 Inclusief omroep en televisie
3 Exploitatieresultaat en winst uit andere hoofde [zie blz 45]

4 Raming voor de jaren 1968 t/m 1970
5 Overschrijvingen, stortingen en cheques

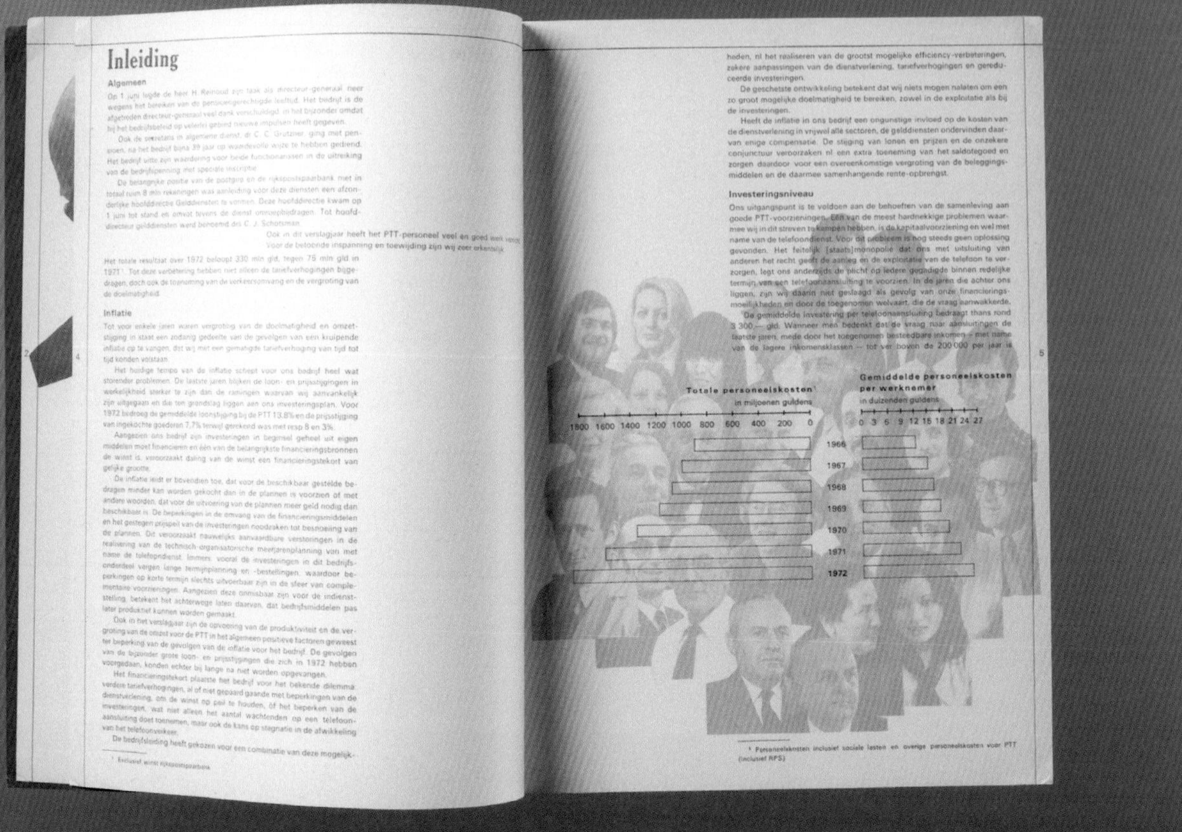

S O C I A A L   J A A R V E R S L A G

Sociale lasten, stuurgroep personeelopbouw, slotvergadering, selectie
overeenkomst, onderwijscontacten
Onregelmatige diensten, overlegstructuur, oudere werknemer, ontplooiingskansen.
carrièreperspectief, contract, collegialiteit, communicatie, competentie
Commissie van beroep, contacten, cursussen, carrièregaranties,
individuele hulp
Internationale contacten, inspraak, inpassing, indiensttreding, introductie.
afscheid, ambtsjubileum, 'aangetekend'
Arbeidssatisfactie, arbeidsmarkt, advertenties, achterban, ambtenaar.
advertentiecampagne
Anciënniteit, arbeidsvoorwaarden, adviseursrol, ambtenarenrechten.
legitimatiebewijs, loonderving
Lange termijnontwikkeling, loonkosten, loopbaan, leeftijdsgrens.
jongerenproblematiek, jaarverslag
Jobrotation, jeugdloon, jaarwedde, jeugdmigratie, jubileum, jeugdige werknemers.
ambtenaar, afkoopregeling
Aanstelling in vaste dienst, arbeidscontractanten, aanwerving, ambtenarenrechter.
afkoopregeling
Arbeidsrechtelijke problemen, aanwerving, aanstelling, afvloeiing.
rangsverhoging, relaties
Röntgenologisch onderzoek, roosterdienst, reorganisatiebegeleiding.
vernieuwing psi-beleid, vertrouwensrelatie, verloop
Verhuiskosten, verplaatsing, verlofregeling, vakorganisaties, vertrouwensman.
externe cursussen, extra verlof
EHBO, examen, evaluatie, ergonomische vraagstukken, eindverantwoordelijkheid.
reorganisaties
Radiotechnici, rangschikking, rechten en plichten, rijwielvergoeding.
studiefaciliteiten, samenwerking, sociaal team
Screening, stakingsrecht, sollicitant, status, scholing, stuurgroep, strafontslag.
leidraad voor sociale en arbeidsrechtelijke aspecten bij veranderingen
Langdurig afwezigen, levensscholen, leiding geven, leerlingenstelsel,
abonnee, afkortingen
Afscheidspenning, arbeidswet, avondwerkers, ambtsjubileum, afkeuring.
gezondheidszorg, gepensioneerd
geoefend werkman, geschiktheid, getuigschrift, gezinshulp, groepswerk,
Georganiseerd overleg, garanties, gratificaties, geneeskundige zorg.

2

3

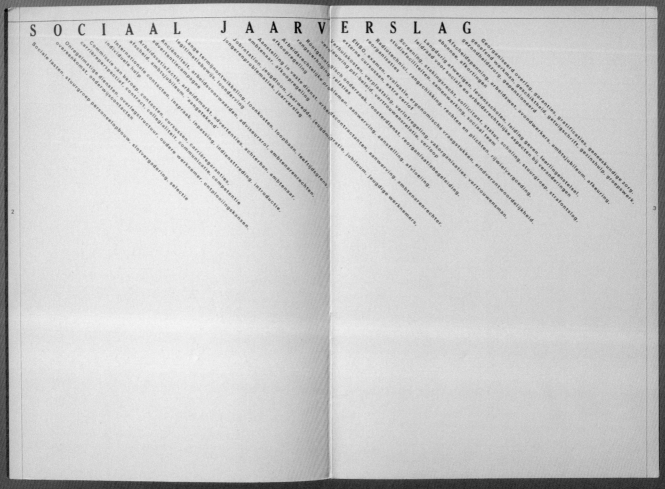

PTT
PTT
PTT
PTT
de mens in het bedrijf

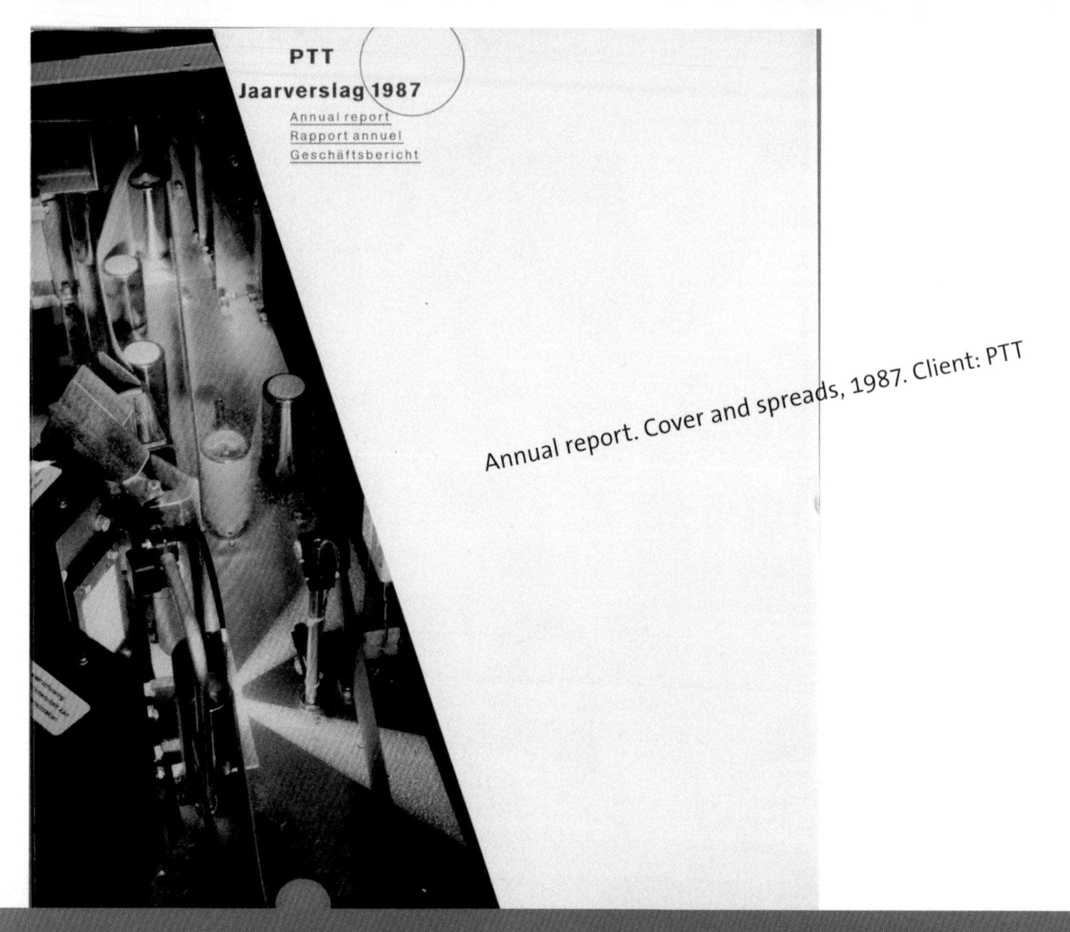

Annual report. Cover and spreads, 1987. Client: PTT

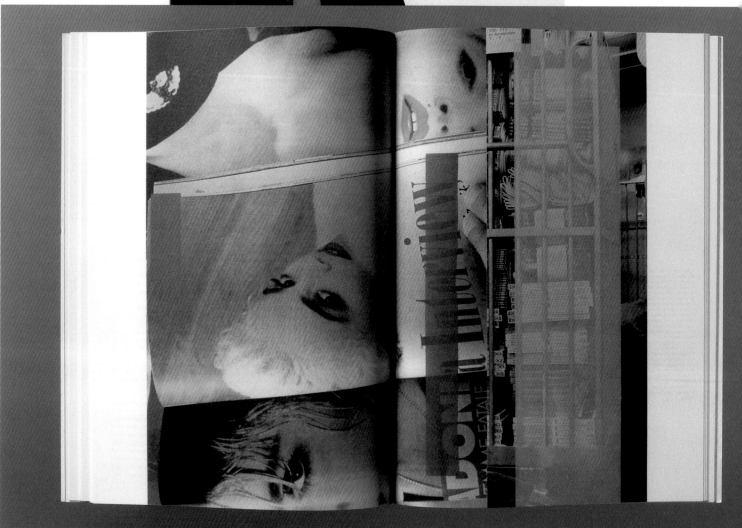

Van Toorn designed the two reports – for 1987 and 1988 – that preceded the PTT's privatization on 1 January 1989. In the 1987 report (this spread), the PTT wanted to show its command of the latest technology and Van Toorn focuses on the communication uses of the equipment in a series of hand-glued photocollages. He juxtaposes an image of Madonna with the means – bulk post – used to distribute this icon of popular culture; and he shows Viditel screens installed at the New York Stock Exchange alongside a trading floor scene from Black Monday (19 October 1987) when the stock market crashed. The 1988 report (pp. 196–7) set out to demonstrate that the PTT had always been at the forefront of technology. Van Toorn employs quotations from earlier designs for the PTT by Piet Zwart and Juriaan Schrofer, and he places a system of reference images in the gutter to document the organization's historical, socio-economic and technological development in relation to the Netherlands and the world. Since this was to be the final report from the PTT operating as a national institution, Van Toorn begins its history with the post's nationalization during Napoleonic times.

PTT Jaarverslag 1988
Annual report
Rapport annuel
Geschäftsbericht

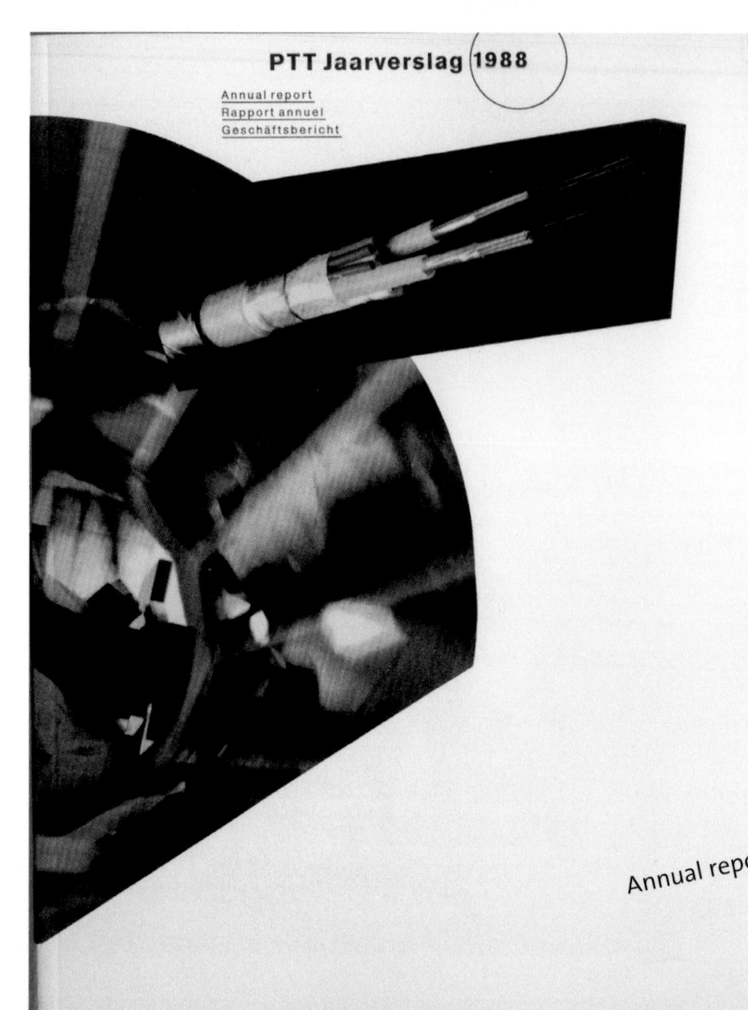

Annual report. Cover and spreads, 1988. Client: PTT

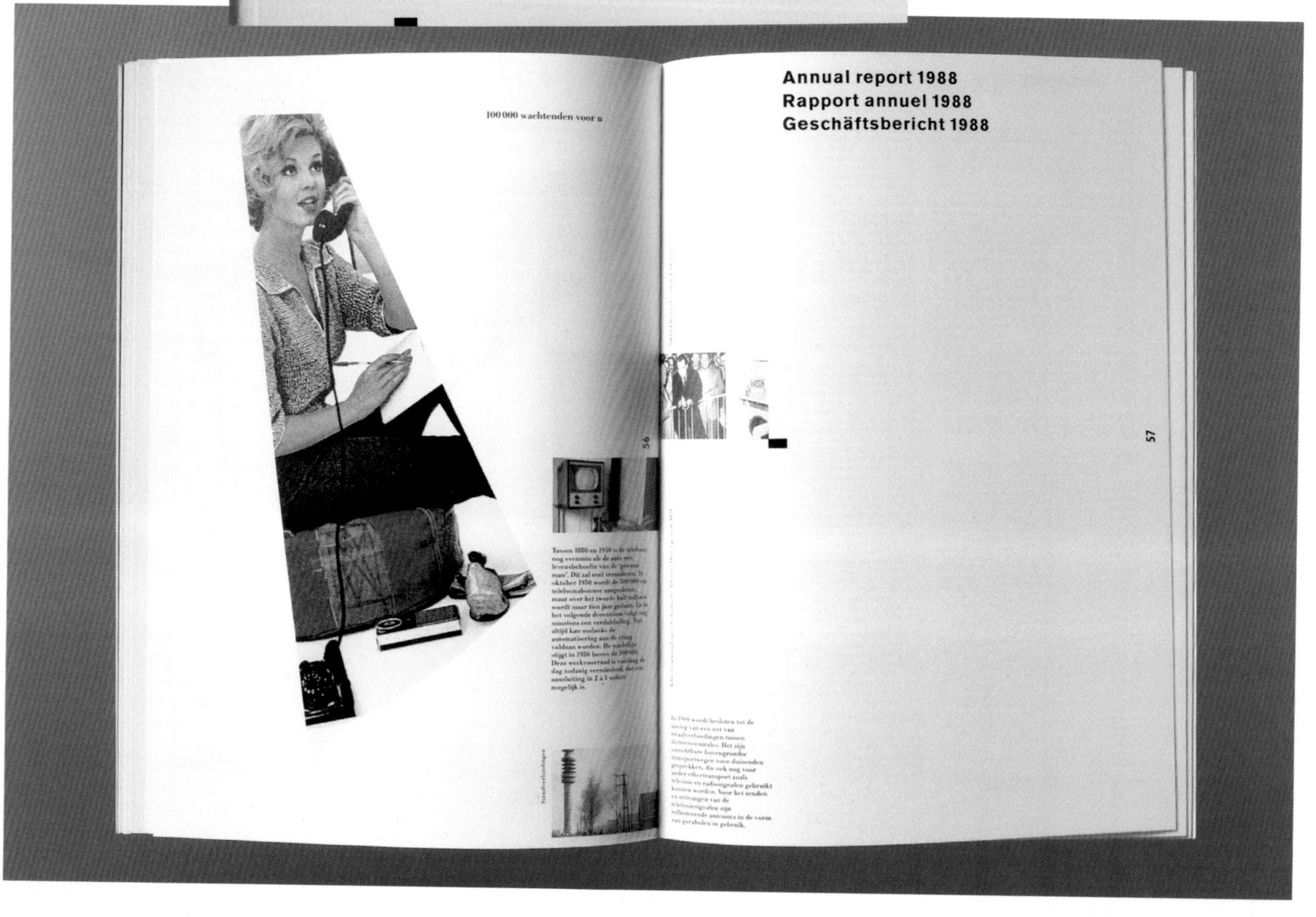

100 000 wachtenden voor u
56
Annual report 1988
Rapport annuel 1988
Geschäftsbericht 1988
57

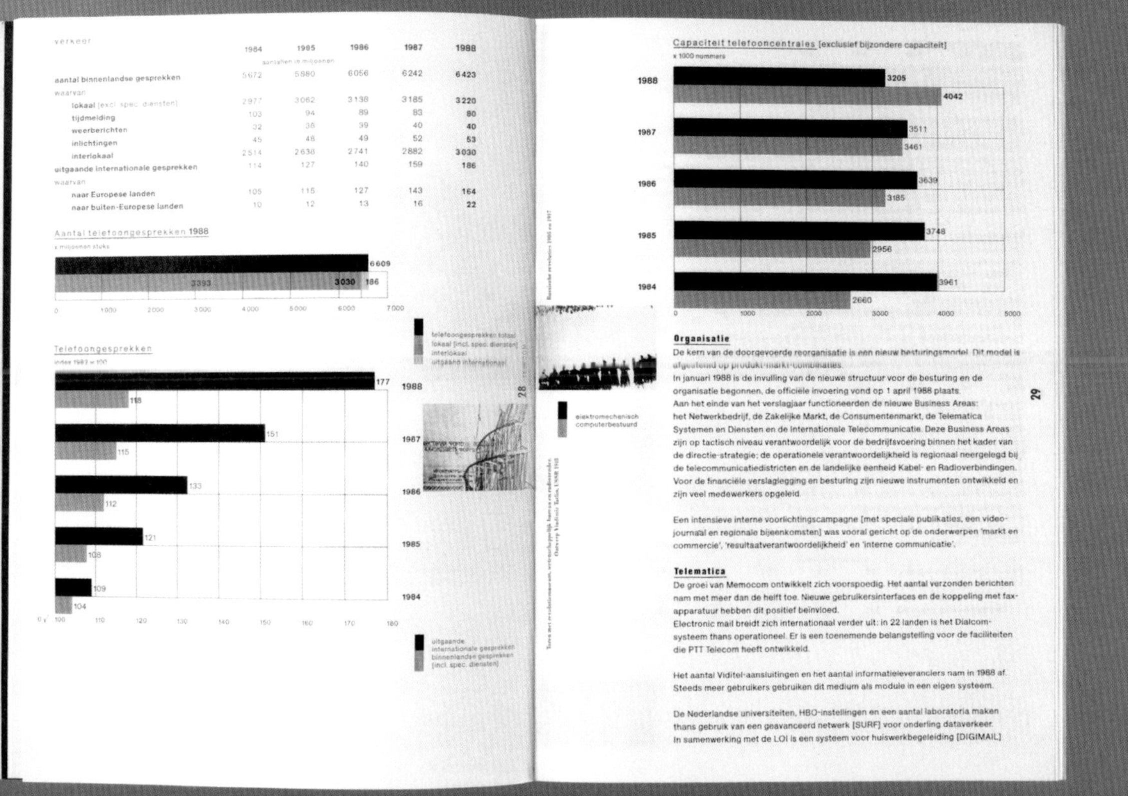

verkeer

	1984	1985	1986	1987	1988
	aantallen in miljoenen				
aantal binnenlandse gesprekken	5672	5880	6056	6242	6423
waarvan					
lokaal [excl. spec. diensten]	2977	3062	3138	3185	3220
tijdmelding	103	94	89	83	80
weerberichten	32	38	39	40	40
inlichtingen	45	48	49	52	53
interlokaal	2514	2638	2741	2882	3030
uitgaande internationale gesprekken	114	127	140	159	186
waarvan					
naar Europese landen	105	115	127	143	164
naar buiten-Europese landen	10	12	13	16	22

Organisatie

De kern van de doorgevoerde reorganisatie is een nieuw besturingsmodel. Dit model is afgestemd op produkt-markt-combinaties.
In januari 1988 is de invulling van de nieuwe structuur voor de besturing en de organisatie begonnen, de officiële invoering vond op 1 april 1988 plaats.
Aan het einde van het verslagjaar functioneerden de nieuwe Business Areas: het Netwerkbedrijf, de Zakelijke Markt, de Consumentenmarkt, de Telematica Systemen en Diensten en de Internationale Telecommunicatie. Deze Business Areas zijn op tactisch niveau verantwoordelijk voor de bedrijfsvoering binnen het kader van de directie-strategie; de operationele verantwoordelijkheid is regionaal neergelegd bij de telecommunicatiedistricten en de landelijke eenheid Kabel- en Radioverbindingen. Voor de financiële verslaglegging en besturing zijn nieuwe instrumenten ontwikkeld en zijn veel medewerkers opgeleid.

Een intensieve interne voorlichtingscampagne [met speciale publikaties, een videojournaal en regionale bijeenkomsten] was vooral gericht op de onderwerpen 'markt en commercie', 'resultaatverantwoordelijkheid' en 'interne communicatie'.

Telematica

De groei van Memocom ontwikkelt zich voorspoedig. Het aantal verzonden berichten nam met meer dan de helft toe. Nieuwe gebruikersinterfaces en de koppeling met faxapparatuur hebben dit positief beïnvloed.
Electronic mail breidt zich internationaal verder uit: in 22 landen is het Dialcom-systeem thans operationeel. Er is een toenemende belangstelling voor de faciliteiten die PTT Telecom heeft ontwikkeld.

Het aantal Viditel-aansluitingen en het aantal informatieleveranciers nam in 1988 af. Steeds meer gebruikers gebruiken dit medium als module in een eigen systeem.

De Nederlandse universiteiten, HBO-instellingen en een aantal laboratoria maken thans gebruik van een geavanceerd netwerk [SURF] voor onderling dataverkeer.
In samenwerking met de LOI is een systeem voor huiswerkbegeleiding [DIGIMAIL]

In 1988 is door PTT, APT Nederland en NKF KABEL BV de stichting NITTC in het leven geroepen, waarvoor NEPOSTEL de management- en administratieve functies verzorgt. NITTC, Netherlands International Telecommunication Training Coordination, stelt zich ten doel opleiding en training aan te bieden en te doen verzorgen voor medewerkers van Telecommunicatiebedrijven in Derde-Wereldlanden.
Dankzij de samenwerking van de opleidingsinstituten van bovengenoemde bedrijven kan het NITTC opleidingen aanbieden die het gehele veld van telecommunicatie omvatten.

38 MET PTT VERBONDEN ORGANISATIES

Jaarrekening 1988

Telefoonnet

In het begin van de twintigste eeuw is de organisatie van het telefoonverkeer bij het lokale verkeer in handen van particulieren of gemeenten en het interlokale verkeer in die van het Rijk. Deze tweedelige exploitatie is zowel technisch als economisch weinig doelmatig. Vandaar dat het Rijk in 1913 begint met de naasting van plaatselijke telefoonnetten. In 1927 zijn alle lokale netten op drie na in staatshanden. Deze naasting is in 1940 afgerond met de overname van de gemeentelijke telefoondiensten van Amsterdam, Rotterdam en 's-Gravenhage.

39

Prins Bernhard Fonds. Stamp, 1971. Client: PTT

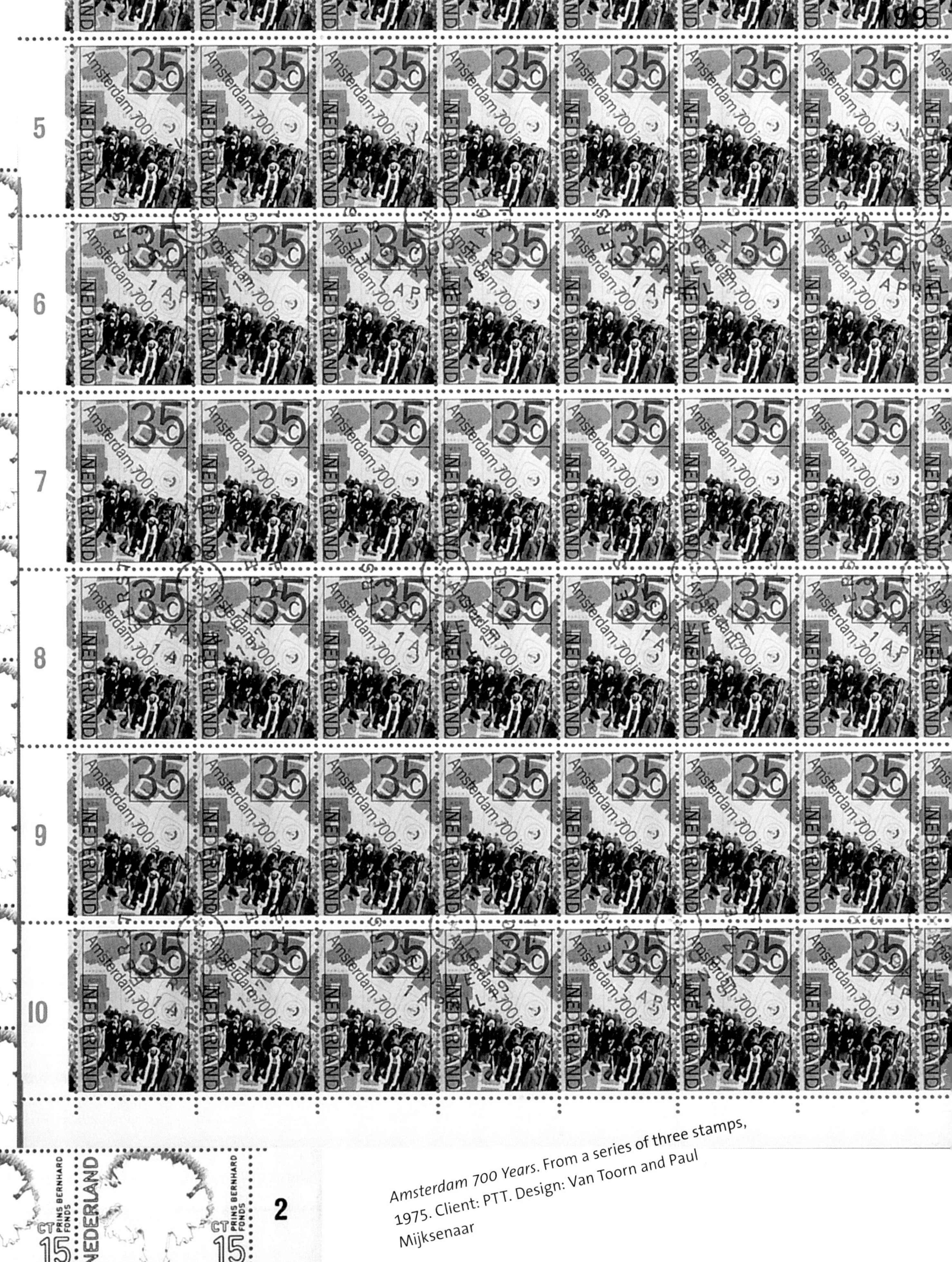

Amsterdam 700 Years. From a series of three stamps, 1975. Client: PTT. Design: Van Toorn and Paul Mijksenaar

Children. Series of four stamps on the occasion of the International Year of the Child, 1979. Client: PTT. Photographs: Willem Diepraam

Rode Kruiszegels 1983
eerste dag van uitgifte
first day of issue

Red Cross. Series of four stamps, 1983. Client: PTT

Red Cross. Series of four stamps, 1983. Client: PTT

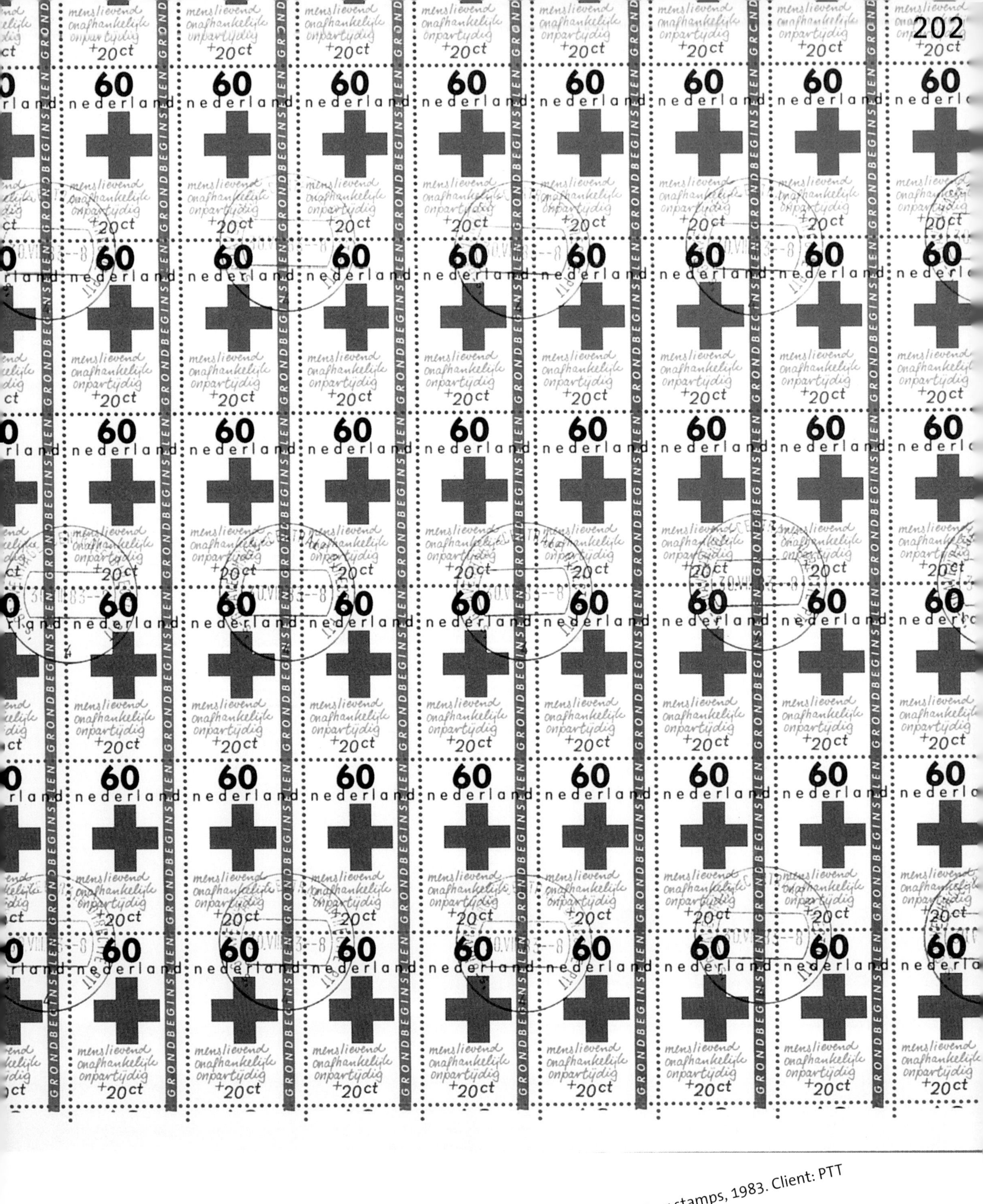

Red Cross. Series of four stamps, 1983. Client: PTT

The social democrat politician Willem Drees, a minister and three times prime minister after the Second World War, introduced a social security system, making him a national hero for many in the Netherlands. Van Toorn's original proposal showed an official photograph of Drees relaxing among sand dunes after playing a ball game with his family. This was rejected by the prime minister's office as an inappropriately informal representation of a politician of such stature. The final design (p. 204), based on another well-known picture of Drees entering parliament to give the Dutch a state pension for the first time, is cropped offhandedly, retaining the colours of Drees's coalition governments as well as the casual typography, resembling a grocery price label, seen in the rejected design.

Rejected design for Willem Drees centenary stamp, 1986. Actual size. Client: PTT

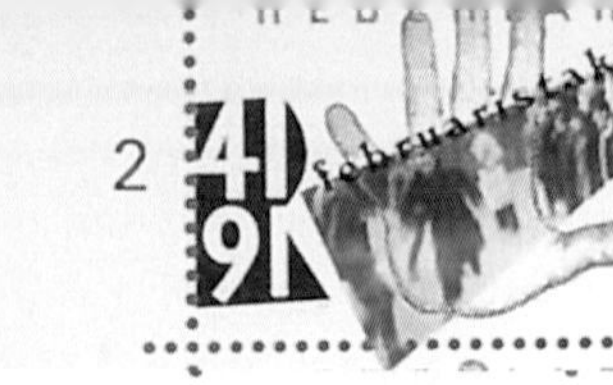

Willem Drees Centenary. Stamp, 1986. Client: PTT

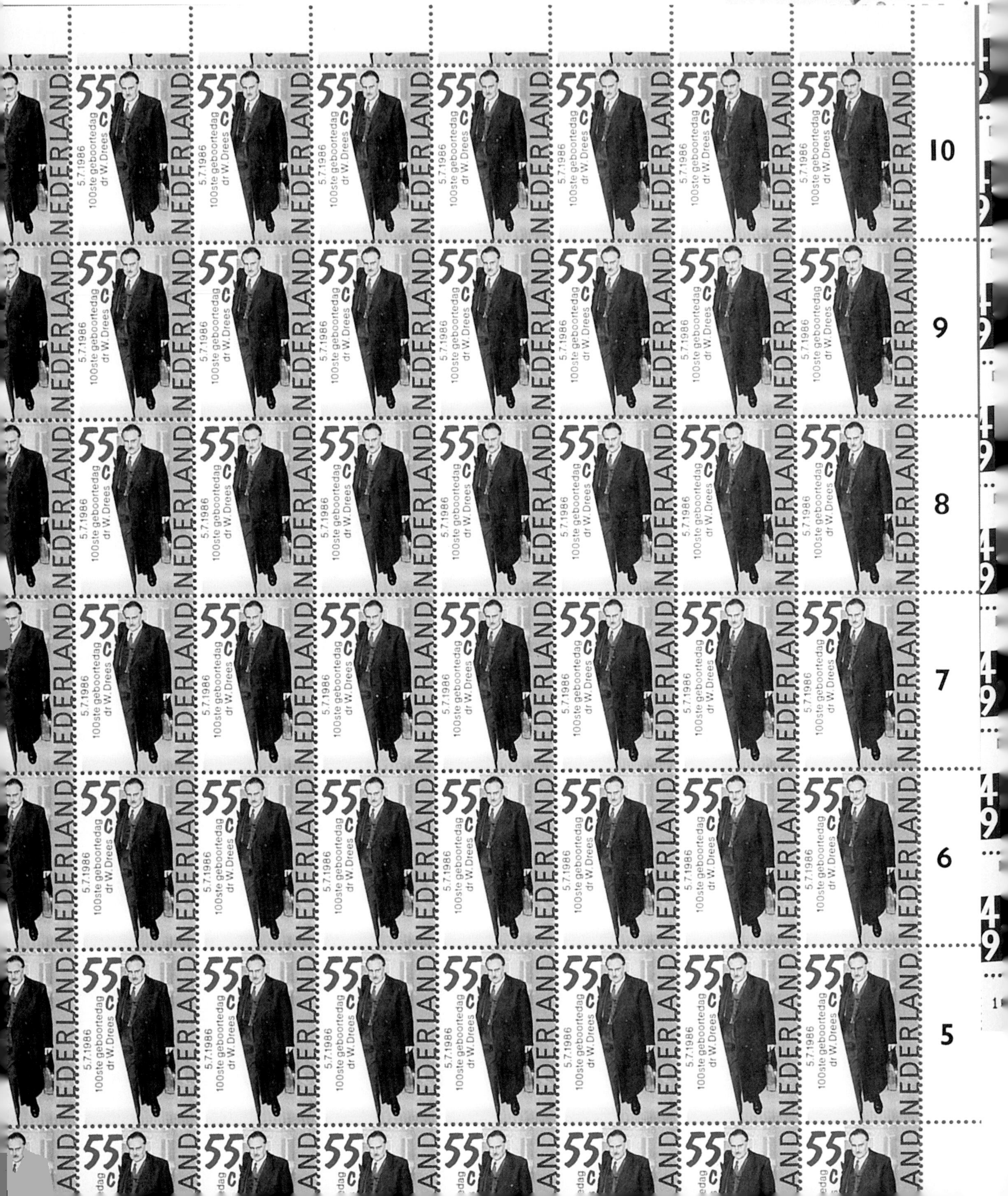

In 1941, the outlawed Communist Party organized a strike in Amsterdam among workers in public jobs in reaction to the first deportations of the Jews. Other members of the population joined the protest. The design, based on an anonymous photograph of Jews being rounded up by Nazis, was intended as a reminder that organized forms of racism were still possible 50 years later. The raised hand featured in anti-racist campaigns throughout Europe. A stylized "R", short for "racism", encloses the dates.

Aanvang verkoop: 25 FEBRUARI 1991

February Strike of 1941. Stamp, 1991. Client: PTT

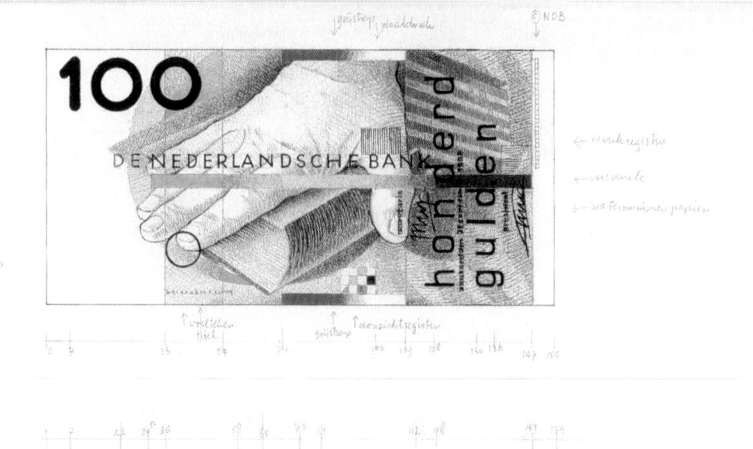

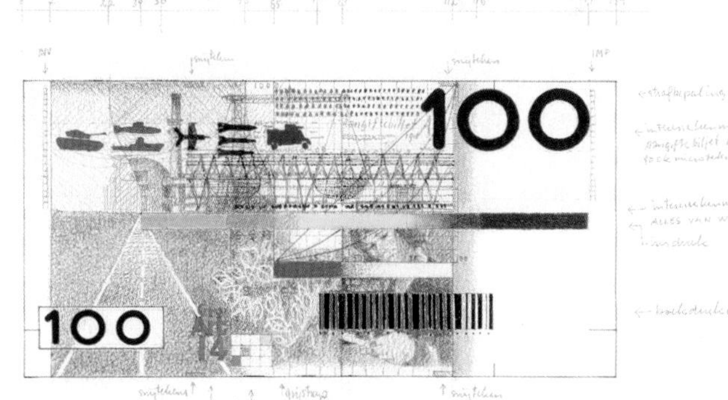

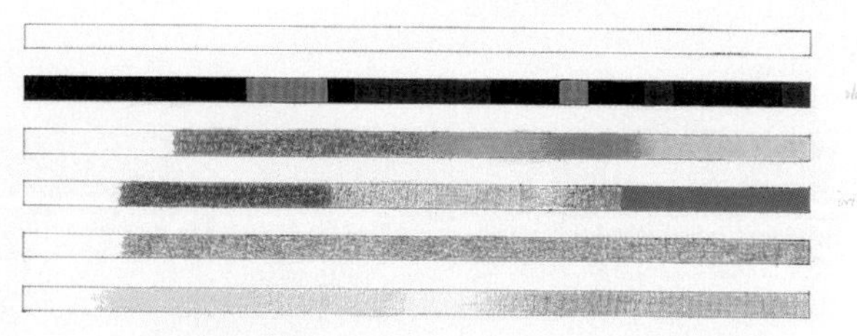

Designs for new Dutch banknotes (unused), 1986.
Client: De Nederlandsche Bank

Van Toorn was one of six designers invited to enter a competition to design new currency and produce proposals for the 25, 100 and 1000 guilder banknotes; the others were Gerard Hadders, Hans Kruit, Rob Schröder, Walter Nikkels and Jaap Drupsteen. Although Van Toorn's designs were not accepted – Drupsteen won the commission – they are notable for the rigour with which he applied his ambition to demystify and reveal hidden systems to the most elementary and ubiquitous form of printed communication. The notes are in every sense reflexive – their subject is money itself – while avoiding decorative symbols in favour of solid, intelligible imagery. The 1000 shows money in its most abstract and liquid state: the financial markets, Stock Exchange, and state and private banks. On the other side, a hand gesture represents the personal transactions that lie behind these systems: here it grasps. The 100 focuses on the role of government, the public sector and economic policy; the hand rests on a law book. The 25 deals with resources, the means of production and commodities such as oil and agriculture; a businessman and worker shake hands. Van Toorn's plans for the 250, 50 and 10, had he won the commission, would have completed a set of images offering a visual summary of the entire economic system, with the 10 representing the individual consumer and private household at its base.

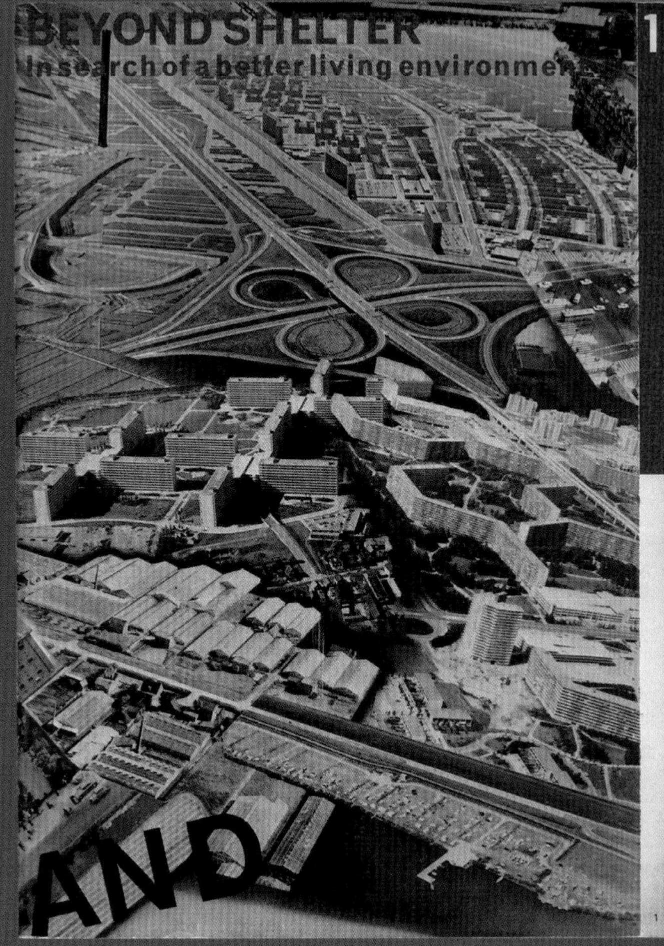

Beyond Shelter: In Search of a Better Living Environment. Brochure cover and spreads, 1976. Client: Visual Arts Office for Abroad, Ministry for Cultural Affairs, Recreation and Social Welfare. Design assistance: Pieter Hildering and Marten Rozenbeek. Photographs: Willem Diepraam, Joost Guntenaar (top, opposite), Pieter Boersma, Violette Cornelius, Cor Jaring, Maarten Kloos, Hannes Walrafen, Willem Vleeschouwer

It wasn't until after the Second World War that Holland was caught in the grip of industrial expansion. This brought on an unprecedented economic boom in the 1960s. The driving force is profit. People's deeper needs are subordinated to it. More and more economic power falls into fewer and fewer hands. People are reduced to the role of immature consumers. They have little hold on the socio-economic system. Unrest grows widespread. Resistance raises its head, first in marginal groups [Provo, students, workers, the Elves Party], then in broader social strata. People start to get more involved in the things that concern them directly: work, the neighbourhood, the environment, and politics too.

5

Living in the Netherlands:
urbanized and industrialized
Sociol-economic system
determines housing
The needs of dwellers
count for less and less
For nearly 14.000.000 inhabitants there are

245.000 hectares[1] for housing, shops etc.
32.000 hectares prepared for building
29.000 hectares for industry
72.000 hectares for transportation
26.000 hectares for recreation
2.516.000 hectares under cultivation
477.000 hectares of natural preserve
314.000 hectares of water

total: 3.700.000 hectares

Living units in 1975, 4,400,000
Built from 1945 until 1975, 2,600,000

Owned by private individuals	2,043,000
private institutions	305,000
housing associations	900,000
government	481,000
Total [according to 1971 census]	3,729,000[2]

Inhabited by owner 38%, rented 62%

Homeless families	44,000
individuals	36,000
Shortage in living units [according to 1971 census] in total	80,000

Involved in the construction industry:

directly	employees	395,000
	one-man concerns	58,000
	man-years	453,000
indirectly	man-years	260,000
		713,000
unemployed construction workers	man-years	32,000
total	man-years	745,000

[total volume of labor in the Netherlands 4,831,000 man-years]

Spent on construction 30.0 billion[3] guilders per year
[total expenditures 288.3 billion guilders per year]

Investment in construction 23.9 billion guilders per year.
[total available for investment 50.2 billion guilders per year].

[1] One hectare is 10,000 square meters, or about 2.47 acres.
[2] broken down by size

1 room	6,095	5 rooms	1,415,300	9 rooms	48,388
2 rooms	54,675	6 rooms	325,250	10 or more rooms	42,600
3 rooms	298,470	7 rooms	315,780		
4 rooms	618,570	8 rooms	109,465		

one-family houses 65%, subunits of houses for more than one family 35%.
[3] [one billion equals one thousand million]

1

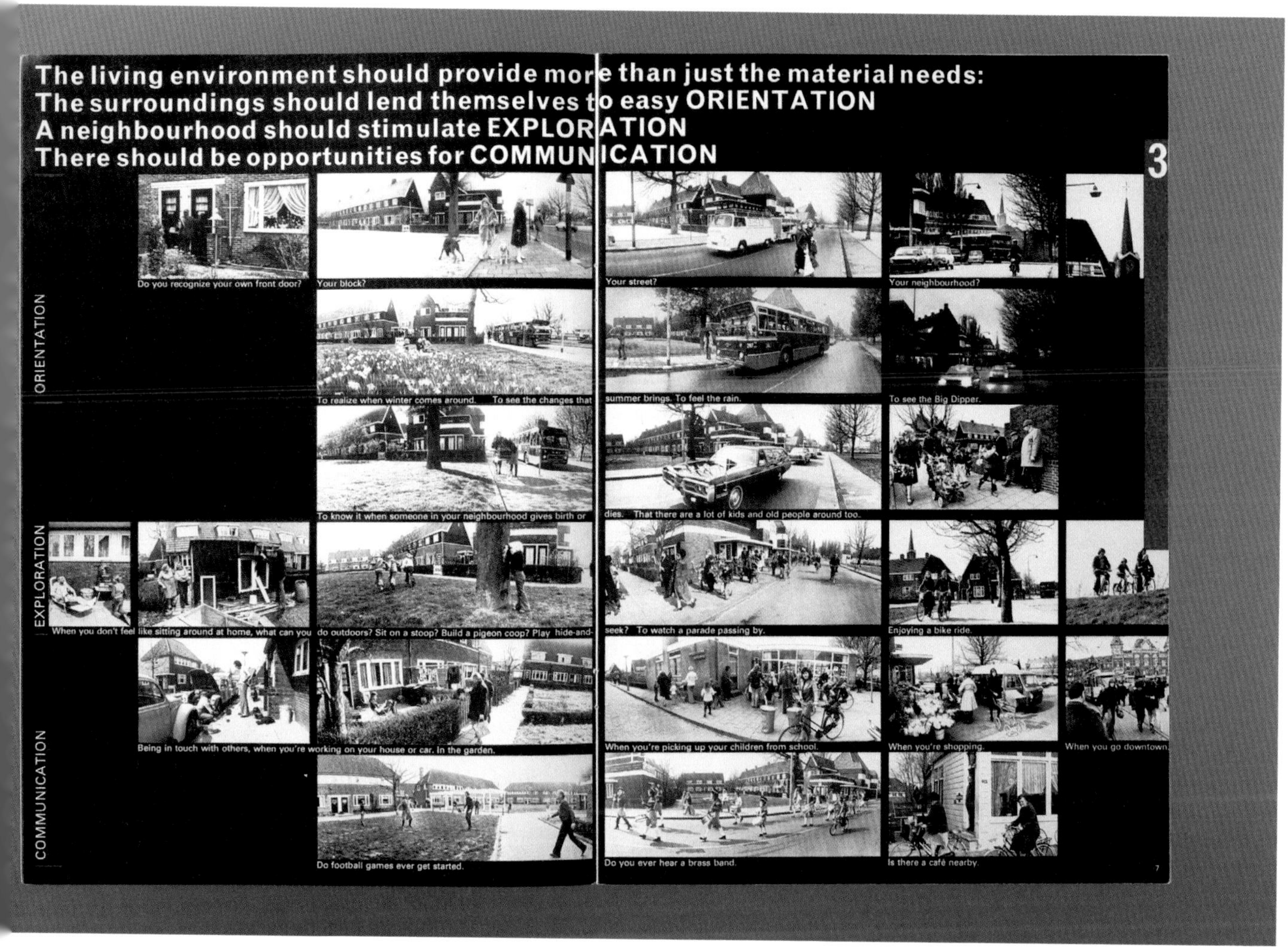

The living environment should provide more than just the material needs:
The surroundings should lend themselves to easy ORIENTATION
A neighbourhood should stimulate EXPLORATION
There should be opportunities for COMMUNICATION

3

ORIENTATION

Do you recognize your own front door? Your block? Your street? Your neighbourhood?

To realize when winter comes around. To see the changes that summer brings. To feel the rain. To see the Big Dipper.

To know it when someone in your neighbourhood gives birth or dies. That there are a lot of kids and old people around too.

EXPLORATION

When you don't feel like sitting around at home, what can you do outdoors? Sit on a stoop? Build a pigeon coop? Play hide-and-seek? To watch a parade passing by. Enjoying a bike ride.

COMMUNICATION

Being in touch with others, when you're working on your house or car. In the garden. When you're picking up your children from school. When you're shopping. When you go downtown.

Do football games ever get started. Do you ever hear a brass band. Is there a café nearby.

7

Beyond Shelter: In Search of a Better Living Environment. Exhibition at Venice Biennale, 1976. Client: Visual Arts Office for Abroad, Ministry for Cultural Affairs, Recreation and Social Welfare

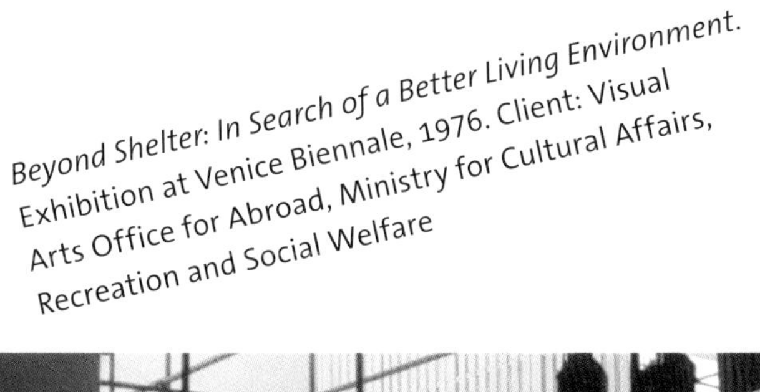

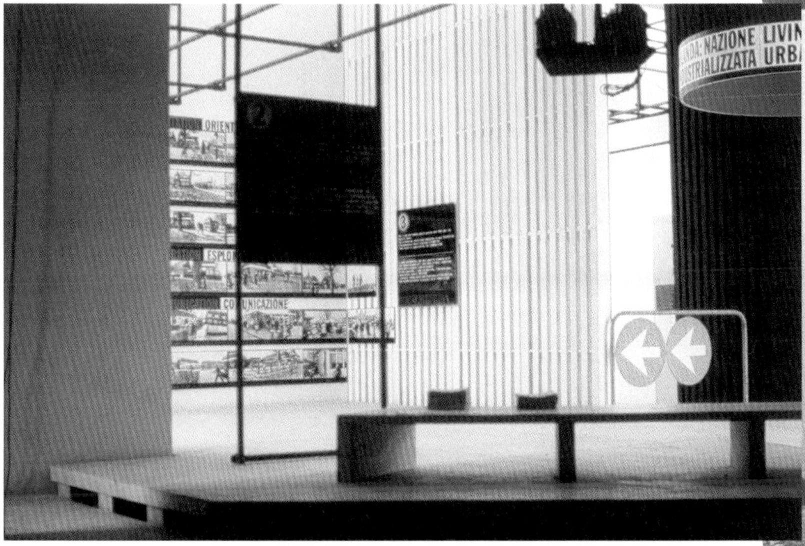

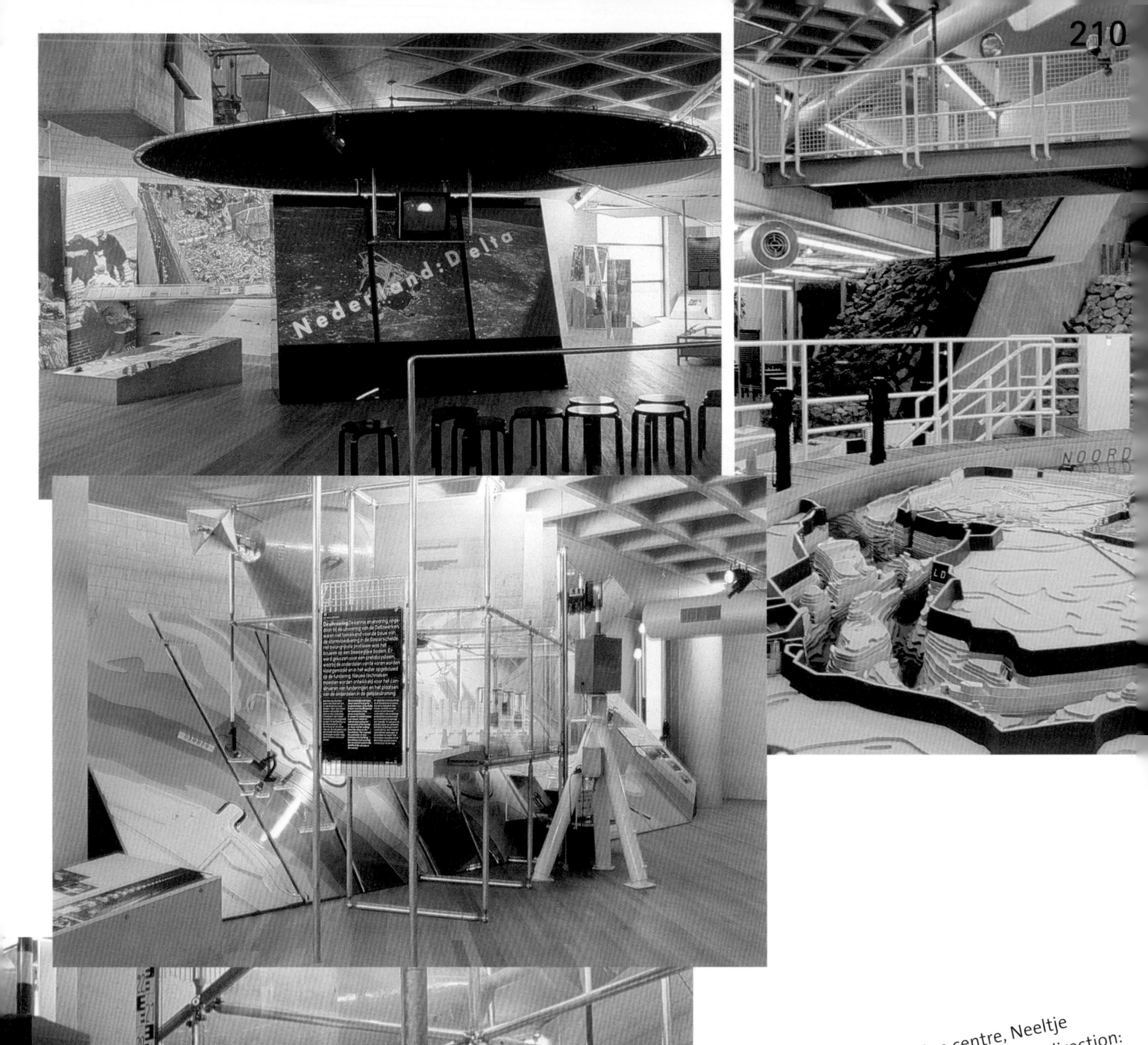

Delta-Expo. Public information centre, Neeltje Jans, 1979–86. Client: Rijkswaterstaat. Art direction: Van Toorn. Designers: Caro de Gijzel, Pieter Roozen, Ko Sliggers, Joke Ziegelaar

After the disastrous flood of 1953 in Zeeland, south of Rotterdam, the Dutch initiated the Delta Works programme of dyke, sluice and barrier building to prevent this happening ever again. In 1981, Van Toorn was appointed art director of the Delta-Expo public information centre housed at the top of a service building on the island of Neeltje Jans. He was part of a working group that included publicity director Leo Kneepkens and Pieter van Koppen, also a designer, who were responsible for the content of the information displays. Van Toorn's team consisted of three designers based at a central studio in The Hague and one at his own studio. Delta-Expo was conceived to provide more than the story of an extraordinary feat of engineering. It illustrated technical developments in relation to social and economic factors, explained the cost of works undertaken on this immense scale and considered their environmental impact; it was also a venue for the promotion of Dutch knowledge, capability and industry. The exhibition was divided into three sections over two floors, reflecting these themes. Its spectacular centrepiece was a 7-metre model with running water, representing the delta from Rotterdam to Antwerp, which had the same compass orientation as the actual works. Some criticized the display for lacking an elaborate sign system, but Van Toorn believed this wasn't necessary if the space was sensitively organized.

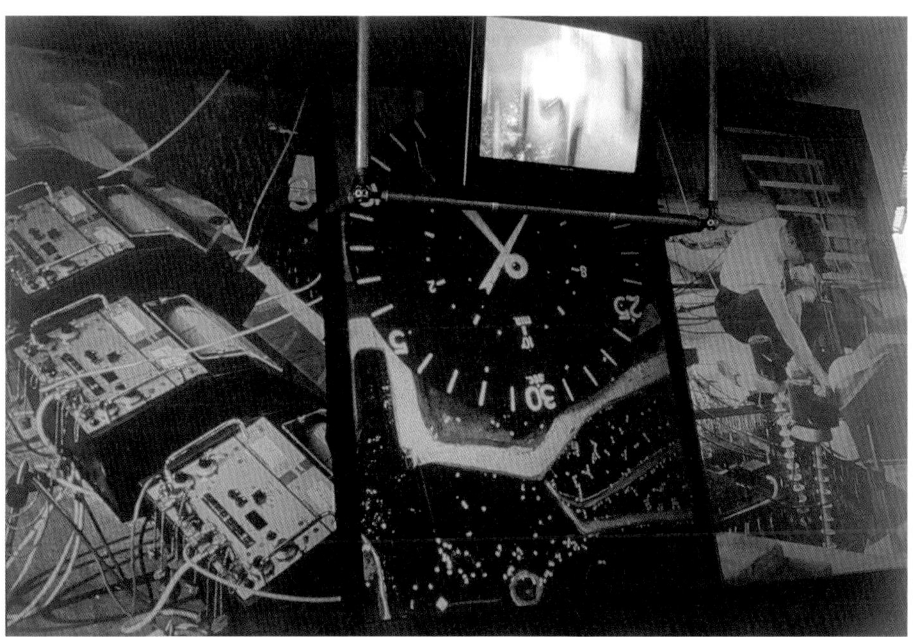

ontwerp Jan van Toorn, Amsterdam druk Steendrukkerij de Jong & Co, Hilversum

Stylos **lezingencyclus / series of lectures 1987-1988**

Het onzichtbare in de architectuur

het verhaal in en achter de façade

The invisible in architecture

the discourse in and behind the façade

deel / part 1

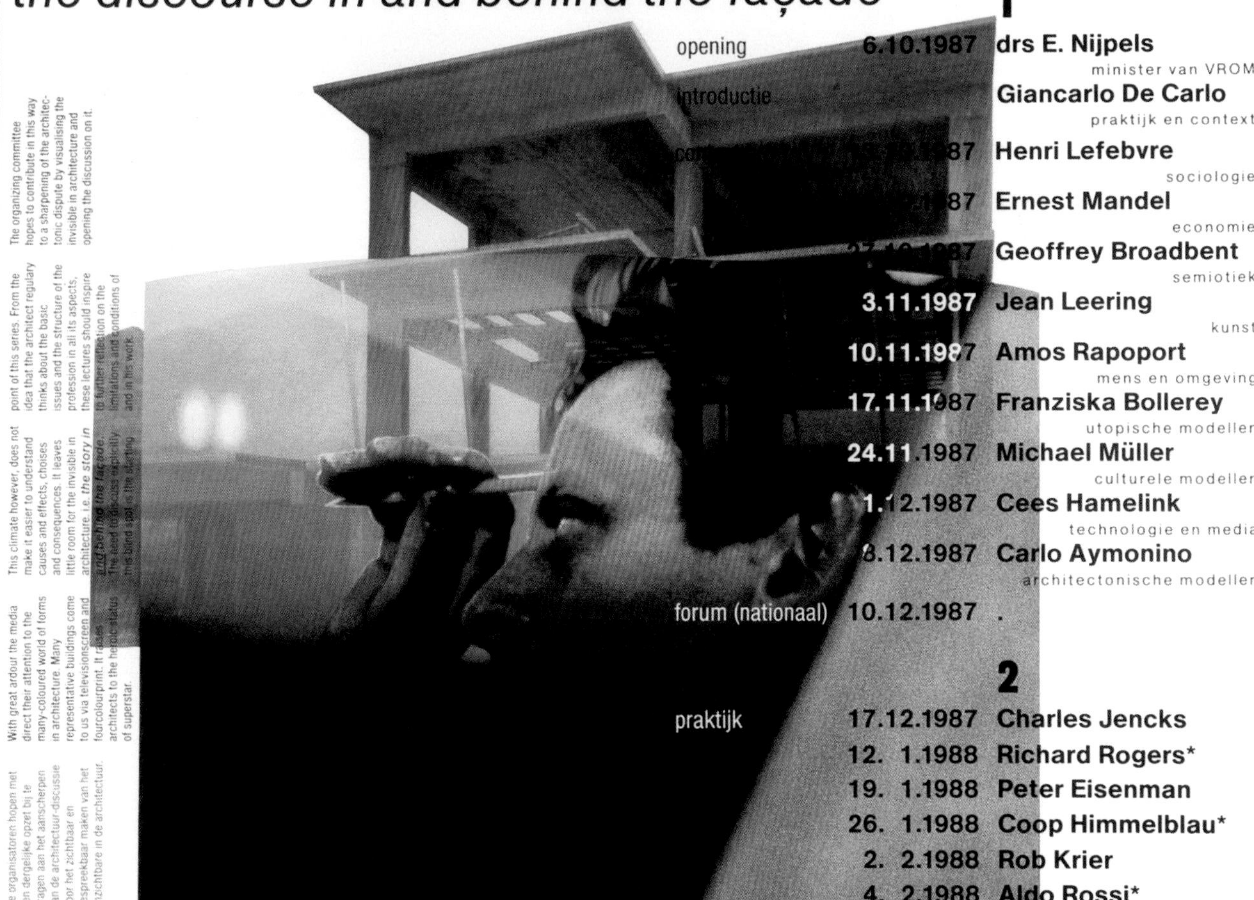

1

opening 6.10.1987 **drs E. Nijpels** minister van VROM

introductie **Giancarlo De Carlo** praktijk en context

Henri Lefebvre sociologie

Ernest Mandel economie

Geoffrey Broadbent semiotiek

3.11.1987 **Jean Leering** kunst

10.11.1987 **Amos Rapoport** mens en omgeving

17.11.1987 **Franziska Bollerey** utopische modellen

24.11.1987 **Michael Müller** culturele modellen

1.12.1987 **Cees Hamelink** technologie en media

8.12.1987 **Carlo Aymonino** architectonische modellen

forum (nationaal) 10.12.1987 .

2

praktijk 17.12.1987 **Charles Jencks**

12. 1.1988 **Richard Rogers***

19. 1.1988 **Peter Eisenman**

26. 1.1988 **Coop Himmelblau***

2. 2.1988 **Rob Krier**

4. 2.1988 **Aldo Rossi***

9. 2.1988 **Ralph Erskine**

*onder voorbehoud

kritiek 16. 2.1988 **Kenneth Frampton**

epiloog 23. 2.1988 .

forum (internationaal) 17. 3.1988 .

Met veel overgave richten de media hun aandacht op de bonte vormenwereld van de architectuur. Veel representatieve gebouwen bereiken ons via beeldscherm en vierkleurendruk. Het verheft architecten tot de heroïsche status van superstar.

Dit klimaat vergemakkelijkt echter niet het begrip van oorzaak en gevolg, keuzen en consequenties. Het laat weinig ruimte voor het onzichtbare in de architectuur: *het verhaal in en achter de façade*. De behoefte deze blinde vlek expliciet aan de orde te stellen is uitgangspunt van deze lezingencyclus. Er vanuitgaande dat de architect regelmatig nadenkt over grondslagen en structuur van het vak in al zijn facetten, moet de serie aanleiding geven tot nadere overpeinzing van grenzen en voorwaarden van en in zijn werk.

De organisatoren hopen met een dergelijke opzet bij te dragen aan het aanscherpen van de architectuur-discussie door het zichtbaar en bespreekbaar maken van het onzichtbare in de architectuur.

With great ardour the media direct their attention to the many-coloured world of forms in architecture. Many representative buildings come to us via televisionscreen and fourcolourprint. It raises architects to the heroic status of superstar.

This climate however, does not make it easier to understand causes and effects, choises and consequences. It leaves little room for the invisible in architecture i.e. *the story in and behind the façade*. The need to discuss explicitly this blind spot is the starting point of this series. From the idea that the architect regulary thinks about the basic issues and the structure of the profession in all its aspects, these lectures should inspire to further reflection on the limitations and conditions of and in his work.

The organizing committee hopes to contribute in this way to a sharpening of the architectonic dispute by visualising the invisible in architecture and opening the discussion on it.

Faculteit der bouwkunde
Technische Universiteit Delft
Zaal A, aanvang 20.00 uur

Organisatie: Stylos (Delftsch bouwkundig studenten gezelschap)
Berlageweg 1, 2628 CR Delft, telefoon 015.784168 /783693

Dit programma wordt mede mogelijk gemaakt door een bijdrage van: Ministerie van Volkshuisvesting, Ruimtelijke Ordening en Milieubeheer; Faculteit der bouwkunde TU Delft; Koninklijke Maatschappij tot bevordering der bouwkunst, Bond van Nederlandse Architekten

The Invisible in Architecture. Poster for lecture series, 1987. Client: Technische Universiteit Delft

“A LİBERATİNG PEDAGOGY SHOULD RECOVER THE FORMS OF MAKİNG AND THİNKİNG, WHİCH HAVE BEEN İNSTRUMENTALİZED BY TRADE AND SERVİCES, SO THAT THEY BECOME USEFUL AGAİN İN THE SEARCH FOR CONDİTİONS THAT ALLOW A MORE TRULY HUMAN EXİSTENCE.”

Jan van Toorn

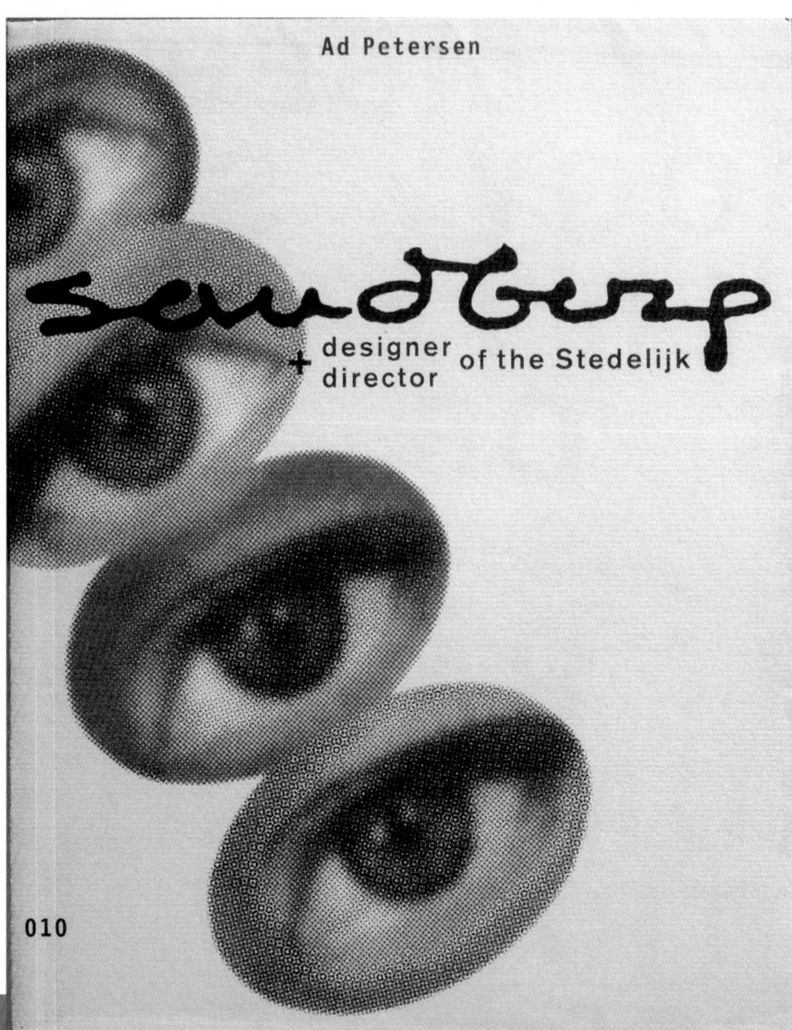

Sandberg, Designer and Director of the Stedelijk. Book cover and spreads, 2004. Publisher: 010. Design assistance: Marten Rozenbeek

1945-54

jaar stedelijk museum

two different catalogue covers and pages 9 jaar **Stedelijk Museum Amsterdam, 1945-'54**, 1954, 48 pp, 26 x 19

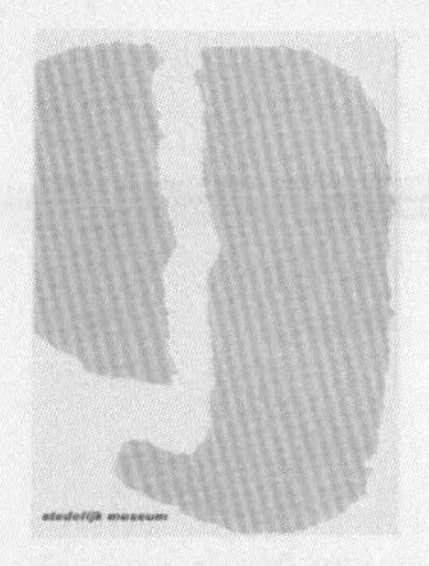

the museum of contemporary art proceeds from
the present to then return step by step into the past.
(...)
the museum confines itself to the visual arts:
architecture, painting, sculpture, graphic art,
the applied arts, photography and film.
the other arts – for example music – can be enlisted
to illustrate parallels.
the task of a museum for contemporary art is to
inform the public in all these fields through
a permanent display of objects, through guided tours
and lectures, film shows, and through its library.
exhibitions can temporarily supplement
the permanent collection.
it is the museum's task to give children
the opportunity to express themselves, to allow
students to study the essence of art and to make
adults aware of the changing face of their own time.

from catalogue foreword 9 jaar Stedelijk Museum Amsterdam

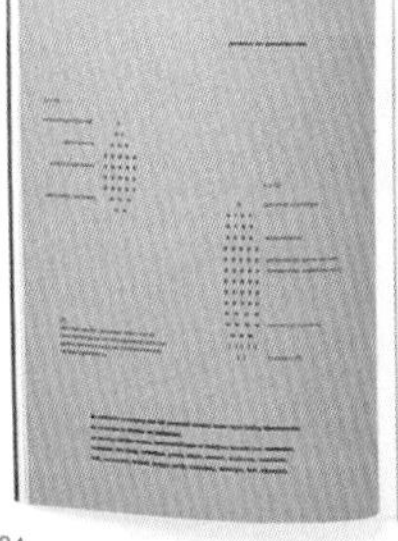

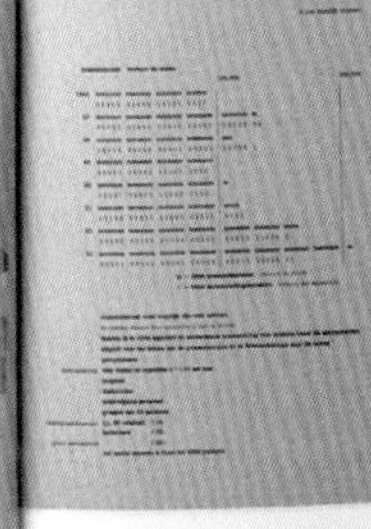

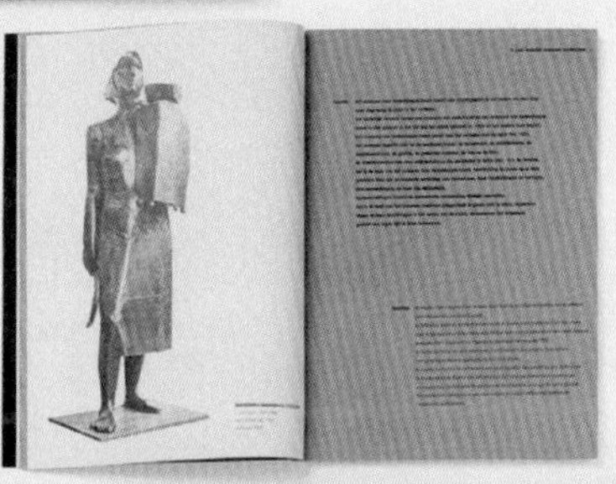

94

95

... the VANK (was) a remarkable association, as it had room for everybody: for Piet Zwart and S.H. de Roos, for Copier and Wijdeveld, for Roland Holst and Rietveld. It was an association in which those who looked forward were allowed as much say as those who looked back, where the avant-garde often made its mark on the manifestations, an association whose progressive plans were consistently considered by the authorities. This miracle was wrought by two men: Van Royen and Gouwe. I can imagine that anyone, looking back on the VANK, might choose the word 'decorative', thinking of Lauweriks and Eisenlöffel, Nieuwenhuis and Lion Cachet; but that would be utterly incorrect, as the functionalists – Gispen and Kiljan, Arie Verbeek and Schuitema – were as much in attendance there as were men from the De Stijl group such as Rietveld and Huszar. The VANK has achieved a very great deal: the consultancy for information and mediation between client and supplier, its intensive involvement with world exhibitions, trade fair stands, its own yearbooks,

57 permanent competition rules, the exhibition council for architecture and allied arts, the code of honour and table of fees. It could achieve all this because it had an excellent administrator who was paid for his work (if poorly). The VANK was dissolved during the early years of the occupation under pressure from the pro-German Chamber of Culture. Why wasn't it simply reinstated in 1945? The VANK was home for many different trends but it lacked one essential element: identity. War is a hard touchstone. It is a time to reflect, a time when the essential can be separated from the non-essential more easily than in the daily round of the duller days of peace. Moreover, in 1945 we still thought that the world had learned something – we saw, wrongly perhaps, the possibility of a change – a change that took place in Asia but not in Europe. The G.K.f thus became a new association of designers of the applied arts, with an identity of its own. We would have to step back further to define that identity – still, we have the definite feeling it's there. The G.K.f operates in an area difficult to define: in this country there are thousands who call themselves advertising designers, hundreds of interior designers and furniture designers, potters, weavers, to say nothing of photographers. It cannot be the intention to bring them all together in one professional association; the differences in quality are too great. So standards are set: skill of course – is that enough? A great many other qualities are also expected of the candidate – we might best describe these as the artist's mentality or 'habitus'. Does this habitus really exist? It does. We are made most aware of it when we compare artists in the G.K.f with groups of craftsmen, photographers and advertising designers external to it. This is why an association in the field of applied arts was set up after the liberation, without a fixed programme but with its own identity. We cannot define that identity, which is the reason for this exhibition. This exhibition we are opening on the 12th anniversary of the liberation we are still expecting.

from Sandberg's introduction to the catalogue of GKf hand en machine

exhibition GKf hand en machine ... designed by Wim Brusse, photo Eva Besnyö

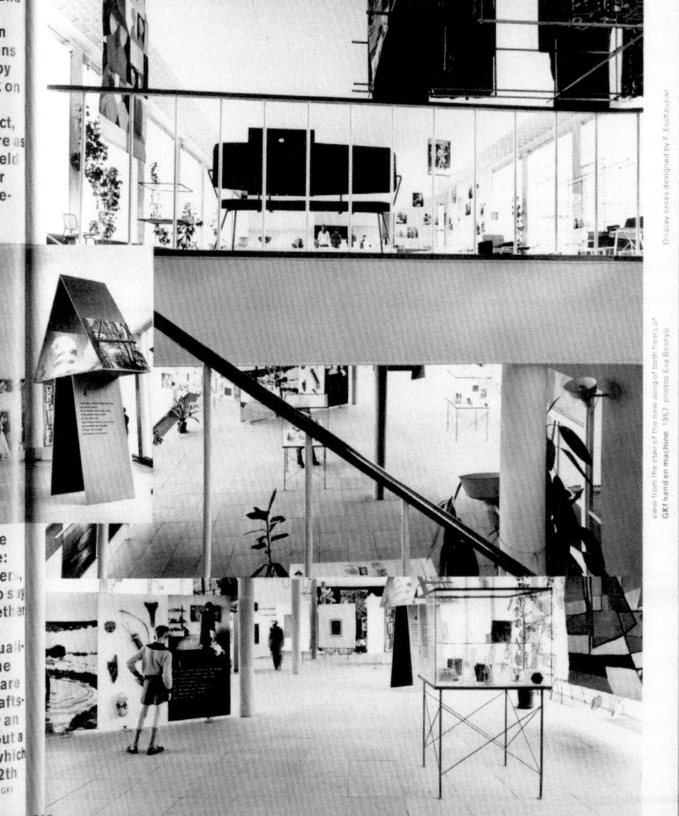

view from the stair of the new wing of both floors of **GKf hand en machine**, 1957, photos Eva Besnyö

Display cases designed by F. Eschauzier

118

119

De BEYERD

ontwerpen van

25.7
12.9.99

otto treumann

affiches, tijdschriften, huisstijlen, logo's, boeken en postzegels

BREDA

Boschstraat 22, 4811 GH, Nederland
open dinsdag tm vrijdag 10-17 uur
zaterdag en zondag 13-17 uur
op maandag gesloten
tel 076.5225025, fax 076.5223842

Gelijktijdig met de tentoonstelling verschijnt bij Uitgeverij 010 Publishers in Rotterdam de monografie Otto Treumann als eerste in de serie Grafisch ontwerpen in Nederland. Initiatief Prins Bernhard Fonds. Tekst Toon Lauwen, ontwerp Irma Boom

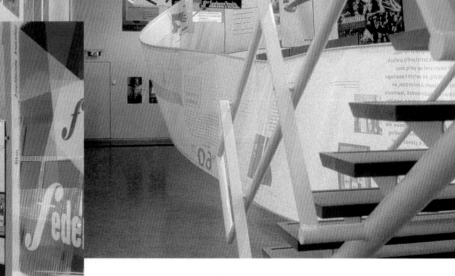

Otto Treuman. Exhibition at De Beyerd and poster, 1999

Chronology

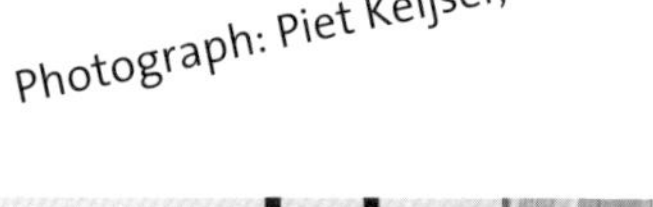
Photograph: Piet Keijser, c. 1960

Book cover, 1962

1932
9 May, born in Tiel, the Netherlands to Anna Maria de Wit and Willem Peter van Toorn.

1935
Family moves to Amsterdam.

1945–9
Attends secondary school in Amsterdam.

1949
Begins work as an apprentice at the printer Mulder & Zoon in Amsterdam.

1949–50
Attends evening classes in design at the Amsterdamse Grafische school.

1950–3
Attends evening classes in graphic art at the Instituut voor Kunstnijverheidsonderswijs in Amsterdam.

1953–4
National service in the Dutch army.

1955
Leaves Mulder & Zoon for a job as a designer of decorated plastic fabrics.

1956
August, marries Wilhelmina Magdalena van Dijk.

1957
Becomes a freelance graphic designer. Clients include Hausemann & Hötte in Amsterdam and Instituut voor Voedingsonderzoek TNO in Zeist.

1959–77
Designs calendars for the printing company Mart.Spruijt in Amsterdam.

1960
January, birth of son, Roemer.

1962–89
Designs for Sikkens Groep/Akzo Coatings, Sassenheim.

1963
January, birth of daughter, Tessel.

1964–70
Designs *Range*, a quarterly journal of telecommunications, for Philips' Telecommunicatie Industrie in Hilversum.

1965
Receives the H.N. Werkmanprize of the City of Amsterdam for typographic work.
Anthon Beeke joins studio as an assistant designer (leaves 1966).

1965–74
Designs posters, catalogues and exhibitions for the Stedelijk van Abbemuseum in Eindhoven.

1966
Kees Zwijgman joins studio as an assistant designer (leaves 1968).

1966–70
Designs for the City of Amsterdam.

1967–70
Teaches at the Royal Academy for Art and Design in Den Bosch.

Van Toorn family camping in Yugoslavia, 1969

With Tom de Heus at a Rietveld Academy workshop, Ardennes, 1972. Photograph: Rob Schröder

Book cover, 1975

Screen shots from *Machiavelli*, 1975–6

1968–85
Teaches evening classes in editorial design at Gerrit Rietveld Academy in Amsterdam. Teaches day school classes at the academy from 1970.
Frans Evenhuis joins studio as an assistant designer (leaves 1970).

1970
Geertjan Dusseljee joins studio as an assistant designer (leaves 1972).

1971–96
Design work for the Dutch PTT.

1972
Co-curates and designs *De Straat: Vorm van Samenleven* at the Van Abbemuseum, Eindhoven. The exhibition subsequently tours to Städtische Kunsthalle, Düsseldorf; Museum de 20 Jahrhunderts, Vienna; Akademie der Künste, Berlin; Kulturhuset, Stockholm.
Marten Rozenbeek joins studio. He leaves in 1974 and they become regular collaborators.
October to December, exhibition of work at the Museum Fodor, Amsterdam.
November, public discussion with Wim Crouwel at Museum Fodor.
Joins the Alliance Graphique Internationale.
Receives the H.N. Werkmanprize of the City of Amsterdam for typographic work.

1974
Jean Leering joins Van Toorn at the Tropenmuseum in Amsterdam as its new director. They resign in 1978 due to lack of management support for their ideas.

1974–88
Designs for the Visual Arts Office for Abroad of the Ministry of Cultural Affairs, including art direction of *Dutch Art + Architecture Today* magazine.

1975
Picture-edits and designs *Frimangron: Reportages uit een Zuid-Amerikaanse Republiek*, the first of five photography books for Willem Diepraam.
Pieter Hildering joins studio (leaves 1978).

1975–6
Designs visual commentaries for the documentary series *Machiavelli* shown on Vpro, the public broadcasting channel.

1976
Art directs and designs *Beyond Shelter: In Search of a Better Living Environment*, the Dutch contribution to the Venice Biennale.

1977
Curates and designs *Kijk Uit! Kiezen is een Keuze*, an exhibition of political posters at the Lijnbaancentrum, Rotterdam.

1978
Publishes *Vormgeving in Functie van Museale Overdracht* with Jean Leering.
Joke Ziegelaar joins studio (leaves 1986).

1979
Co-edits, designs and contributes an essay to *Museum in Motion?/Museum in Beweging?*
Designs *De Kogel door de Kerk: Herdenkings Tentoonstelling Unie van Utrecht*, an exhibition celebrating the 1579 Union of Utrecht at the Centraal Museum, Utrecht.

1980–4
Board member of the Sikkens Prize Foundation, Sassenheim.

1980–6
Art directs and designs the Delta-Expo at Neeltje Jans for the Ministry of Public Works. Co-designers: Caro de Gijzel, Pieter Roozen, Ko Sliggers, Joke Ziegelaar.

1981–2
Teaches exhibition design and methodology at the Institute of Art History, Amsterdam University.

With Anthon Beeke and Ada Stroeve, Amsterdam, late 1980s. Photograph: F. André de la Porte

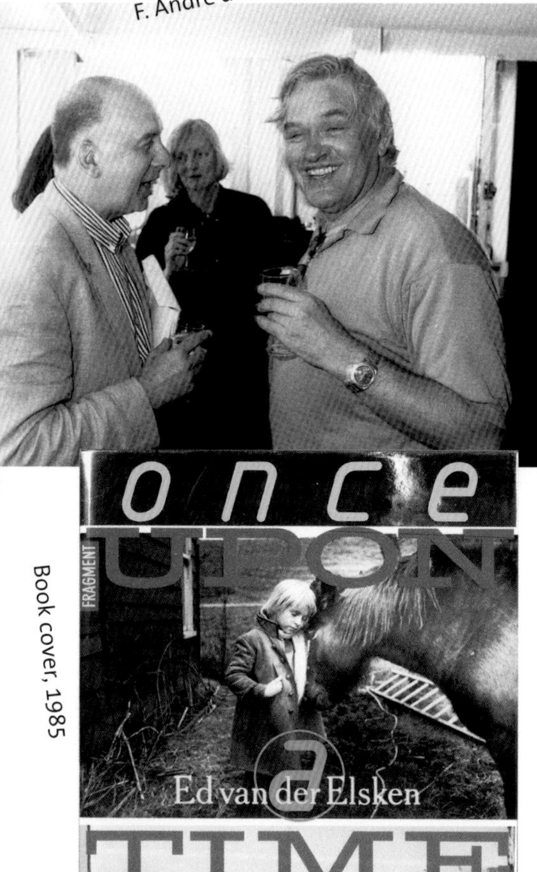

Book cover, 1985

Poster for Jan van Eyck Academy, 1996

1982–3
Guest professor in the achitecture department of the Technical University Eindhoven.

1985
Designs Ed van der Elsken's *Once Upon a Time*.
Contributes photographs of man-made Dutch landscapes to a public art project by Gerard Prent in the new building of the Ministry of Foreign Affairs.
Receives the Piet Zwart Prize from the Total Design Foundation.

1986–7
Ontwerpen Jan van Toorn, retrospective exhibition at De Beyerd, Breda.

1987–9
Head of the multi-media department of the State Academy of Fine Arts, Amsterdam.

1987–2006
Associate professor in the MFA programme in graphic design at Rhode Island School of Design, Providence.
Lectures widely in the US at California Institute of the Arts, Los Angeles; Illinois Institute of Technology, Institute of Design, Chicago; Massachusetts College of Art, Boston; Western Carolina University, Cullowhee.
Member of the American Institute of Graphic Arts.

1989–93
Board member of the Appel Foundation.

1991–98
Director of Jan van Eyck Academy, Maastricht. Appoints Jon Thompson, Heinz Paetzold, Gerard Hadders, Karel Martens and Dawn Barrett as heads of department.
Moves with Wil to Maastricht.

1993
Attends the conference *Positionen zur Gestaltung* at the Hochschule für Künste, Bremen.
Joins the advisory board of *Visible Language*.

1995
Jury member of *The 100 Show*, the Eighteenth Annual of the American Center for Design, Chicago.

1996
Joins the board of the Berlage Institute, Rotterdam (until 2000).
Delivers a lecture entitled "Deschooling and Learning in Design Education" at the *Charting the Future of Design Education* conference, University of Alberta, Edmonton.
Lectures at the Institut Teknologi Bandung, Indonesia.

1997
November, organizes *design beyond Design* symposium at Jan van Eyck Academy. Speakers include Cees Hamelink, Gérard Paris-Clavel, Heinz Paetzold, Susan Buck-Morss, Sheila Levrant de Bretteville, Michael Rock and Susan Sellars.
External examiner on the MA typo/graphic studies course at the London College of Printing (until 2001).
Also lectures at the Royal College of Art, London; Central Saint Martins College of Art and Design, London; Kingston University; Manchester Metropolitan University.

1998
January, returns to Amsterdam and sets up a freelance design studio.
Delivers a lecture entitled "Beyond Design: About the Context of Dutch Design and Architecture" at Southern California Institute of Architecture, Los Angeles.
Joins the advisory board of *Design Issues*.

1999
Edits and designs *Cultiver notre Jardin*.
Co-curates and designs an exhibition about Otto Treumann at De Beyerd, Breda.
Signs the "First Things First 2000" manifesto published simultaneously in the US, Britain and the Netherlands.

2000
Guest tutor at North Carolina State University, Raleigh.

Re: Jan van Toorn exhibition, Kunsthal, Rotterdam, 2004

Catalogue cover, 2005

Guest tutor at Design Academy Eindhoven.
Contributes to the *Icograda Design Education Manifesto* presented at the Icograda Millennium Congress in Seoul.

2001
Lectures at Maryland Institute College of Art, Baltimore.
September, lectures and conducts workshop at University of Western Sydney.
October, delivers a lecture entitled "The Autonomy of Design in the Information Society" at the *Declarations of [Inter]dependence and the Im[media]cy of Design* conference, Concordia University, Montreal.

2002
Joins the honorary board of *Visual Communication*.
November, guest tutor at Christelijke Hogeschool voor de Kunsten Constantijn Huygens, Kampen.

2004
Picture-edits and designs *Sandberg: Designer and Director of the Stedelijk*.
March to June, *Re: Jan van Toorn*, retrospective exhibition at the Kunsthal, Rotterdam.
November, receives Athena Award for career excellence from Rhode Island School of Design.

2005
May, conducts workshop at Festival International de l'Affiche et des Arts Graphiques de Chaumont, France.
Designs *Le Néo-Impressionnisme, de Seurat à Paul Klee* catalogue for Musée d'Orsay, Paris.
September to October, designs a historical timeline for *Catalysts! The Cultural Force of Communication Design*, curated by Max Bruinsma, at the *ExperimentaDesign* biennial in Lisbon.

2006
May, lectures and conducts workshop at *Grafist 10 International*, Mimar Sinan Fine Arts University, Istanbul.
December, publishes *Design's Delight*, a collection of texts, prints and a visual essay.

2007
January to March, *The Visual Journalism of Jan van Toorn*, retrospective exhibition at Maryland Institute College of Art, Baltimore.
Guest tutor in the MA programme of the Utrecht School of the Arts.
Contributes a video montage, with a poem by Willem van Toorn, to the public art project *Beeldenstroom* at the lock in Gaarkeuken, organized by the provinces of Friesland and Groningen.

"THE PROBLEM OF DESIGN TODAY IS THAT IT IS MORE FASCINATED BY THE VISUAL, AS A REALISTIC IMITATION OR DECORATION, AND NOT BY THE IMAGE AS A SUBJECTIVE NARRATIVE AND INTERPRETIVE ELEMENT."

Jan van Toorn

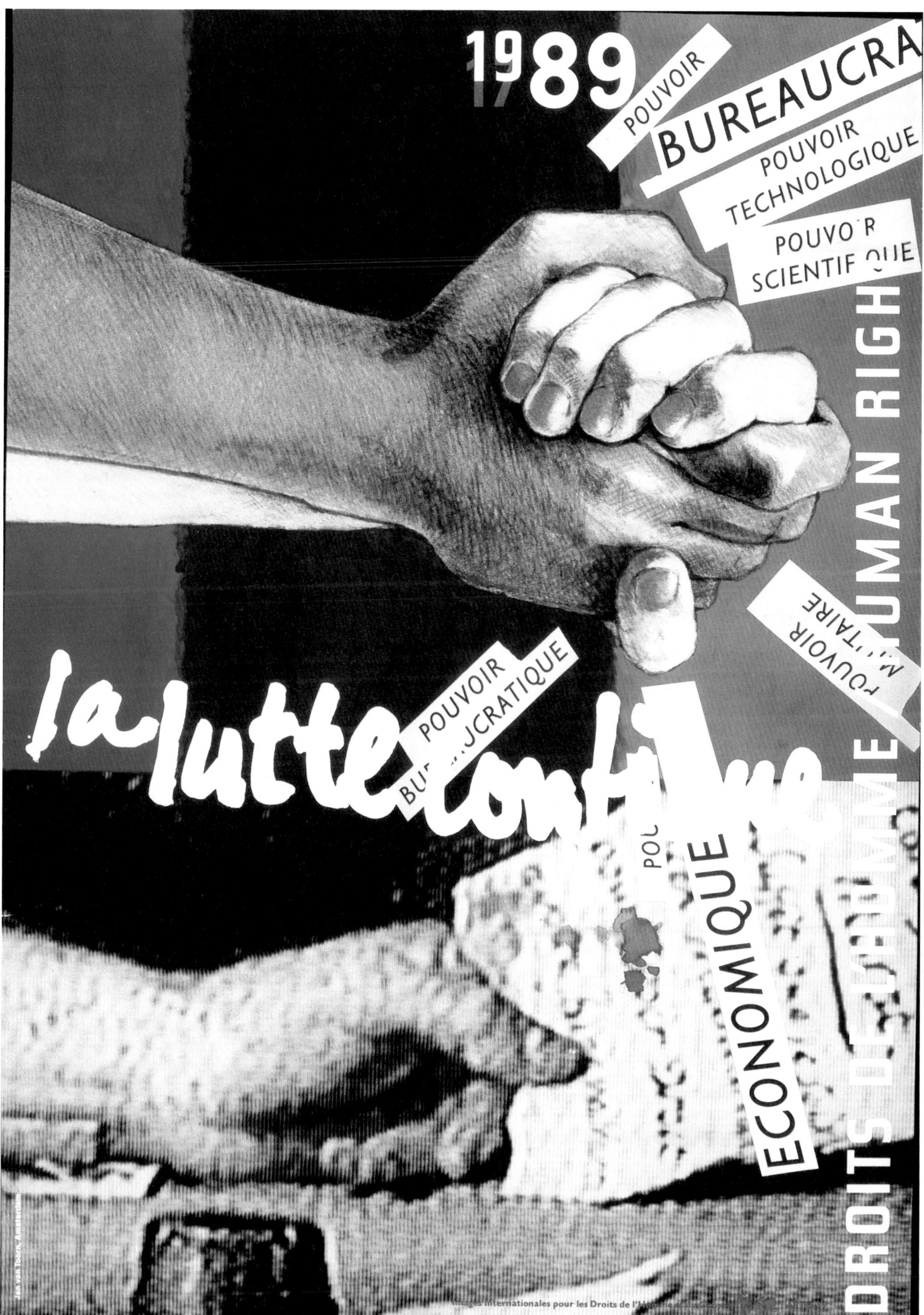

La Lutte Continue. Poster, 1989. Client: Images Internationales pour le Droits de l'Homme et du Citoyen, Artis 89, Paris

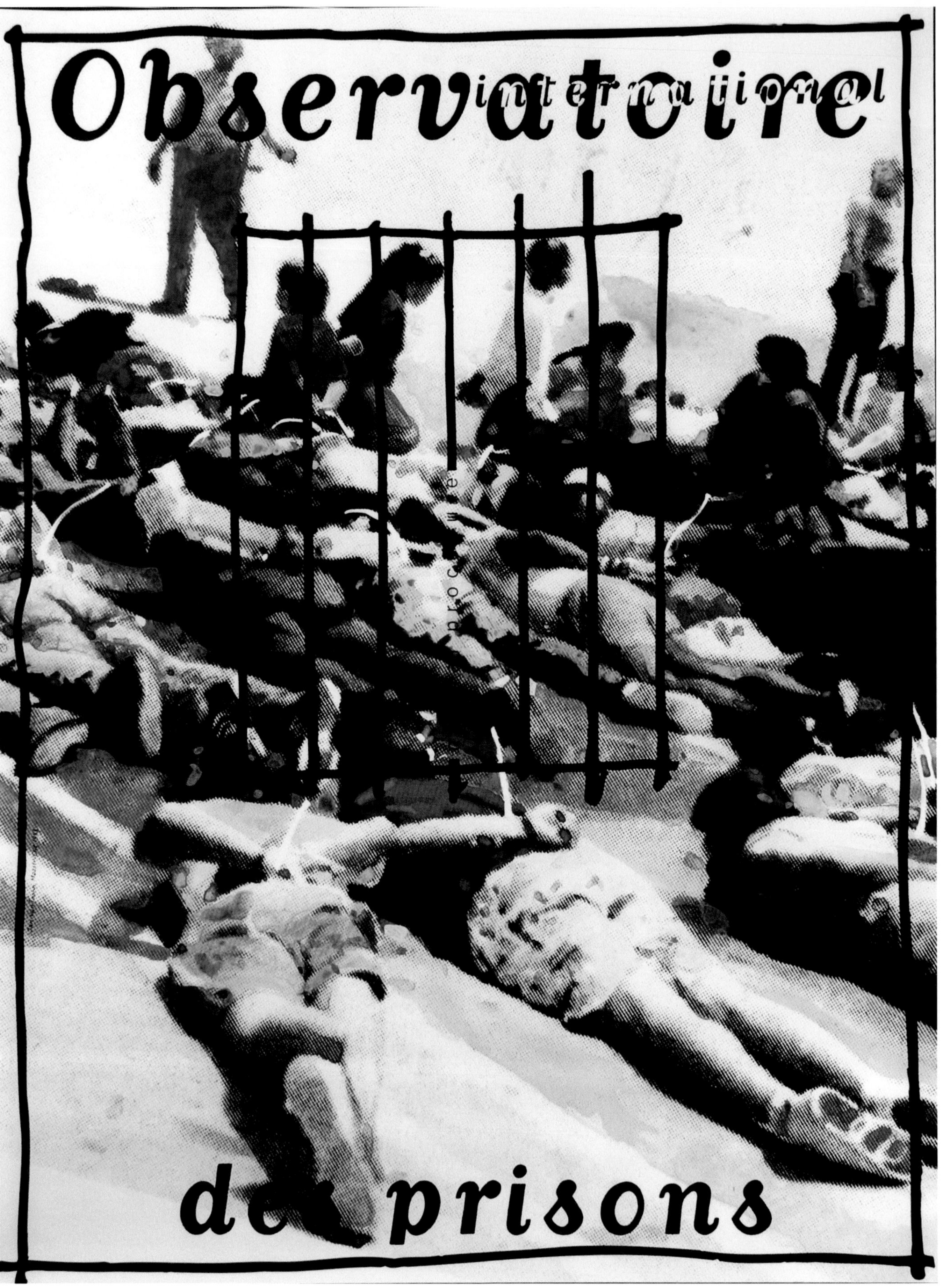

Observatoire International des Prisons. Poster, 1993.
Client: Observatoire International des Prisons, Lyon

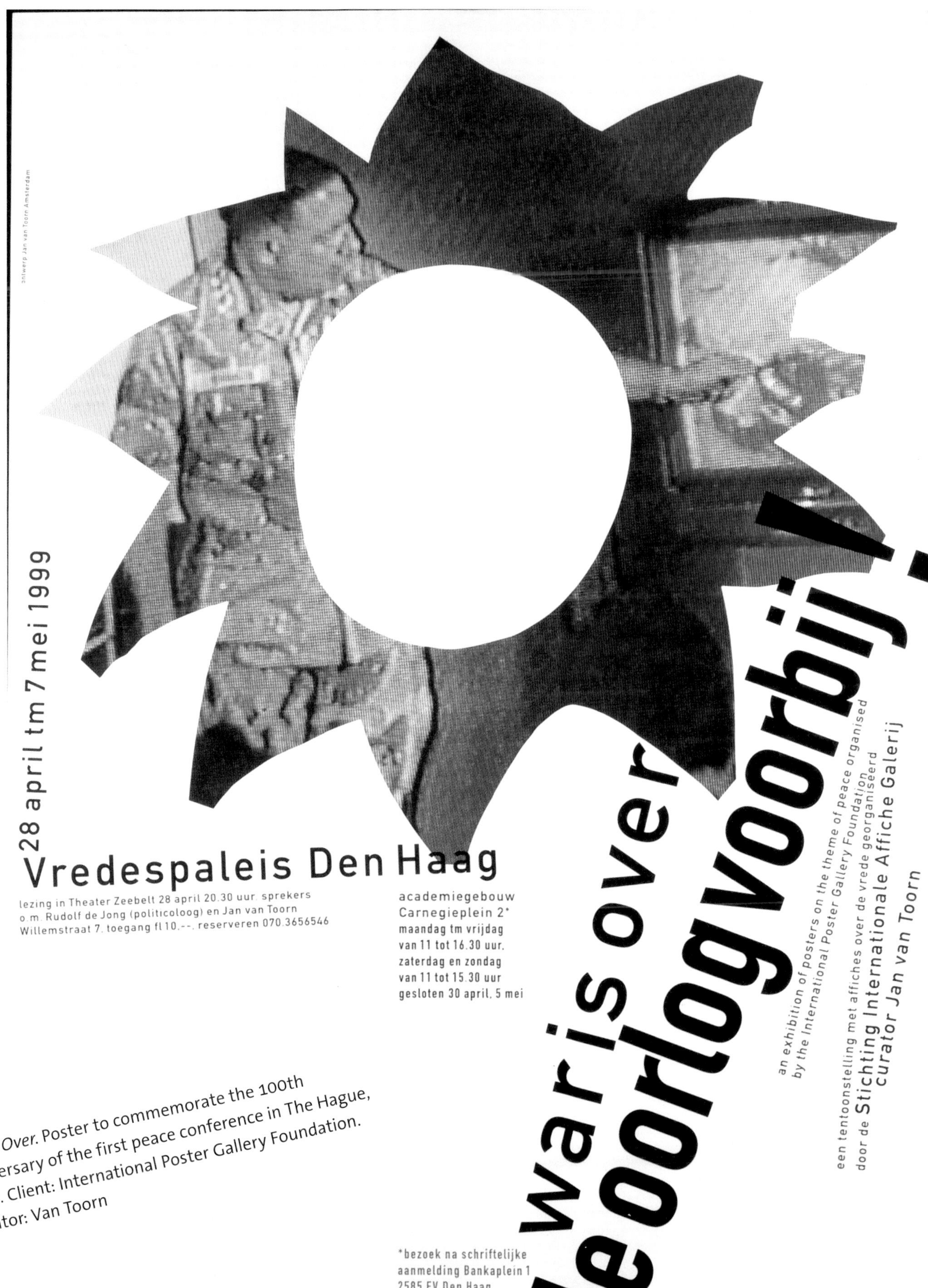

28 april tm 7 mei 1999
Vredespaleis Den Haag
lezing in Theater Zeebelt 28 april 20.30 uur. sprekers
o.m. Rudolf de Jong (politicoloog) en Jan van Toorn
Willemstraat 7. toegang fl 10.--. reserveren 070.3656546
academiegebouw
Carnegieplein 2*
maandag tm vrijdag
van 11 tot 16.30 uur,
zaterdag en zondag
van 11 tot 15.30 uur
gesloten 30 april, 5 mei
*bezoek na schriftelijke
aanmelding Bankaplein 1
2585 EV Den Haag
fax 070.3307546
telefoon 070.3307545
war is over
de oorlog voorbij!
an exhibition of posters on the theme of peace organised
by the International Poster Gallery Foundation
een tentoonstelling met affiches over de vrede georganiseerd
door de Stichting Internationale Affiche Galerij
curator Jan van Toorn

War is Over. Poster to commemorate the 100th anniversary of the first peace conference in The Hague, 1999. Client: International Poster Gallery Foundation. Curator: Van Toorn

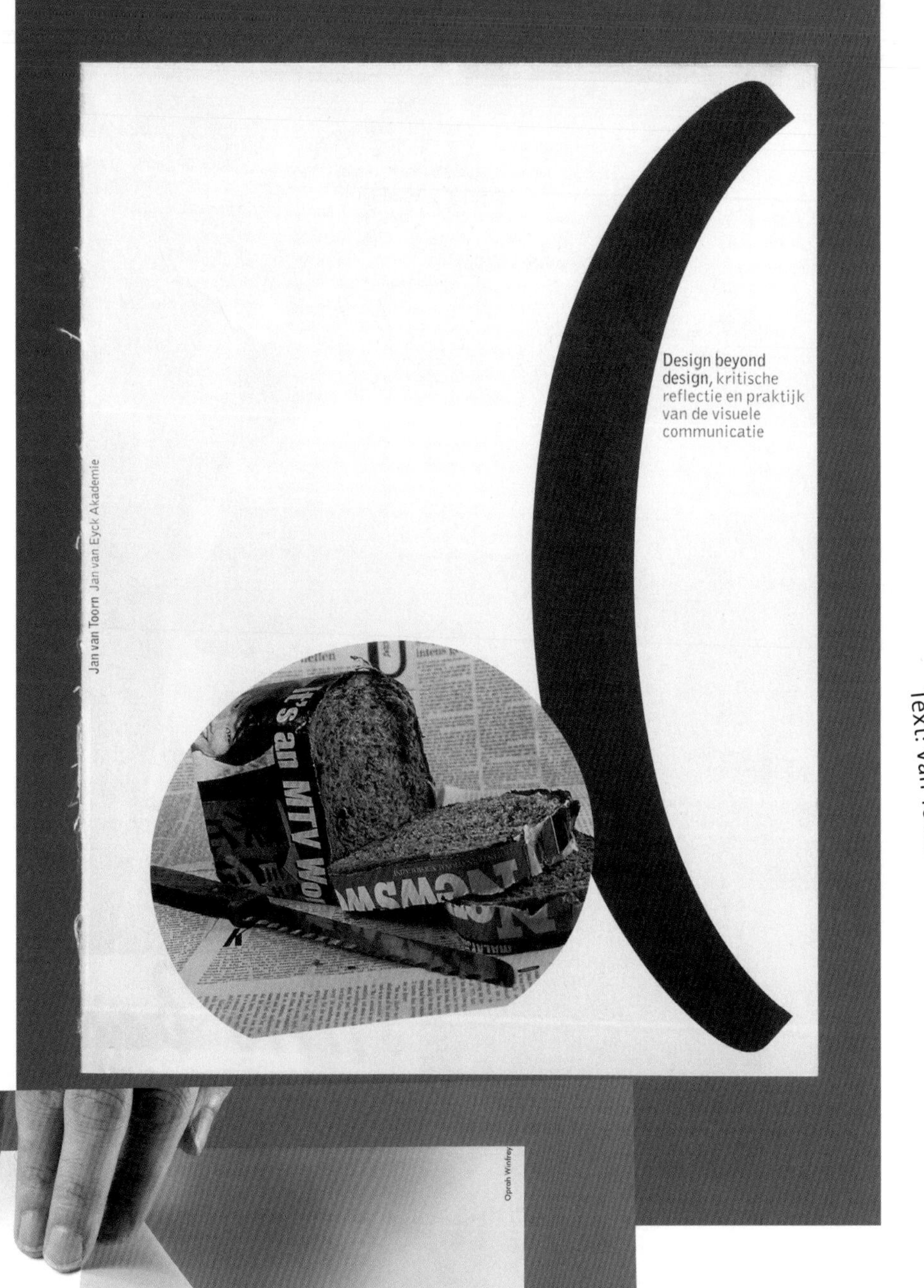

Design beyond Design. Booklet cover, front and back, and spreads, 1996. Publisher: Jan van Eyck Academy. Text: Van Toorn

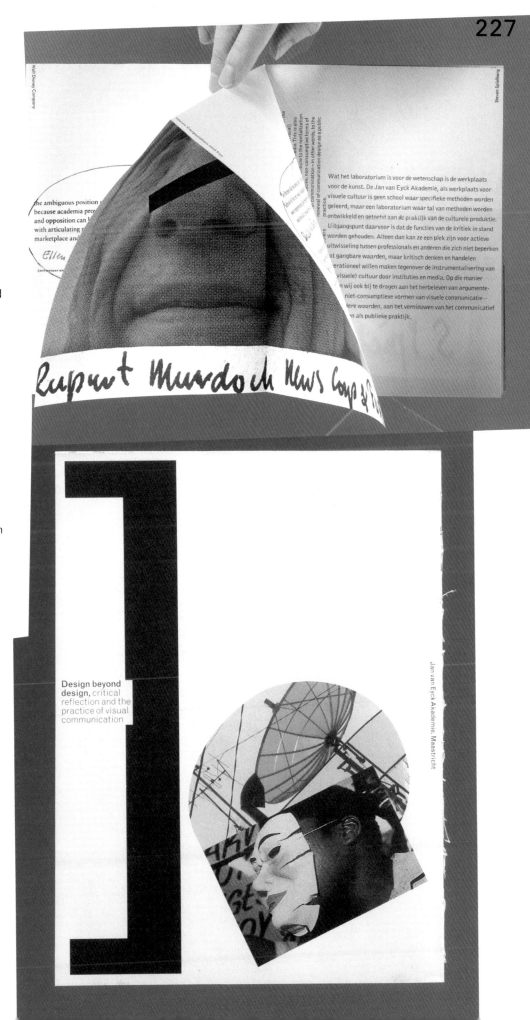

The booklet was an announcement – but more than that, a taster – for the *design beyond Design* symposium held at the Jan van Eyck Academy in 1997. At its spine (quite literally) are a series of short theoretical statements from a lecture by Van Toorn, in English and Dutch, outlining the compromised status of visual communication in a capitalist media society where all forms of information are commodified in the transnational marketplace. On the opposite page, as if cut out, stuck down and encircled in a notebook, are a series of quotations from designers and theorists such as Enzio Manzini, Ellen Lupton, Victor Margolin and Pierre Bernard assembled by Van Toorn as evidence that "there is a serious demand in design for a positive programme of institutional forms connected with an emancipatory reconstruction of society." The reverse sides of the text pages, which are folded at the top, conceal a series of 18 colour photos with an exaggerated halftone dot, like a billboard's, showing leading players within the international media industry, among them Bill Gates of Microsoft, Rupert Murdoch of News Corporation and Fox, Ted Turner of CNN, and Michael Eisner of Disney. Cutting open the pages brings these powerful figures out into the light, a metaphor for the penetrating scrutiny of media ownership and use that must form an essential first step in any reassessment of visual communication's future role.

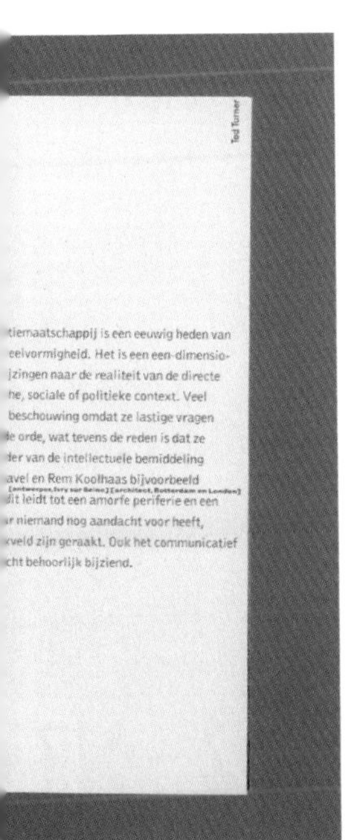

design beyond Design. Book cover and spreads, 1998.
Publishers: Jan van Eyck Academy and De Balie

everything is possible
Gérard Paris-Clavel

Hello,

Here are a few thoughts about the teaching of graphic art and its context. First of all: an educational project supposes a social project in which the discipline to be taught takes its place, a social objective and a pedagogical method. Education in the plastic arts does not begin in art school, it is all around us, in urbanism, architecture, street signs, clothes, objects, journalism, and so on. We can study, invent, and criticise exactly these forms of everyday life, and thereby create memory. We can grasp the origin of images and ideas by coming to grips with the real, in our own history within the community. As the sociologist Pierre Bourdieu has shown, **aesthetic universalism** is an illusion; one must not forget the particular historical and social conditions that have made possible a world view and allowed for the creation of cultural works that may appear perfectly natural and self-evident. Students must learn to shake out of their ingrained habits, to find ways of 'being' in a world that is more and more oriented to 'having'.

School life is a privileged time where personal exploration and social exchange can occur openly, in relative freedom from the divisive pressures of economic necessity and the race for contracts or symbolic power, a time to passionately learn the risks of failure, to make mistakes and start up fresh again.

Social mixtures are what make for a creative, multicultural school. The first culture of all is work, the right to an activity for all is the preamble to the right of access to quality education. Its opposite is unemployment, which destroys the very desire to learn – fine artists too are affected by it, in particular ways. On the contrary, **transforming one's work into a personal activity**,[1] giving it meaning, is the fundamental concern of any truly creative act.

1 André Gorz, *Métamorphoses du travail*, Paris, Galilée, 1988

Intellectuals and social workers

An artistic education implies the ability to challenge taboos, to break through the norm and the average. Education in images means a confrontation with citizenship: critical inquiry and debate. Creativity must step out to meet the world of labour, intellectuals must engage in dialogue with social workers.

Culture should actively participate in social conflict. Art, with its capacity to symbolically express the violence of our contemporary societies, can help question the most difficult problems, and awaken

Let's ask questions about our questions, let's offer ourselves the luxury of taking time, of going back and forth. It takes time for shared thoughts to emerge, for a community to forge its tools of production, and it is indispensable for us to establish a solid methodology of social urgency, to inscribe that urgency in the depth and continuity of time.

I hope this gathering will help construct a space where critical thought on the subject of art and politics can be exchanged. Our association, Ne pas plier, is ready to consider all suggestions.

Ne pas plier [do not bend]

This association was born in 1991 with the objective: **that the signs of poverty not be joined by a poverty of signs, and that the exclusion of language not be replaced by languages of exclusion.** Founded on the energy of a desire, in a relation of friendship with artists, workers, researchers, heads of associations, students, and others, Ne pas plier gathers all those who express their right to exist, in resistance to the dominant discourses. This allows us to enlarge our personal subjects and commissions toward a wider and richer movement of critique nourished on the practices of a collective. With this association I made an essential discovery, which is the necessity of proximity, the urgency of taking your time. I also learned this paradox: the more the means of communication are mass means, the more the meaning is confiscated and coopted. **The institutions filter reality.**

Finally, although I had always been among people, I had few occasions to work with them directly. Rather than continuing on the institutional track, I put myself in the situation of an author-producer, and that did not limit me at all. I already had a certain method, which I brought out onto the terrain of everyday life, where there aren't any commissions. As soon as you have authentic relations between people, the real subjects emerge quickly; it's a chance to work with groups and causes you never encountered before, instead of just reproducing a well-known discourse. The use of the material that we produce stimulates other people's appetites, the material escapes us and that's exactly what I like. **For Ne pas plier, an image is not an inert object to be contemplated, nor is it a political tool in itself. Only when inserted into action or struggle does it produce political effects; only when carried by individuals or groups does it come alive, generating meaning in return. The static image, frozen on the wall, is countered by an image that is carried, used, overwritten, et cetera – drawn into a social and human dynamic. Leave behind the museum space for the stage of social struggle, refuse the rules, values, and categories of the art market, abolish the artist's proud solitude through work conceived as coproduction, reverse the fetishism of the original and of the unique piece by proposing 'images whose original is**

Gérard Paris-Clavel, *Ma ville est un monde*, 1993

Gérard Paris-Clavel, 1996. Poster for Theatre le maillon

Gérard Paris-Clavel, 250 images *Qui se souvient de l'histoire de l'art*. Poster series for the Museum of contemporary arts, Strasbourg, 1996

Paolo Freire: **What fascinates me in reading good books is to find the moment in which the book makes it possible for me or helps me to better my understanding of reality, of concreteness. In other words, for me the reading of books is important to the extent that the books give me a certain theoretical instrument with which I can make the reality more clear vis-à-vis myself, you see. This is the relationship that I try to establish between**

reading words and reading the world.

From **We make the road by walking.**
Conversations on education and social change.
By Myles Horton and Paolo Freire. Edited by Brenda Bell, John Gaventa and John Peters. Philadelphia, 1990.

Design Issues
• History
• Theory
• Criticism

Design Issues Volume XIII Number 1 Spring 1997

Design Issues vol. 13 no. 1. Cover, front and back, spring 1997

Designers are tied to a specific culture, which is strongly defined by the factors of production and distribution of advanced capitalism. Along with other specialists they are part of conventional and institutional systems of representation in mass media. Designers critical of this condition should refrain from the self-referential sign systems which they exploit along with the producers of information in the media.

This does not mean that these sign systems should be abolished in practice. On the contrary: a designer should make his clients' as well as his own manipulation visible in the message by referring to accepted values and visual codes. A strategy that reveals the conditions of production in the mediated display, which enables the message to be experienced as artificial, as an argument: an ideological instrument in the permanent discussion on the contradictions of social reality.

Jan van Toorn

SPIRALS 61 RISD Graphic Design Department

THANKSGIVING 1990 OPERATION DESERT STORM

351

"Thanksgiving 1990 Operation Desert Storm" in *The Tomàs Gonda Prize for Design and Social Responsibility*. Book spread, 1991. Publisher: Rhode Island School of Design. Text: Van Toorn

Visible Language vol. 28 no. 4. Journal spreads, autumn 1994. Text: Van Toorn

Cultiver notre Jardin. Book cover and spreads, 1999. Photographs: Van Toorn and others. Publisher and printer: Drukkerij Rosbeek

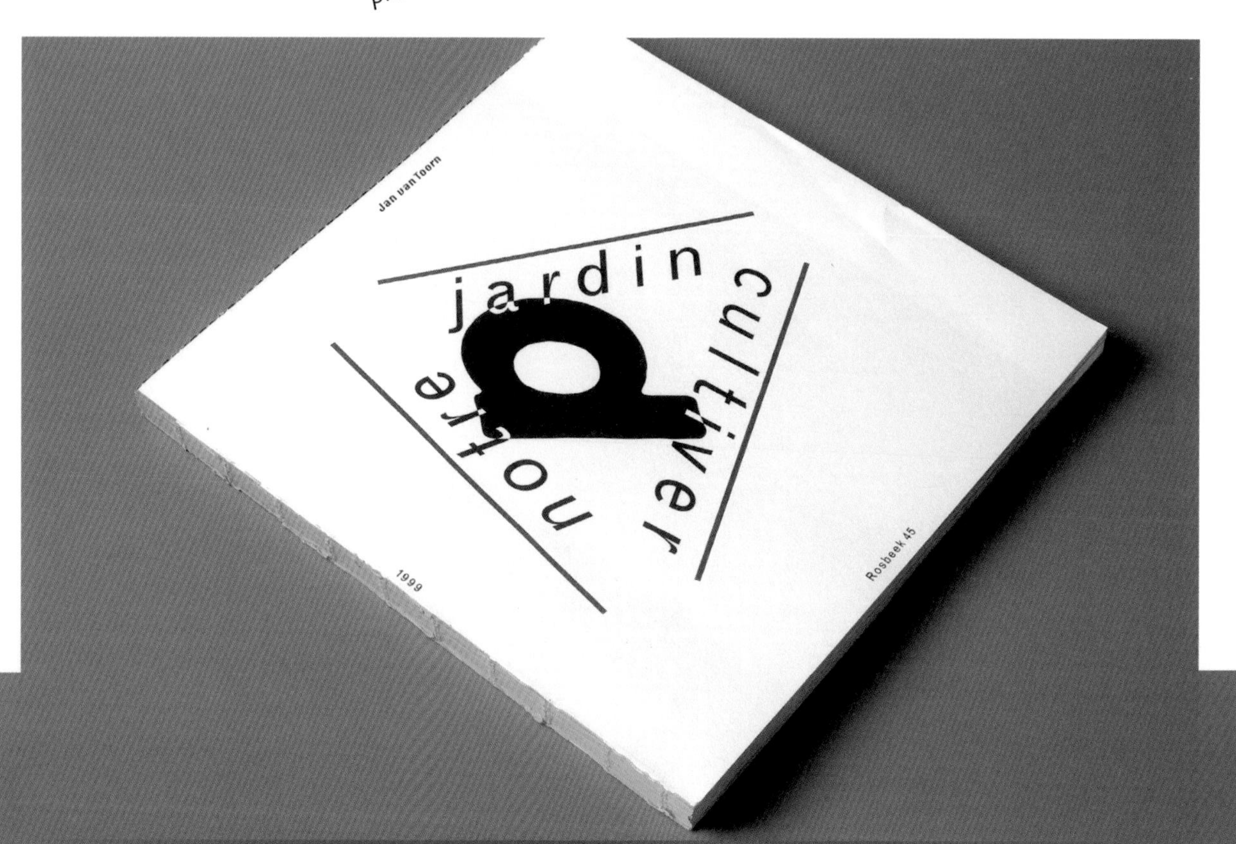

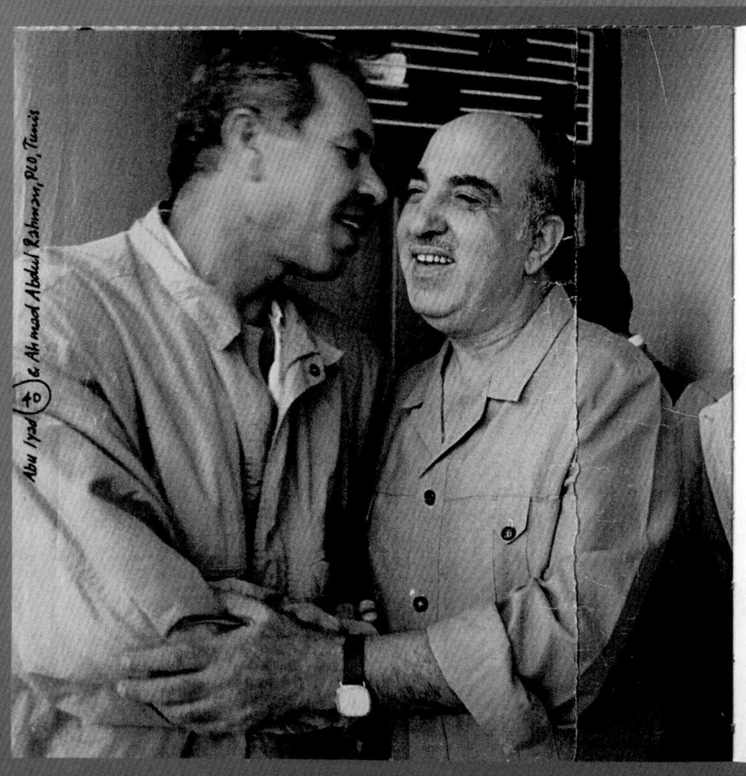

Ernesto Laclau

Is the realm of personal self-realization

really a *private* realm?

It would be so if that self-realization

took place in a neutral medium in

which individuals could seek unimpeded

the fulfilment of their own aims.

But this medium is, of course, a myth.

This book-sized visual essay for Rosbeek's Goodwill series takes its title from Voltaire's famous phrase, *"il faut cultiver notre jardin"* in the novel *Candide* – a defiant counsel against despair. For Van Toorn, these metaphorical gardens represent the small zones of human possibility that remain between the vast global territories occupied today by corporations and conglomerates, and an ordinary alotment garden lies at the book's centre. As with the *Design beyond Design* booklet, alternate spreads are hidden from view by the fold at the top of the page, requiring readers to complete the book by cutting it open. The pages counterpoint unspectacular scenes of people going about their lives, shown in colour, with black-and-white images of the economic and political interests – shopping malls, tourist sites, the media, the military – that lie behind this reality, shaping the direction of everyday life and determining its limits. The interventions that Van Toorn once made manually in the Mart.Spruijt calendars by cutting, pasting and spraying are here performed digitally. The colour in the photos has been adjusted to accentuate certain details and give these scenes a hyper-reality that undercuts their apparent authenticity and begins to reveal the links between the public realm and the society of the spectacle that threatens its freedom.

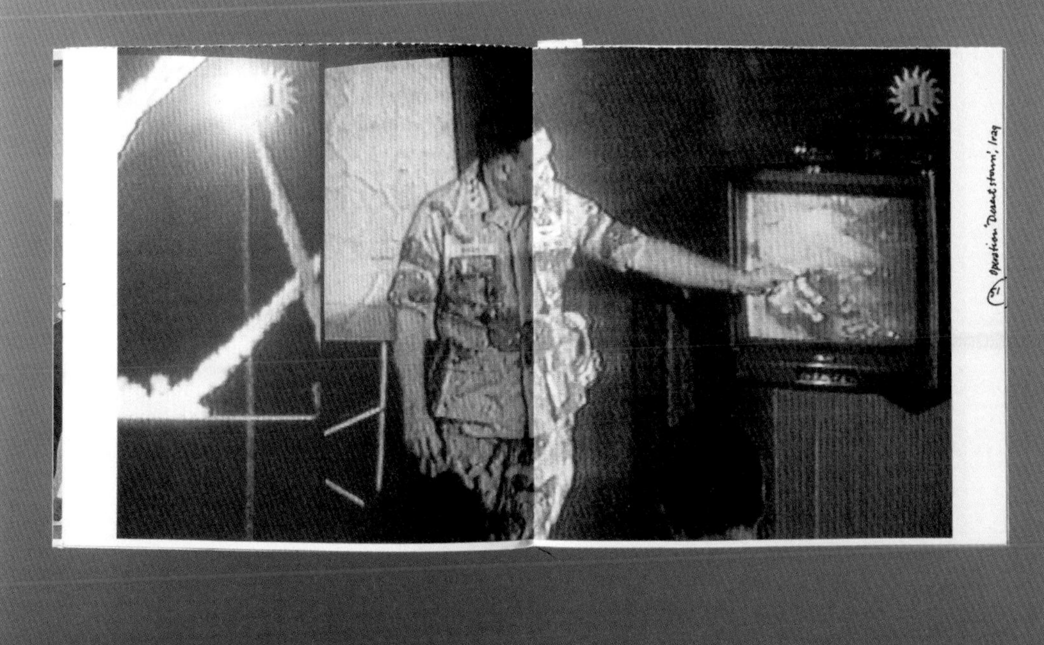

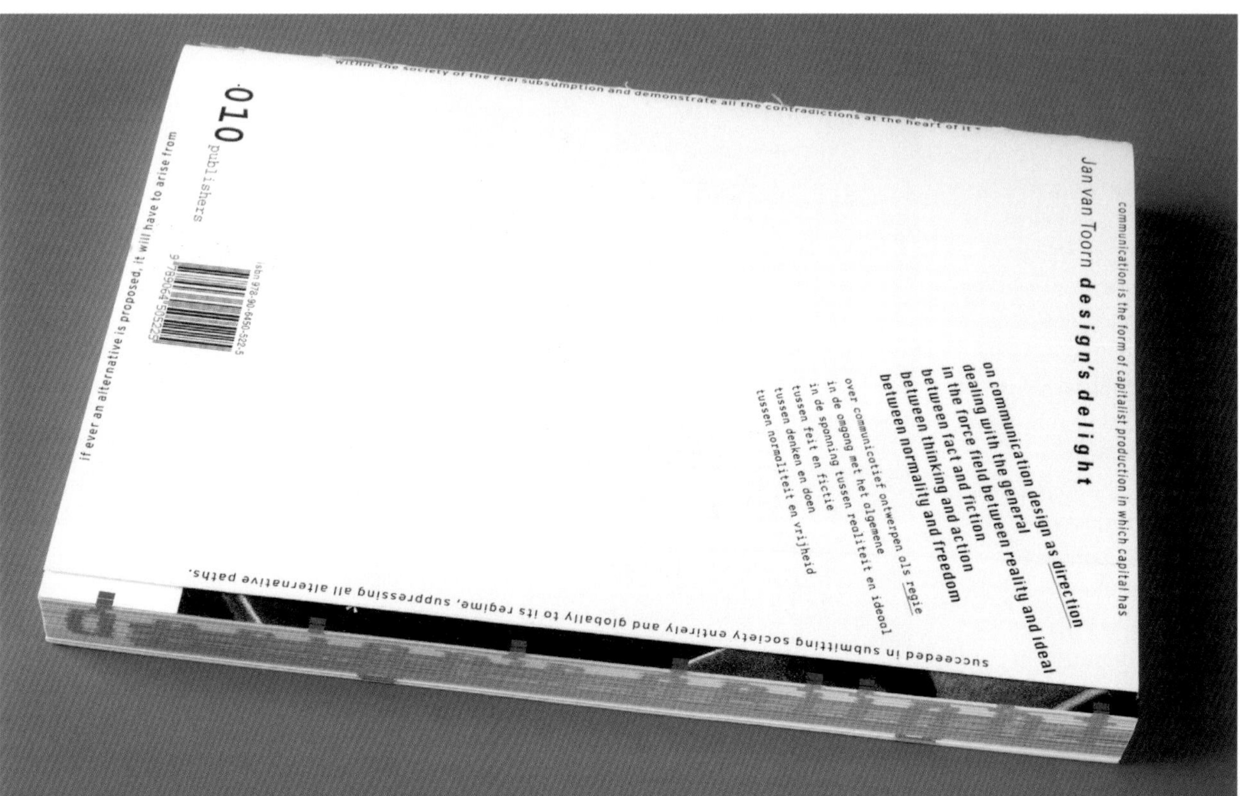

design is a ~~good~~ idea< desperately seeking images

other

and forms

Time warner, Disney, Viacom, News corp and Nbc universal

keep changing position in the top 5 [p 7] and are increasingly partners instead of rivals

10

driftig op zoek naar beelden

en andere vormen

Design's Delight. Book cover and spreads, 2006. Publisher: 010. Text: Van Toorn

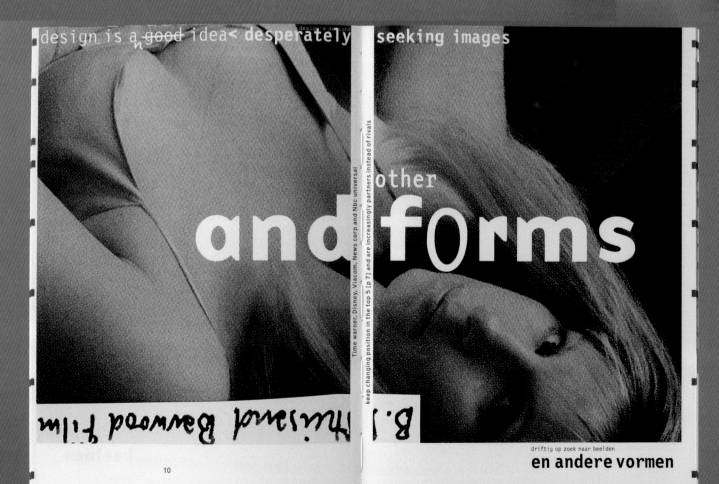

the general move towards visualisation has broad intellectual and practical implications for the conduct and the theory of the humanities, the physical and the biological sciences, the social sciences - indeed, for all forms of education, from top to bottom *

Barbara Stafford

*Good looking. Cambridge and London, 1996

de algemene drang tot visualisering heeft grote intellectuele en praktische gevolgen

the top 5 [p 7] control 90% of all media production and distribution: newspapers, magazines,

books, photo press bureaus, music, cable and satellite networks, tv, radio, new media

for everybody for visual communication

voor het gedrag en de theorie van de menswetenschappen, de natuurwetenschappen, de biologie, de sociale wetenschappen - en niet te vergeten, voor alle vormen van onderwijs, van hoog tot laag

Comcast and Time warner together now own every cable tv network in the US

Dit verhaal gaat over mijn denken als ontwerper [denken over het visuele] van visuele communicatie – over denken als een methode om mijn eigen handelen en rol als specialist te begrijpen in de sociaal-culturele context. Met andere woorden, ik probeer mijn persoonlijk en professioneel handelen in verband te brengen met de kleine en grotere contexten van menselijke activiteit. Dat denken moet wel operationeel zijn: een constructie van begrippen en argumenten die het mogelijk maakt om – als persoon, als sociaal wezen en als professional – te kunnen omgaan met de complexiteit van de wereld waarin wij leven.

Tegen de achtergrond van de libertair-socialistische visie op de wereld van de historische avantgarde waarmee ik me verwant voel, moet dat denken allereerst worden gezien als een poging verbeelding te steken in de tegenstelling tussen traditie en vernieuwing, in de zin van sociale emancipatie en menselijk overleven. Die oriëntatie op maatschappelijke en publieke doelen is meer dan ooit noodzakelijk nu de disciplines van praktisch intellectuelen zich zozeer hebben verbonden met de macht van het geld, de bureaucratie en de media, die weinig overtuigende oplossingen bieden voor de sociale, econo-mische en ecologische crisis.

Om als ontwerpers, architecten, televisiemakers enzovoort, te ontsnappen aan de verstrengeling met de instituties – die nu eenmaal prioriteiten stellen in overeenstemming met hun particuliere belangen – is het zaak te werken aan een denkwereld en strategieën die handelen ten dienste van het publiek belang opnieuw mogelijk maken.

Communicatie bestaat grotendeels uit onberedeneerd handelen. Daarom is bij het formuleren van een concept dat streeft naar meer onafhankelijke meningsvorming, behalve een analyse van de bestaande productieverhoudingen, een constante reflectie nodig op die empirische ervaring. Alleen op die manier is het mogelijk om temidden van de veranderende en tegengestelde corporatieve belangen – waar we tegelijk afhankelijk van zijn – cultuur-politieke criteria en strategieën te ontwikkelen die nieuwe ruimte scheppen voor onafhankelijk professioneel handelen in de media. Een handelen dat uitgaat van een niet-autoritaire houding ten opzichte van het publiek en de eigen rol van de bemiddeling niet verdonkeremaant.

Het ontwerpen heeft, denk ik, niet de aandacht gekregen die nodig is om zijn huidige sociale positie te begrijpen. Ondanks de enorme verspreiding van visuele informatie, worden de complexe factoren van institutionele macht bepalend voor zijn productie grotendeels genegeerd. Het eigentijds ontwerpen

This essay deals with my thinking as a designer of visual communication – with thinking as a method of understanding my own action and role as an expert in the socio-cultural context. In other words I see my personal and professional activity in relation to social reality, in relation to the smaller and larger contexts of human activity. My thinking should be operational in this: a construct of notions and arguments which enables me – as a person, as a social being and as a professional – to deal with the complexity of the world we live in.

Against the background of the libertarian-socialist worldview of the historical avant-garde, with which I feel a close affinity, this thinking should first and foremost be understood as an ongoing attempt to deal imaginatively with the conflict between tradition and innovation, related to the collective interest in the sense of social emancipation and human survival. This orientation towards social and public goals is needed more than ever now that the disciplines of practical intellectuals have affiliated to such an extent with the power of money, bureaucracy and the media, whose solutions for the social, economic and ecological crisis are far from convincing.

For us, as designers, architects, television-makers et cetera, to escape from this entanglement with institutional interests – which wish to set priorities in such a way as to reflect their private interests – it is important to formulate a concept and strategies which once more make action for the public concern possible.

Communication is largely formed by unreasoned action. Therefore the formation of a concept which strives for a more independent forming of opinions, requires besides the analysis of the existing production relations an unceasing reflection on that empirical experience. In this way it will be possible, amidst the shifting and opposing corporate interests – and at the same time being dependent upon them – to develop politico-cultural criteria and strategies which will open new space for professional action in the media. Action starting from a non-authoritarian attitude towards the public and not concealing its own mediating role.

Design, I think, has not received the attention needed to understand its present social position. Despite the enormous dissemination of information, the complex factors of institutional power which definitely contribute to its production have mostly been ignored. Nor has contemporary

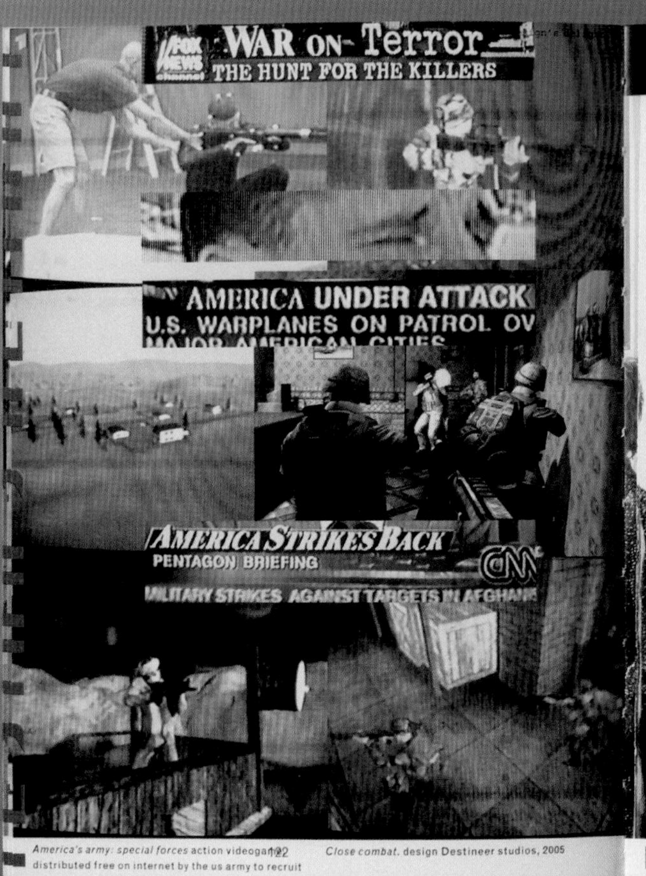

America's army: special forces action videogame distributed free on internet by the us army to recruit volunteers. design Michael Zyda and Michael Capps. 2002

122

Close combat. design Destineer studios, 2005

een markt waarin jaarlijks meer dan $ 2 miljard omgaat

the erasure of memory

THE SPIN TEAM

seeks to reach beyond the military sphere to explain the 'war on terrorism' in terms of economics, culture, diplomacy and law. all five members of the team originate from the media, public relations and culture industry

5 the males of George W. Bush's 'spin team'. 'historic portraits of the White house at wartime'. photo Annie Leibovitz, 2002

Natta, Wto en Ftaa privatiseren de publieke sector waaronder het onderwijs,

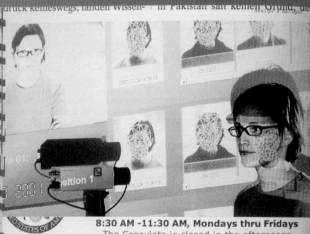

druck keineswegs, landen Wissen- | in Pakistan sah keinen Grund, de

design & delight

8:30 AM -11:30 AM, Mondays thru Fridays
The Consulate is closed in the afternoons and on Embassy and Consulate Holidays

Security Situation in the Netherlands | Latest Worldwide Caution
Homeland Security Threat level announcement

SEVERE
RISK OF TERRORIST ATTACKS

- Effective November 1, 2002, the applicatio... 100 U.S. dollars (100 Euro at the present rate of exchange). The increase from $6... to $100 will bring the MRV (Machine Readable Visa) fee into line with the actual cost of administering nonimmigrant visa services. MRV fee receipts dated on or after Nov 1, 2002 must indicate payment of the Euro 100 fee.
- **New form for Nonimmigrant visa**. effective August 1
  The Department of State announces the introduction of a new form, **Contact Information And Work History For Nonimmigrant Visa Applicant (Form DS-158)**. Effective AUGUST 1st, 2002, all applicants seeking F, J and M visas must complete and submit Form DS-158 in addition to the Nonimmigrant Visa Application (Form DS-156) and, if necessary, the Supplemental Nonimmigrant Visa Application (Form DS-157).
- Important: New passport laws:
- Issuance Rules Effective April 8th, 2002
  - New Law on Passport Applications for Minors under age 14, effective

electronic photometric control at border check 130 website of the us consulate in Amsterdam. 2003

in the US in 40% of secondary schools, on 90% of schooldays, and reach 80% of the classes

quick, light and strong

the 5 levels of risk for terrorist attacks issued by the us Department of homeland security

SEVERE
HIGH
ELEVATED
GUARDED
LOW

6 20,000 police and troops deployed against demonstrating alternative-globalists during the G8 world summit in the 'fortress' of Genoa. 2001

Channel one educational programmes [2 min of commercials for every 10 min of news] are compulsory

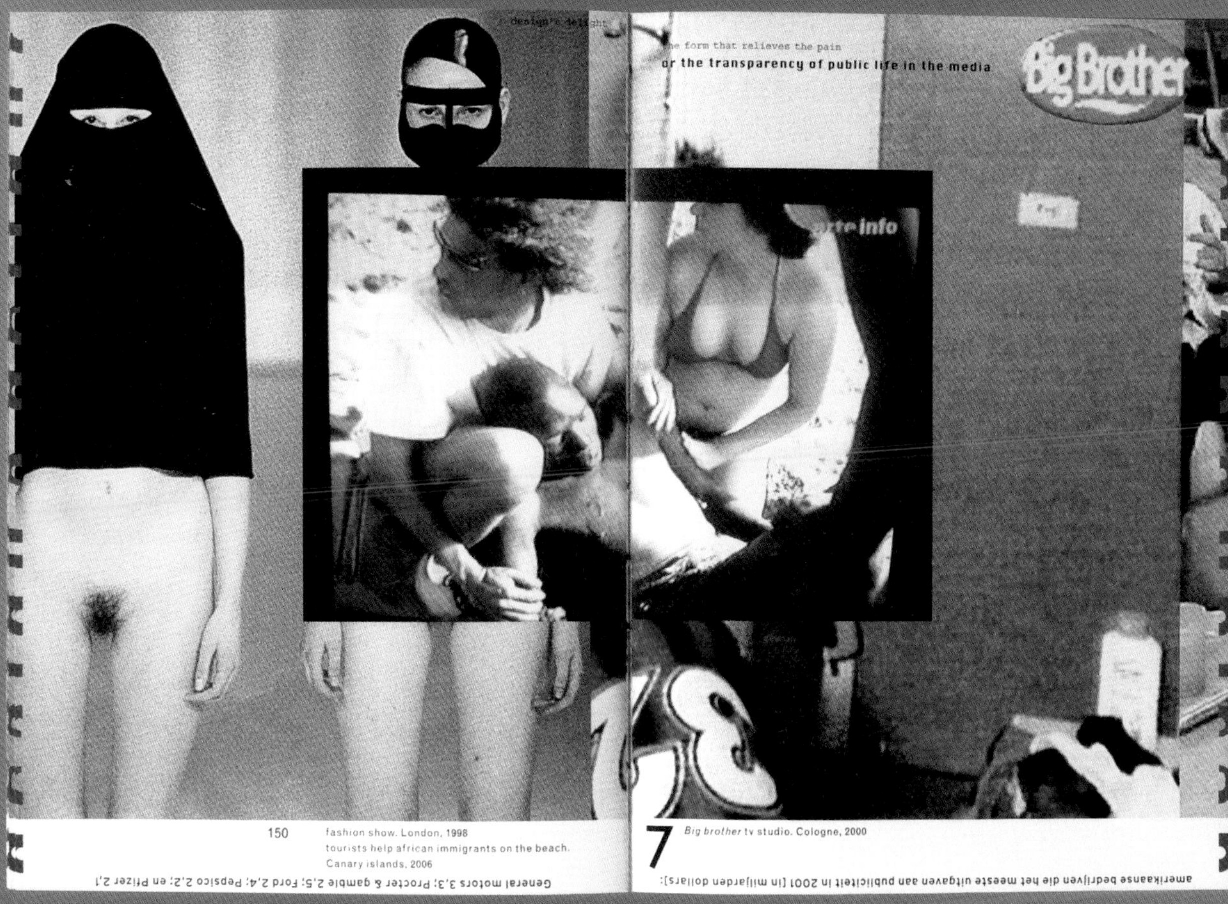

design's delight

the viewer should shift
from receptive watching to
***participating* observation**

Barbara Stafford

Good looking.
Cambridge & London,
1996

de kijker moet omschakelen van receptief kijken
naar *participerend* waarnemen

194

us courts are investigating the merger between Aol and Time warner [$ 106 billion] and other malafide transactions
including those with Bertelsmann [$ 400 million], Monster.com [$ 100 million] and Vivendi universal [$ 25 million]

active spectatorship

by a combinatorial aesthetics
of collage *encouraging*
to make connections,

delightfully inviting
to make our own patterns*

door een combinerende collage-esthetiek
die *aanmoedigt* tot het leggen van verbanden,
enthousiast uitnodigt* tot het maken van onze eigen patronen

Bibliography

Compiled by Els Kuijpers and Rick Poynor

Publications about Jan van Toorn

Books and catalogues

70 Affiches pour le Droit à la Dignité des Prisonniers Ordinaires, Lyon: Observatoire International des Prisons, 1993.

Amstutz, Walter, *Who's Who in Graphic Art* vol. 2, Dübendorf: De Clivo Press, 1982.

Aynsley, Jeremy, *A Century of Graphic Design: Graphic Design Pioneers of the 20th Century*, London: Mitchell Beazley, 2001.

Barnouw, David and Ada Lopes Cardozo, *Herdenken op Klein Formaat: Nederlandse Postzegels over de Tweede Wereldoorlog*, Zutphen: Walburg Pers, 1996.

Beeke, Anthon, *Dutch Posters 1960–1996*, Amsterdam: BIS Publishers, 1997.

——, *Le Nouveau Salon des Cent*, Graulhet: Éditions Odyssée, 2003.

Brattinga, Pieter, *Affiche: Wil Sandberg, Wim Crouwel, Otto Treumann, Pieter Brattinga, Aart Verhoeven, Jan van Toorn, Dick Elffers, Jan Bons, Dick Bruna*, Amsterdam: Nederlandse Kunststichting, 1973.

——, *60 Plakate neun Holländische Graphiker 1956–1970*, Hilversum: Steendrukkerij de Jong, 1974.

Broos, Kees and Paul Hefting, *Dutch Graphic Design*, London: Phaidon, 1993.

Duis, Leonie ten and Annelies Haase, *De Wereld moe(s)t Anders: Grafisch Ontwerpen en Idealisme/The World must Change: Graphic Design and Idealism*, Amsterdam: Sandberg Instituut and Uitgeverij De Balie, 1999.

Fiell, Charlotte and Peter, *Graphic Design for the 21st Century, 100 of the World's Best Graphic Designers*, Cologne: Taschen, 2003.

——, *Contemporary Graphic Design*, Cologne: Taschen, 2007.

Friedl, Friedrich, Nicolaus Ott and Bernard Stein, *Typography: When Who How*, Cologne: Könemann, 1998.

Hollis, Richard, *Graphic Design: A Concise History*, London: Thames & Hudson, 2001 (first edition 1994).

Julier, Guy, *The Thames & Hudson Encyclopaedia of 20th Century Design and Designers*, London: Thames & Hudson, 1993.

Henrion, F.H.K., *AGI Annals: Alliance Graphique Internationale 1952–1987*, Zurich: Alliance Graphique Internationale, 1989.

Khammar, Driss El Yazami, *Pour les Droits de l'Homme: Histoire(s) Image(s) Parole(s)*, Paris: Artis 89, 1989.

Kuijpers, Els, *En/Of, over Tegenspraak in het Werk van Jan van Toorn*, Nuth: Rosbeek Books, 2004.

——, *And/Or, on Contradiction in the Work of Jan van Toorn*, Nuth: Rosbeek Books (booklet), 2006.

Leering, Jean, *Jan van Toorn over Affiches*, Amsterdam: Openbaar Kunstbezit, 1976.

Livingston, Alan and Isabella, *The Thames & Hudson Dictionary of Graphic Design and Designers*, London: Thames & Hudson, 2003 (first edition 1992).

Lupton, Ellen (ed.), *Graphic Design and Typography in the Netherlands: A View of Recent Work*, New York: The Cooper Union and Princeton Architectural Press, 1992.

Noble, Ian and Russell Bestley, *Experimental Layout*, Hove: Rotovision, 2001.

Poynor, Rick, "The Designer as Reporter" *in Obey the Giant: Life in the Image World*, Basel. Birkhäuser, 2001 and 2007.

Purvis, Alston W. and Cees W. de Jong, *Dutch Graphic Design: A Century of Innovation*, London: Thames & Hudson, 2006.

Reitsma, Lex, *Lex Reitsma in Gesprek met Jan van Toorn, Jan Boterman, Karel Kruijsen, Jelle van der Toorn Vrijthoff, Wim Crouwel, Ootje Oxenaar, Paul Mijksenaar*, Amsterdam: Uitgeverij Rietveld Projecten, 1983.

Rodrigo, Evert and William Rothuizen, *Ontwerpen Jan van Toorn*, Breda: De Beyerd (catalogue), 1986.

Soar, Matthew, *Graphic Design, Graphic Dissent: Towards a Cultural Economy of an Insular Profession*, University of Massachusetts Amherst (unpublished PhD dissertation), 2002.

Staal, Gert and Hester Wolters (eds.), *Holland in Vorm: Dutch Design 1945–1987*, The Hague: Stichting Holland in Vorm, 1987.

Ven, Frans van de, *Het Verhaal van Delta-Expo*, Breda: Academie voor Beeldende Kunsten St. Joost (published dissertation), 1992.

Vermaas, Chris H., "De Betekenis en Haar Vorm. Het Werk van Jan van Toorn" in *Jan van Toorn*, Eindhoven: [Z]OO Producties (booklet), 2006.

Articles

Aldersey-Williams, Hugh, "Training Dutch Masters", *I.D.*, January/February 1993, p. 18.

Barten, Walter, "Jan van Toorn", *De Groene Amsterdammer*, 28 November 1972.

——, "Grafisch Ontwerper Jan van Toorn Vrij Tussen de Stromingen", *Het Financieele Dagblad*, 10 and 12 January 1987, p. 11.

——, "Chaos is een Essentieel Gegeven: de Anarchistische Ontwerpen van Jan van Toorn", *De Groene Amsterdammer*, 14 January 1987, pp. 20–1.

Berkhout, Karel, "Van Toorn Maakt Kortsluitung met Details", *NRC Handelsblad*, April 2004, p. 8.

Blauvelt, Andrew, "Towards a Complex Simplicity", *Eye* no. 35 vol. 9, spring 2000, pp. 38–47.

Bojko, Szymon, "Dutch Prints", *Projekt* no. 4, 1973, pp. 10–7.

Bolten-Rempt, Jetteke, "Jan van Toorn, Medium + Message", *Dutch Art + Architecture Today* no. 19, June 1986, pp. 26–31.

Bouman, Ole, "De Noodzaak tot Openbaarheid, een Vraaggesprek met Jan van Toorn", *Beeld* no. 3, 1983, pp. 6–11.

Brattinga, Pieter, "Public and Private: Dutch Design, 1945–1991", *Print* XLV:VI, November/December 1991, pp. 50–9, 144.

Broos, Kees, "From the Fine Book to Visual Communication", *Dutch Art + Architecture Today* no. 3, May 1978, pp. 14–21.

Bruinsma, Max and Pjotr de Jong, "Bij Wijze van Spreken" in *Het Boek*, Hilversum: Steendrukkerij De Jong, 1986.

Bruinsma, Max, "Jan van Toorn: Je ne cherche pas, Je trouve", *Étapes* no. 42, March 2007, pp. 32–42.

Crouwel, Wim, "De Vormgeving en het Museum" in Wim Crouwel (ed.), "Om de kunst", *Documentaires* no. 8, 1978, pp. 15–21.

Erkelens, Rob van, "Dwarse Vormen", *De Groene Amsterdammer*, 29 October 1997, pp. 28–9.

Eun-young-Jung, "Communication Design as a Public Practice: Jan van Toorn", *Design* no. 267, September 2000, pp. 120–1.

David Barnow, "Februaristaking" in Paul Hefting (ed.), *Nederlandse Postzegels 1991*, The Hague: PTT, 1992.

Forde, Gerard, "The Designer Unmasked", *Eye* no. 2 vol. 1, 1991, pp. 56–68.

Sauvage, Anne-Marie and Marie-Pierre Cuvis, "Graphisme(s), 1997–2001: Deux cents Createurs", *Étapes* no. 76, September 2001, p. 30.

Grondel, Annemiek van, "Het DNA van Jan van Toorn", *Identity Matters* no. 7, 2007, pp. 24–31.

Hefting, Paul, "Kinderpostzegels 1979" in Paul Hefting (ed.), *Nederlandse Postzegels 1979*, The Hague: PTT, 1981, pp. 75–80.

——, "Postzegels Nederlandse Politici" in Paul Hefting (ed.), *Nederlandse Postzegels 1980*, The Hague: PTT, 1980, pp. 36–8.

——, "Postzegel Dr. W. Drees" in Paul Hefting (ed.), *Nederlandse Postzegels 1986*, The Hague: PTT, 1988, pp. 57–60.

Heuvel, Jeroen van den, "Training Courses" in *Holland in Vorm: Dutch Design 1945–1987*, The Hague: Stichting Holland in Vorm, 1987, pp. 180–93.

Hubben, Hub, "Twee Keer Kijken", *De Volkskrant*, April 2004, pp. 14-15

Huygen, Frederike, "Geloof in het Denkende Individu", *Het Financieele Dagblad*, April 2004, p. 29.

——, "Verslag van een Bewustmakingsmachine", *Items*, February 2007, pp. 52–5.

Ilyin, Natalia and Katie Salen, "Jan van Toorn" (interview) in Thomas Ockerse (coordinator), *Spirals '91* book 2, Providence: Rhode Island School of Design, 1991, pp. 56–9.

Forbes, Colin, "Graphic Design in Europe", *Idea* no. 150, 1978, pp. 64–5.

Kuijpers, Els, "Pro and Con: Defining Design History, Correctly", *AIGA Journal of Graphic Design* vol. 12 no. 3, 1994, pp. 45–7.

——, "ABC for the Other Reader", *Dot Dot Dot* no. 9, winter 2004/2005, pp. 74–9.

Kuitenbrouwer, Carel, "A Prominent Place", *Dutch Arts* no. 5, "Design in the Netherlands", July 1989, pp. 21–34.

Löb, Kurt, "Kunst Verkaufen wie Margarine", *Novum Gebrauchsgraphik* vol. 43 no. 5, 1972, pp. 10–9.

McCoy, Katherine, "Reconstructing Dutch Graphics", *Industrial Design*, March/April 1984, pp. 38–43.

Olds, Andrew, "The Gospel According to Jan", *Direction*, July 1990, pp. 36–8.

Petersen, Ad, "Van Mind Fucker tot Informant" in Wim Crouwel (ed.), "Om de Kunst", *Documentaires* no. 8, 1978, pp. 7–14.

Poggenpohl, Sharon, "Jan van Toorn" (interview) in Thomas Ockerse (coordinator), *Spirals '91* book 2, Providence: Rhode Island School of Design, 1991, pp. 57–9.

Poynor, Rick, "Why Foucault's Pendulum Swings over Maastricht", *Blueprint*, June 1992, p. 8.

——, "Jan van Toorn: Arguing with Visual Means", *Design Observer*, 21 March 2004. http://www.designobserver.com/archives/000120.html

Purcell, Kerry William, "Delightful Precipice at the Edge of Communicative Reality", *Eye* no. 63 vol. 16, spring 2007, pp. 79–80.

Resnick, Elizabeth, "Keep Your Eyes Open" (interview), *AIGA Journal of Graphic Design* vol. 18 no. 1, 2000, pp. 38–40.

——, "Objetivar lo Social/The Social Context as Objective Reality" (interview), *tpG* no. 52, July/August/September 2002, pp. 14–21.

Rodrigo, Evert, "Grafische Vormgevers en Beeldende Kunst", *Kunstschrift* no. 2, March/April 1986, pp. 56–9.

Rothuizen, William, "Jan van Toorn", *Vrij Nederland*, 15 November 1986, pp. 25–31.
Staal, Gert, "Tegen de Verarming: Jan van Toorn over het Panorama der Gewoonten", *Items*, September/October 2003, pp. 52–7.
Thornton, Richard, "The Nature of Dutch Design", *Print* XXX:VI, November/December 1993, pp. 66–77.
Vrie, Dingenus van de and Titus Yocarini, *Tien Jaar Designkritiek*, Nijmegen, Thieme Projecten, 1980, pp. 27, 29, 30–32, 43, 45, 55.
Toorn, Willem van, "Tekeningen Stop Je in een Plastic Zak. Een Gesprek met Jan van Toorn", *Raster*, no. 72, 1996, pp. 77–97.
Twemlow, Alice, "Theories Look Good on Paper", *Eye* no. 27 vol. 7, spring 1998, p. 85.
Watano, Shiguru, "Typography of Jan van Toorn", *Idea* no. 194, 1986, pp. 67–81.
Westerveld, Wim, "De Dialectiek van Jan van Toorn", *Vormberichten*, July 2004, pp. 16–7.
Vroomans, Margriet, "Over Kleur Bekennen en Objectiviteit", *Haagse Courant*, January 1982, p. 25.
Wilde, Edy de, "Uitgangspunten voor een Museumbeleid" in Wim Crouwel (ed.), "Om de Kunst", *Documentaires* no. 8, 1978, pp. 3–6.

Publications by Jan van Toorn

Van Toorn also designed items marked *

Van Toorn, Jan, *Jan van Toorn*, Amsterdam: Museum Fodor (catalogue), 1972.* (inside only)
Leering, Jean and Jan van Toorn, "Vormgeving in Functie van Museale Overdracht", *Documentaires* no. 7, 1978.*
Van Toorn, Jan, "Anders Zien, Tien Jaar Vormgeving van een linkse Uitgeverij", *Tegenspraak* no. 13, 1979.
——, "De Ondeskundigheid van Museum en Vormgevers"/"Museum and Designer as Non-experts" in Carel Blotkamp, Marjon van Caspel, Frans Haks, Frank van der Schoor, Jan van Toorn and Martin Visser (eds.), *Museum in Motion? The Modern Art Museum at Issue/Museum in Beweging? Het Museum voor Moderne Kunst ter Diskussie*, '-Gravenhage: Government Publishing Office/Staatsuitgeverij, 1979, pp. 162–9.*
——, untitled article, *Quad* no. 2, October 1980.*
——, "Vormgeving, Subjectief, Open en Veranderlijk" in Jan Boterman (ed.), *Rietveld Idiotenband*, Amsterdam: Gerrit Jan Thiemefonds, 1983.
——, "Meer dan Nu"/"More than Now", in *De ene Hemel is de Andere Niet/A Choice of Heavens*, Amsterdam: Gerrit Rietveld Academie, 1989, pp. 78–9.
——, "Designers on Photography, Photographs by Design – A Graduate Seminar Workshop" in Thomas Ockerse (coordinator), *Spirals '91* book 6, Providence: Rhode Island School of Design, 1991, pp. 233–54.
——, "Thanksgiving 1990 Operation Desert Storm" in Thomas Ockerse (coordinator), *Spirals '91* book 8, Providence: Rhodes Island School of Design, 1991, pp. 350–1.
——, "Middelen tot Nadenken", *Bk-info* no. 2, 1992, p. 16-7.
——, *Thinking Design: Issues in Culture and Values*, Cullowhee: Western Carolina University, 1993.
——, "Design and Reflexivity", in Andrew Blauvelt (ed.), *Visible Language*, "New Perspectives: Critical Histories of Graphic Design", vol. 28 no. 4, 1994, pp. 318–327.*
——, Preface and "Thinking the Visual: Essayistic Fragments on Communicative Action" in Ole Bouman (ed.), *"And justice for all . . .*, Maastricht: Jan van Eyck Akademie Editions, 1994, pp. 7–8, 140–52.
——, "Denken über Design: Ideen zum Kommunikativen Handeln" in Melanie Mues and Ulrike Schmidt, *Positionen zur Gestaltung*, Bremen: Hochschule für Künste, 1995, pp. 94–101.
——, "Selections by Jan van Toorn" in *The 100 Show: The Eighteenth Annual of the American Center for Design*, Crans, Switzerland: RotoVision, 1996, pp. 110–143.
——, "Communication, Society and Design Education", *Graphic Design Journal* no. 4, Society of Graphic Designers of Canada, 1996, pp. 11–2.
——, Preface in Jon Thompson (ed.), *Towards a Theory of the Image*, Maastricht: Jan van Eyck Akademie Editions, 1996, p. 6.
——, Preface in Heinz Paetzold (ed.), *City Life: Essays on Urban Culture*, Maastricht: Jan van Eyck Akademie Editions, 1997, p. 5.
——, "Deschooling and Learning in Design Education" in Jorge Frascara, *User-centered Graphic Design: Mass Communication and Social Change*, London: Taylor & Francis, 1997, pp. 126–9.
——, "Frame of Mind", *Typ*, July 1998 (image only, centrefold).
——, Introduction and "Communication Design: A Social Practice" in Jan van Toorn (ed.), *design beyond Design: Critical Reflection and the Practice of Visual Communication*, Maastricht: Jan van Eyck Akademie Editions, 1998, pp. 8–13, 152–67.*
——, "First Things First 2000" manifesto (signatory), *Adbusters* no. 27, autumn 1999, p 57. Also published simultaneously in: *AIGA Journal of Graphic Design*, vol. 17 no. 2, 1999, p. 8; *Blueprint*, September 1999, as a poster; *Emigre* no. 51, summer 1999, front cover; *Eye* no. 33 vol. 9, autumn 1999, pp. 26–7; *Items*, September 1999, p. 73.
——, *Cultiver notre Jardin*, Nuth: Drukkerij Rosbeek, 1999.*
—— and Ewan Lentjes, "Communicatief Ontwerpen" in *Nederlands Ontwerp 2000–2001, part 1/Dutch Design 2000–2001, dl 1: Grafisch Ontwerp/Graphic Design*, Amsterdam: BIS Publishers, 2000.
Katherine McCoy, Teal Triggs and Jan van Toorn, "Undiscovered Delights", *Visual Communication* vol. 1 no. 3, 2002, pp. 326–35.*
——, *Design's Delight*, Rotterdam: 010 Publishers, 2006.*

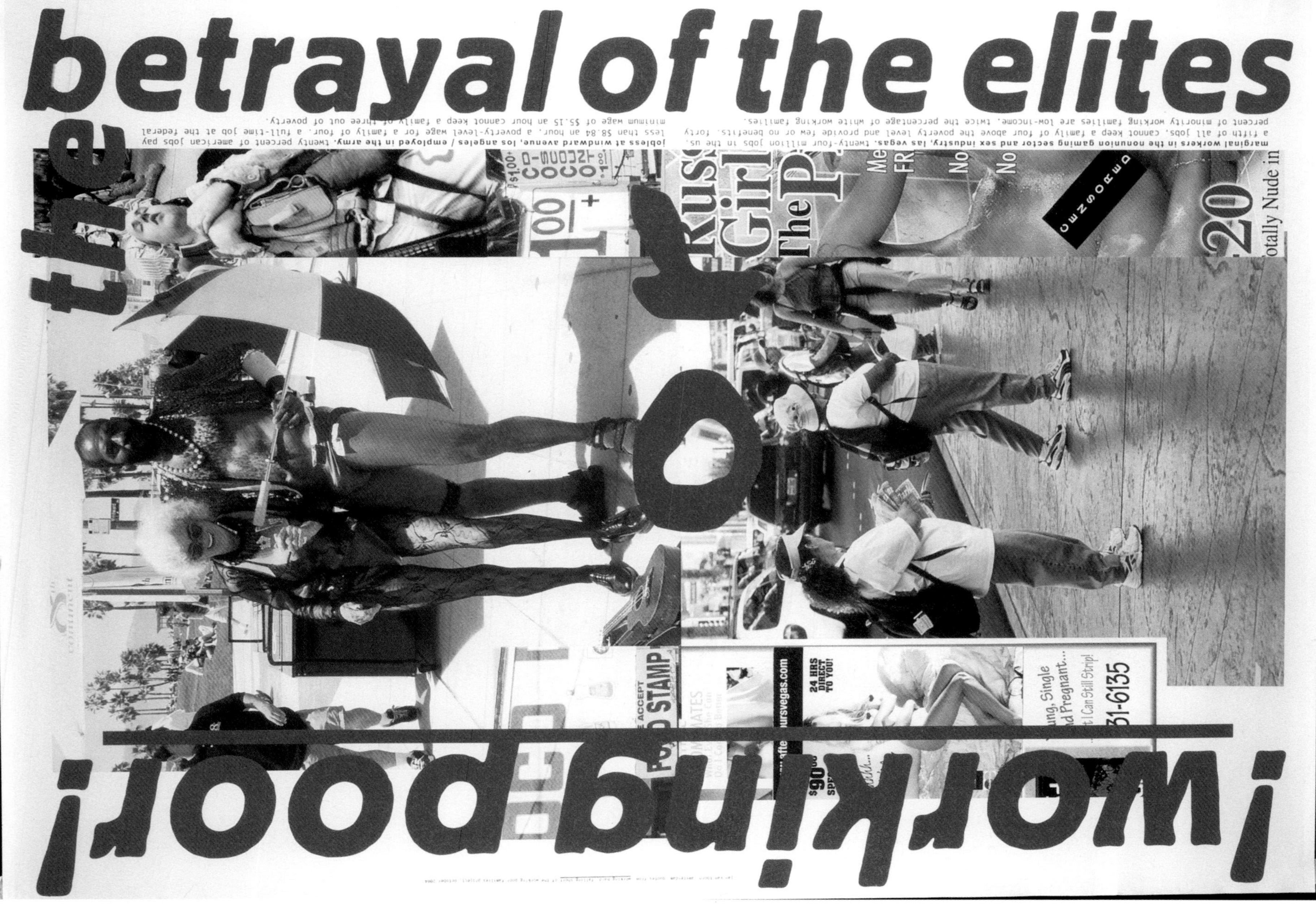

!Working Poor! or the Betrayal of the Elites. Poster for "Not for Profit" exhibition, Laband Art Gallery, Loyola Marymount University, Los Angeles, 2004